Educating the
WholeHearted
Child

A Handbook for Christian Home Education

by Clay & Sally Clarkson

Whole Heart Ministries

We owe a special debt of gratitude to our mothers, Nana and Mimi, for their unwavering encouragement, support and help in giving birth to this book. And thanks to our far away close friends, Karen and Dean Andreola, for their encouragement and counsel. And to Charlotte Mason and to Susan Schaeffer Macaulay for their defining works on whole book education.

Unless otherwise indicated, all Scripture references
are from the Holy Bible: New International Version,
Copyright 1973, 1978, 1984 by the International Bible Society.
Used by permission of Zondervan Bible Publishers

Design, editing and layout by Clay K. Clarkson

Printed in the United States of America

Published by:
Whole Heart Ministries
P.O. Box 3445
Monument, CO 802132

Dedication

This book is dedicated to our wholehearted children—Sarah, Joel, Nathan and Joy. May you all "shine like stars in the universe as you hold out the word of life" to your own generation and to our children's children.

We will not hide them from their children;
we will tell the next generation
the praiseworthy deeds of the Lord,
his power, and the wonders he has done...
so the next generation would know them,
even the children yet to be born
and they in turn would tell their children.
Then they would put their trust in God
and would not forget his deeds
but would keep his commands.
Psalm 78:4,6,7

Table of Contents

Preface and Introduction

Preface

Solomon had it right when he said, "Of making many books there is no end, and much study wearies the body." But in his day of scrolls and scribes, he couldn't even begin to imagine the bookmaking deluge unleashed first by the printing press and movable type, and now by the advent of computers and digital type. It wearies the body just trying to figure out which books (not to mention magazines, newspapers, CDs and cyber-pubs) are worthy enough to be read. All of which begs the question—why *this* book? What will you, a home-schooling parent, find of value in *Educating the WholeHearted Child*?

The answer to that question is simple—you will find a model for home education that will help you sort out the books and materials that weary your body (and your child) from the ones that will enrich you and your child. The Home-Centered Learning model explained in this book will show you how your home can become a heart-filling, rich and lively learning environment where your children will love to learn as naturally as they love to play.

If you flip through the pages, you'll notice that the content is in an outline format. That's because before there was a book, there was The WholeHearted Child Home Education Workshop. The workshop notebook simply grew into a book (and it's still growing!). No matter what age your children may be, we pray that you will find in this notebook-turned-handbook what we ourselves as home-schooling parents are always looking to find—inspiration, encouragement, help, good ideas and godly wisdom. We're just offering back to you what we have found in *our* search.

There is so much more to say about raising wholehearted children than we could put into a single book. And there is still so much more we have to learn! Our family is and always will be a work in progress, and so is this book. Though we both have undergraduate and advanced degrees that included educational studies, we do not pretend to speak as educational "experts." Whatever insight and wisdom we offer has been gained through our own study at home, our experience with our own family, and through talking with other "wholehearted" families. Keep in mind that there is purposefully more to do suggested in this book than any one family (including ours!) needs to do, and yet much more could be said on every topic, and many more excellent books and resources could be listed. We are simply presenting tried-and-true, traditional methods of learning that we have integrated in our Home-Centered Learning model of home education, and suggesting ways and resources to make it work in *your* home.

Which brings us back to Solomon. There truly is, as he says, "nothing new under the sun," especially when it comes to books. And there is no such thing as a truly "original" idea or concept—"what has been done will be done again." The very process of creativity requires grazing freely in the verdant fields of existing ideas, digesting them and synthesizing them into something "new." And so, the underlying concepts and ideas in this book are not original—it is only the way they are synthesized and presented that is new. Our lives have been enriched by the greener pastures where we have grazed in writing *Educating the WholeHearted Child*. We are indebted and grateful to the many authors and publishers whose ideas have nourished our hearts and minds, and are reflected throughout the pages of this book. We wholeheartedly recommend their writings to you.

♥ ♥ ♥

Let's come back to Solomon once more. This time, though, to add some perspective on why we wrote this book. For many people, Solomon's life would be worth emulating—great intelligence and wisdom, immense power, worldwide fame and vast wealth. He seemed to have it all. What he did not have, though, was a wholehearted devotion to God. God filled Solomon's mind with supernatural wisdom, but his heart was divided. He did not prepare his own sons to be God's leaders because he was not, and in the end, Solomon's divided heart resulted in a divided kingdom and, eventually, God's judgment on the nation of Israel. David, Solomon's father and a "man after God's own heart," knew the condition of his son's heart. Near the end of his life, David prophetically admonished him to serve God with *"wholehearted devotion."* Had he listened, perhaps Israel's history would have been different:

> *...acknowledge the God of your father, and serve him with wholehearted devotion and with a willing mind, for the LORD searches every heart and understands every motive behind the thoughts. If you seek him, he will be found by you; but if you forsake him, he will reject you forever. (1 Chronicles 28:9)*

We have very simple goals for our children. We simply want our children to be wholeheartedly devoted to our God, and to have willing minds that seek and serve him. That is what we mean by the "WholeHearted Child." We can raise our children to be Solomons—to be successful by the world's standards—but if their hearts are not turned toward God, we will miss the mark by God's standards. While the world may judge our children against the standards of intelligence, appearance, money, power and fame, God will judge them by their hearts—*"The LORD does not look at the things man looks at. Man looks at the outward appearance, but the LORD looks at the heart."* As their parents, we are raising our children for God's approval.

Our commitment to raising wholehearted children deepens all the more as we contemplate what kind of culture our children will inherit as adults. It will be one of broken, divided hearts, and corrupted minds. As we watch the current generation of children being readied for adulthood, God's words of rebuke to Israel in the opening chapter of Isaiah are too close for comfort—*"Your whole head is injured, your whole heart afflicted."* It is up to us as parents—and especially as dads—to send our children into adulthood with whole and healthy hearts and minds.

We believe God has raised up the home-schooling movement to prepare the next generation not just for spiritual *survival*, but for spiritual *revival*. If there is to be revival, though, there must be those who can provide mature spiritual leadership. *Educating the WholeHearted Child* is one part of our family's efforts to help Christian parents raise mature, wholehearted children who will be *"blameless and pure, children of God without fault in a crooked and depraved generation."* Our message, simply stated, is that a whole and healthy heart guided by a mind filled with God's wisdom is the true goal of home discipleship and home education.

You won't find "the wholehearted child" mentioned on every page of this book. That is because it is a concept that describes the end result, not the process. What you will find in the chapters of this book are some of the principles and the processes that will enable you to raise a wholehearted child. This book presents a model for Christian home education that integrates home discipleship and home education—the shaping of your child's heart to live for God and the strengthening of your child's mind to learn for God.

♥ ♥ ♥

If you are a home-schooling Christian parent, or you are considering home schooling, God has already impressed on your heart the eternal importance of raising godly children. You have considered the costs and committed yourself to the most important stewardship God will ever entrust to your care—your children. That is why you are home schooling—to make sure, as far as you are able, that you give back to God children who are wholeheartedly devoted to him. After all is said and done, the condition of your children's hearts will be the true measure of your success in life.

This book is for you. It is designed to give you, the Christian home educator, greater confidence in the stewardship of your children. The Home-Centered Learning approach of whole books and real life provides a natural way to use your whole home both to disciple and to educate your children—to raise each one to be a wholehearted child.

By the grace of God, you will one day rejoice to see your children graduating from your home school to take places of Christian leadership in the church and in the world. Your wholehearted child will become a mature Christian adult, serving God *"with wholehearted devotion and with a willing mind."* And in God's timing, your sons and daughters will marry and begin their own families to carry on all that you have taught them, and to raise their own wholehearted children. May we all live to see that day.

Oh, that their hearts would be inclined to fear me and keep all my
commands always, so that it might go well with them and their children
forever! Deuteronomy 5:29

With our whole hearts,

Clay and Sally Clarkson

April 3, 1996

CHAPTER ONE

Home Education...
A Step of Faith Toward Home

*I*t's the Right Thing to Do!

Home schooling is the right thing to do. No matter what multitude of reasons may have initially influenced your decision to bring your children home, in the end the only reason that really matters is that *it is the right thing to do*. In your heart, God moved you toward the decision, confirming through a variety of sources that you were doing the right thing. And in your heart, you made the step of faith to do what you knew was right—to bring your children home to disciple and educate them as a family.

That decision, though, was not an uninformed or blind leap of faith. It was guided by conviction, born out of much consideration and research, and shaped in your heart and mind by the Holy Spirit. You have good reasons why home schooling is the right thing to do. You home school because *it is right* to guard your children against the aggressive secular, humanistic worldview of the public school. You home school because *it is right* to shield your children from the immorality that permeates the public school, both the student body and the faculty. You home school because *it is right* to protect your children from the violence and wickedness that inflicts so many public schools. You home school because *it is right* to want your children to receive a better education under your loving guidance than the average public school is providing. You home school because *it is right* for parents to control what their children are studying and are being exposed to without being labeled intolerant and narrow-minded. You home school because *it is right* to decide that learning at home is better stewardship than spending thousand's of dollars for a private school. You home school because *it is right* to follow God's design for family not just in living, but in learning as well. You home school because *it is right* to guide your children's Christian character development at home rather than allow them to be "socialized" by secular, untrained, unsupervised schoolmates. You home school because *it is right* to keep your children under your authority until they are grown, rather than place them under other unknown authorities at a school. You home school because *it is right* to love your children and want to be with them every day of their lives until they are grown—that is what God intended.

For all the right reasons, you have declared your independence from conventional schooling and established a new outpost of spiritual, personal and academic freedom within the walls of your home. You have brought your children home. And now, faced with the task of educating them, you start a whole new round of questions—What is the right way to be sure my children learn what they need to learn? What curricula do I use? What do we do all day? Can I really do this? What do I do now?!

---

3 John 4
I have no greater joy than to hear that my children are walking in the truth.

❝ *We proclaim Christ, admonishing and teaching our children with all wisdom, so that we may present all of our children perfect in Christ. To this end we labor, struggling with all his energy, which so powerfully works in us, their parents.*

Adaptation of Colossians 1:28,29

Comment: It's Your Family
What is right for one family may not be right for another. Our aim in this book is not to tell you what we think is right for your family. Only you can determine that. We don't even want to tell you what books you should read to your children at what age or in what order. You are the best judge of what books your children should read, and when. Neither have we any desire to become yet one more curriculum. You don't need to become dependent on others telling you what to do, whether it is us or someone else. God has given you all you need to train and educate your children at home—it's in real books and real life. Our ultimate goal is to change your way of thinking about home and education—that's all. We want to equip you and other home educating parents to home school with a minimum of "curricular safety nets." We simply want to come alongside your family and others and share some of the things we have learned. You can take it from there.

Home vs. School

It is at this point that most new, and even veteran, home schoolers, having chosen the right thing to do, choose the wrong way to do it. Having chosen to bring their children home, they turn right back around and model their home schooling after the institutional classroom model they have just rejected. They simply accept the default model of learning that they grew up with—classrooms, teachers, and textbooks. But a home is not a school! *Men* designed schools, but *God* designed the home. The home is the *only* institution provided by God for the training of children. It is futile to try to impose an institution of man upon an institution of God. It won't work!

Before you became a Christian, it probably made little sense to you when someone would say that you would no longer think about life the same way once you accepted Christ. Once "converted," though, the Holy Spirit did indeed give you a whole new way of seeing and thinking. "Therefore, if anyone is in Christ, he is a new creation; the old has gone, the new has come!" *(2Cor. 5:17)*. The same is true for "converting" to a home-centered approach to learning. More families are saying *the old way has gone*—no more formal classrooms, graded curricula, tedious textbooks, wearisome workbooks, and long lectures. In their place, *a new way has come*—the home, a God-designed dynamic learning environment, full of real books, real life and real relationships. This book is all about "converting" to that new way of seeing and thinking about home education.

The Liberation of Learning

Your home can and should be a warm, vibrant place where your children love to learn as freely and as naturally as they love to play. In fact, *education should be the natural activity of every Christian home*. That is what God intended in his design for home and family. For many home schooling families, though, the tyranny of textbooks and the rigid rule of school have stolen the joy of home schooling. The freedom that home schooling should bring is held captive by the impersonal formality and constant demands of structured curricula. Families with the right intentions become enslaved to the wrong educational methods—methods designed for human institutions, not for the home.

That was briefly our experience, too, until we realized that textbooks and formal curricula were *artificial* means of education. Rather than unleashing learning potential, they held it back. For us as parents, they created a *false security* that we were doing enough, and a *false confidence* that our children were really learning. For our children, they created a *false dependency* on formal methods of learning, and a *false distinction* between learning and living. We began to see how conventional classroom curricula diluted the wonder and joy of real learning, and turned it into a tedious and burdensome task unrelated to real life at home. Certainly, this was not how God intended children to learn and grow! On the other hand, our children naturally loved reading and being read to, talking about their own insights and ideas, learning through real life, and having time to explore and learn on their own. We knew instinctively this was how God intended our children to live and learn. It was the liberation of learning in our home!

Cooperating with God's Design

Since then, we have been fully invested in a home-centered approach to learning using real books and real life. Every day, we see more clearly how natural and normal it is—something we could not see before we were "converted." For our family, it has been more than just finding the "best way" to home educate—one out of many other good ways. It has been more like finding the "right way," the commonsense way that we sensed must be out there all along. At last, we feel like we are actually cooperating with God's design for our home and children. There is great freedom in knowing that what we are doing is going along with a pattern that is already built into the very fabric and rhythm of our lives. We have come to the place where we can honestly say that there is no distinction in our home school between home and school—we are living to learn and learning to live all at the same time. That is what happens in a home.

You may ask how we know we are cooperating with God's design when home schooling, per se, is never mentioned in Scripture. It's because home *education* is not our primary goal at home—home *discipleship* is, and home education is simply the natural extension of home discipleship. If we are discipling our children to be useful to God's service, part of that process is preparing them intellectually. And, since biblical discipleship is a relational process, then education must be a relational process, too. God designed the home for discipleship, and when we follow God's patterns and principles, the natural and normal fruit will be not only spiritual growth and maturity, but intellectual growth and maturity as well. Scripture allows for no other process for raising and training children—only the family. Your home is a dynamic living and learning environment designed by God for the very purpose of raising your children to become mature, useful disciples of Jesus. When you begin to understand that dynamic, you will find a freedom you never knew was possible in your home education. Home-centered learning helps you discover that dynamic so your home will work *for* you in discipling and educating your children.

Home-centered learning is not just a new perspective on your home and family, though, it is also a new perspective on your children. Not only did God design home and family to be a learning environment, but he also designed children to learn naturally within that environment. Because children are made in God's image, they are already intelligent, creative and curious. No matter what you do (or don't do!), God has already put within them the drive to explore, discover, question and to learn. They do not learn because you show them how to make sense of things...they make sense of things because they are already know how to learn! Your role as a home educating parent, then, is to provide a rich and lively living and learning environment in which your children can exercise their God-given drive to learn, and then to train and instruct your children within the natural context of your home and family life. It's that simple.

Home-Centered Learning is cooperating with God's design for your family, home and children. It is an old model with a new face that is bringing freedom to home educating families. May you find that freedom in *your* home.

66 *Therefore, teaching, talk and tale, however lucid or fascinating, effect nothing until self-activity be set up; that is, self-education is the only possible education; the rest is mere veneer laid on the surface of a child's nature.*

Charlotte Mason, A Philosophy of Education, 1925

Comment: Self-Education
You cannot possibly "teach" your children everything they need to know. But you can give them one thing they need to learn—a positive learning attitude. The attitude that you give your children about learning will stay with them the rest of their lives, and it begins at the earliest ages of childhood. A child with a positive learning attitude will naturally become a self-motivated learner, and will more quickly become a self-educating student. Following are some of the ways you can cultivate a positive learning attitude in your child.

- *Have a positive attitude about learning yourself. Your attitude and example is the greatest influence on your child's attitude.*
- *Let your love of books be infectious. Read many wonderful books to your children from a young age.*
- *Believe in your children. Affirm their worth to you and God; affirm the great potential that you see in them.*
- *Give them freedom to explore and discover. Interact with them about what they learned.*
- *Don't rush learning. Discern the correct pace for each child and let them know they're doing fine.*
- *Express genuine interest in whatever interests your child.*
- *Give your children freedom to ask questions. Always respond seriously to serious questions.*

Be Sure You Have Counted the Cost

Christianity is not a neutral issue. And neither is Christian home education. There is always a cost to accepting the cross, whether it is in your career, marriage, lifestyle or family. If you decide to home school, you will have to make some sacrifices—there will be a cost. A careful examination will reveal, though, that the benefits in your family's life will far outweigh the costs. Before you take the step into Christian home education, be sure you have counted the cost.

❑ The Cost of Ministry

Am I willing to minister to my children...to become a servant like Jesus, giving up my own life for my children?

Christian home education is a ministry of discipleship and education to your children. It is the most biblical way for you to "bring them up in the training and instruction of the Lord." For ministry-minded Christian parents, home education is not simply an "educational alternative." Rather, it is an issue of obedience and submission to God's will for their family. Home education is the natural and logical extension of what God, from the beginning, designed the family to be and do.

❑ The Cost of Lifestyle

Am I willing to accept, along with the joys and blessings, the limitations and sacrifices of the home schooling lifestyle?

Home education will change your life...literally. The good news is, you will be blessed because of it. The not so good news is, you will have to make sacrifices. To be a successful home educating family, you must be ready to continually, and sometimes radically, adjust your lifestyle to the realities of home education. It will impact every area of your life: home life, church involvement, leisure time, income, adult social life, your child's friendships, housekeeping, and more.

❑ The Cost of Commitment

Am I willing to take a step of faith, trusting God to provide and intending in my heart to persevere in that decision?

Home education is not something you casually fit into your calendar, or make room for in your schedule. It is a commitment you make to God and to your family that will require perseverance, energy and patience. You cannot buy a home schooling kit that will make you instantly and easily successful. It is a long term, learning process, both for you and for your children. Only a prayerful, deliberate commitment before God will sustain you through the difficulties and challenges you will face in that process.

*B*e Sure It Is God's Will for Your Family

If you have counted the cost, then you are ready to decide if Christian home education is God's will for your family. Be sure that your decision is a matter of conviction that has come from earnestly seeking God and hearing him speak to your heart through his Word. If home education is not a matter of faith for you, then you very likely will not last as a *Christian* home educator (*Hebrews 11:6*). If it *is* a matter of God's will for you, then step out in faith, without doubting, and do it (*James 1:2-8*). God will honor your faith and enable you to do his will.

The pages that follow contain selected Scriptures to help you discern God's will for you and your family. Listen to and carefully consider what God has to say to you about your child's Christian training, home life and education. Space is provided for making personal notes.

> *"God's will is not something hidden*
> *that needs to be found;*
> *it is something revealed*
> *that needs to be done."*
> *ckc (Hebrews 10:36)*

The following are some biblical insights and principles to help you know how to determine God's will, especially concerning home education.

Stewardship In the case of home education, God's will is mostly a matter of stewardship—what is the best stewardship of the children God has given to you? Regardless of your feelings or circumstances, Scripture calls you to be a good steward, or manager, of all God has entrusted to you. Your children are certainly your most valuable "possessions" in this life. God will require an account of your stewardship of your children. (*Romans 12:1-2*)

Obedience What is God saying to you through his Word? Are you sensing the conviction of the Holy Spirit in the area of becoming a more godly parent? Are there direct commands of Scripture concerning your children that you need to obey? It is God's will for you to obey his leading. (*John 14:15-17*)

Discernment Determining God's will is primarily the exercise of godly discernment concerning the choices and decisions you make. God's Word is the only source for true discernment and wisdom. The more you read and study his Word, the more discerning you will become. (*Philippians 1:9-10*)

Prayer Doing God's will requires fervent prayer. As God speaks to you through his Word, you speak to him about what he is saying to you. Sometimes, praying becomes an act of decision making. (*Philippians 4:6-7*)

Counsel God will use other godly, wise Christians to make his will clear. Seek out the insights of trusted friends, godly home schoolers and wise counselors. Ask them to pray for you. (*Proverbs 15:22*)

Hebrews 10:36
You need to persevere so that when you have done the will of God, you will receive what he has promised.

Hebrews 11:6
And without faith it is impossible to please God, because anyone who comes to him must believe that he exists and that he rewards those who earnestly seek him.

James 1:5-6
If any of you lacks wisdom, he should ask God, who gives generously to all without finding fault, and it will be given to him. But when he asks, he must believe and not doubt, because he who doubts is like a wave of the sea, blown and tossed by the wind.

Ephesians 5:15-17
Be very careful, then, how you live -- not as unwise but as wise, making the most of every opportunity, because the days are evil. Therefore do not be foolish, but understand what the Lord's will is.

Proverbs 3:5-6
Trust in the LORD with all your heart and lean not on your own understanding; in all your ways acknowledge him, and he will make your paths straight.

Matthew 6:33-34
But seek first his kingdom and his righteousness, and all these things will be given to you as well. Therefore do not worry about tomorrow, for tomorrow will worry about itself. Each day has enough trouble of its own.

Romans 12:2
Do not conform any longer to the pattern of this world, but be transformed by the renewing of your mind. Then you will be able to test and approve what God's will is -- his good, pleasing and perfect will.

Matthew 7:24,25
Therefore everyone who hears these words of mine and puts them into practice is like a wise man who built his house on the rock. The rain came down, the streams rose, and the winds blew and beat against that house; yet it did not fall, because it had its foundation on the rock.

Galatians 6:7-9
Do not be deceived: God cannot be mocked. A man reaps what he sows. The one who sows to please his sinful nature, from that nature will reap destruction; the one who sows to please the Spirit, from the Spirit will reap eternal life. Let us not become weary in doing good, for at the proper time we will reap a harvest if we do not give up.

Matthew 6:19-21
Do not store up for yourselves treasures on earth, where moth and rust destroy, and where thieves break in and steal. But store up for yourselves treasures in heaven, where moth and rust do not destroy, and where thieves do not break in and steal. For where your treasure is, there your heart will be also.

Philippians 4:11-13
I am not saying this because I am in need, for I have learned to be content whatever the circumstances. I know what it is to be in need, and I know what it is to have plenty. I have learned the secret of being content in any and every situation, whether well fed or hungry, whether living in plenty or in want. I can do everything through him who gives me strength.

- *Renew your mind (Romans 12:1,2)* Whether you know it or not, your thinking about education, by cultural default, is already conformed to the world. Public education is all we have known as a generation, so it has become the default standard by which we reflexively evaluate "education." But God *commands* you to be transformed by renewing your mind with his truth so you can think like he thinks. He doesn't want us thinking about anything by default. And that includes our thinking about parenting and education.

- *Build on truth (Matthew 7:24-27)* There are some very dangerous cultural storms looming on the horizon. You will face some as a home educating parent, and your child will face them as an adult. These storms will tear many families apart, but you and your children can stand strong in the face of those storms if you build your house on the solid rock foundation of God and his Word. If you build your house on any other foundation, it is sandy ground and your house won't stand a chance against the storms. Build on truth and stand.

- *Sow for Christ (Galatians 6:7,9)* You will reap in your children's lives exactly what you sow in them as a parent. If you want to reap secure, mature adults, you must sow together the seeds of time, togetherness and training. If you want to reap a godly heritage, you must faithfully sow the seeds of godly influence. If you want to reap godly character, you must sow the seeds of a good example. You can no longer sow to please your own desires, but to please Christ. Only he can cause your seed to grow and produce a harvest of blessing.

- *Value the eternal (Matthew 6:19-24)* Your children are your most valuable assets. They are priceless, eternal treasures, entrusted to you by God—yours for a short time, after which you will present them back to God as a gift. If you treasure those young lives, that is where your heart will be—reproduced in their hearts. If you treasure the things of this world, though, you will have missed the opportunity to touch their hearts for God. You must decide what, or who, is going to matter most to you this side of eternity. For where your treasure is, there your heart will be also.

- *Be content in Christ (Philippians 4:10-13)* A decision to home school is also a decision to accept limitations on your life. Your expectations of adult life will be greatly limited by the realities of home education. The more you resist those limitations, the less content you will be. Contentedness grows as you learn to submit to those limitations. God has promised that you can do *everything* through Christ who gives you strength. You can learn to be content with whatever lifestyle God has for you. You can be content as a home educator.

❏ Some Specific Scriptures to Consider

About Parenting

- **Ephesians 6:4; Colossians 3:21** How can I make sure that I am obeying God's command to raise my children for him; to train them in righteousness?

- **Proverbs 22:6** How can I make sure that my child will go in the way he should go so that he will not be misled off the path of righteousness?

- **Deuteronomy 6:4-10** How can I make sure that my children's training in righteousness is consistent and continuous?

- **Psalm 78:1-7** How can I make sure that I pass on a godly and righteous heritage to my children, and to their children?

- **Psalm 127:3-5** How can I make sure that my children know they are valued blessings in my house, and not burdens?

- **1 Timothy 3:4; Titus 1:6** How can I make sure that my household is managed well and my children are "under control" as a testimony of my maturity?

Ephesians 6:4
Fathers, do not exasperate your children; instead, bring them up in the training and instruction of the Lord.

Colossians 3:21
Children, obey your parents in everything, for this pleases the Lord. Fathers, do not embitter your children, or they will become discouraged..

Proverbs 22:6
Train a child in the way he should go, and when he is old he will not turn from it.

Deuteronomy 6:6,7
These commandments that I give you today are to be upon your hearts. Impress them on your children. Talk about them when you sit at home and when you walk along the road, when you lie down and when you get up.

Psalm 78:4
We will not hide them from their children; we will tell the next generation the praiseworthy deeds of the LORD, his power, and the wonders he has done.

Psalm 127:3-5a
Sons are a heritage from the LORD, children a reward from him. Like arrows in the hands of a warrior are sons born in one's youth. Blessed is the man whose quiver is full of them.

1 Timothy 3:4
He must manage his own family well and see that his children obey him with proper respect.

Titus 1:6
An elder must be blameless, the husband of but one wife, a man whose children believe and are not open to the charge of being wild and disobedient.

Proverbs 13:24
He who spares the rod hates his son, but he who loves him is careful to discipline him.

Proverbs 22:15
Folly is bound up in the heart of a child, but the rod of discipline will drive it far from him.

Hebrews 12:9
Moreover, we have all had human fathers who disciplined us and we respected them for it. How much more should we submit to the Father of our spirits and live!

Matthew 18:6
But if anyone causes one of these little ones who believe in me to sin, it would be better for him to have a large millstone hung around his neck and to be drowned in the depths of the sea.

Proverbs 13:20
He who walks with the wise grows wise, but a companion of fools suffers harm.

1 Corinthians 15:33
Do not be misled: "Bad company corrupts good character."

2 Corinthians 6:14
Do not be yoked together with unbelievers. For what do righteousness and wickedness have in common? Or what fellowship can light have with darkness?

2 Timothy 2:16,17a
Avoid godless chatter, because those who indulge in it will become more and more ungodly. Their teaching will spread like gangrene.

- *Proverbs 13:24, 22:15; Hebrews 12:7f* How can I make sure that my children's disobedience and sin are promptly and properly disciplined in love?

- *Matthew 18:5,6* How can I make sure that I am not putting my children in situations where they will be tempted to sin, or worse, which cause them to sin?

- **Proverbs 13:20** How can I make sure that my children walk with "the wise" and do not become harmed as the "companion of fools?"

- *1 Corinthians 15:33* How can I make sure that my children's good character is not corrupted by their falling in with "bad company?"

- *2 Corinthians 6:14* How can I make sure that my children do not become spiritually, emotionally or socially "yoked together with unbelievers?"

- *2 Timothy 2:16-19* How can I make sure that my children are not under the authority and influence of false teachers or false teaching?

- *Romans 12:1,2* How can I make sure that my children do not become conformed to the world, but are transformed by the renewing of their minds?

- *1 John 2:15-17* How can I make sure that my children are taught to love God and to do his will, and are not taught to love the world or anything in the world?

- *Ephesians 5:15-17* How can I make sure that I am being careful with my children's lives, redeeming their time and making the most of my opportunities with them in an evil age?

- *Proverbs 4:23* How can I make sure that I am guarding my children's hearts against all ungodly influences?

- *Ephesians 5:11,12* How can I make sure that my children are not enticed by the "fruitless deeds of darkness" or exposed to those things God calls "shameful?"

- *Philippians 4:8* How can I make sure that my children's minds are filled with and trained to think about only those things that God considers excellent and worthy of praise?

Romans 12:2a
Do not conform any longer to the pattern of this world, but be transformed by the renewing of your mind.

1 John 2:15,17
Do not love the world or anything in the world. If anyone loves the world, the love of the Father is not in him...The world and its desires pass away, but the man who does the will of God lives forever.

Ephesians 5:15-17
Be very careful, then, how you live -- not as unwise but as wise, making the most of every opportunity, because the days are evil. Therefore do not be foolish, but understand what the Lord's will is.

Proverbs 4:23
Above all else, guard your heart, for it is the wellspring of life.

Ephesians 5:11,12
Have nothing to do with the fruitless deeds of darkness, but rather expose them. For it is shameful even to mention what the disobedient do in secret.

Philippians 4:8
Finally, brothers, whatever is true, whatever is noble, whatever is right, whatever is pure, whatever is lovely, whatever is admirable -- if anything is excellent or praiseworthy -- think about such things.

*B*e Confident as a Home-Educating Parent

Comment: Private Schools
This book does not take up the issue of private schools. Our observation has been that, due to the high cost of private school tuition, it is not even an option for most families considering home schooling, so there is little need to address it. Private Christian schools play an important role in the education of Christian children, to be sure, but their Christian leadership and content alone do not negate their weaknesses. Though the content of private Christian education is commendable, in most cases, the form is still the same institutionalized setting that plagues the public school. Consider just a few of the issues, besides the cost savings, that make home education a more attractive choice. When you choose a private school:

- *You are still giving up your ability and privilege to be the primary influence in your children's lives.*
- *Your children will still be restricted by unnatural formality and control at a time when their natural curiosity and creativity is at its peak.*
- *Individualized attention and real life learning will be minimal due to the nature of the classroom.*
- *Even with a heavy dose of discipline, most Christian private schools must deal with children from non-Christian homes. "Bad company corrupts good morals."*
- *Most still rely on lifeless textbooks and workbooks, time-wasting seatwork, and unnecessary homework.*
- *Your children will still have to run in the age and grade treadmill with little or no opportunity or encouragement to linger or advance at their own pace.*

Christian schools are offering a needed ministry, but they are not without drawbacks.

The Scriptures are the basis of your confidence, whatever you do in life. We have found there is only one way to "make sure" that you raise your children according to the principles of Scripture listed in the previous section—by discipling and educating your children at home. If it is biblical, then you can approach home education with confidence because it is God's will. There simply is no defensible argument from Scripture for putting children under the shaping influence of other authorities during the most formative and impressionable years of their lives. American cultural norms notwithstanding, doing so runs counter to the biblical concept of the family, and it is in conflict with how we are wired as mothers and fathers by God. Conventional schooling requires parents to suppress or deny their natural, God-given roles.

On the other hand, keeping your children at home only because you want to keep them out of the public school cesspool is shortsighted. Home education is not just a reaction to the moral decay in public schools—it is a pro-active decision about what is the best way to raise children. The best motivation for home educating is because it is the "right thing to do." Again, the Scriptures are your confidence, not the latest statistics on public school moral and academic failure. In many ways, home education is a gift you give to your children. You give them the opportunity to experience childhood and growing up the way God intended it to be. You give them a sense of wholeness and rightness that only a Christian home can provide. You give them time and space, with you beside them, to become secure, mature Christian adults. If your family is reasonably mature and stable, you can be confident, without apology, that your children will be better off with you at home, than in a public school under the authority of strangers.

God's principles are like a strong river flowing through yours and your children's lives. If you ignore those principles and attempt to swim against their current, you will make little progress. If, however, you submit to those principles and swim *with* the current, you will find a natural strength and power as you are carried along in the flow. As you cooperate with God's eternal design—a design built into our very nature as fathers, mothers, sons and daughters—you will experience an undeniable sense of rightness and release. You will know, deep down, that home education is the right thing to do, because it is what God designed you to do. Unfortunately, even though you may be "going with the flow," you'll soon find that there are some nasty rocks in the river. You're going to run into them from time to time. Those rocks are critics and detractors. The knowledge that you home educate your children will draw several predictable responses from non-home educating skeptics and critics. Their criticisms will nearly always be either biased, reactionary or uninformed. If you have made your decision to home educate based on the Scriptures, you have no reason to let criticism shake your confidence. The following pages suggest five of the most common "indictments" these critics bring against home schooling, followed by a confident home educator's response and defense. You don't need to win the argument, just make the point gently and with the confidence that you are doing God's will for *your* family.

The following are composite examples of the five most common "indictments" charged against home education. These are the kinds of statements that you are likely to hear at one time or another as a home schooler. Just remember, though, that an indictment is not a verdict. In most cases, the one bringing the indictment has not reached a final verdict about home schooling, but is just repeating hearsay charges. You have an opportunity to sway their opinion and win a follower if you know how to present compelling evidence to refute their charges. In the court of public opinion, the jury is always out.

The Legislation indictment:

"I just don't think it's right to keep children out of school. There should be stricter laws to make sure every child gets a proper education."

The Education indictment:

"You just can't provide at home what even an average public school can offer your children. You're neglecting your children by depriving them of a good education."

The Socialization indictment:

"Your kids need school in order to be properly socialized. They won't be able to function in the real world unless they're around kids their own age."

The Qualification indictment:

"You may be a good parent, but you and I both know it takes a lot more to be a good teacher. School teachers have been professionally trained to teach your children."

The Reputation indictment:

"Home schooling is done only by a few fundamentalist extremists. There's a home schooling family in our neighborhood and their kids are just not normal."

The remainder of this chapter presents some of the evidence that counters these five composite indictments. There is much more evidence than provided here, of course, but these responses give you a first response, as well as undergird your own convictions about home education. Perhaps the arguments presented in defense of home education will, in the end, result in freeing home schoolers from false charges, and even convicting those bringing the charges!

Comment: What To Do When Cornered by a Critic

Always remember that vocal critics of home schooling are not neutral. You can generally assume their criticisms have been "cooking" for some time. You just happen to be the one that gets to taste what's been in their mental oven (and it isn't "lovin'"). You don't have to swallow their arguments, but don't throw them back in their face. Here's what to do when cornered by a critic:

- *Above all, be patient and attentive. Let them have their say. Listening to a critic may be the first step toward winning them over.*
- *Consider it an opportunity to gently educate. If they are receptive, suggest a book they might want to read. However, if they are resistant, simply ask about their children and move on.*
- *Stay in control of your emotions. If you become defensive and angry, it will serve only to polarize the issues and convince your critic that home schoolers are extremists. If you answer gently and patiently, but with conviction, you may not win the immediate debate, but you won't lose the opportunity for future discussion.*
- *Don't be overzealous to defend home schooling. Offer responses to criticisms only if there is sufficient time for discussion and you can do so confidently and knowledgeably. Otherwise, suggest you get together to discuss it over breakfast.*
- *Don't let an "itchy trigger finger" cause you to unload on your critic with all your "best shot" arguments for home schooling. They'll start "shooting back." You'll both end up bloodied and angry.*
- *Don't take the criticism personally. De-personalize and generalize your response as much as possible. "A gentle answer turns away wrath."*

❑ Response to the Legislation Indictment:

"Home education is legal in all 50 states. It is widely recognized as a valid educational choice."

Home education is now legal in all fifty states, although specific regulatory policies differ widely from state to state. In some states, there is essentially no regulation; in others there is almost draconian regulation. The issues of legality and validity may be largely settled, but the issue of regulation of home education will be a continuing concern. The ongoing battle against governmental intrusion into your private family life intensifies with the choice to home educate your children. The regulatory tools of intrusion that might be wielded against home educators are myriad—written reports, curriculum review and approval, home visits, attendance and instructional time record keeping, required testing, and on and on. There is no end to the meddling of bureaucrats, educrats and politicians with our constitutional freedoms, and with our children! Regardless of legal conditions, however, home education is always a *valid* form of educating your child. It may not always be validated by the state, but it is certainly validated by Scripture, history, experience, and common sense.

Two areas are of special concern as the home schooling movement matures. The first area of concern is the possibility of state or federal legislation that would attempt to regulate home educators through teacher qualification requirements, mandatory testing, outcome based education (OBE) standards, or other intrusions. The National Education Association, the incredibly powerful and influential public school lobby, is on record opposing home education and will continue its campaign to regulate, and even eradicate, home schooling. The second area of concern is the real threat of aggressive state social and child protective services agencies initiating actions against home schooling families. In most states, these agencies are relatively unaccountable and are able to act on unsubstantiated, anonymous charges. They are very intimidating, and have authority to remove children from the home. The courts are beginning to recognize the unconstitutional scope and power of these agencies, but it is likely to be years before effective safeguards are in place to protect our freedoms.

Because home education is only a tenuous freedom, we strongly recommend all home educating families become members of Home School Legal Defense Association (HSLDA). Since 1983 these dedicated home educators have been fighting the legal battles in every state that secure our freedoms to teach our children at home without governmental intrusion. The $100 annual fee ($85 through some state organizations) is not only reasonable, it's a bargain. If you find yourself unexpectedly on the defensive against an aggressive governmental or educational system, your legal representation and fees are completely covered. HSLDA will handle your case. Even if you never need their services, your fees are a small contribution to the ongoing fight for your freedom to home educate. You are contributing to a greater cause and helping other families like yours fight the legal battles that you don't have to fight. Those battles will help win the war for *your* freedom to home school.

LEGISLATION / REGULATION	STATE
ACADEMIC QUALIFICATIONS: Seven states require a high school diploma or a GED. ND requires either a college degree or passage of a "teachers test." WV allows GED or high school diploma until the child enters high school. Forty-one states do not require specific requirements.	NC, NM, OH, PA, GA, TN SC
COMPETENCY QUALIFICATIONS: Four states require home school teachers to be "competent," "qualified" or "capable of teaching." All require a high school diploma or GED. Less than a GED is required in CA and KS.	CA, KS, NY, OH
APPROVAL REQUIRED: Four states require home schools to be subject to the discretionary "approval" of the local school district, board or state commissioner.	ME, MA, RI, UT
HOME IS PRIVATE SCHOOL: In at least twelve states, home schools may operate as private or church schools.	AK, AL, CA, DE, IL, IN, KS, KY, MI, NE, LA, TX
GROUP IS PRIVATE SCHOOL: In five other states, groups of home schoolers have qualified as private or church schools. SC is the only state where a specific home school association, SCAIS, has been exempted from state compulsory attendance and home school law requirements.	CO, FL, ME, VA, UT, (SC)
OTHER: OK is the only state with a constitutional amendment specifically guaranteeing the right to home school. In ID, home schools must simply be "otherwise comparably instructed," with no approval involved. In NJ, home schools fall under the category "elsewhere than at school." In SD, home schools are "alternative instruction programs" with private schools, and must annually notify and test.	OK, ID, NJ, SD
STANDARDIZED TESTING REQUIRED: Currently, fifteen states require standardized testing or evaluation. MN and GA do not require submission of the test results.	AK, AR, GA, HI, MN, NY, NV, NM, NC, ND, OR, PA, SC, SD, TN
ALTERNATIVE TESTING: Thirteen states provide for an alternative to standardized testing. CO and WA do not require submission of the test results.	CO, CT, FL, IA, LA, ME, MA, OH, VT, VA, NH, WA, WV
EQUIVALENCY REQUIREMENTS: Seven states require instruction or school time to be "equivalent" to public schools. This idea was struck down by courts in MN and MO because it was too vague.	CT, IN, IA, KS, ME, NJ, NV
GENERAL REQUIREMENTS: Three states require instruction to be "regular and thorough."	MD, DE, RI
COMPARABILITY REQUIREMENTS: Two states require instruction to be "comparable" to public schools.	ID, MI
COMPULSORY ATTENDANCE LAWS: Higher courts in six states have ruled that those states' compulsory attendance statutes were vague and, therefore, unconstitutional.	GA, WI, MN, MS, IA, PA

The information in this chart was provided by Home School Legal Defense Association. It is accurate as of June 1995. For an updated summary, or for complete legal information for your state, contact HSLDA.

❝ *I am much afraid that the schools will prove the very gates of hell, unless they diligently labor in explaining the Holy Scriptures, and engraving them in the hearts of youth. I advise no one to place his child where the Scriptures do not reign paramount. Every institution in which means are not unceasingly occupied with the Word of God must be corrupt.*

Martin Luther

❝ *And so, overentertained, pushed, pulled, and tidied up, often the child of today has the rich creative play-response crushed out. Sometimes the only thing his dulled eyes focus on is a premature adolescence which will release him from childhood.*

Susan Schaeffer Macaulay,
For the Children's Sake,
Crossway, 1984

❝ *I would rather my child had a limited curriculum and access to limited educational resources, and yet learned by basking in the atmosphere of someone who had true pleasure in the books that were pursued, than that he should go to some well-equipped and soulless situation where, theoretically, he could 'learn' at optimum speed.*

Susan Schaeffer Macaulay,
For the Children's Sake,
Crossway, 1984

"There is no better learning environment than a loving home and a personal tutor. My children are home because I want them to have the very best education."

Those who oppose home schooling often raise the question of what kind of education your child will receive. Skeptics and critics usually just imply, but often blatantly assert, that you are sentencing your child to a "second rate" education since you cannot possibly, at home, attain the "high standards" of education provided by conventional schools. Though you almost certainly will not be able to convert critics through argument, no matter how well-reasoned your position, your children will ultimately be your defense (*Ps. 127:5*). You can be confident, if you use the educational strengths of your home to their fullest, that your children will graduate from your home school with a superior education. Against a well-educated, well-rounded home-school graduate, critics have no defense.

To expose the illogic of this indictment, simply turn it around. Why should anyone believe that a depersonalized, institutionalized classroom setting is somehow a superior learning environment? To the contrary, it is the least effective setting for developing self-motivated, free-thinking learners. Age-grading, a necessary element of conventional classroom educational strategy, is primarily an administrative technique to maintain order...it has very little to do with true learning. It is a lockstep procedure that results in children being routinely advanced in grade without achieving the competencies required for learning in the next grade. Only the "average" child (whichever one that is) is served—motivated learners are frustrated by the slow pace, struggling learners are frustrated by the fast pace. The institutionalized classroom is a controlled environment with little or no freedom or flexibility, in which the noisiest and the neediest 10% get most of the teacher's personal attention, while the rest of the students are left to fend for themselves. In most conventional classrooms today, whether public or private, there is a copious amount of wasted time, a blind reliance on cold, lifeless textbooks and workbooks, and a self-perpetuating dependency on "the teacher" for learning. It is far from being "the best educational system in the world" and it certainly can't come close to home.

Your home school, in stark contrast, is an ideal learning environment (see chart on the facing page). Remember—God designed homes, not schools, to be the living and learning center of a child's life. When you tap into the natural dynamics of your home, you will liberate learning to be all that God intended it to be for your child. You can balance control and flexibility to meet each child's individual learning needs. You can fill their lives with the best books and resources. You can turn them loose to learn whatever they desire. You can determine readiness for and pace of learning, holding off or jumping ahead of "grade" without concern. Because you are training a child for life, not just preparing them to make a living, you can use all of life as a classroom. "Real life" is always within easy reach. If you use the natural learning environment of your home and family, your home-school graduates will be exceptional people—well-educated disciples, ready to live godly and productive lives. They deserve the best.

Public Education	Home Education
The child is part of the group. Public education focuses on helping the child conform to group standards in order to learn certain things at certain times in certain ways with limited regard to maturity or ability.	The child is an individual. Home education focuses on the development of the whole person, responsiveness to individual learning needs and desires, and guidance in growing in Christian maturity.
Learning structures are created with the need for order, conformity, regimen, and control in mind. Formality is de-motivating, stifling a child's curiosity, creativity and natural desire to learn.	Learning structures are created with the interests of the child, home and family in mind. Time and freedom unleash the child's curiosity, creativity and natural desire to learn.
Instruction is "dumbed down" to accommodate the poorest learners in the class. Motivated learners are frustrated by the slow pace; struggling learners by the fast pace; "average" learners learn to stay average (to keep the teacher's pace of instruction). "Slow" learners are stigmatized, and "fast" learners are ostracized.	Instruction is aimed high to challenge all in the home school. Learning abilities can vary without any attached meaning or stigma. All children advance at their own pace. Each child advances according to his own level of learning and motivation. Each child is treated as an individual without reference to others.
Teacher can give each child only limited individual attention in a class of 15-30 children, and is unable to respond to each child's individual needs and interests. Concentration is hindered by high distraction factor in noisy, uncomfortable or "open" classroom.	Parent is able to give each child unlimited individual attention in a one-to-one tutoring relationship, and to respond to each child's individual needs and interests. Concentration is reinforced by ability to control and even eliminate distractions.
Child must learn how to please various teachers. The authority relationships are unnatural and "formal."	Child instinctively wants to please his parents. The authority relationship is natural and loving.
Routine reliance on mind-numbing, lifeless textbooks and workbooks. The teacher is the authority; classroom setting results in a self-perpetuating and necessary dependency on "the teacher."	Parent is free to choose the best "living" books and curricula available. The parent is a learning facilitator; the child is trained and expected to depend on his own independent learning abilities and skills.
Much wasted time in order to keep students occupied and under control. No real life learning occurs sitting at a student desk. Teach much less in much more time. Most graduate "on time" at 18 years of age.	There is no wasted time. All of life is a classroom, so every activity or involvement is a learning opportunity. Parent can teach much more in much less time. Not difficult to graduate early, even by 13-14 years of age.
Child advances in studies on the basis of age and grade with limited regard to knowledge or competence.	Child advances in studies on the basis of knowledge and competence without regard to age or grade.
Child is tested primarily for short-term linear knowledge (ability to recall facts and information). Retention is low. Written tests, though less effective, are easier to administer and grade; oral testing avoided.	Child is tested primarily for long-term global knowledge (ability to grasp ideas and concepts). Retention is high. Written tests are unnecessary; oral testing is more effective and a better gauge of learning.
Homework is necessary because of the teaching and learning constraints of institutionalized education.	Homework is unnecessary. All learning is accomplished during the teaching/tutoring times.
Grades are necessary for detached teachers to control and track progress of a large class of students.	Grades are largely irrelevant. Parent works with the child until the knowledge or skill is acquired.

❑ Response to the Socialization Indictment:

"The family is God's only authorized institution for the socialization of children. If the goal of socialization is greater maturity, that comes from being around mature adults."

Every home-educating parent hears it with numbing regularity—"But aren't you afraid they won't get enough socialization?" First, you must understand what is being said. To most non-home schoolers, socialization means "regular exposure to peers of the same age and grade," a woefully inadequate definition. A more acceptable understanding is "the process of instilling social skills necessary for relating effectively to other people." *A properly socialized child, then, knows how to relate well to other people, whether young or old, male or female, different or similar.* You can be confident, given the correct definition, that the Christian home is a far better socializing environment than the public (or private) school. In fact, it can be easily argued that public school gets very poor marks in socialization. Research and testing has consistently shown home-schooled children to be significantly above the public school norms for social skills and development, and for "self-esteem."

The reason seems clear. In the home school, the primary models for effective relationships are adults—father, mother, grandparents, family friends. This kind of *age-integrated socialization* simply does *not* take place in a public school where the models are primarily other foolish, immature children, and where supervision and intervention by mature adults is minimal. In the home, in contrast, social skills are constantly and consistently modeled, trained, and corrected. Poor social skills are not allowed to become habituated, and good ones are regularly reinforced.

As to interaction with other children, one wonders how much is enough, and how little is not enough. Why should 4-8 hours *a day* (school) be the norm? Why shouldn't 4-8 hours *a week* be sufficient? It really seems like common sense, but studies show that constant and excessive interactions and activities (such as in school) have a negative impact on children; limited interactional environments (such as a home) have a positive impact. Home schooling families can easily find opportunities for interaction with other children through church, field trips, support groups, lessons, sports and other activities. And all of that time is under the loving supervision of mature adults who have a vested interest in the social development of their children. There is no credible argument that children are better off sitting in crowded classrooms five days a week. They are better off at home.

Those who say that home-schooled children aren't in the "real world" just aren't thinking straight. School is the false world. Never in the rest of their lives will your children be forced to live and interact with 20-30 age-mates in a sterile, isolated classroom totally segregated from real living experiences. The real "real world" of home, family, work and ministry prepares children to work with people of all ages in actual situations that they will experience as adults. School can't even counterfeit that kind of life experience. Tell those naysayers to "Get real!"

Public School Socialization	Home School Socialization
GOAL: To ensure that a child conforms to the social norms of his age mates and school. Other relationships, if addressed at all, are peripheral.	GOAL: To teach and train a child how to relate effectively to other people in all kinds of relationships: siblings, parents, other adults, friends.
SCOPE: Relational experiences with school age mates and a detached teacher...extremely limited range of relational settings.	SCOPE: Relational experiences with family, friends, work, ministry, church, neighborhood, community... wide variety of relational settings.
MODELS: Primarily other immature children	MODELS: Primarily parents and other mature adults.
QUALITY: Peer relationships are shallow and uncertain. The atmosphere is often cool and always competitive. Family is not a factor.	QUALITY: Family relationships are stable and close. The atmosphere is warm and non-competitive. Peer relationships are incorporated into the family.
IDENTITY: Child's identity is developed by attempting to gain acceptance of peers. Acceptance is based on popularity, judged mostly by appearance, intelligence, and abilities. Child wants to become like his peers. Child feels false security or false pride.	IDENTITY: Child's identity is developed as a member of his family. Acceptance is based on mutual, unconditional love of a Christian family. Child wants to become like his parents. Child feels secure and significant, able to act independently of peers.
VALUES: Christian values are in conflict with the secular values of other children and the school; the Christian child can be the object of rejection or ridicule.	VALUES: Christian and family values are taught, modeled and reinforced without conflict; any rejection of Christian values is shared by the whole family unit.
OTHER FACTORS: Respect for authority is constantly challenged among peers. Interaction with other children is rarely supervised; adult intervention is rare.	OTHER FACTORS: Respect for authority is constantly reinforced. Interaction with other children is supervised by mature adults; adult intervention is immediate.
RESULT: This child is a "companion of fools" and suffers harm. The child becomes like other children.	RESULT: This child "walks with the wise" and becomes wise. The child becomes like an adult.

IN OUR HOME...

We believe in "family style" socialization. We try to make our home and family life as entertaining, enriching and enjoyable as we can. We want our children to become "family dependent" rather than "peer dependent," and to prefer our home to any other place they might go. We work hard and make some social sacrifices to build strong family ties. We have a weekly family night with pizza and activities or a movie; we have a weekly "tea time" on Sunday afternoon; we have fun "Bible Times" on some weeknights; we go together on special outings and activities on weekends. All of this, of course, is in addition to play times with friends, support group activities, and church activities. We want to do all we can to so win our children's hearts that they will value and prefer home and family.

□ Response to the Qualification Indictment:

"I am fully qualified to teach my children in my home. They couldn't have a better teacher than a loving parent committed to their best interests."

In recent years the drumbeat of certification has become increasingly loud from the public school educrats, and especially the National Education Association. However, given the increasing success rate of home schooling, and the continuing decline and failure of public schooling, the true intent of the push for certification seems obvious—the regulation of home schools. Teacher certification is the primary strategy of the NEA for extending their control over public education at the Federal level to include the home schooling movement. However, there is no reputable research to support the claim that a teaching degree or certificate makes an individual a better teacher. It is, in reality, simply a state issued "license to teach" in public schools. In reality, much of the training and certification a "professional" teacher goes through has as much to do with classroom control, and the administrative and political aspects of teaching, as it has to do with knowing how to teach. However, a parent's certification is from God, because he has designed you to teach your children. You do not need the state to tell you whether or not you are qualified to train and instruct your children. You are. God has already certified you.

You may be tempted to deny your natural qualifications to teach your child, or to think that there is just too much to teach, so many subjects that you just don't know that much about. The real issue, though, is not how little you know about some general subjects, but how much you know about a few specific subjects. If you are of average intelligence, reasonably mature, can speak, read, write and do math, and you love your children, then you are qualified to instruct them. Many public school teachers do not meet *those* qualifications! With only a good library and minimal curricula for teaching the basics, you can take your children much further than a "certified" teacher ever could in a classroom. There are exceptional teachers, to be sure, but there are many more whose "teaching" consists in passing out textbooks, and giving and grading tests. As a parent, you are qualified to do much more. You see, your goal in home education is not just to make your children good test-takers, but rather to shape their hearts and strengthen their minds to become self-motivated, self-learning students. And because you have a personal, God-given, one-on-one relationship with each of your children, you are much better qualified and equipped to reach that goal than is a classroom teacher whose attention is divided between your child and 20 or more other children.

So, don't confuse qualifications with certification. Education at home is a learning process as much for the parents as it is for the children. Unfamiliar subject areas and problems that you are not able to solve do not reflect on your qualifications to teach your children. They are no more or no less than opportunities for you to learn together. You <u>are</u> qualified. It is <u>not</u> difficult to teach your child. This book will show you how to become an excellent home educator using a very natural approach to learning called *Home-Centered Learning.*

Comment: More Research

As in studies on socialization, numerous studies on qualifications and teaching skills have shown that certification is of no value in teaching effectiveness, and may even have a negative effect. The educational background of the parent has minimal effect on the learning of the child/student. The primary factor is the commitment of the parent.

1 Samuel 16:7

But the LORD said to Samuel, "Do not consider his appearance or his height, for I have rejected him. The LORD does not look at the things man looks at. Man looks at the outward appearance, but the LORD looks at the heart."

❝ *In general the best teacher or care-giver cannot match a parent of even ordinary education and experience.*

Dr. Raymond Moore, *Home Grown Kids*, Word, 1981

Comment: Learning Happens

Family Research Council (Gary Bauer) evaluated research on learning showing that home is the single most important factor in gauging student success (The One-House Schoolroom, Family Policy, Sept. 1995). It is interesting to note that none of the "home schooling" factors involved either curricula or teaching qualifications. They found success is most likely when there is:

- commitment to family routines and meal times
- a limit on outside activities
- an emphasis on self-discipline and hard work
- a high but realistic expectation of achievement
- parental involvement in the learning process
- family reading, writing and discussion
- a wide variety of books and other learning tools readily available
- an involvement with community resources

Public School Teacher	Home School Parent-Teacher
QUALIFICATIONS: College degree, certification, competency requirements, professional experience.	QUALIFICATIONS: Maturity, willingness, leading of the Holy Spirit, life experience.
METHODS: Limited to more formal, group-oriented teaching methods that are suited to classroom setting.	METHODS: No limitation on methods. Able to use informal, individualized teaching methods.
GOALS: Goal of instruction is head knowledge with a focus on the "right answer." Due to the size of the class, learning is measured by knowledge of facts.	GOALS: Goal of instruction is heart knowledge with a focus on understanding. Learning is measured by understanding of ideas.
CONTROL: Must be able to maintain constant control of a classroom of 20-30 young children, many (if not most) of whom are untrained and undisciplined.	CONTROL: Control is already a natural and normal part of the parent-child relationship.
RESOURCES: Limited to the use of approved materials. Not always able to use the best resources available due to budget restrictions, time limitations or size of class.	RESOURCES: Unlimited opportunity to use the very best resources available. Only consideration is the family budget and access.
CURRICULA: Must use the same "one-size-fits-all" curricula and materials with all children in the class, regardless of individual needs and interests.	CURRICULA: Free to use a variety of curricula and materials suited to each individual child's needs and interests.
CONTENT: Limited as to what can be taught and discussed with students (no prayer, Bible, etc.).	CONTENT: No limitations on what can be taught or discussed with children.
TIME: Time with students is limited to the time spent in the classroom. Only problem students receive individual attention. Unable to adjust the pace of instruction—must keep on tight schedule.	TIME: Unlimited time with children in wide variety of learning situations. All receive individualized attention. Can adjust the pace of instruction as needed—scheduling is flexible and non-restricting.
EVALUATION: Limited on means of evaluating student progress primarily to testing and grading. Due to size of class, it is an impersonal process that necessarily excludes learning readiness, maturity, understanding and other individualized factors.	EVALUATION: Children's progress is guided through personal interaction and direction. Evaluation is a very personal process that considers all factors that relate to learning in a particular area of study. Testing and grading is unnecessary.
DISCIPLINE: Limited disciplinary methods due to legal restrictions. Because there are no natural bonds, discipline must be formal, strict and authoritarian in most cases. Discipline is mostly for punishment of unacceptable behavior.	DISCIPLINE: Able to use whatever disciplinary method is most effective. Discipline is always done in love within the bonds of the parent-child relationship. Discipline is mostly for the purpose of training in character and conduct.
CREATIVITY: Unable to cultivate creativity in students due to need for structured learning environment and emphasis on "right answers." Students learn to stay in seats and answer questions.	CREATIVITY: Able to cultivate maximum creativity in children by providing a dynamic, hands-on learning environment at home. Children learn to explore, discover, ask questions and seek out answers.
MOTIVATION: Primary, it's a chosen profession. Secondary, love of teaching (not for all, though).	MOTIVATION: Primary, love of children and obedience to God. Secondary, to provide the very best education for children.

❑ Response to the Reputation Indictment:

"Home education is a rapidly growing and successful educational movement. To many it is a blessing; to some it is a curiosity; to a few it is a threat."

An objective observer of the home school movement would see a steadily growing forest that is strong and healthy. A biased observer will look for one or two diseased trees in order to condemn the entire forest. The best response to biased criticism that attempts to attack the reputation of home education is to change the point of view. Don't allow a detractor to focus on one or two unstable fringe families who give home schooling a bad name. Gently remind them that public and private schools have their bad trees, too. Then, turn their attention to the tens of thousands of normal families (just like them!) who are making genuine sacrifices to obey God's will for *their* families. They, the solid center, are the true measure of the movement's reputation.

TALES FROM THE HOME SCHOOL FRONT

You occasionally will hear the spectacular home schooling war story about vengeful neighbors calling Child Protective Services who take the children away. Our story, though, is probably much more representative of the subtle battles of reputation you will face from wearing the mantle "home schooler." Though not so spectacular, our experience is all too common.

At the time we started "formally" home schooling Sarah, Clay had just taken a pastoral staff position in a church of 1500 in Orange County, California. Soon after arriving, he was told that pastoral staff should expect to work 60-70 hours a week (he didn't). Sally was told that pastoral wives were expected to work outside the home (she didn't). The pastor, associate pastor to whom Clay reported, and the director of the Christian school, were critical of home schooling. And the one other home schooling family in the church was contemplating other options. We were outsiders from the start.

Even though we were extremely quiet about home schooling and always avoided the topic, we were branded nonetheless. When Sally was invited to speak to the women's ministry, the president of the group, an outspoken anti-home schooler, stood up and left the room when Sally got up to speak and did not come back until she finished. This same woman discussed with other women at the church that 3 year-old Joel, who was playing alone one morning in Sunday School, was obviously a home schooler because he was not well "socialized." Clay was taken to lunch by the associate pastor who confronted him with arguments from his doctoral dissertation research for public school and against home schooling. One woman came up to Sally at a meeting without introducing herself and started criticizing home schooling.

When Clay was let go during a staff downsizing, we saw it as God's hand of deliverance. God used our California "wilderness" experience to crystallize our convictions about family, the home and home schooling. Providentially, Whole Heart Ministries, a ministry committed to restoring wholeness in families, was born in a culture characterized by fragmented families. Detractors may use the reputation indictment, but God can use it for his own good!

Point out the scope and reach of the home-schooling movement by emphasizing the factors that underscore its growth and strength.

- ***There are national, state and local organizations to defend, support and assist home-schooling families.*** There is no "national" home education association at this time, and it is unlikely there will be in the near future. However, though they vary widely in scope and purpose, state organizations protect and promote the interests of home educators in the individual states. They often lobby for better home-schooling legislation and cultivate relationships with the educational establishment when possible. These spokespersons, leaders and organizations also sponsor curriculum fairs and home-school conferences with special speakers. Other spokespersons and organizations, such as HSLDA, fight the political and legal battles for the right to home school freely.

- ***There are tens of thousands of godly, Christian families who choose to home school.*** Home education is growing annually. Although hard figures are difficult to come by, estimates range as high as 1,000,000 home-schooling children. Convention attendance, magazine subscriptions, organizations membership, curricula and resources buying, and market research all point to a strong rate of growth and a relatively low attrition rate. Though anyone can home school, home education in America remains largely a Christian movement.

- ***There is a growing nationwide network of home-school support groups.*** Many, if not most, urban and near-urban areas have thriving support groups for home educators. Groups vary widely in purpose, scope, structure, size and quality, but all share common goals and purposes—to provide fellowship for home-schooling families, and to mutually help and encourage one another. Most support groups, which are usually parent-volunteer led, have regular meetings, plan field trips and other activities, and provide other co-operative services. Some provide supplemental classes for the children, keep academic records (depending on the state), or offer teacher-training meetings.

- ***There are professional publications, publishers and ministries to keep home educators informed and supplied.*** Numerous periodicals and publications are available (listed in the appendix). Most are very personal and practical. These publications help home-school parents stay informed about news, speakers, ideas and new products. They provide a kind of ongoing teacher training, as well as a "fellowship in print." Numerous curriculum publishers, product catalogs and other ministries (listed in the appendix) keep a steady stream of new, high-quality materials flowing into the home-school community. There is already a rich sea of good educational resources, and it expands and deepens every year.

Comment: Guarding the reputation of home schooling
To paraphrase, "No home-schooling family is an island unto itself." Whether you want to be or not, you and your children are public relations representatives for the home-schooling movement. It is important to keep some simple guidelines in mind when you are out relating to the public. Your good example can do more to promote the good reputation of home schooling than any other single factor. Don't undervalue the importance of a good witness!

- *In general, don't hide the fact that you home school, but don't flaunt it either. Give a defense when appropriate, but don't create an offense by unnecessarily making it an issue. Channel your strong convictions into the political process, not into winning an argument with a stranger.*
- *Get to know your neighbors and let them know you and your children. Invite them into your home, greet them when you see them, take cookie plates at holidays. Be open and friendly.*
- *Keep your children under control whenever you're out in public. Like it or not, expectations will be higher for home-schooled children.*
- *Limit your out-of-the-house activities during public school hours to educational functions, such as support group, field trips, outings and the like. When possible, let shopping wait until after school hours.*
- *Be discerning about outdoor play during regular school hours. It is the perception (their kids are not in school) and not the reality (they are finished with their school) that some people will see.*
- *Church can be a seedbed of conflict over home schooling. Support the pastor and ministries of the church whenever possible. Reach out in some way to home-school critics. Serve quietly and faithfully with your children.*

Be Ready to Live By Faith

Hebrews 10:35-39
So do not throw away your confidence; it will be richly rewarded. You need to persevere so that when you have done the will of God, you will receive what he has promised. For in just a very little while, "He who is coming will come and will not delay. But my righteous one will live by faith. And if he shrinks back, I will not be pleased with him." But we are not of those who shrink back and are destroyed, but of those who believe and are saved.

Hebrews 11:1,6
Now faith is being sure of what we hope for and certain of what we do not see...And without faith it is impossible to please God, because anyone who comes to him must believe that he exists and that he rewards those who earnestly seek him.

Hebrews 11:13-16
All these people were still living by faith when they died. They did not receive the things promised; they only saw them and welcomed them from a distance. And they admitted that they were aliens and strangers on earth. People who say such things show that they are looking for a country of their own...Therefore God is not ashamed to be called their God, for he has prepared a city for them.

Hebrews 12:1-3
Therefore, since we are surrounded by such a great cloud of witnesses, let us throw off everything that hinders and the sin that so easily entangles, and let us run with perseverance the race marked out for us. Let us fix our eyes on Jesus, the author and perfecter of our faith, who for the joy set before him endured the cross, scorning its shame, and sat down at the right hand of the throne of God. Consider him who endured such opposition from sinful men, so that you will not grow weary and lose heart.

There are many reasoned and rational arguments you can make to justify and defend home schooling. There's only one, though, that closes off debate—*"We searched the Scriptures, prayed about it, and determined it is God's will for our family to home school. For us, it is an issue of obedience and faith."*

We didn't want to end this chapter with the implication that home schooling is "the right thing to do" just because there are so many powerful arguments to be made in its favor. Yes, they are convincing and even encouraging, but those arguments alone will not carry you very far as a home educator. When you're up to your eyeballs with children, housework, home business, activities, responsibilities, bills, broken appliances, car trouble and you-don't-know-the-troubles-I-seen, those nicely reasoned arguments are going to ring pretty hollow. When you're pushed to the limits, only a tested and seasoned faith will take you beyond.

That was where many believing Jews found themselves after being scattered throughout Israel in the persecution that followed Stephen's martyrdom. For a time, they lived by their newfound faith, holding on to the Apostles' teachings. But then they began to grow weary and to "shrink back" from the life of faith. When we find ourselves wanting to "shrink back" from what God has called us to do with our family, we go back and read what the author of the epistle told those Hebrews in chapters 10, 11 and 12. Perhaps the outline and study below will encourage you, too, as you follow the home-schooling path that God has laid out before you. There is no other way but to walk it in faith.

10:35-39   Perseverance: the Mark of Faith
What makes you want to "throw away your confidence"? In what ways do you "need to persevere"? How does the promise of Christ's return and his "rewards" affect your faith?

11:1,6   Belief: the Proof of Faith
What do you "hope for" that you "do not see" (be specific)? Is your faith enough to please God? Do you really "believe that [God] exists"? How, exactly, do you "seek" him?

11:1-38   Faithfulness: the Example of Faith
Which examples touch your spirit? Why? What can you learn from them? What would you want to be said about you?

11:39-40   Hope: the Promise of Faith
What was the promise that kept all those mentioned in chapter 11 living by faith (see verses 1,2,9,10,13-16)? What does that promise mean to you? How does it affect the way you live? Do your children know what the promise means to you?

12:1-3   Trust: the Object of Faith
What "hindrances" slow you down in your "race"? What sins, big or little, "entangle" you and trip you up? Do you "fix [your] eyes on Jesus" or on the distractions around you? Do you think about him when you "grow weary and lose heart"?

Psalm 78:1-7

O my people, hear my teaching;
listen to the words of my mouth.
I will open my mouth in parables,
I will utter hidden things,
things from of old —
what we have heard and known,
what our fathers have told us.
We will not hide them from their children; we
will tell the next generation
the praiseworthy deeds of the LORD,
his power, and the wonders he has done.
He decreed statutes for Jacob
and established the law in Israel,
which he commanded our forefathers
to teach their children,
so the next generation would know them, even
the children yet to be born,
and they in turn
would tell their children.
Then they would put their trust in God
and would not forget his deeds
but would keep his commands.

CHAPTER TWO

Discipleship...
Shaping Your Child's Heart

Shaping Your Child's Heart to Live for God

Solomon knew where the lines were drawn between the heart and the mind. At the very beginning of his book of Proverbs, he says, *"The fear of the Lord is the beginning of knowledge, but fools despise wisdom and discipline."* Solomon told his son that knowledge is useless unless it is acquired by a heart that fears God. And he goes on to tell him that the way to shape a heart that fears God is through "wisdom and discipline." If that sounds a lot like the New Testament concept of discipleship—instruction and training—that's no coincidence. God is consistent, and though the terminology may change over time, the methodology does not. In the parable of the seed and the sower, Jesus made it clear that the "good soil" for the seed of his Word is a "noble and good heart." In other words, God's truth makes its way into the mind only through a heart that fears him.

"But that's different," someone might say. "What does God's Word have to do with education?" Everything! If all truth is God's truth, then all truth must find its way to the mind through a heart that fears God. Otherwise it will be knowledge that "puffs up" but not "builds up" (*1 Cor. 8:1-3*). When you begin to think about how your children learn, you must start where God does...with the *heart*. While the mind is intricately linked to the heart, it is in the heart where God relates to you, and your child, as a person.

That is why your responsibility to disciple your children is so foundational to your responsibility to educate them. If you desire to effectively teach your children, their hearts must first be turned to God. Until your children submit their hearts to God and to your authority, you cannot effectively educate their minds. In fact, in view of eternity, it is far more important that your children become wholehearted disciples of Jesus Christ than it is they become "well educated." *A mature disciple of Jesus Christ with the will and skill to learn is much more useful to God's work than a well-educated but immature Christian.* Discipleship of your children is your first priority as a Christian parent—to shape their hearts to live for God.

Jesus commanded us to *"make disciples,"* and that certainly includes your children. Paul, using the language of discipleship, commanded fathers concerning their children to *"bring them up in the training and instruction of the Lord."* So, discipleship is not a responsibility you can put off or turn over to someone else. It is a biblical priority. And when you make "home discipleship" the priority in your family that God intended it to be, you will find that "home education" will follow naturally and easily. *"The fear of the Lord is the beginning of knowledge..."*

Proverbs 1:7
The fear of the LORD is the beginning of knowledge, but fools despise wisdom and discipline.

Luke 8:15
But the seed on good soil stands for those with a noble and good heart, who hear the word, retain it, and by persevering produce a crop.

❝ *He who knows how to teach a child, is not competent for the oversight of a child's education unless he also knows how to train a child.*
H. Clay Trumbull, *Hints On Child Training*, 1890

❝ *For all the most important things in education we have an inside track, since we reckon with the whole person, including heart and soul.*
Ruth Beechick, *A Biblical Psychology of Learning*, Accent, 1982

❝ *It is, therefore, largely a child's training that settles the question [of what kind of person he will become]...In all these things his course indicates what his training has been; or it suggests the training that he needed, but missed.*
H. Clay Trumbull, *Hints On Child Training*, 1890

Home schooling is where the heart is.

*F*ive Heartbeats of Discipleship

With the ministry of John the Baptist, God began to fulfill the prophecy of Malachi 4:6, the last verse of the Old Testament. Through John, he would begin to "turn the hearts of the fathers to their children" *(Lk. 1:17),* but what about the hearts of the children? The simple reality is that the heart of a child is already turned toward his parents (alternate translation). However, if the parents' hearts are not turned toward the child, that child's heart will turn elsewhere. It is the parents who must first turn their hearts toward their children in order to *keep* their children's hearts turned toward them.

Discipleship is so much more than just a list of spiritual goals to accomplish in your children's lives. It is first and foremost an attitude of the heart toward your children. It is seeing them as God wants you to see them—as future servants and leaders for him in the next generation. That is the "vision" God wants you to have for the emerging adults that he has put into your care. These are not just children, they are adults and leaders in training. That is the purpose for which God has turned your heart toward your children! If you are to keep your heart turned toward them to prepare them for the high calling and purpose God has for them, then your heart needs to beat with God's on the importance of discipleship. These five "heartbeats of discipleship" will help you evaluate the attitude of your heart.

❑ Heartbeat #1: Obedience

God, in his wisdom, gave children only two commands: 1) "honor your father and mother," and 2) "obey your parents." The first speaks to attitude, the second to actions. As a parent, it is your responsibility to make sure that your children honor and obey you. The simple fact is, they cannot grow in maturity until the issue of obedience is settled. If they will not honor and obey you, then they will not honor and obey God. The first beat of your heart for discipleship must be to secure your child's honor and obedience. However, it is all too easy to fall into the pattern as a parent of insisting on obedience, but not honor. You can make a child stop a wrong or unwanted behavior (ex., "Stop whining right now."), but your child may still dishonor you in his heart (ex., by frowning, pouting, sulking, etc.). Being committed to your children's obedience means becoming sensitive to your children's behavior *and* their heart attitudes. Obedience is not complete until it comes from the heart. Otherwise, you are training in your children a superficial obedience that teaches them how to comply outwardly, without ever having to confront their inwardly sinful attitudes. Similarly, if your children do not obey quickly, you are training in their hearts a habit of disrespect. You must always keep your eye on their hearts, but a heartbeat for obedience does not mean that every situation must become a "me parent...you child" confrontation of wills. A heartbeat for obedience also means learning to be sensitive to issues of age, personality and circumstances that will affect your child's obedience. You should not expect the same kind of obedience from a five year-old that you would from a ten year-old, or perfect obedience when your children are tired or overstimulated. Your children's obedience is the way they will show their love for God *(John 14:15).* Your job is to help them love God better.

❏ Heartbeat #2: Discipline

Obedience is secured through discipline. Without a heart for discipline there is no obedience, and no discipleship. Though they are different words in Greek, you cannot *disciple* your children without *discipline*. Unfortunately, many Christians, when they hear the word "discipline," seem to think only of physical discipline, yet that is a very narrow understanding of true biblical discipline. Biblical discipline is a *relational process* of spiritual training that cultivates godliness. A heartbeat for discipline means that you are actively and personally committed to training your child in godly character. Discipline is neither enjoyed nor avoided—it is a commitment.

Discipline, or training, is not an option for Christian parents—it is a command (*Eph. 6:4*). In the same way that God the Father disciplines his children for godliness, you are to discipline your child (*Heb. 12:7-11*). If you fail to discipline your child, he will follow his sinful nature and become a disgrace to you (*Prov. 29:15*), so discipline is an act of love that will save your child from death (*Prov. 13:24, 19:18*). Discipline can be either *directive*, guiding your child into godliness; or, as in most cases, *corrective*, confronting your child with his ungodliness. Both aim at godly character, are done in love, focus on the Word of God, and have as their goal a change of heart, not just a change of behavior. The ultimate goal of discipline is never only to stop or control unwanted behavior. Rather, your goal is godliness—*to strengthen your child's will* to say "no" to ungodliness and to choose to live in a godly way (*Titus 2:11-14*). You are training your child to obey with from his heart, not just with his mind or body. In all discipline, though, the question always on parents' minds is "How do I discipline...what do I do?" Rather than thinking about discipline simply as an *act*, think of biblical discipline as a *process* involving three kinds of disciplinary methods: verbal, behavioral and physical.

Verbal Discipline

Verbal discipline is characterized by *instruction, admonition, reproof and correction* (*1 Tim. 3:15,16*). The purpose of verbal discipline is to instruct your child concerning what God says is right and what is wrong. Scriptural commands and principles are consistently taught, talked about, and learned so that the standard for all behavior is God's Word. Verbal discipline affirms to your children that you are their earthly authority, and God is their ultimate authority. Your authority, though, is never expressed as "parental power" that "lords it over" your children. Rather, it is expressed through love that is willing to serve them (*Matt. 20:25-28*). Christlike love is critical to all effective discipline, but perhaps even more so with verbal discipline. When you verbally discipline your children—whether to confront wrongdoing, or to encourage rightdoing—think about how Jesus would speak to them. He would be gentle, but authoritative; loving, but truthful; gracious, but firm. Gentleness creates a positive atmosphere of grace, even though a discipline might be hard. In contrast, strictness, harshness, anger and judgmentalism create an atmosphere of legalism. Yelling, nagging, blaming and shaming may result in temporarily desirable results, but few parents really want their children to obey out of fear and guilt. Gentleness keeps verbal discipline in the realm of grace, where children learn to obey from the heart, for the right reasons—to please God and their parents.

❝ *Harshness, fear, and autocracy are ruled out if we follow the New Testament teaching that leadership means a serving of the other person. The child is respected, his needs and abilities are considered, and he is lifted up. We are to lead in love.*

Susan Schaeffer Macaulay,
For the Children's Sake,
Crossway, 1984

2 Timothy 3:15,16
But as for you, continue in what you have learned and have become convinced of, because you know those from whom you learned it, and how from infancy you have known the holy Scriptures, which are able to make you wise for salvation through faith in Christ Jesus. All Scripture is God-breathed and is useful for teaching, rebuking, correcting and training in righteousness,

Hebrews 4:12,13
For the word of God is living and active. Sharper than any double-edged sword, it penetrates even to dividing soul and spirit, joints and marrow; it judges the thoughts and attitudes of the heart. Nothing in all creation is hidden from God's sight. Everything is uncovered and laid bare before the eyes of him to whom we must give account.

Titus 2:11-13
For the grace of God that brings salvation has appeared to all men. It teaches us to say "No" to ungodliness and worldly passions, and to live self-controlled, upright and godly lives in this present age, while we wait for the blessed hope -- the glorious appearing of our great God and Savior, Jesus Christ...

Galatians 6:7,8
Do not be deceived: God cannot be mocked. A man reaps what he sows. The one who sows to please his sinful nature, from that nature will reap destruction; the one who sows to please the Spirit, from the Spirit will reap eternal life.

Hebrews 12:11
No discipline seems pleasant at the time, but painful. Later on, however, it produces a harvest of righteousness and peace for those who have been trained by it.

❝ *Every child ought to be trained to conform his will to the demands of duty; but that is bending his will, not breaking it...Training a child's will is bringing such influences to bear upon the child that he is ready to choose or decide in favor of the right course of action...The final responsibility of a choice and of its consequences rests with the child, and not with the parent.... Merely to force one will into subjection to the other is...an injury both to the one who forces and to the one who submits.*

H. Clay Trumbull, *Hints On Child Training*, 1890

Comment: Attitude

It is especially important to discern attitudes in discipline. If there is a resistant "I'll obey with my body but not with my heart" attitude, it must be immediately and directly confronted, and if necessary disciplined. If bad attitude is not redressed, you are allowing your child to slowly harden his or her heart to your authority and discipline. If you discern a resistant attitude, rebuke and admonish your child without hesitation. You need to see godly sorrow and submission. However, be sure the attitude is not just the result of tiredness or over-stimulation. An exhausted child should be put to bed for rest, not disciplined.

Behavioral Discipline

Behavioral discipline focuses on making your children accountable for their own behavioral choices. It is the "if...then" method that is the heart of most parental discipline, or should be. Although it can also provide *incentives* to encourage rightdoing, it more often provides *consequences* to discourage wrongdoing (*Gal. 6:7,8*). The most common expressions of behavioral discipline are *natural and logical consequences*.

Natural consequences follow general foolishness and wrongdoing when there has been no prior agreement concerning a behavior. A simple example would be a child dropping an ice cream cone because he was behaving in a way he knew was foolish. The natural consequence would be the loss of the ice cream. Or, if two children are fussing, they must sit quietly without speaking to one another for 30 minutes. You might also use time outs, loss of privileges, additional work or other "natural" responses. An objectively applied natural consequence teaches your children that they are responsible for their own behavioral choices.

Logical consequences follow specific areas of wrongdoing when there has been a prior agreement concerning certain behaviors. An example would be a child saying unkind words to a sibling. The logical consequence might be a previously agreed upon assignment of writing ten times a verse that talks about speaking only with kind words. Or, if chores are not performed on time, then additional chores are added. Whatever the logical consequence, the effect is to make your children personally accountable for their own actions. It is not you, the parent, imposing discipline—it is they, the children, choosing that consequence by choosing to disobey. It is teaching them to think, *"If this, then that."*

This kind of behavioral discipline begins as soon as a child can understand what you are saying, and continues throughout childhood. "If you continue crying, then Mommy will not listen to you...If you leave your toys outside, then you won't be able to play with them for a week...If you don't complete your assignment, then you will not go on the field trip." In every case, you are making your children take personal responsibility for their own behaviors. It is their choice. The key to making it effective, though, is consistency and follow-through from the very first.

IN OUR HOME...

Household responsibilities (cleaning room, picking up, doing chores) have created a fountainhead of opportunities for discipline. However, we've hit upon a naturally logical consequence that makes sense and makes an impact. If a responsibility is not completed, it is understood that the underlying message is "I need some more practice." So, we have a list of extra chores that provide additional practice for being responsible. The list, of course, is fairly distasteful—cleaning baseboards, washing windows, de-spotting the carpet, and the like. Since the first responsibility is much more desirable, our children are learning that it is better to get it done, than to get some extra "practice."

Physical Discipline

Physical discipline is the ultimate logical consequence. It is the end of a process in which the child has failed to heed verbal and behavioral discipline, and has chosen open defiance or rebellion against parental authority. Unfortunately, rather than reserving the use of physical discipline for the most serious offenses, some minimize its impact by using it for less serious offenses. As we have listened to many parents and teachers, and read numerous books, we have grown concerned about a seeming unbiblical over-emphasis and over-reliance upon physical discipline—the practice of making the "rod" of Proverbs the preferred, default method of discipline. We are concerned because the balance of biblical teaching clearly is being ignored. Reference to the rod as a disciplinary method is found *only* in Proverbs, which is a book of *wisdom principles*, not ethical commands. Of the nine "rod" references, five clearly reference adults, and only four reference a "child" or "son." Even in those four passages, the age of the "child" is not clear, and may be referring to a young man. In addition, there are many, many more passages in Proverbs that deal with verbal and behavioral discipline than there are that deal with physical discipline. Based on the small number of texts, there simply is no biblical justification for making the "rod" a primary focus of discipline. Scripture does not support it. *Overuse* of the rod as a method of discipline is ineffective and counterproductive at best, and unbiblical and destructive at worst. Used properly, it can be biblical and effective, but physical discipline should be reserved for the most serious offenses against your authority. It should be a form of discipline and punishment used with much discretion and great concern.

SOME GUIDELINES FOR PHYSICAL DISCIPLINE

- Physical discipline should be reserved to punish *willful wrongdoing* (*Prov. 22:15; 23:13,14*). While some are uncomfortable with the idea of "punishment," God has no such qualms (*Heb. 12:6*). Physical discipline is clearly punishment. Do not avoid it's use, but use it only when necessary.

- The purpose of physical discipline is to make clear to your child that *rebellion, defiance, and willful disobedience* are serious offenses and they *will be* punished. Avoid arbitrary use of physical discipline by clearly communicating to your children the specific behaviors or sins that will result in physical discipline. Then, be consistent in using it only for those offenses.

- Know your child's threshold of discomfort, the point at which physical discipline becomes effective, and be careful not to exceed it. Physical discipline should never cause more than temporary discomfort.

- Before administering, be sure your child knows why he is being disciplined (have him tell you). After, comfort him, have him pray a prayer of confession to God, and then have him ask forgiveness of anyone who has been offended. Finally, affirm your love and confidence in him, and then resume your normal life.

- Physical discipline should always be administered privately with genuine expressions of love and concern. Never, ever use physical discipline in public or in front of others, and especially not in front of other children. Never, ever use it as a means to humiliate or shame your child. Never, ever use it in anger, or in haste. Never, ever use it as a "convenient" method of discipline.

Proverbs 22:15
Folly is bound up in the heart of a child, but the rod of discipline will drive it far from him.

Proverbs 23:13,14
Do not withhold discipline from a child; if you punish him with the rod, he will not die. Punish him with the rod and save his soul from death.

" *There is a place for punishment in a child's training, but punishment is a penalty attached to a choice; it is not brute force applied to compel action against choice. No child ought ever to be punished, unless he understood, when he chose to do the wrong in question, that he was thereby incurring the penalty of that punishment.*

H. Clay Trumbull, *Hints On Child Training*, 1890

" *No parent ought to punish a child except with a view to the child's good. And in order to do good to a child through his punishment, a parent must religiously refrain from punishing him while angry.*

H. Clay Trumbull, *Hints On Child Training*, 1890

Comment: The "Rod" and the the "Child"
Although the English words evoke images of paddles and young children, the Hebrew terms are not nearly so certain and clear. In most instances in the OT, naar is translated with the meaning of "young man" rather than "child." The context in the discipline passages of Proverbs could just as easily yield "young man," which is more in keeping with the age of the "son" who is being instructed in chapters 1-9. The Hebrew word Shebet,, translated "rod," is the word used for a ruler's scepter (symbol of authority). The punishment in view in Proverbs is the beating of a young man (certainly not a child) on the back with a wooden rod. It is far harsher than our modern day equivalent of paddling on the bottom.

❑ Heartbeat #3: Love

> *It is unquestionably true that in no way can any parent gain such power over his child for the shaping of the child's character and habits of life as by having and showing sympathy with that child.*
>
> H. Clay Trumbull, *Hints On Child Training*, 1890

> *Associations and sympathy have far more influence with children, than argument or reasoning. Or rather, we might almost say, associations and sympathy have all the influence, and argument none at all...If you have no sympathy with [your children's] childish feelings, you can gain no sympathy in their hearts for the sentiments and principles you may endeavor to inculcate upon them. If, however, you can secure their affection and sympathy, your power over them is almost unbounded. They will believe whatever you tell them, and adopt the principles and feelings you express, simply because they are yours. They will catch the very tone of your voice, and expression of your countenance, and reflect spontaneously, the moral image, whatever it may be, which your character may hold up before them.*
>
> Jacob Abbott, evangelical minister and author, ca. 1850

> *How many parents there are...who are readier to provide playthings for their children than to share the delights of their children with those playthings; readier to set their children at knowledge-seeking, than to have a part in their children's surprises and enjoyments of knowledge-attaining; readier to make good, as far as they can, all losses to their children, than to grieve with their children over those losses. And what a loss of power to those parents as parents, is this lack of sympathy with their children as children.*
>
> H. Clay Trumbull, *Hints On Child Training*, 1890

One of the most difficult challenges facing any Christian parent is achieving a satisfying balance between parental love and discipline. The immature and foolish behavior of our children causes us to want to "lay down the law" to control their sin, while at the same time their innocence and immaturity causes us to want to "give them some grace" to allow for their sin. After years of this tug-of-war, we've found ourselves giving more rope to the grace side of the tussle, but only because we had laid down the law earlier in their lives. By giving more weight to corrective discipline with love when they were young, we are able to exercise more grace now that they are older because they are already trained. Had we failed to exercise it earlier, we would be "laying down the law" now.

If you want to imitate Christ in your relationship with your children, let your words and actions be characterized by qualities of love. When Jesus spoke to his disciples and his followers, he was gentle, patient and gracious, even when confronting or rebuking. However, with hard-hearted religious leaders, he was harsh and strict. It should be self-evident, but *you will never reach your children's hearts with harshness and strictness.* Choosing a heartbeat of love means you will train your children with the same kind of loving, tender spirit you would expect from Jesus. The following qualities will keep love alive in your home.

Sympathy

The concept of sympathy tends to fall on unsympathetic ears in our culture. Yet just 100 years ago, it was a guiding principle of biblical child training. Perhaps the word evokes images of the permissive parenting of our parents' generation, so it does not receive the hearing it deserves. But sympathy is not complicated. It is simply the willingness to understand and validate your children's thoughts and feelings. It is an open channel to the inside of your child's heart. It is time to revive the heartbeat of sympathy as a priority in the spiritual training of our children.

"Sympathetic" would describe the parent who is actively involved and interested in his child's life, interests, amusements, concerns, fears and delights. It is the parent who makes time to ask questions, talk, and respond to a child. A sympathetic parent understands that each child's distinctive personality is a gift from God that is to be accepted and affirmed, regardless how "different" it may be from their own. Each child needs a different voice of discipline, a different touch of mercy, and a different word of encouragement. And each child has special potential that the sympathetic parent sees and encourages. However, though sympathy may be uncomplicated, it is not undemanding. It takes time to be a sympathetic parent—to spend enough time with your children to understand their childish thoughts and feelings, and to respond in a sympathetic way. For many busy parents who are in bondage to their calendar, if sympathy is not expedient (which it is not) then it is not expressed. Having a heart of sympathy for your children will mean, by necessity, choosing a less busy lifestyle. It will mean lowering your expectations about what can and must be accomplished in a day. If it means winning your child's heart, though, the trade-offs are well worth the results.

Encouragement

If sympathy is an expression of love that focuses on the present moment, encouragement looks to the future. One of the most loving things you can do for your children is to give them hope. Life is just beginning to stretch out before them with all of its possibilities, mysteries and struggles, and they are looking to you for confidence—to know that there really is a God, that their journey through this life has purpose and meaning, and that there is an eternal home after death. They need to know that you see their potential—that you believe that God will use their emerging skills and interests. They need to hear you affirm their developing maturity, even though they are inconsistent and weak. They need to know that you are proud of their efforts and achievements in learning, whether they come easily or with difficulty. Encouragement is not flattery, which admires superficial qualities only to make one feel good. The aim of encouragement is to strengthen the heart and bolster the spirit—to point your child to God and to God's Word (*Rom. 15:4*). A child who is regularly encouraged this way every day will naturally grow in confidence, with a hopeful outlook on the future.

Affection

We generally think of love as something that is either expressed or done for another person. But children know instinctively that *physical* affection is just as much an expression of love in a family as *words* of affection. Hugs, pats, kisses and squeezes are all part of the language of affection that say, without words or actions, "I love you!" Being affectionate with your children is a non-verbal way of assuring them that you accept them just as they are, that they are special to you, and that there is a spiritual bond and unity in your family that is private and powerful. It is more than just an optional extra in your relationship with your children—it is a necessary expression of love that keeps the doors of their hearts open to you. In that way, it is just as much a part of discipleship as instruction and training.

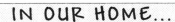

IN OUR HOME...

We are close as a family. As parents, we have warm, loving feelings for our children. But we do not always express our love for them according to the biblical pattern. Every now and then one of us will "lose it" and unload verbally on our kids. Like when Mom gives work assignments three times that don't get done. Or, when one of the children says, "But Mom..." one too many times. Or, when she comes home after a full day of support group, field trip and shopping to find a dirty kitchen (oops, Dad was on the receiving end of that one). Or, when Dad walks into a disaster area at bedtime called the boys' room. Or, when he finds his good tools left in the yard. You get the picture. We have our "bad discipline" days when our otherwise normally gentle, sympathetic, loving spirits seem to go into hiding. Fortunately, our children know that it's a passing phase (although they do get <u>very</u> obedient <u>very</u> quickly on those days). It usually isn't long before we're enjoying one another again. In fact, we usually end up doing something special that evening to compensate. It's all part of the ebb and flow of love in a family. They'll remember the love.

66 *Love should be the silver thread that runs through all your conduct. Kindness, gentleness, long-suffering, forbearance, patience, sympathy, a willingness to enter into childish troubles, a readiness to take part in childish joys,—these are the cords by which a child may be led most easily,—these are the clues you must follow if you would find the way to his heart.*

J.C. Ryle, British minister and author, from *The Upper Room*, 1888

❑ Heartbeat #4: Protection

God wants you to be an overprotective parent! Your children need an "overprotector" who will stand *over* them to *protect* them—to guard their innocence and purity, to prevent spiritual wounds and sinful footholds, and to teach discernment and sensitivity to sin. Unfortunately, it is all too easy to unwittingly or foolishly allow Satan's corrupting influence into your home. You must have a heart to protect your children against two dangerous influences: *unwise relationships* and *ungodly secular media*.

Protection from Unwise Relationships

Your children's personalities and values are powerfully shaped by their relationships, both with children and other adults. Seek out edifying relationships with well-trained, "good and godly" children from trustworthy Christian families. Younger children should always be supervised by mature adults. Entrust your children only to adults you know to be trustworthy believers. Be on guard against four dangerous relationships:

- *Fools* Don't leave your children in the company of other foolish, untrained, unsupervised children, or in the company of a foolish adult. Always monitor the children and screen the adults in their lives. Good training can be quickly undone by fools. (*Prov. 13:20, 22:15*)

- *Unbelievers* Don't allow your children to become emotionally or spiritually yoked to an unbelieving child (i.e., in a close friendship), even if there are no "good and godly" friends around. Your children will grow by waiting and trusting God for a friend. Be very cautious about leaving your children with unbelieving adults. (*2 Cor. 6:14*)

- *Immoral* Don't put your children in the company of other children or adults you know to be immoral or "bad company." Immoral language, attitudes and behaviors are subtle, powerful and spiritually corrosive. You cannot easily erase their effects. (*1 Cor. 15:33*)

- *False teachers* Don't put your children under the authority of an adult you know or even suspect of being a false teacher. Children cannot easily discern false teaching or untruth, especially when promoted by an adult in authority they have been told to listen to. (*2 Tim. 2:16-19*)

❝ *Because a child's companionships are so influential, it is the more important that they be closely watched and carefully guided by the child's parents. It is a parent's duty to know who are his child's companions, and to know the character, and course of conduct, and influence upon his child, of every one of those companions separately. Here is where a parent's chief work is called for in the matter of guiding and controlling his child's companionships...To neglect this agency of a child's training, would be to endanger his entire career in life, whatever else were done in his behalf.*

H. Clay Trumbull, *Hints On Child Training*, 1890

❝ *Keep children as much as possible by themselves, away from evil influences, separate, alone. 'Keep them from bad company,' is very common advice. We may go much farther, and almost say, keep them from company, good or bad...It will be generally found that the most virtuous and the most intellectual, are those who have been brought up with few companions. As an aside, it should be stressed that the most Biblical way for Christian parents to provide their children with quality socialization is for them to act upon the words of Psalm 127 and have large families!...Few companions and fewer intimacies, and many hours of solitary occupation and enjoyment, will lead to the development of the highest intellectual and moral traits of character; in fact, his mental resources may be considered entirely unknown and unexplored, who cannot spend his best and happiest hours alone.*

Jacob Abbott, evangelical minister and author, ca. 1850

IN OUR HOME...

We have found it helpful in our family to illustrate the discipleship process by using the biblical concept of the "path of life" that is pictured in Proverbs 4:18,19 and Psalm 16:11. As their guides on the path, they follow our lead as we direct them, and protect them. As experienced guides, we already know the dangers that must be avoided along the way, as well as the blessings that can be enjoyed by staying on the path. One day our children will be sufficiently trained to walk the path of life without us as guides. Until then, though, we walk together as a family, keeping our eyes on the path laid out before us.

EDUCATING THE WHOLEHEARTED CHILD

Protection from Ungodly Secular Media

Anytime you allow your children to be exposed to the secular media, even if for a "good" show or product, you run the risk of allowing them to be visually, verbally, and spiritually mugged and abused. Most popular media routinely violate biblical standards of what we should allow our hearts and minds to dwell on (*Ps. 101; Eph. 5:8-14; Phil 4:8*). There are plenty of media alternatives, but *secular* media requires your protective oversight:

- *Television* Set a high standard for your children, and for yourself. Never allow them to watch commercial TV unsupervised, or to "graze" or "channel surf" with the remote. If you do watch commercial TV, make it a family rule and habit to mute (or turn off) the commercials. With only a few exceptions, the TV world is violent, sexual and pagan. Use the video recorder to record shows to watch later, or watch pre-recorded videos. As a parent, you must be as disciplined with the television as you want your children to be.

- *Movies* Become an informed and highly selective movie consumer. Don't go to or rent movies just because they are popular, reviewed well, or recommended by other families. And don't trust the movie ratings—today's PG movies are often yesterday's R movies. Remember that movies are messages in film, no matter how innocuous the subject. Most leave God out of the picture...literally. Set a biblical standard of excellence and be wise in movie viewing.

- *Music* Secular radio is a mine field of songs with unbiblical lyrics sung by artists with unbiblical lifestyles. Music is a powerful medium that can go deep into your children's hearts and minds and stay there for a lifetime. Encourage listening to Classical music, and to good Christian music (especially praise and worship, and hymns). Be careful even with "Contemporary Christian" or "Gospel Rock." The messages are good, but the medium may create an undesired appetite for undesirable music. Music can be a powerful tool for discipleship (*Col. 3:16*), but you must use it wisely.

- *Print media* Be careful what you leave on the coffee table. Pictures in magazines can imprint on the brain for life; newspapers are filled with pictures and articles unsuitable for children. Keep your coffee table covered with quality Christian print media, selected children's illustrated story books, unusual art books, interesting Christian publications, acceptable travel magazines, and the like. Beware of other danger zones: supermarket check-out, newsstands and video rental stores.

- *Electronic media* Computer games, edutainment software, CD Rom, TV game add-ons (such as Nintendo, CDI), on-line services, the Internet and other forms of electronic media are both promising and potentially problematic. Be especially careful if your children want to explore the Internet and the World Wide Web. There are places on the net for Christians and home schoolers, but there are also places for degenerates. *You* must monitor the monitor. Whether you slip on a disk or become lost in cyberspace, you can get a lot of nasty bytes if you're not careful.

Psalm 101:3,4
I will set before my eyes no vile thing. The deeds of faithless men I hate; they will not cling to me. Men of perverse heart shall be far from me; I will have nothing to do with evil.

Ephesians 5:11,12
Have nothing to do with the fruitless deeds of darkness, but rather expose them. For it is shameful even to mention what the disobedient do in secret.

Philippians 4:8
Finally, brothers, whatever is true, whatever is noble, whatever is right, whatever is pure, whatever is lovely, whatever is admirable -- if anything is excellent or praiseworthy -- think about such things.

" *The center of companionships in a child's amusements ought to be the parents themselves...No companionship should be permitted to a child in his amusements that is likely to lower his moral tone, or to vitiate his moral taste...It ought to be so, in every well-ordered home, that a child can find more pleasure at home than away from home...Wiser parents secure to their children such home amusements as cannot be indulged in to the same advantage outside the home.*
H. Clay Trumbull, *Hints On Child Training*, 1890

" *I didn't even dream it would be so good. But I would never let my children come close to the thing.*
Vladimir Zworykin, quoted on his 92nd birthday about his invention, the television

" *I have prevented my kids from watching MTV at home. It's not safe for kids.*
Tom Freston, President of MTV

❑ Heartbeat #5: Direction

If you want to "*train a child in the way he should go,*" you must first know the way he should go! A heart for direction means having a clear vision for where you want to lead your children. As obvious as that may sound on the surface, many Christian parents miss that truth because they mistakenly assume that protection is the same as direction. It is not. One of the critical roles you will play in your children's lives is that of spiritual guide. Your job is to guide your children on the path of life. Part of that job is to *protect* them from temptation and sin. However, your real goal is to *direct* them into godliness and righteousness. You can keep them out of trouble for 15 or 18 years, but only a righteous heart will keep them out of trouble after you are out of the picture. If you want your child to stay on the path of life—"*and when he is old he will not turn from it*"—then you must give him direction when he is young. *You* must know where to go if you expect to guide your children in the way *they* should go. You can effectively direct your children using three biblical tools. The more you use them, the more effective your direction will be:

- *Training (Prov. 22:6)* Training, or discipline, is the process of shaping your children's actions and attitudes. Your goal as a trainer is to build godly character and habits in your children.

- *Instruction (Eph. 6:4)* Instruction, or teaching, is imparting Bible truth to your children. Through instruction, you are helping your children grow in understanding, wisdom, discernment and faith.

- *Modeling (Lk. 6:40)* Modeling is being a living example of your training and instruction. You are showing your children what Christian maturity looks like, and encouraging them to imitate your example.

Effective discipleship is always intentional, never accidental. You cannot rely on a passive example to give your children the spiritual direction they will need now and as adults. LifeGIFTS is an uncomplicated plan for active, intentional "home discipleship" that you can use with your children. The five priorities, or *GIFTS*, will enable you to set your children confidently on the path of *Life*. The illustration below visualizes the balance of the five priorities between knowledge and action, one fostering *desire* and the other *ability*. The result is that LifeGIFTS instills *desire-ability* in your children. The five pages that follow expand on each individual priority, explaining how to implement each in your own home and family.

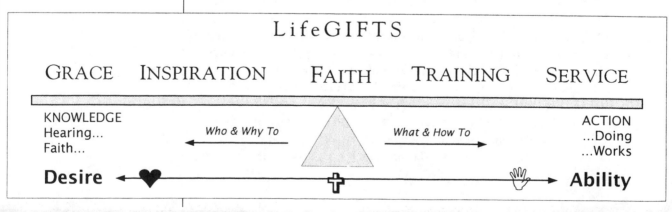

EDUCATING THE WHOLEHEARTED CHILD

LifeGIFTS

GRACE

The gift of grace is *the desire and ability to relate personally and purposefully to God and people.*

- **Training**

    Help with personal devotions.
    Train in gracious behavior (manners).
    Value and pursue priority relationships.
    Train your children how to pray.

- **Instruction**

    About our relationship with God.
    About unconditional love and forgiveness.
    About God's grace.
    About our identity in Christ.

- **Modeling**

    Having regular personal devotions.
    Being gracious to family members.
    Showing loyalty to spouse.
    Praying spontaneously for needs.

The gift of Grace *prepares your children to become channels of God's grace and love to other people. A person who cannot relate personally and purposefully to God or to people will, without fail, be handicapped or even hindered in life and ministry. In order to be channels of grace, your children must be able not only to receive God's grace, but to be able to give it to others. The quality of graciousness will make your children equally at home with both commoners and kings, and will make others they come in contact with feel accepted and valuable. Even simple courtesies become powerful tools of God's grace. Graciousness removes barriers and builds bridges. It opens the channel by which God's grace can flow into a sinful world through your children.*

Matthew 22:37-39
Jesus replied: Love the Lord your God with all your heart and with all your soul and with all your mind. This is the first and greatest commandment. And the second is like it: Love your neighbor as yourself.

❝ *Unless a man is courteous toward others, he is at a disadvantage in the world, even though he be the possessor of every other good trait and quality possible to humanity...Courtesy is the external manifestation of a right spirit toward others.*

H. Clay Trumbull, *Hints On Child Training,* 1890

IN OUR HOME...

We view the ministry of hospitality in our home as God's tool for us to train our children in graciousness. When someone comes to our home, our children know that we expect them to be gracious and quick to serve. That means welcoming adult guests properly, asking if there is something they can get for them, taking their coat, or whatever is appropriate to the visit ("hospitality drills" are a helpful way to train them in this area). Our children know that being well-mannered and gracious is more than just a cultural formality...it is the way we show respect to another person, affirm their value as a person made in God's image, and strengthen our testimony to them not only as a Christian family, but as a home-schooling family. Even when we go to someone else's house, we still practice hospitality. We rehearse with the kids before they leave the car how to be gracious guests who are polite, respectful and helpful.

G □ F T S

The Gift of Inspiration

prepares your children to live with hope in a fallen world. It enables them to view their lives through the unclouded lens of God's past faithfulness, present sovereignty, and future purposes. Inspiration enables your children to see themselves as a part of God's work in this world—that the same God who created them has gifted them for his use and has a special purpose for their lives. It gives them confidence to know that what God has done in the lives of other great Christians and heroes of the faith, he can do in their lives. It gives them the sense that they have a family heritage to share and a legacy of faith to carry on. Inspiration is the flame of faith that burns in their hearts with the truth that they will "believe that he exists and that he rewards those who earnestly seek him."

Hebrews 12:1-3
Therefore, since we are surrounded by such a great cloud of witnesses, let us throw off everything that hinders and the sin that so easily entangles, and let us run with perseverance the race marked out for us. Let us fix our eyes on Jesus, the author and perfecter of our faith, who for the joy set before him endured the cross, scorning its shame, and sat down at the right hand of the throne of God. Consider him who endured such opposition from sinful men, so that you will not grow weary and lose heart.

INSPIRATION

The gift of inspiration is *the desire and ability to view all of life in the light of God's sovereignty and purpose.*

- *Training*

    Have an annual Family Day (God's faithfulness).
    Read Christian history and biographies.
    Create a Family History and Heritage album.
    Play "God's Hands" (I saw God's hands when he...).

- *Instruction*

    About God's sovereignty and providence.
    About God's unique gifts and plan for each child.
    About God's purpose and design for the family.
    About the nature of faith and belief.

- *Modeling*

    Share answers to prayer with your family.
    Trust God for something beyond your current means.
    Thank God often for his faithfulness.
    Talk about the reality of heaven and eternal life.

IN OUR HOME...

Planting seeds of inspiration in our children is a continual process. We look for opportunities to affirm areas of giftedness and talent in their lives that God is using or could use for his glory. We use storytelling to create mental pictures in our children's minds of them as Christian leaders as youths and adults. They especially enjoy stories that have them acting heroically or sacrificing for others. Because there are very few Christian heroes, real or imaginary, for them to emulate today, we diligently search out books and videos that provide good Christian role models. Whenever possible, we try to find stories about people that match one of their current interests (for example music, sports, nature or others). Inspirational fiction provides many good examples of noble Christian character to imitate. We want to secure in their minds that God uses ordinary people to do extraordinary things, and that he can use them, too.

EDUCATING THE WHOLEHEARTED CHILD

Faith

The gift of faith is *the desire and ability to study God's Word and apply its truths to every area of life.*

- **Training**

    Teach your children how to study the Bible.
    Have a weekly Scripture memory challenge.
    Have "Table Talks" about biblical subjects.
    Take advantage of any "teachable moments."

- **Instruction**

    About all areas of Bible doctrine.
    About Bible promises.
    About the reliability of the Scriptures.
    About the Bible (authors, order, themes, dates, etc.).

- **Modeling**

    Talk about what you are learning from Scripture.
    Explain a verse or passage to your children.
    Share meaningful Scriptures you have memorized.
    Take your children to your Bible study.

IN OUR HOME...

As an occasional alternative to church clubs, we have created our own home Bible club called "Pathkeepers." It is centered around memorizing Scripture based on themes (Christian life, character, doctrine, promises, etc.). We open our time with some kind of fun activity and some singing. Then there may be a brief lesson, including review of previously memorized Scriptures, and work on new verses. We close with prayer and a favorite dessert. What makes it especially attractive to the kids is the kinds of awards and prizes we can offer for completing memory goals—books, games, software, and such—much better than the normal club stuff. We don't have uniforms, pins and badges...yet. In reality, it is really just a fancy family night. However, it gives us the opportunity to build our children's faith in an enjoyable and memorable way. It's our family faith night.

G I F T S

The Gift of Faith *prepares your children to bring the truth and wisdom of Scripture to bear on all areas of their lives. In contrast to the more "heart faith" of inspiration, the gift of faith is "head faith." It is the objective truths of God that give content to faith. Paul called it "the faith," the revealed truths of God that needed to be guarded and passed down to others. It is giving your children confidence that God's Word is authoritative, trustworthy and true. It is giving them the ability to gain knowledge and wisdom, and to hear the voice of God in its words. It is giving them the ability to discern truth from error, and right from wrong. It is giving your children a solid foundation on which to build their faith.*

Colossians 2:6,7
So then, just as you received Christ Jesus as Lord, continue to live in him, rooted and built up in him, strengthened in the faith as you were taught, and overflowing with thankfulness.

❝ *From the very beginning the child can take in the great truths concerning God's nature, and the scope of God's power, as fully as a theologian can take them in. Therefore there need be no fear that too much is proffered to the child's mind in this sphere, if only it all be proffered in simplicity as explicit truth, without any attempt at its explanation.*

H. Clay Tumbull, *Hints On Child Training*, 1890

G I F S △ T

The Gift of Training in *righteousness prepares your children to live godly lives. You are doing much more than just training them to do what is right, though—you are training them to choose what is right to do. You are giving them the gift of a trained spirit. You are enabling them to grow in Christian maturity, and to live each day in the power of the Holy Spirit. You are giving them the ability to be self-disciplined, or self-governing, in their Christian walk, not needing others to rule over them to do what is right. You are instilling in them the biblical values and Christian character that will keep them on the path of righteousness throughout their lives.*

Proverbs 22:6
Train a child in the way he should go, and when he is old he will not turn from it.

Ephesians 6:4
Fathers, do not exasperate your children; instead, bring them up in the training and instruction of the Lord.

❝ *Parents, do you wish to see your children happy? Take care, then, that you train them to obey when they are spoken to,—to do as they are bid...Teach them to obey while young, or else they will be fretting against God all their lives long, and wear themselves out with the vain idea of being independent of His control.*

   J.C. Ryle, British minister and author, from *The Upper Room*, 1888

T RAINING in righteousness

The gift of training is *the desire and ability to grow in Christian maturity in the power of the Holy Spirit.*

- *Training*

    Develop your own list of family values/principles.
    Create opportunities to exercise godly character.
    Affirm and reinforce expressions of maturity.
    Gradually enlarge areas of stewardship and responsibility.

- *Instruction*

    About honoring and submitting to authority.
    About walking in the power of the Holy Spirit.
    About growing in Christlike character.
    About being a good steward.

- *Modeling*

    Demonstrate a controlled spirit when under stress.
    Practice any family values or "rules."
    Talk about stewardship of family finances.
    Explain a choice or decision you had to make.

IN OUR HOME...

We wrote Our 24 Family Ways to address six areas of family life: authority, relationships, possessions, work, attitudes and choices. The following are the "ways," or values, that relate to work:

13. We are diligent to complete a task promptly and thoroughly when asked.

14. We take initiative to do all of our own work without needing to be told.

15. We work with a cooperative spirit, freely giving and receiving help.

16. We take personal responsibility to keep our home neat and clean at all times.

With an objective standard for our family, it allows us to avoid nagging and to focus more on positive training. Each way also has a related character quality and Scripture memory verse.

SERVICE

The gift of service is *the desire and ability to minister God's grace and truth to the needs of others.*

- **Training**

  Involve your children in a regular service project.
  Get involved as a family in a church ministry or mission.
  Train children in showing hospitality at home.
  Minister to missionaries (care packages, pen pals, etc.).

- **Instruction**

  About testimony and witness.
  About God's heart for the poor and needy.
  About the ministry of the church.
  About the "Great Commission" and missions.

- **Modeling**

  Create opportunities for hospitality.
  Pray for friends, missionaries, and the unsaved.
  Serve your spouse whenever possible.
  Be involved in a ministry in your church.

IN OUR HOME...

Ministry begins in our home—if we don't minister in our home, then we won't minister away from home. So we come full circle back to Grace in the LifeGIFTS model because the ministry of hospitality we practice at home is the pattern for our ministry and service as a family outside the home—God's way for us to practice serving others in Christ's name. During holiday seasons, we go as a family to sing at local nursing homes. After singing, we all visit with the residents. One Christmas, we took our support group choir to a homeless shelter to minister to homeless mothers and children. We filled stockings with lots of useful and fun items to give away. We also try to keep gift certificates for hamburgers in the car that the kids can give to the "work for food" homeless people we come in contact with. Throughout the year, we look for similar ways to meet needs, encourage the faithful and use our gifts as a family for God.

G I F T

The Gift of Service *prepares your children for meaningful Christlike ministry. It is giving your children eyes that can see needs, hands willing to help meet those needs, and a heart willing to sacrifice and serve in the name of Christ. It is easy to be self-centered in this world, looking out only for our own interests. But Christ wants our families to serve others. He wants us to be servants, like him, who look out for the needs and interests of others. If our children will one day lead, they first must learn to serve. They can learn that first at home in a family that serves others—whether helping the poor, reaching the lost, or building up the body of Christ.*

John 12:25-26
The man who loves his life will lose it, while the man who hates his life in this world will keep it for eternal life. Whoever serves me must follow me; and where I am, my servant also will be. My Father will honor the one who serves me.

" *One of the greatest powers for good is a family whose members respect each other and who have learned to function, however poorly, with the rich concepts of the Word God gives us as human beings. It is almost incredible to think of the stabilizing effect ordinary families can have: not only for themselves, but as a light in a troubled generation.*

Susan Schaeffer Macaulay,
For the Children's Sake,
Crossway, 1984

It All Starts In $Your$ Heart

Deuteronomy 6:1-9

*These are the commands, decrees and laws the LORD your God directed me to teach you to observe in the land that you are crossing the Jordan to possess, so that you, your children and their children after them may fear the LORD your God as long as you live by keeping all his decrees and commands that I give you, and so that you may enjoy long life. Hear, O Israel, and be careful to obey so that it may go well with you and that you may increase greatly in a land flowing with milk and honey, just as the LORD, the God of your fathers, promised you. Hear, O Israel: The LORD our God, the LORD is one. Love the LORD your God with all your heart and with all your soul and with all your strength. **These commandments that I give you today are to be upon your hearts.** Impress them on your children. Talk about them when you sit at home and when you walk along the road, when you lie down and when you get up. Tie them as symbols on your hands and bind them on your foreheads. Write them on the doorframes of your houses and on your gates.*

❝ *Instruction, and advice, and commands will profit little, unless they are backed up by the pattern of your own life. Your children will never believe you are in earnest, and really wish them to obey you, so long as your actions contradict your counsel...Think not your children will practise what they do not see you do. You are their model picture, and they will copy what you are...[Your children] will seldom learn habits which they see you despise, or walk in paths in which you do not walk yourself.*

J.C. Ryle, British minister and author, from *The Upper Room*, 1888

You may know discipleship up, down, backward and forward, and you may even be a great discipler and teacher. But one thing is certain—no matter how much you know or are able to do, *your children will want to become only as mature as you are willing to become.* Jesus taught, *"A student is not above his teacher, but everyone who is fully trained will be like his teacher" (Luke 6:40).* Your child is not above his teacher (that's you), and will in fact become like you when his education is completed. It should be a sobering thought that most of what your child eventually becomes will result not from what you say and do, but from what you are. *You are your child's standard for Christian maturity.*

Before they were to cross the Jordan into the land God promised to them, Moses gathered all the people of Israel together and addressed them *as parents.* He admonished them to love and serve God, to obey his commands and teachings, and to *"impress them on your children."* But there was one stipulation: *"These commandments that I give you today are to be upon your hearts."* They were to be on *the parents'* hearts first. It wouldn't be enough for them to simply *tell* their children how to live; they must also *show* them. Simply put, *you cannot impress on your children's hearts what is not already on yours.*

It is possible that Christian home education is a spiritual awakening through which God is restoring families and preparing for revival. The home-schooling movement may be the first fruits of a greater movement of God's Spirit in our country that is yet to come, and our children may be the seeds of a new and godly generation. However, *if our children are to be lights in their generation, we must be lights in ours.* If, indeed, we are preparing our children to become the Christian leaders of the next generation, then our goal must be no less than to raise up godly men and women who will be totally, wholeheartedly devoted to God and to living only to please him. We need, then, to seriously consider what qualities of godliness we want to develop in our children. *For whatever goals we set for our children, we must also set for ourselves. Whatever we want to be on our children's hearts, must first be on ours (Deut. 6:6).*

Even though impressive people with recognizable names still recite the axiom, "Christianity is more caught than taught," the truth is more accurately expressed, "Christianity is best caught when taught." A passive Christian example pales in power and impact in relation to an active, verbal one. If you want to provide a true biblical model, whatever is on your heart must also be on your tongue. If biblical character and values are on your heart, then biblical teaching about them will be on your tongue in instructing your children. Wholehearted Christian children come from homes led by wholehearted Christian fathers and mothers. We must take the gospel to the nations, but the home will always be God's primary tool for reproducing believers in the world. And it all starts with your heart.

Jesus pictures God in Matthew 7:9-12 as a good father. If asking for a fish, the child knows he will receive a fish, not a snake. If asking for bread, the child knows he will receive bread, not a stone. Your children are asking you to give them a taste of real spiritual life. They want to learn from you how to live for Christ. Your passivity is the same as a snake or a stone to your child. You must decide what you will give them, and then determine to provide it. And like the five loaves and the two fishes offered in simple faith by a child, God will take what you have and multiply it to spiritually feed your family and many others through you. The following acronyms of "fish" and "bread" provide some simple goals for Christian character (what is important *about* me) and values (what is important *to* me) you can begin to cultivate in your own heart, and to teach to your children.

❑ Christian Character (FISH)

- *Faithfulness*...to God, to his Word, to his cause, to your family, to your church, to his will for your family, to ministry, to witness.

- *Integrity*...in personal character, in family matters, in work, in finances, in ministry, in relationships, in agreements, in difficulties.

- *Self-Discipline*...to live righteously, to be contented, to persevere under trial, to resist temptation, to fulfill responsibilities.

- *Humility*...in relationships, in disagreements, in serving others, in being available, in being teachable, in asking forgiveness.

❑ Christian Values (BREAD)

- *Bible*...reading it, studying it, memorizing it, talking about it, obeying it, believing it, trusting in its promises.

- *Relationships*...spending time with your family, enjoying your children, fellowshipping with friends, reaching out to lost people.

- *Eternal perspective*...having a biblical worldview, trusting God for daily and future needs, longing for heaven.

- *Authority*...submitting to authorities, taking biblical authority seriously, speaking positively of leaders, submitting to elders.

- *Disciplines*...having regular devotions, praying alone and with children, worshipping God, serving others, confessing sins.

2 Chronicles 16:9a
For the eyes of the Lord range throughout the earth to strengthen those whose hearts are fully committed to him.

2 Peter 1:3-11
*His divine power has given us everything we need for life and godliness through our knowledge of him who called us by his own glory and goodness. Through these he has given us his very great and precious promises, so that through them you may participate in the divine nature and escape the corruption in the world caused by evil desires. For this very reason, make every effort to add to your faith goodness; and to goodness, knowledge; and to knowledge, self-control; and to self-control, perseverance; and to perseverance, godliness; and to godliness, brotherly kindness; and to brotherly kindness, love. **For if you possess these qualities in increasing measure, they will keep you from being ineffective and unproductive in your knowledge of our Lord Jesus Christ.** But if anyone does not have them, he is nearsighted and blind, and has forgotten that he has been cleansed from his past sins. **Therefore, my brothers, be all the more eager to make your calling and election sure. For if you do these things, you will never fall, and you will receive a rich welcome into the eternal kingdom of our Lord and Savior Jesus Christ.***

CHAPTER THREE

Education...
Strengthening Your Child's Mind

Strengthening Your Child's Mind to Learn for God

Learning is a mysterious process. Researchers examine it, scholars attempt to explain it, and teachers try to stimulate it, yet no one except God knows exactly how we learn. However, for our purposes, there are two broad views of learning that summarize the crowded spectrum of educational philosophies and methodologies—secular and biblical. Ask a proponent of each about learning and you will receive two very different answers.

If you ask a secular educator about learning theory, he would likely describe learning as a *mental process* centered on the child's *material brain*, and measured by the *retention of discreet facts and information*. He would emphasize the role of the teacher and the acquisition of knowledge. The secular educator would acknowledge neither the existence of a Creator God nor the existence of an immaterial heart and mind (the soul). Instead, he would view a child's mind as an empty vessel waiting to be filled. The educator might describe the child as a wonderful and complex human organism. But when all the educational rhetoric is stripped away, to the secular educator the child is still just a smart animal, the product of evolution in a godless, material universe that just happened by cosmic chance.

As a Christian home educator with a biblical view of education, your answer to the same question about learning theory should be very different. You would describe learning as a *personal process* involving both your child's *heart (or, soul) and mind*, and measured by *wisdom, understanding and knowledge of truth*. You would emphasize the role of the child as a whole person with an innate, natural appetite for knowledge and a limitless capacity to learn. You would be more concerned with your child's understanding of important ideas and concepts, than with the accumulation of discreet knowledge. Your child is not just a soulless brain that needs to be filled up with facts by a teacher, but a person in relationship with you and God, who has eternal value, dignity and purpose because he or she is made in the image and likeness of their Creator.

Contrary to the secular educator's view, a child is not educated just because he has logged enough time in classrooms, or performed well on certain tests, or completed a formal curriculum. In God's economy, to be "educated" is not a matter of something you know or have achieved. Rather, to be educated is something you become. A truly educated child is one who has the *desire* and the *ability* to learn and to grow. The desire to learn (will) is from the heart; the ability to learn (skill) is in the mind. An educated child has strong mental muscles.

> 66 *Modern research and theories do give various views of man and his learning, but the Bible gives the 'soul' view. And that is too important to leave out of a learning theory...Piaget, who more than anyone else worked at breaking down children's learning into bits and describing them, came to the conclusion that it is not possible to lay bits out in linear fashion for children to learn...In short, there is no scientific explanation of learning. Many people have argued that it's a fallacy to call education and psychology sciences. They are not sciences in the sense that physics is. And when they do behave like sciences, they leave out heart and soul, the most important ingredients. So it is right for our theory of learning to draw from the Bible more than from science. A Bible figure for learning is 'growth.' Growth happens all over, at the same time.*
>
> Ruth Beechick, *A Biblical Psychology of Learning*, Accent, 1982

> 66 *Our belief, or lack of belief, in the child's human heart will completely determine the way we teach that child.*
>
> Mary Pride, *Schoolproof*, Crossway, 1988

> 66 *The purpose of education and the schools is to change the thoughts, feelings and actions of students.*
>
> Prof. Benjamin Bloom, the "father of O.B.E." (Outcome-Based Education, a comprehensive secular methodology that emphasizes attitudinal and values conformity over traditional educational goals)

*B*uilding Mental Muscles

Our culture is obsessed with measuring learning—Achievement Testing, PSAT, SAT, IQ, test grades, report cards. The problem with all this measuring is that it has convinced us as a culture that we should compare our children to other children when it comes to learning. That is not only an unfair burden on your children, it is a poor measure of true education.

The true test of a child's education is not what he or she knows at any one time relative to what other children know. It is whether or not the child is growing stronger in all of the most important learning skills. We have found it helpful to think of those skills in terms of *muscles*. In the same way we want our children to develop their physical muscles, we also want them to develop their mental muscles. But, just as children have varying physical abilities, they also have varying mental abilities. Some children are going to have stronger leg muscles than others, some stronger arm muscles than others, but it does no good to compare all children's arm muscles. Neither should we compare and judge all children on the basis of one or two mental muscles only (such as IQ, which focuses on reasoning). The goal should be to exercise all of a child's mental muscles so they enter adulthood with a strong mind, with the will and the skill to learn whatever is necessary. Schools do not have the time nor the resources to give each child the individual attention such a goal would require, so they focus on the measurable goal of knowledge retention. However, a home is an ideal environment to build your child's mental muscles.

Mental *strength* is not the same as mental *capacity*. In fact, you probably know adults whose mental capacity for knowledge is adequate, maybe even exceptional, but who are nonetheless mentally weak—they cannot make a decision, present an idea, be creative. Regardless of the mental capacity of your child, it is the strength of his or her mental muscles that will have the greatest impact on their success in life. In the same way that stronger physical muscles enable you to do more, strong mental muscles will enable your child to *learn* more, and even to expand their mental capacity. *The goal of education is not to raise a child who does well on the tests of secular educators; rather it is to raise a child who does well on the tests of real life.* When they need to research an issue, they will have the discipline and ability to find and analyze relevant information. When they need to present an argument, they will know how to use language persuasively. When mediating a problem at church, they will know how to apply wisdom and find a creative solution.

Learning is far too complex to reduce it to just seven mental muscles. Nonetheless, these seven provide a useful way of looking at your children that can free you from the culturally conditioned dependence on testing to evaluate your child's progress. Your children are persons, made in God's image, not just products of an educational system. At the end of the day, when you release your children into adulthood, measurements and tests will be of little importance. If you have shaped their hearts to live for God, and strengthened their minds to learn for him, then you can rest assured that you have successfully "educated" your child.

❏ Mental Muscle #1: Habits

Habit is the ability to act upon common duties or tasks without the necessity of deliberation. It is doing what should be done without having to think about it. Of all the mental muscles, habit is perhaps the most noticeable, regardless whether it is weak or strong. You know quickly whether a child has formed good mental habits or not. Most good habits are the end-product of discipleship and discipline of your children. Once formed, though, they can become powerful drives in the learning process, even stronger than many natural drives. Whatever the habit, though, *it is not the child who forms habits; rather, it is the parents who form habits in the child*. Whether actively or passively, knowingly or not, it is in your power to form habits, both good and bad, in your child. To the degree that you fail to instill good mental habits, you will find yourself needing to govern your child's mental habits where they are yet unformed. Your child needs strong mental habits in order to become self-governing. The following are just a few of the more important habits related to an effective education.

- *Attention/Concentration* The habit of attention enables your child, for example, to hear and retain information without you having to re-read, question, or summarize. You can, in fact, train your child to a habit of inattentiveness by allowing any more than a single reading. Your child has an enormous capacity for attention and retention, but it must be trained into a habit in order to be harnessed for learning.

- *Excellence* The habit of excellence expresses itself in an unwillingness to do less than one's best. You develop this habit in your child by not excusing poor work (i.e., less than the child's ability), and by expecting and affirming real personal effort, whether in reading, writing, math, art, music or other subjects.

- *Orderliness/Neatness* The habit of orderliness is more noticeable by its absence...sloppiness. It is expressed not only in neatly written papers and projects, but in proper use and storage of materials, careful use of books from your library, and care for the home.

- *Truthfulness* The habit of truthfulness affects your child's attitude toward learning and knowledge. It is necessary to train the habit of being truthful about what is actually known or not known, accomplished correctly or poorly, and so on. It is easy to fall into the negative habit of self-deceit concerning learning.

- *Self-Control* The habit of self-control enables your child to do work, even when it seems hard or he doesn't feel like doing it. Although temporary diversion is sometimes necessary for allowing the mind to rest, the habit of self-control enables the child to return to the task willingly. It is the ability to govern one's inner thoughts and feelings.

- *Diligence* The habit of diligence keeps a child moving forward on studies or reading, even when there are distractions. It also spurs him to work hard, not just to get by or do as little as possible. A child with the habit of diligence does not need to be told to do his work.

> ❝ *Hardly anything can be more important in the mental training of a child than the bringing him to do what he ought to do, and to do it in its proper time, whether he enjoys it or not. The measure of a child's ability to do this becomes, in the long run, the measure of his practical efficiency in whatever sphere of life he labors."*
>
> H. Clay Trumbull, *Hints On Child Training*, 1890

> ❝ *Our generation is prone to amuse itself with fragmentary information and resources. We flip on the TV for brief programs, and then we think we know about the subjects they dealt with. A few paragraphs in a magazine, and we think we've formed an opinion. What is happening so often is that we are merely forming a habit of amusing our interest, and then forgetting the fragments. This is not education.*
>
> Susan Schaeffer Macaulay, *For the Children's Sake*, Crossway, 1984

> ❝ *No intellectual habit is so valuable as that of attention; it is a mere habit but it is also the hall-mark of an educated person. Use is second nature, we are told; it is not too much to say that 'habit is ten natures'...We have lost sight of the fact that habit is to life what rails are to transport cars. It follows that lines of habit must be laid down towards given ends and after careful survey, or the joltings and delays of life become insupportable. More, habit is inevitable. If we fail to ease life by laying down habits of right thinking and right acting, habits of wrong thinking and wrong acting fix themselves of their own accord.*
>
> Charlotte Mason, *A Philosophy of Education*, 1925

❑ Mental Muscle #2: Appetites

Appetites in education are closely related to influences in discipleship. Whatever you encourage your children to consume is what will train their appetites, or tastes. A child's mind has a natural appetite for all knowledge, yet too often we satiate our children's intellectual appetites with nutrition-less mental junk food that appeals only to their immature childishness rather than to their developing maturity. With adults, "you are what you eat;" with children, "they become what you feed them." Your children will pick up their appetites from what *you* value, not just from what you *want* them to value. If you want to cultivate their appetites to prefer the best foods for learning then you, too, must value them.

In all appetites, the guiding biblical principle is found in Philippians 4:8,9. The ultimate goal is to train your children's spirits not only to be discerning, but to desire: whatever is *true*, rather than counterfeit; whatever is *noble*, rather than common; whatever is *right*, rather than just acceptable; whatever is *pure*, rather than corrupted; whatever is *lovely* (and beautiful), rather than base and ugly; whatever is *admirable*, rather than just different or clever. You are training appetites in your children to prefer *excellence* over mediocrity, and *praiseworthiness* over market-worthiness.

- *Literature* Great literature is the natural food for your child's mind. It is complete (a whole book), satisfying (real words and ideas; complete sentences and thoughts), and interesting (a complete, complex, well-told story). You do not have to convince or bribe a child to like good literature. Even appetites trained on inferior books will turn very quickly to feed on good literature if given the opportunity. Children have an innate desire for good literature.

- *Living Books* Books on a wide variety of interesting subjects can be either lifeless or living. Lifeless books dwell on dry facts and details, reducing their subjects to snippets of often disconnected information. Living books relate their subjects to real life and real experiences, drawing the reader into a slice of life. Pieces of information will soon be forgotten, but real life insights from a living book will be locked into a child's memory. Living books live on in a child's mind.

- *Art* Children already have a natural appetite for and appreciation of art and beauty. However, the relentless barrage of mass-produced art, digital art, and commercial media dulls their artistic senses. They need a steady diet of quality and classic art to grow in their ability to distinguish good art from mediocre, and to enjoy the full range of artistic styles and abilities. As that ability is sharpened, their appetite and taste for quality art grows and deepens.

- *Music* There is a sea of tasteless, childish, children's music today, and it is getting bigger. However, there is an ocean of great, inspiring music, whether it is classical, praise and worship, inspirational, hymns or other genre. You have the power to shape your children's musical appetites by defining the standards of "excellent" music in your home and then feasting on the best whenever you are able.

Philippians 4:8,9
Finally, brothers, whatever is true, whatever is noble, whatever is right, whatever is pure, whatever is lovely, whatever is admirable -- if anything is excellent or praiseworthy -- think about such things. Whatever you have learned or received or heard from me, or seen in me -- put it into practice. And the God of peace will be with you.

Psalm 101:3,4
I will set before my eyes no vile thing. The deeds of faithless men I hate; they will not cling to me. Men of perverse heart shall be far from me; I will have nothing to do with evil.

Proverbs 15:14
The discerning heart seeks knowledge, but the mouth of a fool feeds on folly.

❝ *A love of reading is an acquired taste, not an instinctive preference. The habit of reading is formed in childhood; and a child's taste in reading is formed in the right direction or in the wrong one while he is under the influence of his parents; and they are directly responsible for the shaping and cultivating of that taste.*
    H. Clay Trumbull, *Hints On Child Training*, 1890

❝ *If I were to label much educational material today, I'm afraid a large percentage would definitely be twaddle. How colorfully and scientifically our generation talks down to the little child! What insipid, stupid, dull stories are trotted out!*
    Susan Schaeffer Macaulay, *For the Children's Sake*, Crossway, 1984

❝ *We have never been so rich in books. But there has never been a generation when there is so much twaddle in print for children.*
    Charlotte Mason, *Home Education*, 1935

- *Video* If ever there was a vast wasteland of childishness, it is the video tape desert filled with poorly written, cheaply produced children's videos. There are, however, excellent video products for children that are mentally stimulating high-quality productions. Even so, limit video viewing. As a totally passive medium that has a dulling effect on mental faculties, watching videos too much can create a negative effect on other habits and appetites as well. If you own a TV and video, use it sparingly only for learning opportunities, strategic times or special privileges. You must control it, not the other way around.

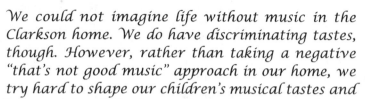

IN OUR HOME...

We could not imagine life without music in the Clarkson home. We do have discriminating tastes, though. However, rather than taking a negative "that's not good music" approach in our home, we try hard to shape our children's musical tastes and appetites with a positive "that's good music!" approach. We started them all out young listening to good Christian music at bedtime—Maranatha Praise tapes, Michael Card, hymn tapes, other adult artists, and the like. We also keep a selection of good music to listen to when we're in the car. The Classical Kids recordings have really piqued their interest in classical music. As new parents, we were drawn to the typical cheery children's tapes such as Psalty, Kids' Praise, Donut Man and others. Now, though, the more their tastes have been trained to "adult" music, the more they prefer it and ask for it. At meal times, we often put on praise and worship, Classical (usually Baroque), contemporary hymns, or good Christian artist recordings. For fun, we have a variety of genres and artists ranging from hammered dulcimer to Christian country and cowboy music. In all, we unashamedly hold to high standards of quality in composition, performance and production. By consistently exposing our children to the "real thing" we are training their appetites to enjoy "real" music, and developing their abilities to discern mediocre from excellent. We've been startled at times at the songs they know (hymns and choruses they've never sung in church), and at the Scriptures and biblical concepts they know just because of a song. We also greatly enjoy as a family viewing well-done videos. Since we want to limit TV viewing, though, we try to be very discerning about the videos we allow in our home. The video wasteland is growing at an alarming rate, and very little of it is worth viewing. We have to search hard for videos with quality content and production values, that also are not offensive. We have begun to build a family video library of good movies, Christian productions, science series, historical productions, good PBS and BBC productions, and a few feature-length animated shows. We have discovered video jewels that have inspired us, touched our hearts, taught us, challenged us and just plain entertained us. Video will be a part of our children's lives when they grow up. We are training their appetites now to guide their choices as adults.

Comment: Discernible Appetites
There is a close relationship between discernment and appetites. It has been likened to the training agents receive for recognizing counterfeit bills. Rather than studying the counterfeits, they intensely study the real bill. They instinctively know the counterfeit bill because it falls so short of the real thing. The best way to teach your children discernment in the area of appetites is to saturate them with the "real thing"—beautiful, excellent music, art, writing or whatever it may be. Then, they will instinctively discern what is base or mediocre by how far short it falls from the real thing.

Psalm 101:1-8
I will sing of your love and justice; to you, O LORD, I will sing praise. I will be careful to lead a blameless life -- when will you come to me? I will walk in my house with blameless heart. I will set before my eyes no vile thing.

Comment: Image and Imagination
Feeding an appetite in your children with the entrancing images of video and television can suppress and distort their appetites for works of good literature that engage the imagination. Consider how image subtly overrules imagination with, for example, Anne of Green Gables. Who can read the book without thinking about the characters from the mini-series. The images have "programmed" the imagination, so the imagination is no longer fully engaged when the book is read. It can become "lazy." Also, research has shown that television has a hypnotic, dulling effect on children viewers that depresses mental functioning. A diet of images that require no mental work will weaken the imagination, which needs mental effort to function well. Starve an image, feed the imagination.

❑ Mental Muscle #3: Language

Your child may grow up to become a well-educated follower of Jesus Christ, but if he arrives at adulthood unable to articulate or communicate what he knows, then you will have provided an incomplete education. You will have given your child a *message*, but failed to make him a *messenger*. It would be like having a battery for your car with no terminals to which you could attach the cables—plenty of "power" but no way to release it to its intended use. It would be useless to you. The mental muscle of language will allow your children to release their spiritual and intellectual power to noble use under the control of the Holy Spirit.

When you think about language development in children, you realize that it is an innate ability designed into our mental abilities by God, the source of all language. How else, with no real instruction, can a child learn such a complex skill? In a few short years beginning at around two years of age, children experiment and expand the language abilities almost exponentially. That a young child can cover such an enormous amount of linguistic ground so rapidly is almost miraculous. But that's just the beginning.

It is not enough simply to teach your child to say words, read words, or to write words. The *power* of language is in the ability to *use* words to move people—to cause another person to learn, to change, to act, to resist, to believe, to follow. That is true of your children as well—whatever they become will be because of the power of language influencing and changing *their* lives. Everybody uses language as a utilitarian means of information exchange, but those who understand its power use it to change lives and even influence history. Whatever impact your children will have for God—how *they* will change lives and make *their* mark on history—will be because of the power of language that you give to them. The following are some of the ways you can strengthen their mental muscles of language.

- *Create a verbal environment* It would seem self-evident, but it cannot be said strongly enough that children's verbal skills grow in proportion to the amount of verbal stimulation they receive in their environment. The more they hear language used, the more their language skills will grow. Begin talking to your children in full sentences very early, even in responding to "baby talk." Talk *with* them, not just *at* them. As they grow, engage your children in conversation whenever possible, especially at meal times when everyone is relaxed. Discuss interesting topics on trips in the car. Look for opportunities to ask open ended questions—What did you think about the sermon? Why do you want to be a fireman? What would you do if that happened to you?

- *Create a print-rich environment* Research shows that one of the common characteristics of geniuses is that they were raised with many books available to them. Don't be stingy on your library—have as many books at home as you possibly can. Have a wide variety of kinds of books. Leave them at strategic reading spots throughout the house. Make all of your books accessible. Every time your child opens a book to read, it is a lesson in language—how someone else used it to express a thought, story, idea or insight.

- **Read, read, read!** The single best way to strengthen your child's language muscle and even expand their capacity for language is to read aloud to them, and have them narrate what they have heard you read. The combination of hearing well-written language spoken aloud, internalizing those words, and then verbally restating what has been heard is an almost ideal language learning method. And it is not just for while your children are young, but for all through their childhood and teens. Also, encourage them to read as much as possible.

- **Write on!** Give your children real life reasons to write—devotional thoughts, a daily journal, a nature notebook, letters. Writing develops their language skills by helping them to think about what they want to say in an orderly and understandable way. Writing poetry is also a richly rewarding language-building exercise. Writing of any kind is the best way to "fine tune" language skills.

- **Limit television** It is tempting to think that television, as a verbal medium, would strengthen a child's language muscle. Just the opposite is true. Because it is a totally passive medium, television actually retards language development because it requires nothing from the child. Without verbal interaction, verbal skills are not exercised or strengthened. Keep TV time limited.

IN OUR HOME...

When we lived in Nashville, we became friends with Dean and Karen Andreola. Our children enjoyed playing with theirs whenever we could get together and were greatly disappointed when the Andreolas decided to move to Oregon. Some time after the move, the kids received a package with an audio tape in it. They were anxious to hear it, so we listened in the car. When we turned it on we were so surprised to hear this perfectly lovely child's voice with a delicate British accent (just like Karen's) reading aloud from a good book. She read so well, with appropriate expression and dramatic timing, that we were all held spellbound for a moment. "That's Sophia! She's a good reader," someone offered. Soon, another sweet voice came on with another wonderful reading. "That's Yolanda! Isn't she great?" We were captivated by their readings—we could count on one hand the number of children we knew whose language skills were so evident. But upon further reflection we realized that we should not be surprised. These children were being raised on good literature read aloud to them by their mother and father. Their home was full of verbal interaction and good language. We were simply seeing the fruit of that environment. With a good example ringing in their ears, our children were motivated to create their own tape of readings and other offerings, which they did with admirable verbal skill. The whole episode was a real-life confirmation of the effectiveness of a verbal environment for building language skills. We could hear it with our own ears.

♥ **Verbal Books**—We have observed that children who are raised in a verbally enriched environment are not put off by books with a bigger vocabulary than their own. As they listen to them read aloud, or read them alone, they may not comprehend all the vocabulary, yet it is going into their minds as food. It is like adding nutrients to the soil of your garden. You won't see immediate results, but the eventual fruit will be much more bountiful than if you had not enriched the soil. The following are some of the books that we have found uniquely enrich our children's language.
- The Lambs *Tales From Shakespeare*
- *Dangerous Journey (Pilgrim's Progress)*
- *The Wind in the Willows*
- *James Herriott's Treasury for Children*
- *Children's Stories from Dickens*

♥ **Words to Grow On**—There is a definite link between vocabulary and intelligence. The best way to increase your children's vocabulary is to read good books aloud. However, you can also have fun learning new words with one of many vocabulary builder products, calendars or lists. The challenge is to use the word without getting "caught" using it. The challenge grows daily because any word from the past week (or month) can be used. Everyone keeps score by awarding themselves one point for each time a word is used without being noticed. Another good source for making vocabulary games is *From the Roots Up*, by Joegil Lundquist, which teaches the Latin and Greek roots of common English words. Points are scored for hearing any words during the day that use the same root words studied. Young children, of course, get a handicap of several free points.

❑ Mental Muscle #4: Creativity

Your children are creative. In fact, *all* children are innately endowed with creativity. As image-bearers of the Creator God, we all reflect a part of his creative nature and power, even though that reflection is blurred and crippled by sin. Redeemed creativity, though, is a powerful mental muscle that allows even children to reflect the glory of God, not just through artistic expressions, but through any endeavor of life. Never allow yourself to think, "My child just isn't creative." There is no such thing as a "creative personality" that some children possess and others do not. Every personality is capable of different expressions of being creative. Your child *is* creative, but that creativity must be nurtured if it is to grow and be expressed.

A common notion of creativity seems to be that it is some kind of mysterious, mystical inspiration that exudes from certain individuals. It is true that some people are endowed with more natural intuition than others, but even intuitive insights are not *ex nihilo*—they do not come from nothing. Creativity never really produces something new that never was before—that is what God alone could do, and did at creation. True creativity draws upon what already exists and finds a *new or better way* of doing something. Far from being a mysterious special gift, it is a process that can be cultivated and trained in all children.

Left to their own interests, children will naturally find ways to express their innate creative drive. Some studies have sadly shown that children enter grade school with a full tank of creativity, but by late elementary the regimented, limited, only-one-right-answer classroom environment drains their tanks nearly dry. Fortunately, the home environment stimulates creativity. The more opportunities your children have to exercise their creativity, the more their creative tanks will stay full. Similarly, the more knowledge, experience and skill they acquire, the more productive their creative process will become. The following are ways you can strengthen the mental muscle of creativity in your children.

- *Provide tools* Like any skill, creativity requires good tools. For children, the tools may be simple, but they are necessary for expressing creativity: good library of books and resources, good computer software, creative writing materials, arts and crafts materials, creative play resources (Lego®, Dacta®, blocks, play bricks, etc.), musical instruments, cooking utensils, gardening tools, dress-up clothes, carpentry tools, sewing materials, science and nature equipment, and so on (see sidebar).

- *Allow free time* One of the most basic characteristics of creativity that research always confirms is the need for lots of free time. Creativity needs time to incubate in the mind before it is "hatched." Along with that free time, your children also need freedom—to explore, to try out different creative ideas, and to simply enjoy the creative process. Creativity is not a totally "unstructured" process, so you can provide structure and guidelines to be sure they are using materials correctly and safely, and aren't expressing ungodly ideas. However, be sure to give your children lots of freedom beyond those reasonable limitations.

Comment: Creativity Is God's Idea

God's pattern of creation in Genesis 1 provides a four step model for our own creative endeavors.

*1. **Information** First, there must be information, or knowledge, upon which to draw ("the earth was formless and empty"). Ex: What kinds of houses can I build?*

*2. **Imagination** Second, imagination is engaged to consider possible new ways to accomplish a task, express an idea, or solve a problem ("let there be"). Ex.: This is the kind of house I would like to build.*

*3. **Realization** Third, there must be a realization of the new idea so that it is expressed in some way; it becomes a reality ("and it was so"). Ex.: Build the house.*

*4. **Evaluation** Fourth, there must be evaluation of the realized idea to determine its validity and usefulness, and if necessary, to improve it ("it was good"). Ex.: What can I do to improve the house?*

Comment: This Is Creative?

Creativity may express itself in your children in ways that are annoying to you as an adult—messy paintings, noisy instruments, outdoor construction eyesores, Lego® fungus (it's everywhere!), smelly nature finds—but it's all a part of the creative process. In the beginning, it may seem "formless and void" to you, but it is the necessary first step for your child. Just hold your critique, or your nose, and give it some time.

EDUCATING THE WHOLEHEARTED CHILD

- **Develop imagination** Imagination is the internal work of the creative process. It is mental vision—the ability to see with your mind's eye. Some children have a more active imagination than others, but all must engage the imagination when listening to a story, wondering about a far-off land, or thinking how to solve a problem. However, unbridled imagination can lead to unbiblical thought-life, so the imagination must be kept subject to the Spirit and to biblical principles. Reading is the single best way to exercise the imagination in a positive way. Your child cannot read or listen to a book without engaging the imagination in some way. Let the book provide an arena for their imagination, envisioning what the people, life and times of the book were like. Especially read the kinds of books that will feed their "moral imagination" with positive role models of virtue, sacrifice, faithfulness, courage and the like. Your goal is to keep your child's imagination active so that it can be called into service for the creative process. A dormant imagination will cripple creativity.

- **Give guidance** Guide your children into areas of creative expression that you see developing in their lives. Be sensitive to their feelings, and certainly don't "push" your child into something that they do not seem interested in, but suggest different creative areas to them and then "try them on" to see if they fit. If they don't, try on something else. Encourage their creative expressions by displaying them, using them, or recording them on cassette, video or film. You may not always be able to praise their creative output, but you can always affirm the creative *process* in your child that brought about the creation. When a creative delight emerges as a potential skill or long term interest, invest in lessons to develop it.

- **Model creativity** If you don't value the creative process, it is not likely your children will. Choose an enjoyable hobby or pastime that exercises *your own* creative gifts (yes, you *do* have them). Display or use your creations just like you would your children's.

IN OUR HOME...

We use holidays to let our children exercise their creative muscles. We'll give them a box of decorations and let them decide how to use them. Or, one of them will create a centerpiece for the table that reflects the holiday or season. For instance, for Presidents' Day Sarah used an antique log cabin model, some books on Lincoln and Washington, coins and bills with their portraits on them, and some other symbolic and decorative items, all placed in a visually pleasing way. We also use our Sunday tea time to exercise creativity by allowing the children to make a special dessert without parental help. Whether it's oatmeal-apple muffins, or instant chocolate-vanilla pudding swirl with chocolate chips and topping (all low fat, of course), or strawberry shortcake, or cookies, it is their way of making a creative contribution to our special time together.

> 66 *[Every] child should leave school with at least a couple of hundred pictures by great masters hanging permanently in the halls of his imagination, to say nothing of great buildings, sculpture, beauty of form and colour in things he sees. Perhaps we might secure at least a hundred lovely landscapes, too—sunsets, cloudscapes, star-light nights. At any rate he should go forth well furnished because imagination has the property of magical expansion, the more it holds the more it will hold.*
>
> Charlotte Mason, *A Philosophy of Education*, 1925

> 66 *Shakespeare, Leonardo da Vinci, Benjamin Franklin, and Abraham Lincoln never saw a movie, heard a radio, or looked at television. They had loneliness and knew what to do with it. They were not afraid of being lonely because they knew that was when the creative mood in them would work.*
>
> Carl Sandburg

> 66 *Creativity is a God-given ability to take something ordinary and make it into something special. It is an openness to doing old things in new ways...The creative spirit is part of our heritage as children of the One who created all things. And nurturing our creativity is part of our responsibility as stewards of God's good gifts.*
>
> Emilie Barnes, *The Spirit of Loveliness*, Harvest House, 1994

❏ Mental Muscle #5: Curiosity

❝ *Equally strong, equally natural, equally sure of awakening a responsive stir in the young soul, is the divinely implanted principle of curiosity. The child wants to know; wants to know incessantly, desperately; asks all manner of questions about everything he comes across, plagues his elders and betters, and is told not to bother, and to be a good boy and not ask questions. But this is only sometimes. For the most part we lay ourselves out to answer [the child's] questions so far as we are able, and are sadly ashamed that we are so soon floored by his insatiable curiosity about natural objects and phenomena.*

Charlotte Mason, *Parents and Children*, 1904

❦ **Just Curious**—Cultivate your children's curiosity by giving them lots of room and resources to explore and discover. Let them take apart old dead appliances to see what is inside them. Crack the case on the computer and give them a tour through its insides. Get some science kits to play with—magnets, electrical circuits, and chemistry are always interesting. Have a star watching party during the Perseid meteor shower. Help them plant an herb garden. Do whatever will stimulate their curiosity and desire to know more.

God has put into children a nearly unquenchable thirst for knowledge. As a parent, you want your children to have strong mental muscles of curiosity that compel them to become self-directed learners. Curiosity—the drive to know—is in many ways the source of all learning. However, in children, who lack the natural discernment that comes with maturity, curiosity is a thirst that can lead them to drink from contaminated wells as readily as from mountain springs. As a parent, you must learn how to channel that God-given curiosity into pure, clean waters. It is true with adults, and doubly true with children, that what we *choose* to know, whether good or bad, determines what we *want* to know. If you let your child choose to know about great missionaries, then the more he or she will want to know about missionaries. If you let your child choose to know about movie stars, then the more he or she will want to know about movie stars. And the more deeply your child drinks from any well of knowledge, the more they will want to drink. Ultimately, the knowledge that your curious child retains will shape what he or she becomes—*we are what we think about!* So, carefully satisfy their thirst for knowledge by directing them to the best wells.

God is concerned not just about the quality, or purity, of knowledge, but also about the kind of knowledge we pursue. Too much knowledge "puffs up" (with pride), but it does not "build up" (*1 Cor. 8:1-3*), and it may even keep a person from coming to a knowledge of the truth (*2 Tim. 3:7*). Any pursuit of knowledge can become empty and vain if it does not lead back in some way to a knowledge of God as the source of all that is good and true. Even Bible knowledge can become a source of "prideful puffery" if it becomes separated from the God who spoke it. That is why discipleship (shaping the heart to live for God) must undergird education (strengthening the mind to learn for God). It is the heart that directs the pursuit of knowledge, and the heart must be turned to God so that curiosity is channeled into knowledge that builds up—*"The fear of the Lord is the beginning of knowledge..."* The following are some ways you can direct your children's curiosity into good wells of knowledge.

- *Model discerning curiosity* Be curious about life and seek out knowledge about new things that interest you—news stories, how something works, historical events—*with your children*. Discuss with them the meaning and impact on your life as a Christian of what you learn.

- *Provide lots of resources* Fill your home with lots of good "cisterns" of knowledge from which your children can drink—interesting books, encyclopedia, "how to" books, hands-on projects, computer, science experiments, telescope, microscope, and the like.

- *Directed studies* Look for areas of interest in your children. Harness their curiosity about that area by creating a unit study that will broaden their understanding of it and apply it to their lives as Christians.

- *Strategic field trips* Select field trips that will tap into your children's curiosity and open up new topics to investigate. Have interesting resources available after the field trip. Discuss their interest in the topic.

❑ Mental Muscle #6: Reason

Language and reason are the arms and legs of the mental muscles. Language is the ability to reach out; reason is the ability to go in the right direction. We don't consciously think about the importance of reason that much, any more than we think about the importance of our legs while we are walking, yet we are exercising reason all the time—evaluating options, making decisions, weighing alternatives, arguing a point, planning a meal, reading an article, explaining something to a child.

Sometimes, when we just can't seem to break through with our children about how reasonable our parental opinion of a matter is, we are apt to think that they must have missed out on some reasoning genes at conception. Yet God designed within them an innate reasoning ability which is the imprimatur of his image in us as his creations. Our children are born with the capacity to reason—it is a part of God's image that sets us apart from the rest of creation. It grows quietly until around 11 or 12 years-of-age when it breaks the surface and shows itself more forcefully, but it must be fed and strengthened from birth if it is to become a strong and useful mental muscle in adulthood.

Home education is uniquely suited to strengthening reason. You can provide your child a great pool of ideas, concepts and knowledge on which their growing reason can draw, and you can train their powers of reason in the context of their home schooling. As you demonstrate to them how reason comes into play in every area of life and learning, they begin to see the patterns that they will use as they begin to reason more on their own. The following are some ways you can reinforce reason at home.

- **Dialogue** Talk with your children about their concerns and questions—choices they are making, spiritual questions, observations they make about life. Resist the temptation to be the "answer-man-or-mom" and, instead, gently probe your children to do their own reasoning. Dialogue with them as they think aloud about their concerns.

- **Problem solving** When you have a real life problem that needs solving—how many gallons of paint to paint the garage, how to double a recipe, what kind of car to buy, planning a room addition—get your children involved. Let them develop and present their solutions. Encourage team problem solving, too. Use their solutions if you are able.

- **Opinion formation** Even a child experiences the personal satisfaction of having a reasonable opinion. Encourage your children to persuade you why they think their opinion of a matter is right. The end product may be childish reasoning, but affirm the process nonetheless. Let them have a voice in discussions as long as they honor and respect you.

- **Thinking skills** Most children enjoy mental challenges. There are many good supplementary workbooks that will stretch their thinking skills. The workbooks are mental work outs that help strengthen reason through analogies, sequences, similarities and differences, spatial reasoning, deduction, logic and others. They're fun and very reasonable!

2 Timothy 2:7
Reflect on what I am saying, for the Lord will give you insight into all this.

1 Corinthians 2:14-16
The man without the Spirit does not accept the things that come from the Spirit of God, for they are foolishness to him, and he cannot understand them, because they are spiritually discerned. The spiritual man makes judgments about all things, but he himself is not subject to any man's judgment: "For who has known the mind of the Lord that he may instruct him?" But we have the mind of Christ.

❝ *The child must think, get at the reason-why of things for himself, every day of his life, and more each day than the day before. Children and parents both are given to invert this educational process. The child asks 'Why?' and the parent answers, rather proud of this evidence of thought in his child. There is some slight show of speculation even in wondering 'Why?' but it is the slightest and most superficial effort the thinking brain produces. Let the parent ask 'Why?' and the child produce the answer, if he can. After he has turned the matter over and over in his mind, there is no harm in telling him—and he will remember it—the reason why. Every walk should offer some knotty problem for the children to think out—"Why does that leaf float on the water, and this pebble sink?" and so on.*

Charlotte Mason, *Home Education*, 1935

❑ Mental Muscle #7: Wisdom

1 Corinthians 1:25
For the foolishness of God is wiser than man's wisdom, and the weakness of God is stronger than man's strength.

1 Corinthians 1:25
For the foolishness of God is wiser than man's wisdom, and the weakness of God is stronger than man's strength.

Comment: Keep Wisdom In Mind
From a New Testament perspective, wisdom begins with a redeemed heart—the heart is turned to God, bondage to sin is broken, the Holy Spirit indwells the new believer making him a new creation with the mind of Christ. But receiving the "mind of Christ" is not the same as receiving God's wisdom. The former must be exercised for the latter to grow. As a "new creation," you are set free from sin in order to choose to listen to and learn from God, rather than from the world. Making that choice every day requires a mental fitness beyond just knowing a few precepts and principles of Scripture. It requires an ongoing renewal of the mind to prevent conformity with the world. That ongoing "renewing of your mind" is the daily exercise of the mental muscle of wisdom.

Romans 12:2
Do not conform any longer to the pattern of this world, but be transformed by the renewing of your mind. Then you will be able to test and approve what God's will is—his good, pleasing and perfect will.

1 Corinthians 2:14-16
The man without the Spirit does not accept the things that come from the Spirit of God, for they are foolishness to him, and he cannot understand them, because they are spiritually discerned. The spiritual man makes judgments about all things, but he himself is not subject to any man's judgment: "For who has known the mind of the Lord that he may instruct him?" But we have the mind of Christ.

Jesus grew in it. Paul preached it. Solomon sought after it. James asked for it. It is acquired by study. It comes from God. It is more precious that wealth, available to all, a supernatural gift, but only for the humble. What is it? If you said "wisdom" you're partially correct. It is *godly* wisdom. Not the world's wisdom, but God's wisdom (*1 Cor.1:18f*). Children can learn the world's wisdom and be very intelligent, knowledgeable and bright, but only the world will be impressed, not God (*Jer. 9:23,24*).

Most discussions of wisdom focus on it as a godly character quality that is the result of training and discipleship. However, that is not all there is to wisdom. You cannot train into your child all the wisdom necessary to address every situation they will face. When they enter young adulthood, and you're not always there to help them, they will need to know how to seek out wisdom and apply it to their lives on their own. Even in childhood wisdom is a mental muscle that must be exercised and strengthened!

When Moses prayed that God would "*teach us to number our days aright, that we might gain a heart of wisdom*" (*Ps. 90:12*), he was acknowledging that godly wisdom takes work and discipline, and that we have only a few days on this earth, in view of eternity, to acquire it. Your task as a parent is to "number your child's days" so that you ensure that they gain a heart of wisdom while in your home. The following are some of the ways you can help your child learn to acquire and grow in wisdom.

- **Discernment** The most fundamental quality of wisdom is the ability to discern right from wrong, what is pleasing to God from what is not, what is biblical from what is not. Teach your children how to use a concordance and a topical Bible to do their own search of the Scriptures for godly discernment on various subjects such as friends, television, money, music, and activities. For practice, have them create a topical index of the book of Proverbs, or of the parables of Jesus.

- **Understanding** Books and commentaries can often help deepen understanding of a subject. Whenever possible, involve your children in locating a helpful book or resource, and in seeking a better understanding. Talk about it, then have your child express what he or she learned.

- **Wise people** "*He who walks with the wise grows wise*" (*Prov. 13:20*). Train your children how to seek wisdom from other godly, wise people. Have them interview a mature believer to learn more about a chosen subject—relationships, work, walk with the Lord, or others.

- **Prayer** Encourage your children, before they do anything else, to pray for wisdom (*Jas. 1:5*). Make a notebook to record wisdom they learn in answer to their prayer. Model praying for wisdom for your family.

- **Stewardship** Give your children gradually expanding stewardships to exercise their wisdom, such as in the area of money. Have them find out what Scripture says about money, then help them develop a budget and justify where they apportion the monies they receive.

You Set the Pace for Learning

You can exhort, cajole and harangue your children all day long about getting regular exercise to have fit bodies, but if they don't see *you* exercising you'll be fighting a losing battle. It is the same with education. If you want your children to value and pursue learning—to build strong mental muscles—then your first priority as a home educator is to set the pace for their learning. Your example will be their model. So before you exhort your children about strengthening their mental muscles, be sure to evaluate your own heart for learning.

- Are you developing good mental *habits*—do your children see you working to strengthen your habits?

- Are you feeding good mental *appetites*—do your children see you choosing what is excellent over what is mediocre?

- Are you improving your *language* skills—do your children see you speaking more with expression and conviction?

- Are you expressing *creativity* in your life—do your children see you enjoying a creative pursuit?

- Are you cultivating *curiosity*—do your children see you seeking out knowledge about areas of interest?

- Are you strengthening your powers of *reason*—do your children hear you reasoning through problems and issues?

- Are you growing in *wisdom*—do your children see you seeking God's wisdom on important questions in your life?

One of the extra benefits of home educating is that it restores to the whole family the excitement and pleasure of learning—fathers, mothers, daughters and sons all learning and growing together. *God never intended for parents to retire from learning.* In the biblical family model, parents continue to learn and pass their learning on to their children. We can read the Proverbs in an offhanded, detached sort of way that doesn't let the truth sink in, but the exhortations in Proverbs to seek wisdom, knowledge and understanding were meant for adults, and probably in most cases, for parents. God wants us to be fervent learners all of our lives.

God never meant for learning to become a burden, either for children or for parents. He meant it to be a natural, enjoyable part of family life. Our culture has wrested education from families and turned it into an unnatural, tedious drudgery of classrooms, textbooks and tests. And as children's minds and hearts wilt under the crushing conformity of "school," parents likewise begin to wither intellectually as the roots of learning are severed from the family tree. As you bring education back home, bring with it the joy of learning, both for you and your children. Set the pace by showing them, by your example, that you value learning, and they will follow. If your children are growing strong in these seven mental muscles—if you are strengthening their minds to learn for God—then you will have little reason to be concerned about their "education."

Proverbs 24:3-4
By wisdom a house is built, and through understanding it is established; through knowledge its rooms are filled with rare and beautiful treasures.

❝ *In the [Old Testament], the goal of education is a godly life, one that expresses the believer's loving fear of the Lord....Thus while teaching and learning involve the word coming from outside, that word is sharply focused on the moral life. To learn is to attain wisdom, discipline, and insight and to acquire prudence so that one does what is right and just and fair...[Because] learning is viewed as shaping values, character, and lifestyle itself, the content must be processed in a life-transforming way. It is not enough to gain mental mastery of biblical information. The divine word must be taken into the heart of the learner and expressed in his every choice and act...Moreover, unlike teaching in our culture, teaching as envisioned in the OT does not presuppose a classroom. Rather, the OT presupposes a distinctive community and a distinctive interpersonal setting for teaching and learning...That is, as life is lived by adult and child, the recurrent experiences they share are to be constantly interpreted by the divine Word. Thus, learning does not take place in classrooms but in the cycle of ordinary events.*

Lawrence O. Richards, *Expository Dictionary of Bible Words*, Zondervan, 1985

EDUCATING THE WHOLEHEARTED CHILD

CHAPTER FOUR

Teaching Models...
Learning At Home, Naturally

Home Centered Learning ~
Giving Your Children a Designer Education

Christian Home Education is the original "Designer" education. More than any other approach to education, each new Christian home school bears the imprimatur of *The Designer*. It is significant to remember that God did not institute schools. It is clear from Scripture that God designed and instituted *families* for the education of children. And, since he has given us great freedom in how to use our homes to raise our children, Christian home education is also a "designer" education. Every home school can be *custom-designed* with learning structures that are tailor-made to suit the unique educational needs of each individual child in the home. Your home school differs in some degree from every other home school because your family, children, and home are different. Some families insist on a structured, formal curriculum approach, and some resist any kind of pre-designed approach. However, more and more home educators are discovering the natural strengths of a "designer" education. They are designing their own educational program, picking and choosing the best resources and methods that fit their own unique family situations.

This book was written to guide you in implementing what we call a *Home-Centered Learning* model which integrates the major priorities and goals of home education within a "whole book" or "literature-based" approach. What is generally called the "whole book" approach is rapidly gaining wide acceptance in the Christian home education movement because many are finding it is a natural and effective approach to education. Because it is designed to be both comprehensive and flexible, the Home-Centered Learning model can be implemented in any home setting. It is a one-size-fits-all designer (and Designer) education for the Christian home.

The first part of this chapter will briefly introduce you to the most commonly adopted home education models (profiles provided are in summary, review form only). Each has its relative advantages and disadvantages in comparison to the others, and all are valid, acceptable means of educating your children. Add a dedicated home educator to any of the models and you will get the job done. Nonetheless, we are convinced that a "real books, real life" approach is the best. The Home-Centered Learning method, which is rooted deeply in the Living Books and Life Experiences method credited to Charlotte Mason, will liberate learning in your home and free you to become the teacher God designed you to be and the parent your children need. It gives you a natural, home-centered framework for shaping your child's heart to live for God, and strengthening your child's mind to learn for God. Its goal—to raise wholehearted Christian children.

Proverbs 23:12-19
Apply your heart to instruction and your ears to words of knowledge...My son, if your heart is wise, then my heart will be glad; my inmost being will rejoice when your lips speak what is right. Do not let your heart envy sinners, but always be zealous for the fear of the LORD. There is surely a future hope for you, and your hope will not be cut off. Listen, my son, and be wise, and keep your heart on the right path.

❝ *...the truth is mothers — and fathers — exert far more influence over their children's intellectual development than is commonly realized. In fact, more than three decades of research shows that families have greater influence over a child's academic performance than any other factor — including schools.*

Family Research Council, "The One-House Schoolroom," Sept. 1995 issue of Family Policy

There's no place like home school.

Schools of Home Schooling

❏ The Curricular Approach

Bob Jones, A Beka, Alpha Omega, A.C.E., Christian Liberty, Calvert, Mott Media, Rod and Staff, numerous others

This traditional schooling approach is highly structured and formal. It relies nearly entirely on textbooks and workbooks. Many new home schooling families choose the curricular approach more by default than by design since it is what they are most familiar with from their own school experience. Formal curriculum represents a "safe" choice to them at a time when all the other options are unfamiliar. The textbooks are age-graded with a scope and sequence based upon generally accepted public and private school subject areas and standards. They generally reflect a particular doctrinal or theological viewpoint. Most private Christian schools use these as their primary curricula. Textbooks are generally "fact" oriented, making up in breadth for what they do not provide in depth. A teacher is required to plan and guide textbook studies to ensure that all the material is covered. Some curriculum publishers use consumable workbooks or worktexts containing both instructional text and lessons designed for independent pacing and study. These require less preparation and supervision than a textbook only approach. Some companies sell "classic curricula" from the 1800's (McGuffey Readers, Ray's Arithmetic).

Strengths: Comprehensive, systematic studies.

❏ Unschooling

John Holt, David and Micki Colfax, Growing Without Schooling magazine

Unschooling is the opposite end of the spectrum from the Curricular approach. It is totally unstructured and informal. John Holt, though not writing as a Christian, was an educator and a pioneer of the modern home education movement. He believed that children possess an innate desire to learn, that their desire and natural curiosity would drive them to learn on their own in their own way and time, and that conventional methods of teaching destroyed their desire to learn. He advocated using minimal structure, instruction, or intervention in order to allow children maximum time, freedom and creativity. "What children need is not new and better curricula but access to more and more of the real world." Unschooling influence is noticeable in home education models that allow children to pursue their own interests with parental support and guidance. The distinctives of this approach include: free access to good books and learning resources; a trust in the child to learn; interaction with adults and real life; formal academics only when the child indicates interest or need.

Strengths: Encourages child to become a natural, self-motivated learner; all of life is a classroom.

Comment: Curricular Approach

Curricular studies publishers are part of a multi-million dollar industry that serves both the Christian school and home school movements. As an approach to home schooling, its methodology is really a classroom approach that has migrated into the home. Most curricular publishers employ textbook and workbook intensive methods that were designed for age-graded, large classroom schooling conditions. Advocates of curricular studies promote their approach as being a tested, proven, effective way to teach your child.

❝ *What children need is not new and better curricula but access to more and more of the real world; plenty of time and space to think over their experiences, and to use fantasy and play to make meaning out of them; and advice, road maps, guidebooks, to make it easier for them to get where they want to go (not where we think they ought to go), and to find out what they want to find out.*

John Holt, *Teach Your Own*

❑ Delayed Academics

Dr. and Mrs. Raymond Moore, Hewitt-Moore Child Development Center

Many home schoolers trace their start in home schooling to Dr. Moore's books. Dr. Moore is a leading educator and advocate of "better late than early" home education. His research led him to conclude that children are not emotionally, physically, spiritually or mentally ready for the stress of academic studies until around 8-12 years of age (different times for different children). He advocates delaying formal academics until the parent discerns the time is right. Until then, parents should focus on balanced development of "head, heart, hand and health" by reading good stories and literature, and developing good habits, routines, and responsibility. Children need lots of love, discipline, real life experiences, and time to explore and learn. When ready to learn, Dr. Moore recommends using multi-sensory learning resources and unit studies, in addition to drill and review type material. According to Dr. Moore, children will catch up on learning in a very short period of time once they signal their readiness to learn. He believes every child has a specific area of genius or giftedness that needs to be nurtured and encouraged.

Strengths: Sensitivity to child's learning readiness; whole book approach; giftedness of each child.

❑ The Classical Approach

Dorothy Sayers; Douglas Wilson (Canon Press); Harvey/Laurie Bluedorn (Trivium Pursuit)

The Classical model of education has produced many of the world's greatest scholars. Its goal is to teach children how to think. Its distinctives include Latin at an early age, and "conversation" with great minds of the past through extensive reading of great literature and writings. The Classical approach revives a Medieval form of education that taught children under 16 years of age the tools of learning in a three-stage process known as The Trivium (and later, the Quadrivium).

- *Grammar Stage (age 6-10): Mastery of the Facts* The student studies the fundamentals of reading, writing and spelling; Latin; memorization and thinking skills; Bible and history; math. These studies lay the groundwork for future studies.
- *Dialectic Stage (age 10-14): Study of Logic* The student learns to discuss, debate, interpret, draw out correct conclusions supported by facts, discern fallacies in an argument. He continues Latin study and adds Greek and Hebrew; interpretive history; higher math; theology.
- *Rhetoric Stage (age 14+): Use of Language* The student develops proficiency in the use of written and spoken language to express himself with eloquence and persuasion.

Strengths: Emphasis on languages, thinking, speaking, reading, and history.

❝ *For the first eight to ten years at least—until their values are formed—most parents, even average parents, are by far the best people for their children...In general the best teacher or care-giver cannot match a parent of even ordinary education and experience...Children under eight are seldom, if ever, able to reason consistently about why they should or should not behave as parents see best, and sometimes cannot do so until eleven or twelve. So a reasonably consistent, continuing adult example is important if they are to get on a track toward sound character and personality values.*

Raymond Moore, *Home Grown Kids*, Word, 1981

❝ *For we let our young men and women go out unarmed in a day when armor was never so necessary. By teaching them to read, we have left them at the mercy of the printed word...They do not know what the words mean; they do not know how to ward them off or blunt their edge or fling them back; they are a prey to words in their emotions instead of being the masters of them in their intellects...We have lost the tools of learning—the axe and the wedge, the hammer and the saw, the chisel and the plane—that were so adaptable to all tasks. Instead of them, we have merely a set of complicated jigs, each of which will do but one task and no more, and in using which eye and hand receive no training, so that no man ever sees the work as a whole or 'looks to the end of the work.' What use is it to pile task on task and prolong the days of labour, if at the close the chief object is left unattained?*

Dorothy Sayers, *The Lost Tools of Learning*, 1947

❑ The Principle Approach

James Rose, Stephen McDowell, Rosalie Slater, F.A.C.E., The Pilgrim Institute, The Mayflower Institute, The Providence Foundation

The Principle Approach attempts to restore three vital concepts to American Christianity: knowledge of our Christian history; understanding of our role in spreading Christianity; and the ability to live according to the Christian principles upon which our country was founded. It identifies seven key principles governing all areas of life. Subjects are studied in the light of one or more of these principles. Students learn to think "governmentally" to determine who or what is creating, preserving, guiding, nurturing, controlling, restraining, directing, or regulating any area of life. The student learns to take responsibility for his own learning and life. The goal is to become self-governing and self-determining. Study of any subject involves recording in a notebook the "4R's": *Researching* God's Word; *Reasoning* from biblical truths and principles; *Relating* truths to personal life; *Recording* conclusions in a student notebook. The Principle Approach is as much a way of living as it is a way of educating children.

Strengths: Emphasis on principles of self-government and self-motivation; Providential history and the Christian history of America; writing and thinking skills.

❑ Unit Study

Konos, The Weaver, Alta Vista, ATIA (Bill Gothard), Delight Directed Studies (Gregg Harris), Valerie Bendt, Katherine Stout, others

Unit study integrates and relates several subject areas of study around one common theme, subject or project. One topic then can be studied intensively over a period of time covering language arts, math, science, nature, history, social studies, fine arts and whatever other subject areas might apply, or be made to apply. Unit study advocates believe that it is more natural to study one topic from several related perspectives, than to study several unrelated subjects in isolation from one another. It is argued that knowledge is more easily learned and remembered when interrelated. Unit study is said to work well in home schools because it can be easily adapted for age-integrated learning where each child can learn at his own level. Unit study also can be used to supplement other approaches (ex., doing a 2-week "unit" on the human body). The amount of preparation and time involved in unit study varies depending on the level of complexity and activity you create or plan into the study. However, unit study tends to be more time and preparation intensive than other approaches. Unit studies by Christian publishers are typically organized around Bible chronology, Bible themes, passages of Scripture, Christian character, and history, among other themes. If you design your own unit study, you can determine whatever theme you desire or that you think may be of interest to your child.

Strengths: Interactive, multi-sensory studies; integrated studies.

Comment: Unit Studies
Because unit study is such a flexible methodology, every advocate seems to approach it from a slightly different perspective. Like curricular studies, it is very difficult to find one approach that represents the whole Unit Study school. Loyalty to the method, though, is nearly universally based on thematic, integrated study. Cathy Duffy (The Christian Home Educator's Curriculum Manual) says, "God's direction is much more evident when we design our own unit studies than when we use formal curriculum." The appeal for Unit Study advocates is that it is natural, child-centered and informal.

❏ Computer-Based Education

School of Tomorrow, A-Plus, Home Quest Academy, Scholars Online Academy, curriculum publishers, software publishers

As computers move into more and more households, they will play an increasingly important role in home education. Some families will look to computers to provide an entire K-12 curriculum, much like a digital worktext. Some will use programs that supplement and enhance print-based curricula and study, such as math and language programs. Some will use the computer primarily as a research and writing tool. Some will use the computer as a tool for exploring the rapidly expanding universe of information available on CD ROM, through on-line services, and through the Internet. The digital revolution has only just begun so it is impossible to predict the many possibilities of computer-based education. Those who advocate computer learning agree that computers loom large in their children's futures, whatever life calling they may choose. It is in their best interest, then, to become confident and competent computer users now, so they can keep pace with the changes that will come. However they are used for home education, computers are excellent teaching tools. Their interactivity is tailor-made for self-paced learning, and their ability to store and retrieve large amounts of text, audio and video opens the world to young learners like nothing before.

Strengths: Interactive; breadth and depth of information; automate routine educational tasks

> 66 *"By the time your grand-children start school, the tedious part of your life as a home schooler should be fully automated. Lesson plans, record keeping, drills, spelling lists—all of this you shouldn't have to do! Some of this software already exists, or is being developed right now for the home school market."*
> Scott Somerville, "Computerized Education," Practical Homeschooling, Fall 1994

❏ Accelerated Education

Joyce Swann, Alexandra Swann, Doreen Claggett

This approach, which is closely related to the concept of "never too early" academics, starts early and advances rapidly. Those who subscribe to accelerated education believe it is in the best interest of their children to help them move through formal schooling as rapidly as possible in order for them to begin adult life fully educated. An accelerated education might mean completing High School requirements as early as 10 years old and then moving on into college courses and even graduate courses by mid to late teens. The approach is based on a 12-month school year, five days a week, three hours a day. The schooling time each day is structured, concentrated and intense, but then the rest of the day is free. The approach is based on the use of a structured curriculum. In theory, however, any approach to education could be accelerated if specific goals were set and the same steady pace of study were maintained. Adherents see in accelerated education a way to provide maximum academic achievement, with greater time and opportunity to explore occupational interests and skills. The emphasis of this approach is on academics and educational standards.

Strengths: Efficiency of time and effort; early completion of schooling; expanded opportunities during young adult years

> 66 *Accelerated education gives a young person an early start on life. A young man or woman goes into the workforce and begins carving out a career. Not only does that individual learn what he or she would like to do in life but, just as importantly, that individual is able to eliminate those things which he or she does not want to do. Before marriage, before children, before making those commitments that limit the direction of a person's life, we are able to find out what we are best suited to do, to become established in a career and to realize some dreams of our own.*
> Alexandra Swann, "I Was An Accelerated Child," Practical Homeschooling, Winter 1994

❑ Charlotte Mason Method

Charlotte Mason, Susan Schaeffer Macaulay, Karen Andreola, Ruth Beechick, David Quine, others

Charlotte Mason (1842-1923) was a turn of the century educator who had great influence on British education in her time. She rejected the traditional, institutional education of her day as a soulless system that depersonalized children, viewing them only as containers to be filled with bare facts (*"It cannot too often be said that information is not education."*). She eschewed that system's reliance upon textbooks full of pre-digested bits of information she called "snippets," inferior and dull books she labeled "twaddle," and unnatural, artificial learning experiences. ❧ In contrast, she viewed education as the "science of relations." While British culture tended to view children as sub-persons that needed to be formed and civilized, Miss Mason viewed each child as a whole, maturing person with an active intelligence and an enormous capacity for learning. The role of education was to lead children into learning through the many natural relationships with things, thoughts, people and ideas they were already exploring. She championed an approach to education that emphasized character development, or "habits," basic learning skills (reading, writing, arithmetic), the reading of many "living books," the study of the fine arts (art, music, poetry), and learning through real life experiences (nature, museums, etc.). She stressed reading and reading aloud, and the regular practice of narration—saying back, or writing, what has been read or heard. She rightly saw in narration a proven instructional method that helped internalize and personalize learning, and that also developed attending, thinking, and speaking abilities. ❧ Miss Mason provided the children in her schools with ample opportunities to interact with the very best literature, art, and music. She believed that children had a God-given thirst for knowledge no different than an adult had. Instead of lifeless, pedantic textbooks and workbooks that expected children only to remember the right answer, she insisted on reading only *living books* that made literature, history, geography, and science come alive, and that focused more on insights and ideas about the subject than on dry and lifeless facts. Nature study was a regular part of her students' education, consisting of long walks in the outdoors observing nature and wildlife, collecting specimens, and keeping a nature journal of their observations, including sketches. ❧ Miss Mason saw in children an unlimited capacity to learn that needed to be nurtured and stimulated, not controlled and conformed. She argued that traditional structured classrooms and teacher-dependent education "get in the way" of learning, impoverishing children's intellectual development and preventing them from pursuing their own innate and natural desire to learn, and from drawing their own conclusions about what they are learning. ❧ The current "whole book" movement in home education today has been fueled by the voluminous writings of Charlotte Mason. Her ideas and principles of education are the seeds from which numerous new expressions of whole book education have grown.

Strengths: Emphasis on living books; fine arts, music and poetry; verbal and writing skills; self-motivated learning; real life; dignity of the child.

❝ *We hold that the child's mind is no mere sac to hold ideas; but is rather...a spiritual organism, with an appetite for all knowledge. This is its proper diet...(we take) care only that all knowledge offered him is vital, that is, that facts are not presented without their informing ideas...Our business is to give children the great ideas of life, of religion, history, science; but it is the ideas we must give, clothed upon the facts as they occur, and must leave the child to deal with these as he chooses.*

Charlotte Mason, *A Philosophy of Education*, 1925

❝ *Christians can't develop a Christian view of education by accepting the usual aims and views of our society and then adding a 'Christian message' or interpretation. No, we start from a different basis. We have another world view—another people view! When a baby is picked up, spoken to, and loved, he is starting his education as God planned it. For all our lives we are human beings, in an active state of learning, responding, understanding. Education extends to all of life. In fact, an educational system that says, one bright summer's day in the dawn of my youth, 'There. Now you are educated. This piece of paper says so,' is doing me a gross disfavor. The truly educated person has only had many doors of interest opened. He knows that life will not be long enough to follow everything through fully. This broad view of true education as the sum of all life meant that Charlotte Mason first turned her attention to the parents...(She) never spoke of education as merely taking place behind the walls of the schoolroom. She saw the home as the basic educational environment.*

Susan Schaeffer Macaulay, *For the Children's Sake*, Crossway, 1984

❑ Charlotte Mason's Philosophy of Education

Masterly Inactivity

Charlotte Mason encouraged what she called "masterly inactivity" as a teaching methodology. She believed that adults do not really teach children anything, and may even hamper their natural desire to learn by making them dependent upon textbooks and teachers to tell them what to think. She insisted that children possess the same appetite for ideas as adults, and viewed the teacher's role as a guide into learning. She held that *"once we receive an idea, it will work itself out, in thought and act, without much after-effort on our part."* Masterly inactivity means providing children with a rich pool of books, arts, experiences and ideas and then getting out of their way, trusting them to search out knowledge that is meaningful to them, and to come to their own conclusions about what they are learning.

Instruments of Education

Miss Mason also recognized that every educational methodology was limited to some degree because of the many differences in children's personalities. She proposed three "instruments of education" that would apply to all children regardless of personality. *"Seeing that we are limited by the respect due to the personality of children we can allow ourselves but three educational instruments...Our motto is,—'Education is an atmosphere, a discipline, a life.'*

- **Atmosphere** (the atmosphere of environment)
  Education requires an atmosphere in which the child is accepted and valuable; that is non-judgmental and realistic; that is stimulating, positive and enjoyable. *"It stultifies a child to bring down his world to the 'child's' level."* Education should look to the home, which is a natural learning environment. *"We foresee happy days for children when all teachers know that no other exciting motive whatever is necessary to produce good work in each individual...than that love of knowledge which is natural to every child."*

- **Discipline** (the discipline of habit)
  Education requires disciplined habits. A critical part of education is the formation of good habits *"definitely and thoughtfully, whether habits of mind or body."* No matter how strong or weak the natural tendencies, habit is stronger (*"Habit is ten natures."*). Key disciplines, or habits, include: attention/concentration; truthfulness; self-control; unselfishness, and many others. *"No intellectual habit is so valuable as that of attention; it is a mere habit but it also the hall-mark of an educated person."*

- **Life** (the presentation of living ideas)
  Education happens in real life, not in isolated, artificial classroom experiences. All of life is meant to be used for learning. Children will learn to feed their own minds with the best intellectual food—literature, art, music, history, science and nature—and come to their own conclusions without being told what to think. *"Education is a life. That life is sustained on ideas. Ideas are of spiritual origin, and God has made us so that we get them chiefly as we convey them to one another, whether by word of mouth, written page, Scripture word, musical symphony; but we must sustain a child's inner life with ideas as we sustain his body with food."*

> ❝ *For this reason we owe it to every child to put him in communication with great minds that he may get at great thoughts; with the minds, that is, of those who have left us great works; and the only vital method of education appears to be that children should read worthy books, many worthy books.*
>
> Charlotte Mason, *A Philosophy of Education*, 1925

> ❝ *The fundamental idea is, that children are persons and are therefore moved by the same springs of conduct as their elders. Among these is the Desire of Knowledge, knowledge-hunger being natural to everybody. History, Geography, the thoughts of other people, roughly, the humanities, are proper for us all, and are the objects of the natural desire of knowledge. So too, are Science, for we all live in the world; and Art, for we all require beauty, and are eager to know how to discriminate; social science, Ethics, for we are aware of the need to learn about the conduct of life; and Religion, for like those men we heard of at the Front, we all 'want God.' In the nature of things then the unspoken demand of children is for a wide and very varied curriculum...Children no more come into the world without provisions for dealing with knowledge than without provision for dealing with food. They bring with them not only that intellectual appetite, the desire of knowledge, but also an enormous, and unlimited power of attention to which the power of retention (memory) seems to be attached, as one digestive process succeeds another, until the final assimilation."*
>
> Charlotte Mason, *A Philosophy of Education*, 1925

*H*ome-Centered Learning ~
Ten Distinctives for Home Education

This handbook explains and develops the *Home-Centered Learning* model of home education. We have drawn key elements and strengths from most of the above approaches, drawing most deeply from the Charlotte Mason Whole Book approach. The *Home-Centered Learning* model integrates these various elements in a comprehensive model of home education. The ten distinctives that follow are the guiding principles for the model.

1 Children need a home and family.

God designed families to raise children. To paraphrase Pascal (with apologies), there is a home-shaped vacuum in the heart of every child that can be filled only by a father and a mother. It is natural and normal for children to want to stay with their parents until they are grown. It is *un*natural and *ab*normal to believe others should or must raise your children for you. Only the love and stability of a godly family can provide the solid center all children need and deserve to grow up wise and godly.

2 Children need to be discipled by their parents.

The first responsibility of Christian parents before God is to "make disciples" of their children. As a child's heart is turned toward God and his feet are put on the path of life, his mind then begins to grow in godly wisdom. Discipleship is the process of bringing up children in the "training and instruction of the Lord" in order to bring them under God's authority. Until your child's heart is submitted to you and to God, you cannot effectively educate their mind.

3 Children need to be accepted as persons.

The child you disciple and educate is no less a *whole person* than a fully grown adult. Everything that defines person-ness— intelligence, curiosity, creativity, reason, will—is present in your child. God's image and likeness is complete in your child. Children deserve respect as persons based on their emerging maturity and God-given capacity to learn and grow, rather than belittlement based on their childish immaturity.

4 Children need purpose and hope.

Christian home education is the shaping of a life, not just the preparation for a living. Your child needs to see that home education is preparing them for a higher purpose in life, and that their real hope is heaven, not the riches of this world. They need to know that their purpose in life is to serve God, not to make money and buy things. If you set their hearts and minds on things above, not on earthly things, then they will find fulfillment in whatever they do in this life because it is a means of serving God.

---

66 *It is not enough for parents to have a lofty ideal for their children, and to instruct and train those children in the direction of that ideal. They must see to it that the atmosphere of their home is such as to foster and develop in their children those traits of character which their loftiest ideal embodies. That atmosphere must be full of pure oxygen of love to God and love to man. It must be neither too hot in its intensity of social activities, nor too cold in its expressions of family affection, but balmy and refreshing in its uniform temperature of household living and being. It must be gentle and peaceful in its manner and movement of sympathetic discourse. All this it may be. All this it ought to be.*

    H. Clay Trumbull, *Hints On Child Training*, 1890

66 *It is not merely that the child is to be [someday] the possessor of a marked and distinctive individuality, and that therefore he is to be honored for his possibilities in that direction; but it is that he already is [now] the possessor of such an individuality, and that he is worthy of honor for that which he has and is at the present time.*

    H. Clay Trumbull, *Hints On Child Training*, 1890

5 Children need many relationships.

Life is a series of relationships, and we learn from all of them—family, God, siblings, spouse, friends, church, teachers, employers, employees, customers, and on and on. Exposure to many kinds of relationships prepares a child to better relate to and learn from others as an adult.

6 Children naturally love to learn.

Children do not have to be told to want to learn—they can be trusted to learn. They will innately pursue knowledge without constantly being made to or told what to think. The key to their learning, then, is to create an environment rich with whole books and real life that provides opportunities to exercise their natural desire for knowledge.

7 Children learn from real life.

Seeing and holding a garden snake discovered on a nature walk is infinitely more interesting and educational to a child than being told in a classroom what a garden snake is like. There is more to learn from observing or doing real tasks than from only reading about or hearing someone else's experience. Children need much free time and real life experience to grow.

8 Children learn from real books.

It is natural for a child to prefer a whole book. One of the keys to true education is to feed a child's natural desire for knowledge with lots of good food, rather than starve it with bits of inferior, tasteless food. Whole and living books are deeply satisfying to children. When children are allowed to taste and sample of a wide selection of whole books, their appetites will be trained and they will want to come back for more.

9 Children learn from the fine arts.

It is in the study of the fine arts that a child is introduced to the passion, power and beauty of life expressed through the eyes of artists, musicians and poets. The integration of intellect and emotion in the fine arts is a dim but true reflection of God's creative nature that is part of his image in man. Children learn to express it as they become more aware of it in others.

10 Children learn from ideas.

A steady intake of lifeless facts and data will dull a child's mind and senses. Emphasis on knowing the "right answers" reduces education to little more than data processing. Children, like adults, think and feel deeply—they need to feed mentally on ideas and concepts that help them to understand and make sense of their world. Facts, without the ideas that give them meaning, add little to a child's growth.

> **❝** *This broad view of true education as the sum of all of life meant that Charlotte Mason first turned her attention to the parents. She believed that they had the most interesting and valuable vocation that exists among mankind. Into their love, care, and responsibility this person was placed. Charlotte Mason never spoke of education as merely taking place behind the walls of the schoolroom. She saw the home as the basic educational environment.*
>
> Susan Schaeffer Macaulay, *For the Children's Sake*, 1984

> **❝** *Therefore, the selection of their first lesson-books is a matter of grave importance, because it rests with these to give children the idea that knowledge is supremely attractive and that reading is delightful. Once the habit of reading his lesson-books with delight is set up in a child, his education is not completed, but ensured; he will go on for himself in spite of the obstructions which school too commonly throws in his way.*
>
> Charlotte Mason, *Home Education*, 1935

> **❝** *The aim of education then...must be complete living. But ordinary education, instead of seeking to develop the life of the child, sacrifices childhood to the acquirement of knowledge.*
>
> Rousseau

*T*he Home-Centered Learning Model

God has given you a family and a home. A home is a place where a family is grown, just like soil is where a tree is grown. Your task is to use your home to its fullest measure to grow a family that will stand strong and long for God. The Home-Centered Learning model describes one way to use your home to disciple and educate your children. There is, of course, much more to family life than is contained in this model. If, though, you are committed to educating your children at home, this model provides a wholistic, comprehensive way of looking at your home as the center of living and learning for your children. It will provide rich soil for growing mature, well-educated disciples of Jesus Christ.

Home-centered Learning is structured much like a house. First, just as a house needs a strong foundation to be stable, your children need a strong spiritual foundation to be stable (Discipleship Studies). Then, just as the interior of a house is built with different rooms for different purposes, your children's "mental interiors" have different but connected rooms of learning. One room is for more structured learning (Disciplined Studies); one is for more relational learning (Discussion Studies); and one is for more self-directed learning (Discovery Studies). Finally, just as the roof unifies the house, your children are progressively building their unique gifts and skills that will bring all their learning together "under one roof" (Discretionary Studies).

❏ Five Focused Study Areas

The five focused study areas of the Home-Centered Learning model provide an integrated plan of home education. The house illustration on the facing page shows how the five areas work together.

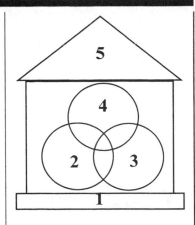

The Home-Centered Learning Model

1 Discipleship Studies

The solid foundation of the house.
The study of the Bible.
Doctrine, wisdom, Bible knowledge.
Purpose: To shape your children's hearts to love God and to study and know his Word.

2 Disciplined Studies

The first central study focus.
The study of the "basics."
Learning skills (reading, writing, math, thinking)
Purpose: To develop your children's foundational learning skills and competencies in language arts, math and reasoning.

3 Discussion Studies

The second central study focus.
The study of the humanities.
Literature, history, fine arts
Purpose: To feed your children's minds by giving them the best in living books and the fine arts.

4 Discovery Studies

The third central study focus.
The study of learning.
Nature, science, creative arts, all interests
Purpose: To simulate in your children a love for learning by creating opportunities for curiosity, creativity and discovery.

5 Discretionary Studies

The unique finishing of the house.
The study of living.
Home and community life, field trips, life skills
Purpose: To direct your children in developing a range of skills and abilities for adult life according to their gifts and your family's circumstances and resources.

The model is designed so that you provide a range of coordinated learning experiences for your children, moving from more structured learning to more unstructured learning, and from more teacher-directed learning to more child-directed learning. This kind of balanced approach allows you to have input and direction at any level in your children's lives, while at the same time giving them freedom to explore and discover on their own. That balance is important for your child to develop a self-motivated desire to learn, independent of always being told what they must think and study. It gives them the freedom to discover the person that God is making them.

The pages that follow describe each of the five focused study areas in more detail. The lists on each page are representative only, not comprehensive.

Discipleship Studies:
The study of the Bible

All true education begins with God, who is the source of all that is true. Discipleship Studies are the foundation of the Home-Centered Learning model upon which the rest of the house is built (Matthew 7:24f). The emphasis of Discipleship Studies is more than just Bible knowledge, though—it is developing a vital relationship with God through his revealed Word. It includes understanding the Bible as a book, studying it as truth from God, and reading it devotionally to hear God speak through it. The goal of Discipleship Studies is to train your children's hearts to seek God and his truth. You are building a secure foundation so the house you build—your child's life— will stand strong.

DISCIPLESHIP STUDIES

Focus:

The study of the Bible
Doctrine, wisdom, Bible knowledge

Purpose:

To shape your children's hearts to love God and to study and know his Word.

Learning Objectives:

To read the Scriptures regularly.
To develop devotional habits.
To memorize selected Scriptures.
To understand basic Bible doctrines.
To know Bible facts.
To know how to study the Bible.

Suggested Methods:

Bible Reading
Bible Devotions
Bible Study
Personal Reading
Reading Aloud
Narration
Memorization & Recitation
The Fine Arts
The Expressive Arts

Suggested Materials:

Personal Bible
Bible study notebook
Devotional notebook
3x5 cards (Scripture memory)
Bible marking pen

Suggested Resources:

King James Version Bible
New King James Version Bible
New International Version Bible
New American Standard Bible (updated)
New International Readers Version Bible
The Narrated Bible
The International Children's Bible Dictionary
The International Children's Bible Handbook
What the Bible Is All About for Young Explorers
The Child's Story Bible (Vos)
The Children's Illustrated Bible
Every Day With God: A Child's Bible
Our 24 Family Ways (Clarkson)
Leading Little Ones to God (Schoollhand)
LifeGuide Family Bible Studies (IVP)
The Life and Ministry of Jesus Christ (NavPress)
Greenleaf Guide to Old Testament History

DISCIPLINED STUDIES

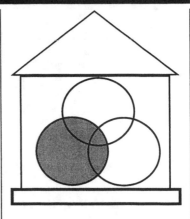

Focus: **The study of the "basics"**
Learning skills (reading, writing, math, thinking)

Purpose: To develop your children's foundational learning skills and competencies in language arts, math, and reasoning.

Learning Objectives:
To learn to read phonetically.
To develop reading skills.
To strengthen language arts skills.
To develop handwriting skills.
To develop writing skills.
To learn keyboarding skills.
To master basic math skills.
To strengthen thinking skills.

Suggested Methods:
Beginning Reading
Reading Aloud
Pesonal Reading
Creative Writing & Composition
Language Arts
Math
Thinking Skills
Context Study
Asking Questions
Scope & Sequence

Suggested Materials:
Lots of good books
Math workbook or notebook
Math manipulatives
Flashcards
Computer
Drill & review sheets

Suggested Resources:
Teach Your Child to Read in 100 Easy Lessons
Noah Webster's Reading Handbook
Classic American Readers series
Learning Language Arts Through Literature
English From the Roots Up
Simply Grammar~An Illustrated Primer
The Italic Handwriting series
Wordsmith series (creative writing, composition)
How to Teach Any Child to Spell
Saxon Math
Making Math Meaningful (Cornerstone)
CalcuLadder (math drills)

Disciplined Studies:
The study of the basics

Learning begins in earnest when a child acquires the skills of reading and writing (and mathematical computing). A world of information and ideas opens to him with the development of these basic learning skills. Disciplined Studies focus on developing the foundational skills and competencies required for education and learning—language arts, math and reasoning. They are called "Disciplined" studies because they require a significant amount of commitment and work from both the parent and the child. A disciplined study of these basic learning skills, though, will set the pace for the self-motivated learning that is to come.

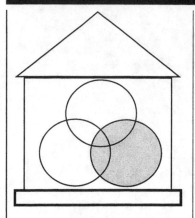

Discussion Studies:
The study of the humanities

Once your child has acquired the skill of reading and language, he needs good food in order to satisfy his appetite and to grow. Discussion Studies provide the very best food for your child's growing heart and mind through what is called, generally, the Humanities—the best of literature, poetry, art and music. These are called Discussion Studies because, through discussion and narration, your children learn to express back verbally what they are reading, hearing and observing. It is a wholistic method of learning that naturally integrates the written and spoken word, and internalizes learning. It is the heart and soul of your home educational program.

DISCUSSION STUDIES

Focus: **The study of the humanities**
Literature, history, fine arts (art, music, poetry)

Purpose: To feed your children's minds by giving them the best in living books and the fine arts.

Learning Objectives:
To read and discuss great literature.
To read and discuss historical literature.
To study and discuss world history.
To study and discuss American history.
To read and discuss poetry.
To study and discuss music and art.

Suggested Methods:
Reading Aloud
Personal Reading
Narration
The Fine Arts
The Creative Arts
Storytelling
Memorization & Recitation
Speaking & Presentation
Context Study
Unit Study
Home Workshops
Age-Integrated Studies
Library
Study Groups

Suggested Materials:
Home library
Public library
Art posters and books
Classical music tapes
Chalk and marker boards

Recommended Resources:
Children's Classics books
Quality illustrated storybooks
Historical novels and literature
Kingfisher Illustrated History of the World
Classical music collection
Classical Kids series
Famous Children/Artists series
Lives of the Musicians/Writers/Artists
Spiritual Lives of the Great Composers
Come Look With Me art book series
Fine arts books of all kinds
A Child's Treasury of Poems

DISCOVERY STUDIES

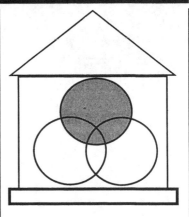

Focus: ***The study of learning***
Nature, science, creative arts, all interests

Purpose: To stimulate in your children a love for learning by creating opportunities for curiosity, creativity and discovery.

Learning Objectives:
To experience, explore and discover.
To develop and express creativity.
To know how to use a library.
To know how to use learning tools.
To know how to do simple research.

Suggested Methods:
The Creative Arts
Storytelling
Speaking & Presentation
Context Study
Unit Study
Nature Study
Creation Science
"Hands On" Science
Computer
Library

Suggested Materials:
Home library
Cassette tape and CD players
Musical instruments
Computer
GeoSafari
Educational games, puzzles, models
Arts/crafts materials
Historical dress-up costumes
Work bench with tools
Nature "museum" display shelves

Recommended Resources:
Books on tape (unabridged)
Your Story Hour Living History tapes
Moody Science videos
Pocket-sized field guides (various publishers)
Nature Friend Magazine
Legos®, Lego Technics®, Lego Dacta®
Piano and/or electric keyboard
Learning Seeds Activity Cards (Home Team Press)
Aristoplay games
Creative software for computer
Mark Kistler's Draw Squad

Discovery
Studies:
*The study of
learning*

The desire and ability to learn is, in itself, a learned trait. Discovery Studies are directed experiences in self-learning. They are opportunities for your children to discover the world around them through independent exploration, research, experimentation, observation and study. There are many ways to learn, so there is a freedom built into Discovery Studies that allows your children to pursue their own learning interests. Creativity and curiosity are allowed fuller expression. "Discovery corners" in the home provide plenteous resources for self-directed learning to take place. Field trips expand the scope of discovery. The goal is to cultivate in your child a natural excitement about and love for learning.

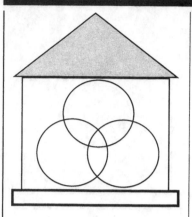

Discretionary Studies:
The study of living

Every child is different. Every family is different. That is why these are called Discretionary Studies, because it is up to your discretion as to how to develop the unique gifts and abilities of your children. Your family circumstances and resources will be different from other families, but God has put your children in your family for a purpose. You prayerfully determine a direction and then marshal the resources available to you to prepare your child for adult life. Your goal is to give your child a broad experience in a wide range of life skills.

DISCRETIONARY STUDIES

Focus: **The study of living**
Home and community life, field trips, life skills

Purpose: To direct your children in developing a range of skills and abilities for adult life according to their gifts and your family's circumstances and resources.

Learning Objectives: To develop personal interests, gifts, skills, interests.
To develop general life and living skills.
To study occupations and careers.
To understand how to make/earn money.

Suggested Methods: Live and Learn
Field Trips
Library
Lessons
Study Groups

Suggested Materials: *The options are infinite. The materials you need will depend entirely upon what you pursue. A few general examples would include:*
Hobby supplies
Individual sport supplies
Gardening supplies
Cooking supplies
Chores/responsibilities charts
Ad infinitum

Recommended Resources: How-To books (age appropriate)
Books on children's business ideas
Private lessons (music, art, etc.)
Family members
Community resource people ("experts")
Your own experience

Setting Up Your House for Home-Centered Learning

Setting up your house for home-centered learning is something like decorating your home, as opposed to only furnishing it. You can put all the right things in all the right places and get the job done. Or, you can look at the whole house and aim to create an *environment* that makes everything work together in unity. In Home-Centered Learning, your goal is to create a *learning environment* that causes your entire home to work together to help you achieve your home education goals.

The image of home schooling at the kitchen or dining room table emerged early in the movement, and continues to be reinforced in both the Christian and secular media. It is a relatively harmless stereotype, but it no longer represents the reality of a maturing movement. Home education should not be relegated to a *temporary* location in your home. The not-so-subtle message to your children is that what they are studying must not be that important if it must be done quickly between meals on the kitchen counter or dining room table.

However, when an entire room or area is *permanently* dedicated to home education, it speaks volumes to your children that their learning is so important that you want to give them a special place for it. Learning is something that goes on all the time, not just between meals. And when the whole house is used for learning, then home education takes on a whole new meaning. It is not just education done *at* home; it is education done *through* the home. Home is not just a *place* where education happens— it is your primary *means* of education.

Creating a learning environment is the key. Make your entire home an exciting, vibrant place where learning is happening all the time. Make it a child-friendly environment that is rich in interesting, inspiring, mentally stimulating options at every turn. Use your home to engage your children's senses in the learning process and to strengthen their emotional ties to the home—the smell of fresh bread baking, the sounds of Baroque chamber music, the sights of beautiful Scripture calligraphy and interesting artwork. Your entire home should reflect your home schooling values, from the way you arrange your furniture, to the books you leave out on tables, to the pictures and verses you hang on the wall, to the way you use your kitchen. There should be no discernible dividing lines between "home" and "education." The natural atmosphere of your home should be alive with learning and life.

When learning becomes truly "home centered," then the environment you have created begins to work *for* you. Your children enjoy learning and discovering because that is what happens in a home. You know that when they are in your "learning room" or are actively engaged in one of the "discovery corners" that home education is happening without you. Home education should be happening all the time without you because learning is what happens in a home. That is *Home-Centered Learning*.

Proverbs 24:3,4
By wisdom a house is built, and through understanding it is established; through knowledge its rooms are filled with rare and beautiful treasures.

Comment: Spaced Out!
Home schoolers, in general, are no strangers to sacrifice. Moms sacrifice their expectations for the sake of their children. Families nearly universally sacrifice financially by choosing a one-income lifestyle. Many home schoolers have larger families and cheerfully accept the accompanying financial and space sacrifices. And, for all these, many home schoolers sacrifice the ability to have a larger home with adequate space for learning and living. The concept of a separate Learning Room is an ideal that may not be possible for many home schooling families with smaller homes and no ability to expand. However, you can still accomplish it in principle, if you're willing to look at your home creatively and to accept a little bit more sacrifice, or ask your children to. Is there an area in one room that can be carved out and dedicated to home education? Can your children sleep together in one room to free up a bedroom that can become your learning room? Can some furniture or possessions be stored or sold to make additional room? Whatever your situation, with a little creativity and ingenuity, you can turn your home into a vibrant learning center for your children. If home schooling is God's will for your family, then he will provide a way for your to do it effectively. Whatever God has entrusted to you, he will show you how to use it.

❏ Designate a "Learning Room"

Every modern house has either a living room, a great room, a family room, or a recreation room in its floor plan because family togetherness is a value for most families with young children. If you are a home schooling family, though, it's time to consider another room for the basic family house plan—a *learning room*.

If you are committed to discipling and educating your children at home, you need a separate room dedicated to home education. Ideally, it should be comfortable, roomy, well-lighted, and have storage for books, materials and other learning resources. Individual student desks (the kind with the attached writing surface and storage shelf) may seem like fun to your classroom-deprived children, but they are not necessary and the novelty grows thin quickly (they're just vestiges of public school rooms). Instead, there should be *several* writing, reading, and drawing spaces available with plenty of tabletop area for spreading out projects (rectangular utility tables work well). A big, inviting reading couch, or some overstuffed reading chairs, allows everyone to get comfortable for read aloud or for reading alone. Other rooms are used for education, too, but the learning room is like the hub of a wheel—everything centers around that room and emanates from it.

You may not be able to designate a learning room in your house. If not, try to replicate its features in a part of your largest room, or in other rooms. The key is to create one area in your home that is the permanent hub of your home education, then to make as many discovery corners as you can throughout the house. No matter what your house is like, with a little creativity you can fine tune it for home centered learning.

IN OUR HOME...

We've learned a lot about creating an atmosphere in the 11 homes we have lived in since we were married. When Sarah was approaching school age, we began the practice of setting aside one room as a Learning Room. Now it is the center of our home school. Our Learning Room contains our primary library (hundreds of books and growing), our BIG reading couch, and personal study areas for each child. It also has several discovery corners: computer and printer; GeoSafari with assorted cards; music (keyboard, rhythm instruments); creative corner ("Lego® lab," games, puzzles, etc.); a writing and drawing corner; and a fine arts corner (we keep art books open on the coffee table and on mini-easels to display interesting pieces of art). We have other discovery corners elsewhere inside and outside of the house— piano, music and video, arts & crafts, workbench—but everything flows out of and back into our primary learning room. The great thing is, they're learning all the time they're there and we don't even have to tell them to. It's as natural to them as breathing. Learning is the atmosphere of our home.

❣ **Learning Tools:** Create a basic reference section in your home library to keep important information within easy reach:

- Bibles (NIV, KJV, NKJV, NASB update, NIrV)
- NIV, KJV, NAS Concordances
- Topical Bibles
- Children's Bible handbook
- Children's Bible dictionary
- Children's Bible atlas
- Children's dictionary
- Children's thesaurus
- Advanced dictionary and thesaurus
- Atlas, almanac and globe
- Child-friendly encyclopedia
- Informative topical books
- Historical reference books
- Nature guides (wildlife, plants, weather, stars, etc.)

❣ **Organizing Tools:** Keep some basic organizational helps on hand to help keep order in the Learning Room:

- desktop hanging files (for misc. drawings and papers)
- drawer organizers (for pencils, pens, etc.) or desktop drawers
- pencil cups and desktop organizers
- divided horizontal or flat files (for various kinds of blank paper)
- paper boxes (for bulk paper)
- magazine holders or boxes (for each child's current work)
- metal bookends (for library)
- waste baskets

❣ **Hang It On Your Wall!:** Learning Room walls should say, "Look at me and learn!"

- History time line
- Posters of historical events and people
- Scripture verses, books of the Bible
- Fine art and music posters
- Maps—world, US, Holy Land, historical
- Language arts posters

❑ Create "Discovery Corners"

A *discovery corner* is a designated space that is dedicated to a general learning focus. The more discovery corners you are able to create in your home, the more choices your children have for Discovery Studies and self-motivated learning. Discovery corners are generally scattered throughout the house wherever you can create the spaces. Several of them will likely be located in your learning room. Use your creativity in setting them up. Each corner should be a distinct place, well-supplied for the learning activity to which it is dedicated, comfortable and well-lighted. It is best to have them in "public" areas, rather than secluded, so you can monitor learning activities as necessary. Following are some examples:

Drawing and Design Corner Tabletop area supplied with paper (lots of it), pencils, colors, erasers, stencils, coloring books, sketch and tracing books, rulers, and so on. Use files or boxes for storage of drawings.

Computer/Electronic Media Corner Multi-media computer loaded with a variety of educational and creativity software, a scanner, and a printer.

Creative Play Corner Legos, Lego Dacta, blocks, educational games, puzzles, creative play items.

Story Tape Corner Audio cassette player with dramatized Bible, history and biography tapes, classical books on tape, classical music and character story tapes.

History Dress-Up Corner A trunk or box full of historical dress up clothes, uniforms and accessories for creative play and historical studies role play.

Music Listening Corner A good stereo cassette or CD player, and a wide selection of good music of all styles, Christian and secular.

Music Making Corner Piano, keyboard, guitar, dulcimer, autoharp, recorders, rhythm instruments and whatever other musical instruments are handy. Sheet music and collections. Also, a Karaoke (accompaniment trak player) is excellent for encouraging singing and performance. The key is availability.

Geography Corner Globe, maps, atlases and geography books that tell the stories of different lands. A *GeoSafari* with Geography cards is a very inviting and effective educational product.

Crafts Corner An area where a mess is allowed, stocked with a wide variety of craft materials and tools.

Carpentry Corner Don't forget to use the garage! Set up a long work bench with tools, scrap wood, nails and fasteners. You can also put broken appliances there to be "fixed," studied or recycled in new creations.

Comment: The Price of Education

Since you aren't able to declare a tax on your neighbors to pay for your children's education at home, you will have to purchase supplies and resources yourself. One basic rule of thumb in supplying your home is: don't try to do and buy everything all at once. Think of your home learning environment as a flower garden you are just beginning to plant. At first, it's going to look a bit thin, but it's going to grow over the years into a beautiful, colorful, growing showplace. There is no need to rush out and buy everything you need to stock every discovery corner you want to have. You will only end up spending more money than you need to on things you might not yet need. Slowly, but steadily, cultivate your home environment and let each new discovery corner bloom over time. It has taken us several years to get our home learning environment to the place where it is now—but it's still not "done." In fact, it is never completed. We are continually cultivating, pruning and improving our discovery corners. Much of our discretionary income is set aside for improving the learning environment of our home for our children. Christmas and birthday gifts add to the discovery corners. When we can afford it, we do a little bit more; when we can't, we wait. And like a garden, we've planned ahead what comes next and what we'll want to have in the future. That way, we can channel our limited funds toward resources and materials we know are strategic and desirable. It has taken time, but our home garden is blooming quite nicely now.

A growing home library is absolutely essential for a home-centered learning approach to home education. It is said about some home-school booklovers that when the paycheck comes, they buy books first, and if anything is left over they buy food and clothing! Building a library is a way of life and a way of thinking (and a way of frustration if you don't have adequate bookshelf space). Just remember, books are an investment. They have intellectual asset value. They are non-consumable curricula that can be used with every child, and then with *their* children. Books are worth it. Here are a few tips for building and maintaining your library:

- Support home businesses and ministries by buying from home school family-owned-and-run book catalogs whenever possible. Keep your money in the family!

- Learn where to buy new and used whole books at discounted prices; get to know the antique book stores, book search services, and specialty catalogs for buying hard-to-find reprints and books; know when library sales and used book fairs are held; pick up bargain books at garage and estate sales; raid your parents' unused library; get to know teachers who might have used book sources.

- Start a book buying and trading co-operative. Members gather to discuss books in their libraries, trade and sell books, and share useful information on the various catalogs and suppliers. Start an annual used books and curricula fair in your area.

- Ask parents and relatives to give books for Christmas and birthday gifts (plastic toys last a few months; books last a lifetime!). Be bold— give them a list of special books you want for your library.

- Your books are special, so lend them out with due caution. Keep a list or a 3x5 file to record who borrowed which book when. Invest in a self-inking rubber stamp and put your name in any and every book that leaves your house. *Be especially cautious when lending out-of-print, rare or hard-to-find books that cannot be easily replaced!*

- Don't do Dewey Decimal unless you have the heart and patience of a librarian. You want your children to use the library and enjoy it, not admire it or be intimidated by it. Just get the books in general categories and you'll be in good shape: literature, history, geography, reference, science/nature, art, preschool/early reader, and so on.

- It is inevitable that you will acquire duplicates, or books that aren't what you thought they'd be. You've got to make space for the next round of book purchases anyway, so plan to periodically purge the extras. Sell them, store them, trade them, or give them away. Consider a garage sale, trading with a used book store, putting them on consignment at a children's resale shop, or selling them at home school events in your area. Consider donating some or all to your church library, an overseas mission or a local charity needing books.

♥**Book Search**—You'll know you're a true booklover when you start looking out for out-of-print books for your library. You can still search the old way, using a search service that will do the work for you and add a commission, fee or mark-up. Your local antique or used bookstore can do this for you (they're usually listed under antique, antiquarian or used books in the Yellow pages). Or, you can search the new way, using the internet. You do the searching, find the best value, and place the order yourself, all through easy search sites on the internet. However, not all bookstore inventories have been cataloged on the internet yet, so some books you'll still have to find through traditional search methods. Here are a few places to start your search:

ABE Books
www.abebooks.com
Consortium of thousands of antiquarian book dealers. Good member features and interface.

Bibliofind
www.bibliofind.com
Owned by Amazon.com. Thousands of dealers. More search parameters and very fast.

Book Finder
www.bookfinder.com
Multi-site search engine that searches several top sites and summarizes its finds. Good interface but somewhat slow.

Abracadabra Booksearch International (3827 West 2nd Ave., Denver, CO 80211) (800) 545-2655, (303) 455-0317

BookSearch International. (P.O. Box 120862, Nashville, TN 37212) (615) 298-3804

❑ Create a Learning Environment

A house is more than just a place where you live. If that is your concept of home, then your vision for what happens there won't reach much beyond what furniture should go in which rooms. Home-Centered Learning, in contrast, views your house as a living and learning environment. Consequently, everything in your house either enhances that environment, or it does not. Webster's Collegiate Dictionary defines "environment" as "the circumstances, objects, or conditions by which one is surrounded." In your home *environment*, you want to consider how to *surround* your children with *circumstances* that stimulate and invite their inquiry and investigation, *objects* that reinforce truth and knowledge they are learning, and *conditions* that motivate them to want to learn. In general, the environment is the *physical* surroundings of your home; the atmosphere (discussed in chapter 8) is the *emotional* surroundings. The following are some ways your can set up the living and learning environment in your home.

- *Walls* What hangs on the walls is the first indicator of a Home-Centered Learning environment: Scripture calligraphy, historical time lines, maps, artistic creations, calendars and goal planners, classical artwork posters, nature posters, visual aids for learning, family-affirming art, and any number of other objects. Use your walls to their maximum, and periodically draw your children's attention to what is there. Walls are one of your best teaching tools.

- *Furniture* Furniture should be comfortable, inviting and child-friendly. If your children feel like certain furniture is more important to you than they are, they will mentally cordon off and avoid those parts of the home—they will be lost as areas of living and learning. Arrange the furniture to provide maximum room for naturally energetic children—don't inadvertently create obstacles and then make them fearful of being children. If you need to, make room for them to move by moving some furniture, or storing it.

- *Table Tops* Make maximum use of your table top spaces. Tastefully display appropriate magazines, art books or special books on coffee tables for casual reading. Decorate your dining room table with a centerpiece and arrangement that reinforces a current holiday or area of study. In your Learning Room, leave out reference and reading books for current areas of study. Display an open art book flat, or on an book easel, on a corner table.

- *Yard* From a child's perspective, the home environment extends beyond the "four walls" of your house to the "unseen walls" that enclose your property (including the garage). Your yard can become an important part of the living and learning environment of your home. Aside from recreational areas, create areas for learning and creativity: a kids' vegetable garden, a place for building materials, a workbench with tools and discarded machines and appliances, birdhouses and feeders for observation, and so on. It should also be, as much as possible, a fun place to play with a fort or play area, rope swing, basketball goal and other popular play options.

❧ **Lost in (no) Space**—If you plan to start building a library of good books, then plan to build a library of good bookshelves. You need shelf space! Built-ins of some kind will give you the most bookshelf space for the buck, but not everyone has the room, money and/or inclination to go that route. Finished or unfinished wood or veneer bookshelf units are an alternative to built-ins if you value quality and beauty. KD (knock-down) bookshelves of laminated particle board are heavy as bricks, but they are moveable, affordable and easily sold if you decide later to go for the built-ins. Bricks and boards will do in a pinch, but for a starter library only. Other handy-man variations work, too, depending on just how handy the man is in your house. As a very last resort, you can use banker boxes, corners, and tables, but it's much harder on the books and on you.

📖 *How to Stock a Home Library Inexpensively (Jane A. Williams)*— Excellent resource for every book lover. All you need to know to build a great home library without raiding the retirement fund.

❧ **Print-Rich Environment**— We aim to create what we call a 4-A book environment in which our books are:
- *Available* We want to provide a wide range of books to meet any reading or research desire
- *Accessible* We want all of our books to be easily accessible to the children for their use
- *Appropriate* We choose books that are suited to our children's needs and reflect our values
- *Abundant* We provide as many books as we can and as our bookshelves will hold

Selecting the Best Materials

You need and can buy only a small portion of what is offered to the growing home-school market, so it is helpful to have some general criteria in mind for evaluating the countless choices for where to invest your home schooling dollars. The following principles and lists will help to guide your desires and decisions when you're perusing a catalog, browsing the bookstore, or cruising the curriculum fair. Always remember, "First, the best. Then, the rest. Books are best."

❑ Books

What qualities to look for in a good book:

- **Ageless** The story and/or illustrations are appealing both to children and to adults. The book possesses a distinctive verbal power, visual beauty, or both, that is recognizable by an eight year-old or an eighty year-old reader.

- **Timeless** The characters and themes of the book transcend time and culture. It appeals to the higher ideals and virtues of the human heart, mind and experience that are meaningful from one generation to another. It is not dated by passing cultural terms and references.

- **Living** It is filled with concepts and ideas that touch the heart and mind. Whether fiction, non-fiction, or history, it holds up a mirror to real life and living ideas. It makes its subject "come alive" with enlightening insights about real people, places and things. It captures the imagination.

- **Literary** It is well-written with a natural flow of narrative, dialog and description. The writing is engaging, clear and grammatically acceptable. It is a worthy model of the English language used well.

- **Whole** It tells a complete story that is interesting and satisfying. The characters are developed, the plot is clear, and the story has a beginning and ending. It appeals to both the heart and the mind. There is a sense of satisfaction and closure when it is finished.

- **Inspiring** It is morally uplifting, providing literary models of sound moral character. It feeds the moral imagination and inspires the reader to higher ideals and virtues. It touches the Christian's spirit, regardless of its "Christian-ness" as a literary work, because it depicts true, honorable and noble ideas.

- **Creative** It stimulates the imagination through creatively developed concept, characters, plot and action. It reflects the creative spirit of the image of the Creator God in the writer. You are drawn into the writing by the author's creative use of words and writing style.

What kinds of books to avoid:

- *Abridged classics* If you are trying to decide between an abridgment and a whole book, always read the whole book! An abridgment tends to take out the literary qualities that make the book both whole and good, leaving only the bare bones of the story. It strips a classic book of the qualities that made it a classic in the first place! Abridgments also tend to remove spiritual and Christian elements in a story, such as testimonies, biblical references, and prayers, in order to focus primarily on the action. Keep in mind that there are two kinds of abridgments. In a *textual abridgment*, both language and concepts are rewritten and "dumbed down" for easy reading. Avoid these mutilations. In a *condensed abridgment*, the original text, style and language of the author are retained while non-essential content is either condensed or left out. These are often acceptable, though not necessarily desirable. Your best choice—the whole book.

- *Formula fiction* Don't waste your children's time and minds, and your money, on mass market fiction. Assiduously avoid modern romance themes for your daughters, and violent or action/adventure themes for your sons. The feminine and masculine types they promote are flawed and fleshly at best; pagan and unbiblical at worst. And the tastes and appetites they create are enduring and hard to satiate. Be cautious even about Christian and historical fiction series. Also avoid science fiction or science fantasy for children, especially stories involving intelligent life from other planets, "UFOs" or "aliens" of any kind. Reading science fiction can lead early to a very strong appetite for stories that will lead your child away from God.

- *Commercial books* Just say "No!" to all the cartoon and media character books that are thinly veiled advertisements for tie-in products, publications and productions. They are cheap, mass-produced products for the consumer market. Don't be fooled—labeling twaddle as "educational" or even as "Christian" (and there is *lots* of Christian twaddle!) will not make it any less twaddly.

IN OUR HOME...

We do whatever we can to encourage our children to think very positively about book ownership. They are beginning to get a kick out of building their own libraries, so we always give special books for birthdays and for Christmas. Whenever we get new books, we spend a long time handling, admiring and talking about them (we stop just short of book lust and idolatry). The kids naturally let us know which ones they want to read first without our prompting. We will sometimes talk up a really good book, but hold off on reading it for awhile. We'll save it for a rainy day, or for a trip, or as a reward for finishing a project. By the time we get to reading it, everyone is champing at the bit. And, of course, library day is a big deal. I think we hold the record for most books checked out in a single visit! And it's all for the love of books.

> " *A book which is enjoyed only by children is a bad children's story. The good ones last. A book which is not worth reading at age 50 is not worth reading at age 10.*
>
> C.S. Lewis, "On Three Ways of Writing for Children"

❦ **Run for the Cover!**— Children's book publishing is a breeding ground for all kinds of awards, honors and lists. To paraphrase an old saying, though, *"You can't tell a book by what's on its cover."* When it's time to spend money on a book, remember: it is the content that makes a book worthy of *your* library, not the accolades. Following, in no particular order, are a few of the more visible awards:

- *The Caldecott Medal* (Gold), for illustration
- *Caldecott Honor Book* (Silver), for illustration
- *John Newbery Medal*, for children's fiction
- *Parents' Choice Honors*, by the Parents' Choice Foundation.
- *Reading Rainbow Book*, featured on the PBS series
- *The Horn Book Award*, by Horn Magazine and the Boston Globe
- *ABBY*, by American Booksellers Assoc./International Reading Assoc.
- *IBBY Honor List*, by the International Board on Books for Young People
- *The Whole Heart Award*, by Whole Heart Ministries, for inspirational and family-affirming children's books

Comment: Basal Readers
No matter how "cute" or popular those early readers may seem, your children do not need basal readers to learn how to read. They are sugar to minds that need protein. Your children need to hear and read real language in age-appropriate whole books, or in collections of real stories and excerpts.

What makes a "living book" alive:

The current emphasis on "whole book" education has grown out of a renewed interest in the writings of Charlotte Mason. She was an articulate promoter and defender of what she called "living books," or books with "literary power." She considered living books the worthiest intellectual food for the minds and hearts of children hungry to learn. Her language about books is fast becoming a part of the *lingua franca* of the home school community, but the question arises, "what makes a living book alive." A living book is the literary expression of insights and ideas in a single work, by a single author, who knows and loves the subject about which he writes. It is a *living* book because the author touches the heart of the reader—the emotions and feelings. In contrast to living books, Miss Mason excoriated "textbooks" as lifeless, fragmented collections crammed with bare facts and boring information, all at the expense of the ideas that give facts meaning. These lifeless books lack the touch of human emotion. Children are sustained by *ideas*, and ideas are found in living books written by individuals with something to say, not in textbooks written by committees with something to design. The terms "whole book" and "real book" are also often used to express Miss Mason's idea of a "living book."

- All of the great literary "classics" are whole, living books. They contain stories that feed your child's moral imagination, touch the heart, and challenge the intellect. They are classics, not simply because someone decided they should be, but because they are enduring stories with a life of their own. They are classics because they are living books, not the other way around.

- Many of today's children's books may be *whole*, but they often are not *living*. In other words, it may be a literary work by a single author, but the writing does not touch the heart or emotions. For example: historical accounts often fall into a mind-numbing, lifeless factualism. Those that *live* are lively accounts full of narrative, dialogue and description.

- If a book is new to you, whether it is fiction or non-fiction, the easiest way to test it for signs of life is a one-page reading. Read the first page aloud to your children. If they show an interest and want to hear more, then it has touched something in their hearts and it shows signs of life. Keep on reading.

Living Book	Text Book
Written by a single author, a real and knowable person.	Written by various authors or contributors, usually unknown.
Literary expression of the author's own ideas and love of the subject	Non-literary expression of collected facts and information.
Personal in tone and feel. Touches the heart and emotions, and the intellect.	Impersonal in tone and feel. Touches only the intellect.
Author addresses the reader as an intelligent and capable thinker.	Looks down on the reader as one needing to be instructed.
Ideas are presented creatively in a way that stimulates the imagination.	Facts are presented without creativity in a way that deadens the imagination.

How to evaluate "imaginative" literature:

Every family will have a slightly different level of tolerance or contempt for some forms of imaginative literature. However, the real issue is rarely the *form*, but rather the *content* of the work. Whatever the literary form may be—fiction, fantasy, fairy tale, fable, myth, allegory—Philippians 4:8 provides a general principle you can apply to evaluate the appropriateness of imaginative literature for your family. *Taken as a whole*, is the work characterized by what is true, noble, right, pure, lovely, admirable, excellent and praiseworthy? That does not mean a story with no evil characters, which would be a very unrealistic and unsatisfying story! Rather, it is one in which the main story line is about a character who represents good, the lines of good and evil are sharply drawn, and the symbols and images used are clear and unconfused (e.g., witches and serpents are always evil; angels and lambs are always good). Train your children to look for "red flags" in the content of various forms of imaginative literature. When you are evaluating imaginative books, talk with your children about why a book's content is or isn't appropriate.

- *Fable* Fables, similar in form to the parables of Jesus, illustrate and teach a timely lesson or timeless truth. Because fables are expressions of wisdom, it is rare to find unacceptable ones. In addition to the venerable *Aesop's Fables*, many of the classic children's stories fall within this form, such as Beatrix Potter's animal fables. It is an excellent literary form for teaching biblical truth and wisdom.

- *Allegory* All forms of imaginative literature can use allegory. In its purest form, though, allegory is a story in which the imaginary elements and characters represent real things and persons. The purpose of allegory is almost always to illustrate or instruct. *Pilgrim's Progress* is an allegory of the Christian life. Personified animals are often used in allegory, such as in the *Chronicles of Narnia*.

- *Fairy Tale* The fairy tale is a story populated by "imagined" creatures, but the story more often than not takes place in a true-to-life setting. As a bridge to truth, a fairy tale can help children learn to think about spiritual realities that they cannot see; as a wall, it might confuse a child about spiritual realities. Hans Christian Andersen used fairy tales to creatively teach Christian truths and values.

- *Fantasy* Fantasy, like fairy tale, is populated by "imagined" creatures, but its story usually takes place in an imaginary setting as well. This detachment from reality makes fantasy difficult to evaluate. Pure fantasy that provides no overlap with the real world of a child should raise caution flags. Use of allegory might bring balance to an otherwise pure fantasy story. An appetite for fantasy is difficult to satiate.

- *Myth* Myths, legends and folklore are "bigger than life" stories that usually find their origins in an oral storytelling tradition. They can be just for fun, "historical" stories, or they might provide insights into an ancient culture's beliefs and false views of God and man. They contribute to your child's "cultural literacy."

❤ **Whole Book Fever**—This affliction is spreading rapidly throughout the home schooling community. It is contracted through frequent contact with whole books. There is no known cure. Symptoms include the following:

- You lose the motor function needed to close a good book and put it down.
- You have an insatiable desire to browse in other people's libraries.
- You hyperventilate with a rapid heartbeat upon finding a whole set of mint condition Landmarks with dust jackets at a garage sale.
- You are physically not able to pass by a stack of old looking books without stopping to look at them.
- You schedule your vacation around the annual community used book sale.
- You begin stacking books horizontally in your bookshelves to make room for more books.
- You fail to tell a friend about the library sale for fear of missing a rare find
- You buy a fourth copy of *Johnny Tremain* at a library sale because you forgot you had the three others.
- You actually worry about which child will get which books from your home library when you die.
- You start a booktable business just so you can buy more books at dealer's cost.

❏ Curricula

If you have ever wandered the aisles in a large curriculum fair, then you know the temptations of curricula. Whether it is full-color products from a big publishing house, or a photocopied and hand-bound product from a small family business, the lure is the same. It's neat, it's clean, it's a just-add-child learning resource. Curriculum, by its nature, holds the promise of easy teaching, but does it really deliver on that promise, or is it just a "curricular safety net" to spread out beneath your uncertainty and insecurity? It is so easy to become "curriculum dependent" either by default, because it is what you were raised on, or by accident, because you fail to break the curriculum habit. If you have made the switch to a whole book approach to home education, then you don't need to be tempted by curriculum any more. You're beginning to discover that books are a much better investment of your educational funds than yet one more curriculum that equates learning with filling in blanks and choosing multiple choices. The liberation of learning in your home means throwing off the tyranny of textbooks and breaking the grip of curriculum. Enjoy your freedom! You and your children need never be enslaved by curriculum again. However, if you are tempted by a curriculum, be sure to ask yourself a few questions.

What to ask yourself when considering curricula:

• Can I teach this subject naturally without a curriculum? What will this curriculum do for my children that I, or they, cannot do without it?

• What good books on the subject could I buy with the money it would take to buy this curriculum?

• Am I just attracted to its packaging and promotion? Am I judging the book "by its cover" or by it contents? Is it effective, or just clever?

• Do I know anyone personally who is using or recommending this curriculum? Have I read any good reviews on it?

• Does the tone of the writing appeal to my children's maturing appetites, or to their immaturity and childishness?

Some parting thoughts about curricula.

There is a booming cottage industry among home schoolers selling "used curriculum." You can occasionally save some money by shopping at the used curricula tables at book fairs, but you can save even more by observing what is on those tables. It is nearly a rite of passage for new home-schooling families to buy curricula that ends up gathering dust on the shelf. Usually, it turns out to require more preparation and involvement than they are willing to invest, or it just doesn't fit their lifestyle. It becomes an investment in experience. What we all learn, though, is that any curriculum is only a tool—it doesn't really "teach" anything. The attitude and commitment of the teacher is far more important than the tool. So if it doesn't work, don't worry. Put your unused used curriculum on the table with everyone else's and buy real books next time. You're experienced now.

❑ Materials and Supplies

There is always the temptation to want to recreate the classroom in the home. If you've ever browsed through one of those classroom supplies catalogs or stores, you surely know the lure of all those cute, brightly colored, creative and *expensive* educational do-dads. The math section is particularly enticing with all those counters, attribute blocks, base ten boards and cubes, Cuisenaire rods, and the countless books and workbooks for using them all. The bottom line is, schools have lots of money (yours!) to throw away on those things...you don't. Just keep in mind all the great books you could buy with the same money.

- The basic principle governing all this "stuff" is that you can nearly always a) do just fine without it, b) find an inexpensive alternative, or c) duplicate the stuff at no cost using materials you have at home. An obvious example: you don't need cute little rubber bears for counting. Marbles, beans, candy, or any number of things will do just fine. Construct your own "Cuisenaire" rods or "interlocking counting cubes" with the jillions of Lego® or Duplo® blocks you probably already have. Be creative!

- Some educational stuff can be good and useful, to be sure. However, it is rarely necessary. So don't buy too much of a good thing. A nice set of shape and attribute blocks is interesting and fun. However, you don't need a 200 piece set—that's for a whole elementary classroom! Just get the basic starter set.

- Colored pencils are better than crayons and markers. European kids, who've known this for years, carry their colored pencils in nifty little pencil boxes with pop-up pencil holders. Colored pencils last a long time, sharpen easily with less mess, allow for much more precision and artistic expression, don't smear, and provide truer colors. Also, they don't break in half like crayons and, because they have no cap to get lost in the couch cushions, they don't dry out like felt markers. And they don't melt when left in the crease of the car seat in the heat of summer. You can start with inexpensive colored pencils ("map colors") for everyday drawing, or start your children early discovering the wonder and beauty of art-quality colored pencils. In either case, go with the colored pencils—they make a point!

- If you have children who enjoy drawing and doodling, buy your paper in bulk. If you want quality, your local office or paper warehouse will have inexpensive, off-brand bond (copier) paper in 500 sheet reams. Or, buy newsprint sheets from a moving company or U-Haul and cut them to size. Check at your newspaper for newsprint roll ends, too. If you have a source of used computer paper or copy center discards, you can collect and use it for everyday drawing. And don't forget to recycle your own computer paper discards—your children can use the unprinted side for when they are doodling or sketching.

Basic supplies to keep on hand:

- pens, pencils, colored pencils, felt markers
- rulers, scissors, tape, glue, hole punch, pencil sharpener, erasers, compass
- paper—white bond, lined writing paper, colored construction sheets, newsprint
- poster board
- loose-leaf notebooks
- report covers, ringed binders
- chalk board (chalk, erasers), white board (dry erase markers, eraser)
- bulletin board(s) with map tacks

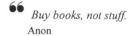

❝ *Buy books, not stuff.*
Anon

Comment: Art Quality Colored Pencils
There is a huge difference between "map colors" and "art quality" colored pencils, such as Design Spectracolors or Berol Prismacolors. Art quality pencils use wax-based pigment that yields rich, true colors. Unlike map colors, the better pigments can be blended together into new colors. Also, they are very responsive to pressure so a light touch yields a soft, gentle hue, and a firmer stroke leaves a bold, brilliant hue, giving your children far greater flexibility and range of expression in their artistry. If you want to create an appetite for artistic expression in your children, start them out with art quality colored pencils.

CHAPTER FIVE

Teaching Methods...
Instructing Your Child

Making Methods Work for You

Methods are all the things you do to teach your children. Your methods may even be defined by things you *don't* do. They are the *how* you teach of *what* you teach. You may not be consciously aware of it, but you are using a method whenever you read aloud to your children, or help them with a math problem, or tell them to go work on the computer. How you do the tasks of teaching are your methods, whether you are systematic and predictable, intuitive and spontaneous, goal-oriented, or non-structured. It is impossible to teach without using methods.

No matter how you teach, understanding teaching methods will help you become a better home educator. As you discover the methods that reflect your philosophy of teaching and learning, or that just seem to work better with your children, it makes sense to try to understand and master those methods so you can be more effective. However, your goal is always to master the methods without letting them master you. The methods you use should never become more important than what is being learned. Use specific methods only if they work for you and your family, and only if they are serving your purposes (instead of you serving them). Different methods work differently in different families. You will have to discover for yourself what works best for *your* family.

The methods discussed in this chapter are what we use in our Home-Centered Learning approach. These are not classroom teaching techniques—they are personal tutoring skills. These methods emphasize the *relational process* inherent in home learning, as opposed to the *instructional procedures* of a classroom setting. The relationship you enjoy with your children is, by God's design, the most powerful factor in your child's education. These methods reinforce that relational strength. In fact, many of the methods in this chapter have the positive result of not only helping your children learn the subject matter, but of helping both you and your children learn how to better relate to one another. These are family-building learning methods.

One final thought. Your attitude towards the methods you use is at least as important as your skill in using those methods. If you project a negative attitude toward a method, your children sense it and reflect your own negativism. It is better to use a less-desirable method with a smile, than a great method with a scowl. Your attitude should be enthusiastic and positive about the methods you choose and use. Before we talk about the methods themselves, we thought it was important to talk about how we "think about" those methods.

> *The horse-in-a-mill round of geography and French, history and sums, was no more than playing at education; for who remembers the scraps of knowledge he laboured over as a child?*
>
> Susan Schaeffer Macaulay, *For the Children's Sake*, Crossway, 1984

Proverbs 1:8
Listen, my son, to your father's instruction and do not forsake your mother's teaching.

> *[M]ethod is natural; easy, yielding, unobtrusive, simple as the ways of Nature herself; yet, watchful, careful, all-pervading, all-compelling... The parent who sees his way—that is, the exact force of method—to educate his child, will make use of every circumstance of the child's life almost without intention on his own part, so easy and spontaneous is a method of education based on natural law. Does the child eat or drink, does he come, or go, or play—all the time he is being educated, though he is as little aware of it as he is of the act of breathing.*
>
> Charlotte Mason, *Home Education*, 1935.

Home Schoolers Have Class!

Thinking About Methods

When I think of teaching methods, I think of the bread recipes we use at home. Each kind of bread—whole wheat loaf, dinner rolls, pizza dough, cinnamon buns, herb bread—shares the same basic ingredients, but proportions and seasonings differ, and the way each one is put together differs. But they all make bread. It's the same with teaching methods. There are some basic methods that you will always use, there are less common methods you will use only occasionally, and the mix you use will vary depending on the result you want to achieve. With a standard curriculum, it's the same recipe, and the same old plain white bread every time. But you are a master baker, an inspired teacher. Think about methods as your ingredients for creating a mind-watering, soul-fulfilling, heart-stirring learning experience for your children. Your special recipes will leave them asking for more because what they just consumed was *so good*. That is your goal as a home educator. Use your creativity to make learning delicious!

Think simple and natural. Like the rest of us, your thinking about learning has been deeply influenced by a formal, institutional model of education. It may take a step of faith for you to leave the familiar old world and false security of textbooks, workbooks and classrooms, and step into the new world of real books and real life. Once you do, though, you will find a refreshing new freedom in home educating your children. You and your children will be able to relax and genuinely enjoy learning. The old way will seem like so much regulated drudgery; the new way will turn home schooling into a joyful, natural part of family life. So don't be afraid of methods that are simple and natural—that is how learning should be.

Think informal and creative. It's not uncommon, once you have "converted" to an informal, whole book approach to learning, to slowly slip back into the "old ways" of formal classroom and curricular education. You can avoid that, though, if you train yourself to think creatively about the methods you are using, and to maintain an informal learning atmosphere. Remember, God has put your children into a *home* to learn, not into a school. Use methods that reinforce the natural strengths of your home, and appeal to the home-centered interests and desires of your children.

Think confidence and success. The more comfortable you become with home-centered learning, the more you can relax and focus more attention on your children, rather than on curricular demands. Your goal is to build their confidence in their own learning skills and abilities. By selecting methods that encourage them to do their own learning and thinking, you are training your children to be independent learners—not dependent upon you teaching them, or upon curricula and textbooks, for them to learn. You are also guiding their learning by setting them up to succeed, not to fail or to settle for mediocrity. Use methods that encourage good effort, challenge weak areas, and reward progress and accomplishment, not just "right answers." You are more than a teacher. You are your children's discipler and guide, showing them the way to maturity not only in Christian living, but in learning, preparing them to live wholeheartedly for Jesus Christ.

*H*ome-Centered Learning Methods

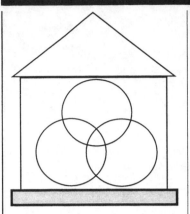

DISCIPLESHIP STUDIES METHODS

❑ Bible

The Bible is God's wholly inspired revelation to mankind. In it, God has spoken, and we must listen. But it is also an inspired "whole book" library in one volume. God has spoken through great historical literature, compelling storytelling, beautiful poetry, inspiring ideas and ideals, stimulating biography, and all variety of creative writing styles. In other words, the Bible is a "holy whole book." It should be your first, last and best resource for whole-book reading, and the standard against which all other literary works should be judged. It should be the starting point for giving your children an appetite for books, because it is the "book of books."

Of all the appetites for life and learning that you instill in your children's hearts, let a love for God's Word be one that you feed and stimulate every day. Let all others be be minimized until you see the signs in your children's hearts of a godly "hunger and thirst for righteousness." As you cultivate your children's appetite and love for the Word, be careful to avoid two extremes that will leave a bad taste, or no taste, for Scripture in their mouths. On the one end, avoid overemphasizing "grace" by treating the Word primarily as a collection of inspiring stories and moral ideals. At the other end, avoid overemphasizing "truth" by treating the Word primarily as a book of rules and principles that must be learned and obeyed. The correct attitude is found in the middle, where "grace and truth" meet in the person of Jesus Christ, "the Word became flesh." You should treat the Word as a personal message from the heart of God.

When you read and study the Bible with your children, remind them you are carrying on a conversation with the God of the universe. When you open the Bible to read God's words, remind them to open their hearts to hear God's voice. Remind them often that the Bible is not just an inspired curriculum, or a heavenly story book, but it is God speaking to them through his revealed Word.

> ❝ *But if you love your children, let the simple Bible be everything in the training of their souls; and let all other books go down and take the second place.*
> J.C. Ryle, *The Duties of Parents*, 1888

John 1:14
The Word became flesh and made his dwelling among us. We have seen his glory, the glory of the One and Only, who came from the Father, full of grace and truth.

Hebrews 4:12
For the word of God is living and active. Sharper than any double-edged sword, it penetrates even to dividing soul and spirit, joints and marrow; it judges the thoughts and attitudes of the heart.

> ❝ *In regard to this great book I have but to say it is the best gift God has given to men. All that the good Saviour gave to the world was communicated through this book.*
> Abraham Lincoln

> ❝ *The study of God's Word for the purpose of discovering God's will is the greatest discipline which has formed the greatest character.*
> Anonymous

IN OUR HOME...

We are awash in Scripture in our home. Our children can't turn anywhere that there doesn't seem to be a Bible or a Bible book of some sort. It is a continual reinforcement of our commitment to God's Word and its importance to our lives. If there is a question or need for Bible wisdom, there is always a Bible handy. We keep several versions on hand so we can get different insights on a passage we're talking about. Rather than leave it only to the church, we've even tried having a home Bible club, with Bible activities and singing, Scripture memory and prizes to earn. We also keep the Word in view with calligraphic renderings of verses hanging on the walls. In the end, though, all those efforts are just reinforcement. The reality is, our children value the Bible because their parents value the Bible.

Bible Reading

Bible reading used to be a mainstay in Christian families. The entire family would gather together in the evening to listen to the Bible read aloud, usually by the father. Unfortunately, in a culture characterized by too many activities and too much television, it is rare to hear of Christian families who take the time for family Bible reading. In an age of information fragmentation and saturation, though, our children need to have their hearts and minds trained to listen to long readings of God's Word. They may have *quality* in their devotions and Bible study, but they also need *quantity* in their Bible reading.

- Above all other books, the Bible should be honored in your family as the "Book of books." It is the very Word and words of our God. Make it a regular part of your required reading for your children. And when you read aloud the Bible, always read it with expression, energy and pacing that says, "This is worth listening to!"

- Your children will value the Bible as a source of reading pleasure only if you do. Make Bible reading a regular part of your daily routine. Set aside special time to read longer passages of the Bible. Talk about the Bible to your children the same way you talk about favorite books.

- In the elementary years, give your children realistic Bible reading assignments. Be selective in suggesting which books and passages they should read. Focus on historical narrative, selected Psalms, Proverbs, the gospels, Acts, and selected passages from the epistles. Assign blocks of reading but allow them to read at their own pace. Or, create Bible reading goals for a quarter or for a year.

- Be sure to provide opportunities for your children to be the ones who read aloud the Bible. Let them read long passages (chapters or short books), but guide them in reading with expression, energy and pacing.

- Bible on tape is an effective way to expose your children to long readings of the Bible. Their attention can be focused on some other project while they listen in order to reduce distractions. They can do other schoolwork, color in a Bible stories coloring book, write letters, or whatever keeps their ears open and the hands busy.

COMMON BIBLE TRANSLATIONS FOR FAMILY USE		
Version	Level	Comment
KJV	Gr.12	King James; many prefer for memorization and study; difficult to read.
NASB	Gr.11	New American Standard; literal translation; updated version excellent.
NKJV	Gr.8	New King James; updated language easier to read and understand.
NIV	Gr.8	New International; equivalent translation; popular and widely used.
NCV	Gr.5	New Century; equivalent translation; "gender neutral."
CEV	Gr.5	Contemporary English; equivalent translation; "gender neutral."
NIrV	Gr.3	New Int'l Readers; simplified NIV for family reading and read aloud.

♥ Best Reads—Children enjoy some parts of Scripture more than others. Stick with what will stick with them—the rest will come later:
Genesis and Exodus
Historical narrative (stories)
Gospels and Acts
Parables (selected)
Proverbs (selected)
Psalms (selected)
Key OT and NT passages

📖 *The Child's Story Bible (Vos/Eerdmans)*—All the stories of the Bible told in narrative with interpretive insight.

📖 *Leading Little Ones to God (Schoolland/Eerdmans)*— Time-tested doctrinal devotionals for young children.

📖 *Every Day With God: A Child's Daily Bible (NCV)*—Bible stories with devotional content.

📖 *Stepping Stones to Bigger Faith for Little People (Herzog/Greenleaf)*— Biblical devotionals for younger children

♥ Bible On Tape—There are numerous products that are just Bible readings (often pretty dull ones). Two audio Bible products stand out:
- *The NIV Dramatized Bible*— A dramatic reading of the actual NIV text by a team of actors, with music and sound effects.
- *The World's Greatest Stories*—Totally unique one-man interpretive, dramatic reading of selected Bible stories (NIV or KJV text) with music and effects, by George Sarris.

♥ Chalk Talk—For Bible read aloud time, use a good descriptive story Bible and have the children illustrate the reading on the chalk board.

Devotions

The purpose of a family devotional is to model for your children how to hear God speak through his *Word* and how to respond to him in *prayer*. You are training your children how to relate to God and how to appropriate his grace for daily living through personal Bible reading (God speaking to us) and prayer (us speaking to God). Many parents (especially dads) wrongly assume that biblical instruction is a substitute for devotions, but it is not. With instruction, your focus is on the mind. In devotions, your focus is on the heart—knowing God, not just knowing about him.

- The most effective method for developing the *personal* devotional habit in your children is for them to see *you* have personal devotions. If they observe you reading and praying in the morning or evening, they will more readily agree to begin doing it for themselves.

- The next best method for developing the personal devotional habit in your children is to have daily family devotions at a regular time (such as breakfast, dinner or bedtime). Choose a time (or times) that allows for the greatest consistency and priority.

- Once your children are reading confidently and well, encourage them to have a daily personal devotional time. Select a Bible-based devotional guide, or create your own readings for them on a one-month calendar. Create a simple prayer list also. Ask them to spend 5-10 minutes daily in reading and prayer. Make it a habit to ask them how God spoke to them in their devotion (to narrate it to you).

- Soon after your children begin reading, give them an inexpensive Bible of their own. Encourage them to take it to church each week. Show them how to underline and make notes in it. Teach them proper Bible care and respect, but be careful not to make the Bible itself an object of veneration ("bibliolatry"). We take care of the container because the contents are holy, not the container.

- Turn your own personal devotions into a family devotional. Share what God is saying to your heart in your daily devotions.

❣ **The Family Devotional A.R.T.S.**—Create a family devotional on a minute's notice with this simple outline:

Ask a question.
...ask it personally.
...ask it simply.

Read the Bible
...read it persuasively.
...read it slowly.

Talk about it.
...talk about principles.
...talk about stories.

Speak to God.
...speak with praise.
...speak with submission.
Select a paragraph or passage suited to the ages of your children. Start with an opinion-type or thought-provoking question that piques their interest. Personalize it ("If you were a giant, what would you do..."). After reading the Bible, have them narrate the reading to you (the story of David and Goliath). Then talk about what principles can be learned and applied (courage, trust), and tell a brief family story to illustrate. Finally, end with a prayer about the passage (for courage and trust).

❣ **The Three-for-Me Personal Devotional**—Use this simple three question Bible study and devotional outline to teach your children how to read the Scriptures for personal application:

1. Is there something in this passage God wants me to know? (Is there truth, doctrine, principle, wisdom, instruction, insight?)

2. Is there something in this passage God wants me to do? (Is there a command, admonition, exhortation, advice to obey or follow?)

3. Is there something in this passage God wants me to be? (Is there a character quality, example, virtue to grow in or practice?)

IN OUR HOME...

No matter how good we think we're becoming in the family devotional arts (see column), there are times we wonder. We were having a lively devotional discussion one morning about Paul's admonition to the Thessalonians "to keep away from every brother who is idle and does not live according to the teaching you received from us." We had followed the ARTS outline to the letter and were rolling along just fine until we asked four year-old Nathan what he thought God was saying to us as a family. His reply, though perfectly correct, put the brakes on our devotional—"Keep away from idols!" We gladly settled for a good chuckle and a short prayer.

Bible Study

The primary purpose of Bible study for your children is not simply to pour knowledge about the Bible into their brains—it is first and foremost to instill a love for God's Word, and to teach them how to acquire wisdom from it. You are training your children how to search the Scriptures in order to find answers and guidance for their lives. Knowledge *about* the Bible is important, too, but knowledge *from* the Bible is the goal.

- No matter how many colorful, illustrated, child-friendly Bibles, Bible supplements and materials are created and marketed, there is no substitute for direct interaction with the Word of God. Despite a flood of children's Bible products, we have found very little that takes our children seriously in Bible study. Even the few that do a good job can tend to become a substitute for the Bible, rather than a supplement to it. Give your children the real thing—study the Bible, not Bible books.

- Bible knowledge of books, authors, people, events, general doctrines, and key passages is a necessary foundation for meaningful Bible study. However, whatever isn't picked up in read aloud and devotions, can be easily learned through discussion, assignments and self-study.

- Because writing is necessary to Bible study, wait until your child's handwriting has developed enough so that it is not a frustrating experience (9 or 10 years old). Buy or create a simple Bible study form for him to use in recording his own Scripture discoveries.

- Teach your children as soon as possible how to use some of the basic Bible study tools: Bible dictionary, concordance, topical Bible, encyclopedia of the Bible, Bible handbook. There are good child-friendly versions available to get them started.

- Teach your children how to do a *topical* Bible study as soon as they achieve some "biblical literacy." This is the easiest and most fundamental form of Bible study to learn. The purpose of this study is to train your children how to search and survey the Scripture with a concordance to gain wisdom concerning a specific topic or doctrine (faith, love, patience, friendship, Christ's return, baptism, and so on).

- Teach your children how to do an *inductive* Bible study as soon as they show readiness. This is the best method for systematic Bible study. It uses three basic methods: 1) *Observation* (what does the passage say?), 2) *Interpretation* (what does the passage mean?), and 3) *Application* (what does the passage say and mean to me?). Start your children on individual verses, and work them up to paragraphs and passages. It's the pattern of study that counts, not just the product of it.

- Teach your children how to synthesize what they are learning from their topical or inductive Bible studies into a guiding principle or principles. In other words, show them how to define a personal application that is derived from several passages, not just one. Give them a Bible Study Notebook to record all their studies and applications.

The International Children's Bible Handbook (Word)—Child-friendly handbook covering all books of the Bible and more.

What the Bible Is All About for Young Explorers (Scripture Press)—Good Bible handbook for kids.

The Read 'N Grow Picture Bible (Word)—Good illustrated resource for studying Bible chronology and events.

LifeGuide Family Bible Study series (IVP)—Devotional/Bible study guides for ages 4-8, with insight, text, questions, prayer, activity, and commentary.

❣ **Wisdom to Grow On**—Create topical studies for your children to address their spiritual growth needs. For example, if your son is having trouble with patience, create a topical study with ten passages on patience or self-control that he is to look up. Help him distill several principles that will help him become more patient. Memorize one of the Scripture passages studied.

❣ **Word Processing**—Bible software for 8-12 year-olds makes Bible study interesting and fun. Look for more and better quality software in the near future.

Logos products

Parsons products

NavPress products

❣ **Keep It In Context**—Study the historical context surrounding a reading of a Bible story or passage. Where was the author writing? Why and to whom was he writing? What were the cultural conditions at that time? What other people are involved?

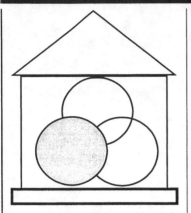

DISCIPLINED STUDIES METHODS

❏ Beginning Reading

Reading is a mysterious process. Although various schools defend their respective methods, no one really fully understands how a child learns to read. What is a certainty, though, is that God has created your child with intelligence and an innate ability to learn language. The ability to read is *already there*—it is not something that you will *teach* your child, but something that you will *release* in him. In other words, the power to read is not in the rules or the methods, it is in the child. In helping your child learn to read, you are simply cooperating with God's design.

* The goal of a good reading program should be to lead your child to read, and then get out of the way. Don't burden your child with memorizing dozens of phonics rules, an emphasis which can turn reading into a tedious, frustrating effort, and result in a child who only deciphers words instead of reading for meaning and enjoyment. Reading is not that difficult! Phonics *principles* will enable your child to read well. Phonics *rules* can help them spell better, but the rules can wait until they are 10 or 11, and then only if they are needed. The best way to learn to read is...to read.

* Choose a phonics-based reading program that focuses on reading, not just on phonics rules. It will teach your child naturally, in the process of actual reading, how to "de-code" the actual letter and word symbols on the page. However, don't be surprised when your child reads by pattern memory, too ("Look-Say"). It is a natural part of learning to read, especially in the exception-ridden English language.

* You don't need gimmicks to teach your child to read. The simple, inexpensive methods work. Don't be intimidated into thinking complexity means effectiveness—it doesn't. Complicated games, flashcards, songs and colors do not teach reading—you do!

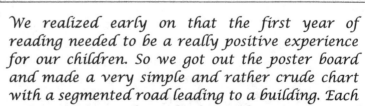

IN OUR HOME...

We realized early on that the first year of reading needed to be a really positive experience for our children. So we got out the poster board and made a very simple and rather crude chart with a segmented road leading to a building. Each of the 100 segments represented one book, or about 30 pages of reading. We let Sarah, who was nearly seven, decide on the reward. She wanted to spend the night at a hotel with her mother, and eat out for dinner and breakfast. As a typical first child, she got the best deal. Joel got a day at Opryland with his dad. Nathan will probably get a night out for Ranger baseball. Actually, it wouldn't really matter what it is, just so it seems special. So far, it has worked quite well. That challenge set the pace for what continues to be a steady run at reading. Try it!

📖 *Teach Your Child To Read In 100 Easy Lessons (Fireside)*—This uncomplicated phonics-based reading curriculum works! Applies phonics principles in a graduated learning approach.

📖 *AlphaPhonics*—Popular resource using a linguistic (word family) approach.

📖 *Noah Webster's Reading Handbook (Christian Liberty Press)*—Updated and illustrated. Great for review of phonics basics.

📖 *The Christian Eclectic Readers (McGuffey)* — Upadated with Christian supplemental material.

❝*Even speaking with scientific logic, it is an impossibility for the mind of man to search and understand the mind of man. Thus we Christians, more than others, ought to be humble about our knowledge of teaching and learning language. The answers are not all in. They likely never will be. And someone who thinks differently than us about these matters may very well have something valuable to share with us. This is a time to keep open minds on language teaching.*

Ruth Beechick, *The Language Wars*, Arrow Press, 1995

- The most important role you play as your children's reading teacher is not just teaching them to read—it is making each individual child feel successful as a reader. Offer lots of praise and encouragement during the learning process, even if there is only a little progress. Always tell your child what he is doing well when learning to read; don't focus on areas of struggle or on what he is not yet able to do. And never use reading as a threat—"You may not ride your bike until you read this to me well!" Always present reading as a wonderful, pleasurable experience that your child is going to greatly enjoy.

- Some children start reading later. Don't worry, and don't push—just keep reading aloud to them until they signal their own readiness to read (asking about words, reading signs and boxes, "reading" books). If you encounter resistance, put away the lessons until the child is ready to try again. When the time is right, the process will be natural and enjoyable. Resist the cultural pressure to be sure your child learns to read "on schedule." Your child may read much earlier or much later.

- Reading skills are developed progressively and incrementally, so make it a habit to practice with your child a little bit every day. And just as important, read aloud to him every day. Research confirms that hearing language is an important part of learning to read. There is always a certain amount of tension when a child is learning to read. He will be coming up against barriers that can be frustrating, even though they are not that formidable. It is the tension that draws a child forward in the learning process. As a parent, your job is to discern when that tension is healthy and normal, and when it is becoming unhealthy and counterproductive. When it does, you need to be ready to ease up and take a break. Be sure to affirm your child's progress when you do.

- Create a mini-library of books for early reading practice. Choose readers that will stimulate an appetite for real books. Avoid basal readers and primers, which are usually just twaddle. Provide books that are well-written, with larger print and fewer words on a page, and challenging vocabulary (it can be a little beyond your child's reading level). Books like the *Classic American Readers* series, the *I Can Read* series, and *Billy and Blaze* books are good starter books.

- When children discover a book they like, they will want to read it over and over. Repetitive reading reinforces reading development and should be encouraged, not discouraged. Your child's confidence grows as he "masters" a book through repetitive readings, just as he would master getting a basketball in the goal by repeatedly throwing the ball.

- Before the teaching of beginning reading became an industry, children learned very naturally with no formal curricula. In a more literate time, they would grow up immersed in language and books, and reading was simply taught in a natural, commonsense way. Reading was learned by reading, not by learning reading "skills." If you want to give your child the best reading curriculum possible, fill their world (your home) with language. Let them explore books with you. Talk with them often. Tell them what you are writing. You will be preparing them to read.

> 66 *Many persons consider that to learn to read a language so full of anomalies and difficulties as our own is a task which should not be imposed too soon on the childish mind. But, as a matter of fact, few of us can recollect how or when we learned to read: for all we know, it came by nature, like the art of running; and not only so, but often mothers of the educated classes do not know how their children learned to read...Whereby it is plain, that this notion of the extreme difficulty of learning to read is begotten by the elders rather than by the children.*
>
> Charlotte Mason, *Home Education*, 1935

> 66 *How much time for the fluency stage? Two years. One full year at the least. For instance, if children learn basic phonics in first grade they can spend second and third grades reading widely in easy books... Even with good readers, there is no need to push on with what textbooks call reading skills. When children read real books, they get practice in the skills. Reading is learned by reading.*
>
> Ruth Beechick, *The Language Wars*, Arrow Press, 1995

> 66 *In concentrating exclusively on teaching the child <u>how</u> to read, we have forgotten to teach him to <u>want</u> to read...Somehow we lost sight of the teaching precept: What you make a child love and desire is more important than what you make him learn.*
>
> Jim Trelease, *The Read-Aloud Handbook*, Penguin, 1985

□ *Common Sense Press language arts workbooks*—CSP materials for language arts (*Learning Language Arts Thru Literature*), grammar (*Great Editing Adventure* series), spelling (*How to Teach Any Child to Spell*) and creative writing (*Wordsmith* series) are well-designed, child-oriented, and focus on real rather than artificial activities.

□ *The Italic Handwriting series*—A contemporary handwriting curriculum based on classic italic lettering that creates a fast, legible hand. Basic and cursive letter forms are the same, so it is much easier to learn.

□ *Simply Grammar~An Illustrated Primer (Andreola, Charlotte Mason R&S Co.)*— Updated and illustrated oral grammar used by Charlotte Mason. No writing required. Useful for primary instruction or for review in later grades.

□ *English from the Roots Up*—Interesting studies of word origins from Latin and Greek.

□ *Draw Write Now (Barker Creek Pub.)*—Introduction to handwriting for K-3 that integrates handwriting practice with simple art instruction.

❏ Language Arts

The art of language is the expression of thoughts and ideas through speaking, reading and writing. Language arts, on the other hand, is the group of skills that help you speak fluently, read proficiently, listen carefully and write clearly. The term usually encompasses phonics, grammar, spelling, vocabulary, writing mechanics (punctuation), and handwriting. Your child learns to speak fluently without any formal instruction because God designed his mind for language. If your home environment is rich in language and good books, your child will, in much the same way, naturally pick up language arts without the necessity of formal instruction. However, it is at this point that many parents fall prey to their fears and spread the curricular safety net—a comprehensive graded grammar curriculum, graded spelling lists, phonics workbooks, and so on. There is a much better way. It is unnatural and burdensome to segregate each element of the language arts in order to study it separately and out of the context of its use in real language. A better way is to immerse your child in reading and writing, creating an environment rich in language usage. If you want to use a curriculum, choose materials that integrate several areas of language arts studies, or that parallel the natural learning methods already in place in your home.

You can teach language arts very easily and effectively without any curriculum. For example, have your children read aloud a piece of literature, or a Bible passage (reading). As the selection is read, put new words on a marker board (vocabulary). When completed, have each child narrate the passage to you, from the youngest to the oldest (speaking). Then choose a paragraph or passage to dictate that your children will write down (handwriting), which you will check and correct (spelling, grammar and mechanics). The language arts lesson is complete.

Grammar

Grammar is to writing what phonics is to reading. The goal is to learn how to write well, not to learn how to be a good grammarian. The best way to help your child acquire a good grasp of grammar is by the reading of good literature and hearing it read aloud. The more language your child is exposed to in the early years (3-8 years-old), the more he will naturally acquire good grammar. Grammar rules, which will never by themselves make any child good at grammar, can wait until your child is writing easily and well at around 10 years-old, and then only if they are needed. Grammar studies, like phonics, should move aside once your child is actively writing. Your child will learn grammar by using it, not just by studying it. And, in fact, too much emphasis on grammar will quickly kill an appetite for writing by turning it into a technical, academic exercise.

Mechanics

Although it may seem redundant, the best method for teaching writing mechanics is to have your children read many good books. They will see punctuation, capitalization, formatting and other mechanics at work. Then, mechanics are learned by using them, not just studying about them.

Whenever you child writes in a journal, or creates a report, scan the page for writing mechanics errors. Never simply tell your child what the error is—mark the line or paragraph in pencil (lightly, so it can be erased) and have your child find and correct the errors. Of course, you can also check for grammar and spelling errors in the same way. Dictation is an excellent way to drill for mechanics. Read a selected paragraph which your child copies and do the same as above. Choose a selection rich in mechanics to get an indication of how your child interprets what he hears..

Vocabulary

If you are reading quality literature, there is no need to wonder if you need to be drilling your children from vocabulary lists. You will find so many new and infinitely more interesting words in your reading than a curriculum could ever offer. Whenever you come upon an unfamiliar word in reading, stop reading and ask if the children know what it means. Write the word on a marker board, then define it for them, or have them look it up in the dictionary. Have them say the word out loud and then use it in a sentence. Then continue reading. Keep the words on the board for a few days to periodically review them. For fun, challenge your children to use the word during the day without getting caught. Bottomline in vocabulary: words in context increase vocabulary, not words in lists.

Spelling

Research is indicating that some children are naturally good spellers, and some are not. However, good readers are generally good spellers because they are constantly reviewing words visually in their reading. If your child is having difficulty spelling, don't panic. First, give your child freedom and encouragement to keep writing. Spelling is learned by writing, not by list-memory. Then, start to focus only on the words he is using that he is misspelling, not on isolated lists of words he might someday misspell. Memorizing spelling lists is tedious, distasteful and not all that effective. Have your child start a notebook to record misspelled words. A newly misspelled word should be written correctly 3-5 times to reinforce the correct spelling. When your children are writing easily and well at around 10 or 11 years-old, you can also review the rules of phonics with them then.

Handwriting

There are scores of handwriting curricula, any one of which will help your child develop a legible hand. It matters very little what "school" of handwriting your child learns from since they will eventually develop their own preferred "hand." A handwriting workbook helps by giving your child a standard against which to measure his own handwriting. The reality, though, is that a workbook just points the way—real learning comes from using writing for real tasks. A practice paragraph in a workbook has little lasting impact on handwriting skills in comparison to writing in a journal, or writing a letter, or writing out a list. So don't let a handwriting curriculum put you on an obsessive quest for perfection—it will greatly frustrate both you and your child! Handwriting is a means to an end, not an end in itself. Your child's handwriting will mature as he matures.

Comment: Keyboarding
In a computer-based culture, keyboarding (typing) is a form of language arts. The ability to use a keyboard will remain the entry point for computer use for a long time to come. In a way, it is electronic handwriting. Get your children started early on a simple "typing" computer program.

❣ **Computer Language**—If you own a computer, there are numerous excellent programs that teach and reinforce language arts skills. Many of them are published by The Learning Company, Davidson & Assoc., Edmark, and Broderbund, all well known for their high quality and thoughtfully designed educational software products.

Comment: Oral Test
Language arts can also be studied orally, and often should be. A child's mental ability to understand concepts typically far exceeds his physical ability to write. So, if writing is tedious and difficult for your child, simply have them answer questions orally. Oral examination is much more accurate as a means of determining if your child knows or has learned something. This can be an especially helpful method for boys, whose fine motor skills (handwriting) develop more slowly than those of girls.

Comment: Boys and Girls
In general, boys are slower to develop in fine motor and verbal skills than girls. Parents who understand this will adjust their expectations of their sons to prevent unnecessarily frustrating them by expecting more than they are capable of doing or expressing. If you have a boy who is slower, don't worry about it, just give him space to grow and time to mature. Fill that space and time with lots of good books and real life experiences.

❑ Creative Writing & Composition

📖 *Teaching Your Child to Write (Cheri Fuller)*—A parent-friendly guide filled with practical suggestions for encouraging writing skills for school, work and life.

📖 *Any Child Can Write (Harvey Wiener)*—A highly acclaimed book with a multitude of ways to encourage and cultivate your child's ability to write.

📖 *Wordsmith Series (Cheany, Common Sense Press)*—*Wordsmith Apprentice* makes writing fun for the younger child. *Wordsmith*, for the older child, is an easily-paced one-year workbook for creative composition. *Wordsmith Craftsman* is a high school workbook for report and essay writing. Least burdensome of the many writing curricula available. Each provides the foundational instruction, then encourages real writing, not just workbook busywork.

Comment: Writing Freely
Guiding your child to become a good writer requires you to maintain a delicate balance of freedom and structure. You want to give them maximum freedom to express themselves with the voice God has given to them, not to you. But that freedom will be expressed through a structure— grammar, mechanics, spelling and so forth. Your goal is to build a solid structure with them on which their expressive freedom can stand. Too much structure will overpower it; too little will undermine it. The right balance will release it. Avoid workbook-style curricula that keep your child dependent on tedious "exercises." The best "practice" is in doing real, meaningful writing.

Writing is the highest expression of language. It is the ability to communicate thoughts and ideas in a medium that is both permanent and transferable. John wrote "For God so loved the world..." one time two thousand years ago, but it is still changing lives today. Giving your children the ability to write clearly and powerfully will allow them to communicate far beyond the range of their spoken words, perhaps even to future generations. Most writing, of course, is purely utilitarian—lists, forms, information and the like—and for that your children need know only handwriting. Writing to communicate, though, requires much more—orderly thinking, proper mechanics, good vocabulary, creativity and imagination. And it will require more of you as a parent. But you do not need to resort to a formal curriculum to guide your child in developing the ability to write well. In fact, trying to reduce writing to an academic exercise may be counterproductive, giving your child technical proficiency yet nothing to write about. Good writing begins long before your child ever picks up a crayon to scribble his name and an "i luv yu."

The essence of good writing is clear thinking. The best way to prepare a child for writing is through "oral composition," or what is referred to as "narration." The practice of reading aloud good literature and then having your child narrate back to you what he has heard is foundational to good writing—it is your child's first steps at ordering his thoughts to communicate clearly and logically. The same process can be applied to narrating personal reading and life experiences, as well. You are training your child to think about *what* is best to say and *how* to say it best—that is composition. If a child learns to think clearly and logically about speaking, it is a natural step to thinking the same way about writing. The grammar, mechanics, and spelling may not be perfect (and probably won't be until a later stage of their maturity), but that is a minor concern that can be easily fixed over time. However, if a child does not learn early how to think clearly and logically, it is very difficult to remedy that deficiency. It is critical to create an environment rich in good books, writing and language to lay the foundation for your child's writing abilities. If you want writing to be important to your children, it must be important to you first.

IN OUR HOME...

Writing is a time intensive exercise for children, no matter how good they are. We try to personalize the process to make writing something they actually choose to do. We keep a collection of rubber art stamps, quality paper and card stocks which our children know how to use to make their own cards and notes. Writing a note on a handmade card doesn't seem like a writing assignment to them, but just one more step in the creative process. They also make their own stationery, stamped all over with boy stuff (cars and planes) or girl stuff (flowers and cute animals). Since they already want to write to their friends, we just consider that to be another writing exercise.

- Don't rush writing. It is difficult and frustrating for a young child to write very much until he or she has developed the necessary hand strength and coordination. Early writing experiences should be short—notes to friends, copy work, short dictation, Scriptures to memorize, a nature journal, a commonplace book, or other similar writing activities. Older children can take on longer writing exercises and projects—written narration of a book or experience, article for a family newsletter, an imaginative story, poems, longer letters and such. The more natural and personal the subject of the writing experience, the more motivated your child will be to write.

- You are your child's writing coach. One of the most important things you do is keep your child motivated to write. He needs to feel confident that his communications are acceptable, even though you know they are full of errors. Whenever your child is making errors in an *emerging* skill area, be very slow to correct those areas (if it is something they already know, correct it). For instance, there is no need to correct a pre-schooler's invented spelling words. He will soon pass out of that phase and want to become proficient at spelling. At first, though, he is simply motivated to communicate and will attempt phonetic reconstructions of the words he does not know. Focus on the communication, not on the mechanics. Or, don't be overly concerned about a bit older child who isn't getting all the mechanics quite right yet. Focus first on the content and quality of the composition itself.

- Learning to write well is a gradual process. It takes time and practice—lots of both. Have your child do some kind of writing every day, whether it is a letter, in a journal, a list or whatever it might be. In any writing time or exercise, be sure to allow time for "mental composition"—time to think. If you want your child to write well, give him time to think well. Also, be sure that the environment is conducive to writing—quiet, low distraction level, comfortable, and not rushed.

- There is no formula for learning to write. Would that it were as simple as an arithmetic equation—grammar + vocabulary + spelling + mechanics = writing! In writing, the sum of the parts may be more or less than the whole. One thing is certain, just as it is with other language arts, the best way to learn writing is not by studying all the parts separately. The best way to learn writing is to write.

- In all writing, whether creative or compositional, have your child write about what is interesting to him. There is no gain in forcing a child to write a tedious report about Rome if it holds no interest to him. Instead, tie it to an interest—Roman Transportation for a boy who likes cars, or Roman Homes for a girl who loves homemaking. In creative writing, encourage your child to write from personal experience or knowledge. Keep good reference materials handy, especially a child-friendly dictionary and thesaurus, for help in making their writing more precise and descriptive. Take some time to dialog with your child about the subject to draw out impressions and perspectives. Direction is always more positive than correction. For younger children, have them dictate a story which you write down for them, word for word.

❣ **Write Now!**—There is no shortage of possibilities for natural writing opportunities for your children. You can probably come up with many more:

- letters to friends and family
- thank you notes
- "article" for family Christmas letter
- start and international chain letter (yes it's legal)
- write to new "pen pals"
- "how to" instructions for a newly learned skill
- make a book (staple or tie sheets together with an illustrated cover)
- illustrate a story on the computer
- favorite recipe cards
- directions to your home or favorite restaurant
- classified ad to sell something
- favorite Scripture passages
- greeting cards and placecards
- best memories
- captions for family photo album pictures
- personal or devotional journal entries
- opinion letter to a magazine or newspaper

❣ **Write Together**—Gather around the dining room table once a week for a creative writing time. Have several topics ready. Poll the family as to their choice of topic. Everybody writes something. Everybody reads their writing aloud. Parents offer suggestions on grammar, style and expression. Everyone edits or rewrites until their piece is polished. (Note: This same idea is developed as Workshops in the Right Words writing curriculum.)

❣ **Write Away**—*Free Stuff for Kids* is a year-round writing project for your children. They are naturally motivated to write away for something free, so they will keep writing as long as there are things they are interested in getting.

Saxon Math—K-12 text-books, workbooks with tests. Widely used and recommended. Written for classroom use.

Making Math Meaning-ful—Complete math curriculum emphasizing understanding and manipulatives. David Quine.

Miquon Math—K-3 consumable workbooks. Good introduction to Saxon Math.

Math-U-See—Focuses on understanding using video instruction and manipulatives.

CalcuLadder—Pencil and paper timed drills for basic math through fractions and pre-geometry.

❧ Handy Manipulatives—
Some math manipulatives you might want to keep on hand for hands on:
- attribute blocks
- pattern blocks
- counters
- Cuisenaire rods
- base ten blocks
- geometry peg board

Comment: Math 2000
Math will undoubtedly play a large role in our children's lives. However, not every child needs to learn higher math. If your child has a proclivity for math, let him or her go as far as possible with it. If not, there is no reason to go beyond Algebra and Geometry. The goal should be familiarity and experience with common mathematical concepts, not mastery of the disciplines. Let your children excel where they are strongest and most motivated. If math, great. If something else, it's OK. Don't let math become a source of stress and anxiety because you're afraid you're going to handicap your children if you don't push them. You won't.

❑ Math

Math is a big bugaboo for many home-school parents. It doesn't need to be, though. Once you choose a curriculum or approach, if you stick with it, your children will learn. In most cases, the curriculum chosen probably has less to do with the children, and more to do with what the teaching parent is willing to use. No matter what approach your primary math curriculum takes, you should try to provide in addition to it a variety of methods in your math instruction—paper problems, manipulatives, word problems, drills, practical math and, especially, real life math experiences

- During the early years of math study, look for practical, hands-on ways during the day to demonstrate math concepts the children are learning. Math is everywhere—measuring foods, counting money, figuring square footage, sorting and counting common items (clothes, silverware, mail, etc.), counting minutes before and after on a clock, and so on. In addition to learning math concepts, they will also learn the practical necessity of knowing how to use math as part of real life.

- Let your children set their own pace for learning—if it is too easy, let them work ahead as they are able; if it is too difficult, slow down for a while. Be aware that most math curricula, due to learning lost over summer break in conventional schools, contain as much as 70% review of previously learned material (i.e., very little new material). If you home school year round, this is unnecessary and tedious repetition. If it's already known, move on. Most children will hit occasional roadblocks when new mathematical concepts or functions are introduced (multiplication, fractions, geometrics, etc.), but that is natural. Go to another area of study and come back to it after a while.

- To a child, math can require a frustrating amount of abstract thinking. Numerals (3 is a symbol for three things) and function signs (in written equations) are symbolic and abstract. Rather than frustrate your child with mathematical abstractions, translate the problem for him with concrete images instead of symbols—"If you have three apples and I give you two more, how many do you have?" This kind of oral and mental math helps your child focus on the actual problem, rather than on translating the abstract symbols in an equation.

IN OUR HOME...

God has made our children's parents good at words, but not at numbers. We rely on formal curricula to get the job done. We also harness their love of the computers to math. They love climbing a ladder to higher levels of recognition (from "rookie" to "star detective"), or racking up points based on accuracy and speed of computation. We, of course, monitor the skill levels so the problems reflect their current abilities. They like getting the certificates of achievement generated by the programs, which makes math more enjoyable and affirming.

❑ Thinking Skills

Exercising and strengthening your children's thinking skills will prepare them for solving problems, and for expressing their thoughts in written and spoken words with clarity, logic and persuasiveness. *Logical thinking skills* enable your children to address issues and problems based on facts and accuracy of thought. *Evaluative thinking skills* enable your children to reach conclusions based on values and clarity of thought. Generally, a child will have a natural preference for one or the other, but both are needed for communicating well.

- Avoid the temptation to always tell your children what to think, or to play the "Answer Man" to all their questions. Encourage and help them to think through their questions to allow them to reason or research their way to an answer. Validate their thinking process, even if you can't always validate the conclusions they may reach.

- Most bookstores, educational stores and teacher supply stores offer a good selection of helpful thinking skills workbooks that exercise problem-solving and logical skills, visual skills, and mathematical reasoning skills. Children usually enjoy the mental challenges they offer.

- When there is a real life problem at home, involve your children in finding a solution—how to plant the garden, fixing something that is broken, making room for more books on the bookshelf. The purpose is not necessarily to have them solve the problem, but to play a role in *thinking* about solving the problem.

- Develop evaluative thinking skills through the use discourse and discussion. Ask questions that are open-ended and allow for opinion and evaluative thought. Create hypothetical situations, talk about current events, or discuss a real experience. Stay away from topics that will be morally vague or ambiguous. Children need practice in thinking about and applying the moral principles and precepts they are learning. However, fill-in-the-blank questions looking for "the right answer" do not train thinking skills. Dinner time or long trips in the car are natural opportunities for this kind of discussion.

IN OUR HOME...

Opinion is not in short supply at our house. As parents, we have to guard against "parental intimidation" when it comes to opinion formation in our children. The dinner table is a good place for discussion since eating keeps everyone in one place. We try to elicit opinions on various subjects, track their reasoning (mostly evaluative), and interact about the topic. Humor keeps the discourse enjoyable and blunts the intimidation factor. The value in these times is not in the conclusions they reach, but in the process of reaching those conclusions. We have to be careful to keep the discussion general, and not to encourage argumentativeness, but verbal interaction is just a part of our home atmosphere.

✎ *Critical Thinking Press (CTP)*— Offers numerous workbooks filled with page-based thinking skills problems.

📖 *Building Thinking Skills (CTP)*— Series of graded, easy to use workbooks using similarities and differences, sequences, classification and analogy to build thinking skills

📖 *Mathematical Reasoning (CTP)*— For your "math minors." Two volumes of graded problems to stretch thinking and reasoning skills.

📖 *Developing the Early Learner, vols. 1-4*— Consumable workbooks for pre-reading and early thinking skills.

📖 *Connections: Working with Analogies (Continental Press)*— Age-graded, consumable workbooks.

📖 *Gifted and Talented Series*—A wide variety of workbooks for thinking skills and other areas.

❝ *Reading consists mainly of thinking; only a small part consists of the reader's eyes moving across the page. If children are going to become good readers, they need many opportunities to dialogue and practice critical thinking.*
Cheri Fuller

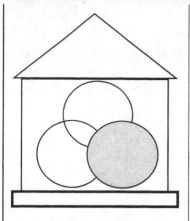

DISCUSSION STUDIES METHODS

❏ Reading

The ability to read is foundational to all education. Literacy is the power to acquire knowledge and learn. But your efforts at giving your children the *ability* to read will be in vain if you do not also give them the *desire* to read. If you do nothing else in home education, raise your children to love reading. A "heart for reading" is the key to self-education, your ultimate goal for your children.

In a home where parents value reading, and reading is a natural part of life, the question "why should I read" is rarely asked. The reasons are plain to see. There are three to keep in mind as you cultivate your children's desire to read. First, *we read because that is how we can know God's truth.* In the early years of our country, the main reason parents taught their children to read was so they could read the Bible on their own. God has revealed himself through the written Word—it must be read in order to "correctly handle the word of truth." Second, *we read because we want to learn and grow.* Reading will enable your children to continue the education you begin while they are at home. You are equipping them to learn and grow on their own through books. Third, *we read because it is enjoyable and fulfilling.* Reading is an adventure of the heart and the imagination. A well-written book is a joy to read, whether it is fiction, inspiration, biography, history, poetry or any of a multitude of writings.

Your children will naturally imitate you and adopt your values. If you want your children to have a heart for reading, then they must see that *you* have a heart for reading. If you love to read, your children will love what you love. The best way to create a desire to read in your child is by modeling a genuine interest in a wide range of reading materials—the Bible, history and biography, inspiring fiction, interesting magazines, letters, poetry, reference resources, reports, instructions, recipes, newsletters, instruction manuals and on and on. And don't be only a passive reader. Whenever you have the opportunity, involve your child in what you are reading—read a passage out loud, ask him to read a selection, explain what you are reading and why, share an interesting insight you just learned. Always emphasize that reading is not just something you *have* to do, it is something you *want* to do—that you can't imagine what it would be like to live without reading. Become a dedicated promoter of books in your family, always talking positively about them and pointing out their benefits.

Reading is much more than simply an academic discipline. It is the doorway between a life of dependency on others on one side, and a life of spiritual and personal freedom on the other. If you cannot read the Bible for yourself, then you must depend on someone else who can. If you cannot read an instruction manual, then you must depend on someone else who can. Without literacy, there is no liberty. By instilling deep in your child's heart both the desire and the ability to read, you are leading them through the doorway to a life of personal freedom. You are giving them the assurance that, with God's help and good books, they can succeed in life.

📖 *For the Children's Sake (Macaulay, Crossway Books)*—The philosophy of Charlotte Mason distilled into one book by the daughter of Francis and Edith Schaeffer.

📖 *Books Children Love (Wilson, Crossway Books)*— Reading list for children. Companion book to *For the Children's Sake.*

📖 *Honey for a Child's Heart (Emily Hunter)*— Good insights on reading with a recommended reading list for children.

📖 *A Family Program for Reading Aloud (F.A.C.E.)*—Book list for the Principle Approach.

📖 *Books That Build Character (Kilpatrick, Simon & Schuster)*— Books for children and youth that reinforce character and virtue.

📖 *The Original Home Schooling series (Charlotte Mason)*— Six volumes of all you want to know about the Charlotte Mason whole book approach to education in her own words.

Personal Reading

Your children will read more books during their years at home than at any other time for the rest of their lives, and most of them they will read silently. With their minds set by God for peak learning, they can learn more from reading good books than you can ever hope to teach them. In a whole book approach, personal reading is the primary source of learning.

- To ensure the best use of personal reading times, you need to provide both structure and freedom. You provide structure—a scheduled reading time and selected books to read—to make your children accountable to you for what they are reading and learning. You provide freedom—to make their own choices for reading as long as they are age-appropriate and acceptable to you—to encourage your children to follow their own interests in reading.

- For personal reading to become habitual, you need to create designated daily reading times. Make it a priority for your children to read during these times. With so many distractions vying for your children's attention, you must be consistent at keeping the reading time a priority or else it will be pushed aside by lessons, activities, field trips or whatever other option that comes along. Make your children be disciplined to read. It should become an unquestioned expectation. During the reading times, be sure to keep distractions in your home to a minimum. Choose a time that is generally quiet when all (or most) of the children can participate. Require everyone to read or rest (which do you think they'll choose?) quietly for an hour, and limit any distracting noises during the time.

- Some parents worry that a whole book approach will leave "holes" in their children's education. But it's really just the opposite—personal reading fills in so many holes that you will never be able to cover as a "teacher." The reality is that children who are widely read have no more or less holes than conventionally schooled children. The difference is, as readers, your children will know how to fill holes.

IN OUR HOME...

With all the baskets lying around our house, one might think we like to shop at the local Farmers' Market. Except for one thing...they are all filled with books! Next to just about every comfortable couch or overstuffed chair, there is a big wicker basket sitting on the floor filled with "fruits and vegetables for the mind." The baskets can be filled with random or topical selections of books (holiday, illustrated stories, heroes, pre-school, etc.). Recently, we've turned them into personal reading baskets, one for each child (and one for library books). We change the selection periodically with input from the children. It's so fulfilling to see our children grab books to read alone or together stretched out on the couch, or overstuffed in the overstuffed chair. Now if we can just find a good Farmers' Market for books.

❣ **Required Reading**—Your child should always have a required reading list that he or she is working on. These books will be read during the daily designated reading time, so you do not need to establish a time frame for completion of the list. Only required reading books should be read during that time. Any other time, they may read any approved books (including from the reading list) of their choice. Each required reading assignment might include one book for each of the emphases listed below. Three might be selected by the parent, and two selected by the child (with parent's approval):
- one history or biography
- one science or nature
- one fiction
- one Christian history
- one Bible related

❣ **Snoozin' to Perusin'**—Convert your child's nap time in the afternoon into a daily one-hour reading time.

❣ **Reading Chart**—Rewards are not necessary to get your children to read, but they can be an effective source of positive motivation. Create a simple "Reading Challenge" chart on poster board. Establish a reachable goal, and a modest, meaningful reward for meeting the challenge.

❣ **Book It!**—Plan ahead for Pizza Hut's Book It program. Have your Support Group sign up 6 months in advance. Focus on the Family also has a reading challenge (but they don't have pizzas!).

❣ **Ho-Ho-Whole Books**—Choose humorous books from time to time to read or read aloud. It will help lighten the weightiness of the more serious reading. Everybody loves to giggle and laugh through a good book.

Reading Aloud

Countless studies over the past several decades have confirmed over and over again the undeniable impact of reading aloud on a child. Apparently, God has designed the minds of children to grow when watered with words from good books, his words being the best. It is impossible to overstate the influence you can have on your children simply by reading aloud to them regularly. It stands alone as an educational tool that is nearly universal in its effectiveness. Beyond that though, there is also a bonding that takes place when a family shares the experience of reading aloud. It is a unifying experience. Some are apt to be suspicious that such an uncomplicated means can produce such complex ends, but sometimes God uses the simple things to confound the wise. Reading aloud is just that.

- The art of listening is inextricably linked to the art of reading aloud. If you want your child to learn to *listen* well, you must learn to *read* well—to capture and hold your child's attention, interest, and imagination. You're not reading interpretively merely to entertain your children, but to train their attention, and to teach them by example how to be expressive in speech and mannerisms.

- Read expressively. If the passage is sad, sound sad. If a person is angry, show anger. If there is joy, be joyful. Use your voice to interpret. Try to give characters different voices and personalities—high voice, low voice, accents, fast and slow. Vary the speed, intensity, tone, inflection and volume with which you read. Set a moderate pace to begin with so you can slow down or speed up from it. Vary other elements to reflect the atmosphere and literary tone of the story.

Our Top Twenty Top Rated
Family Favorite Read Aloud Books
(Enjoyed equally well by everyone in the family!)

- *The House on Pooh Corner* (A.A. Milne)
- *The Wind in the Willows* (Kenneth Graham)
- *Treasures in the Snow* (Patricia St. John)
- *Chronicles of Narnia* (C.S. Lewis)
- *Dangerous Journey* (Pilgrim's Progress, J. Bunyan)
- *All Things Bright and Beautiful*, and others (James Herriot)
- *Little House on the Prairie*, and others (Laura Ingalls Wilder)
- *Little Women* (Louisa May Alcott)
- *Heidi* (Johanna Spyri)
- *The Secret Garden* (Frances Hodgson Burnett)
- *Freckles* (Gene Stratton Porter)
- *A Girl of the Limberlost* (Gene Stratton Porter)
- *Black Beauty* (Anna Sewell)
- *Hans Brinker, or the Silver Skates* (Mary Mapes Dodge)
- *Where the Red Fern Grows* (Wilson Rawls)
- *Summer of the Monkeys* (Wilson Rawls)
- *Benjamin West and His Cat Grimalkin* (Marguerite Henry)
- *Johnny Tremain* (Esther Forbes)
- *Caddie Woodlawn* (Carol Ryris Brink)
- *Great Dog Stories* (Albert Terhune)

❦ The Moral of the Story— Select read aloud books that are morally and spiritually inspiring. Discuss the characters in the story—their moral character, their choices and their companions. Look for Christian types, symbolism and metaphors. Identify principles of wisdom and life found in the book. Use the characters and events of the stories as illustrations for teaching and talking about Scriptural principles and truths.

❝ *Morality is not rule-keeping, but role-playing. Great literature can provide our children with models of ethical behavior that will inspire them and challenge them to view their own lives and behavior differently.*

Terry W. Glaspey

📖 *The Read-Aloud Handbook (Jim Trelease, Penguin)*—Excellent case for reading aloud. Lots of research. Secular in persuasion but still recommended reading.

When mother reads aloud, I long
For noble deeds to do—
To help the right, redress the wrong;
It seems so easy to be strong,
So simple to be true.
Oh, thick and fast the visions crowd
My eyes, when mother reads aloud!

Author Unknown, excerpt from *When Mother Reads Aloud*

EDUCATING THE WHOLEHEARTED CHILD

- Immerse your children in a rich pool of "living books" from all streams of knowledge: fiction, history, historical fiction, biography, science, nature, myths and legends, essays, and of course the Bible. Because we are awash in books in our day—many good, multitudes not—be especially discriminating of the books you read aloud or make available to your children for reading. Cultivate their literary appetites with only the best in age-appropriate whole, living books.

- Establish a regular routine for read-aloud times. Select times that work best for your family—morning, mealtimes, bedtime. Select locations where distractions will be at a minimum, and where the children can be comfortable. Set aside a time when you can read undisturbed for up to an hour or more. Also, set aside an evening for a regular extended read aloud time together as a family

- Whenever you return to a story, have your children review (narrate) what has happened up to that point—characters, plot development, setting. There's no need to re-tell the entire story, just enough to catch up. Before reading, have them imagine what they think might happen next.

- Establish eye contact whenever possible. It keeps your children more alert, and it enables you to gauge their attentiveness. Put your entire body into the reading—facial expressions, hand and arm movements, body movements. If you do all that and interest in the story seems to be waning, set that book aside. Select another book more attuned to their interests or reading levels. If you have both sons and daughters, read a "girl" or "boy" book occasionally

- Have your children read aloud from time to time to develop their oral reading skills. Reading aloud is excellent training for speaking and presentation. Expect them to read aloud expressively and dramatically. Be sure they read the Bible aloud regularly.

♆ Play Aloud Books—The "books on tape" market is still in its growth phase. Although there is a scarcity of unabridged children's classics on tape for the present, there are enough to start building up an audio-tape book library. Like books, though, they can go out of print unexpectedly, so don't wait if you run across a book on tape your family will enjoy. When you need some time, let a book on tape do your read-aloud. Long drives are great times for listening to an "audio book." We "read" the following books during about a six-month period:

- *Where the Red Fern Grows*
- *Trumpet of the Swan*
- *Silas Marner*
- *Les Miserables*
- *Cheaper by the Dozen*
- *Great Expectations*
- *Call of the Wild*
- *Swan Princess*
- *The Secret Garden*

❝ *If children haven't been read to, they don't love books. They need to love books, for books are the basis of literature, composition, history, world events, vocabulary, and everything else.*

Edith Schaeffer

IN OUR HOME...

The simple, venerable "bedtime story" is becoming a regular fixture in our home. I (Dad) sort of feel like it is my thing—I like it so much I don't want to share it. We recently read a children's novel about a boy from Greece who is captured by slave traders and sold. It was a well-told adventure story full of interesting insights about the culture. Now we're reading "Trumpet of the Swan" by E.B. White, a rich, allegorical fantasy fiction about a voiceless Trumpeter swan. Next we'll probably read a historical children's novel set in the Colonial or Revolutionary period. I get real satisfaction from the children's enjoyment of our time. I love hearing them get tickled when I do a funny character voice or expressive reading. I have found that when I read for 20-30 minutes at bedtime, the kids seem to settle down faster. It's a good feeling, too, that everybody hurries to get ready and to get comfortable when they know I'll be reading. It is a special time with my children that is deeply satisfying for me.

Comment: Literature Study Guides

There is nothing magical about study guides for books. Even though they are built around good literature, they are still just a "curricular safety net." The more confident you become in "the book, the whole book and nothing but the book," the less you will feel a need for written curricula. Study guides always contain useful insights about a book, to be sure, but that information is usually readily available elsewhere. The unfortunate effect of a study guide, even though it is not usually the writer's intent, is to take a whole book and dissect it into a number of discreet lessons, usually one per chapter. Rather than training your children to read the "whole book," you are training them, inadvertently, to think of a book in terms of its parts, rather than as a whole. The book's author did not intend for each chapter to be reduced to a lesson, any more than a poet would intend that each stanza of his poem be studied separately. Using a study guide also has a tendency to reduce the amount of actual reading aloud that you do, as you are spending more time on the study guide rather than on the book. Finally, a study guide perpetuates a dependency on "experts" rather than on your own insights. You are telling your child that you need someone else to guide you through a book, rather than reinforcing your child's own confidence in being able to understand a book. Narration is a much simpler, more natural means of extracting meaning from the reading of literature. It does not detract from the unity of the book, it allows maximum reading time, and it affirms the natural intelligence of your child. The intent of study guides is right, but the method is unnecessary. You don't need a curricular safety net—just a good book.

- Younger and active children can become distracted during reading aloud. Allow them to play quietly with something that will engage their hands yet leave them free to listen—a toy, a ball, colors. It will actually help them to concentrate on the reading. Even if you have a terminally wiggly child, the key is whether or not they are listening and paying attention to what you are reading. Whatever position they assume for listening—sitting down, lying down or standing on their heads (common for little boys)—it's okay as long as they can narrate back to you what has been read.

- Attention spans will vary greatly with children, but all children can be trained to listen attentively to progressively longer and more advanced readings. Don't wait to start training until they start school—start reading very early in your child's life with interesting picture and story books. They will progress naturally to chapter books.

Why Read to a Reader?

Reading aloud is an effective educational method at all ages, even into adulthood. Rather than diminishing your older children's reading skills or boring them, as some fear it would, reading aloud improves their skills and captivates their imaginations. The following are just some of the reasons to read to readers, no matter how old they are.

- **Emphasis:** When you are reading, you are able to emphasize words and concepts that your children would not always understand if reading alone. You can also point out recurring themes, symbolism and types in literature that might otherwise go unnoticed by an immature reader.

- **Insight:** You know much better what portions of a book to read interpretively, and when. How you read will make the book more understandable and interesting to your child.

- **Vocabulary:** Listening vocabulary, especially in children, is much larger than speaking vocabulary. Reading aloud enlarges their listening vocabulary by allowing them to hear new words in context.

- **Variety:** Children develop their own appetites for reading which often do not include challenging new types of reading materials. Reading a new kind of book aloud with your child expands their reading horizons in an enjoyable way.

- **Discussion:** Reading aloud sparks conversations at all age levels. A good story provides a wealth of examples to discuss godly character, good and bad choices, the uncertainty of life, and the importance of family and friends.

- **Appetite:** You can stimulate your children's appetites for quality literature through reading aloud. Your reading can set the standard for excellence, especially with older children as they begin to make their own reading choices.

- **Comprehension:** Through narration and evaluative questions (those that ask for an opinion), you can raise your children's level of reading comprehension. You are modeling how to understand an author's intent.

- **Togetherness:** Above all, your children will never grow too old to enjoy the warm feeling of gathering together as a family to read aloud a good book. The shared memories of those hours will last a lifetime.

❏ Narration

Narration—*the telling back or writing down in your child's own words what has been heard or read*—is the best way for a child to acquire knowledge from books. As a "teaching method" it is as old as language itself. Cultures through the centuries that relied on oral tradition were using narration—telling back and writing down accurately and clearly what had been heard. In our media-flooded times, oral skills have declined, but the practice of narration from books of literary quality can reclaim them for your children. And not just oral skills, but the powers of attention and retention that are fundamental to learning, and to the ability to sort, sequence, select, connect, reject, classify, visualize, synthesize and communicate knowledge from books. The uncomplicated method of narration releases the powers of reasoning and self-expression in your children that are left untapped by textbooks, worksheets and lectures. Charlotte Mason has revived the forgotten simplicity and power of "telling" that teachers from Socrates onward have known. It is brought to life through narration.

- Narration is a progressive skill. Before age six, let your children simply talk—do not ask for narrations. At around age six, though, your children can begin narrating shorter readings of children's stories, Bible stories, and the like. From age seven and on, provide the best in classic children's literature for read aloud and silent reading. As your children age and mature, you can progressively increase the amount and complexity of material to be narrated. By age nine or ten, the narrative ability is well developed.

- Narration develops language skills in the ability to express whole thoughts and sentences well before the ability to write is developed. When mechanical writing skills are more fully developed, compositional skills are already in place from narration. From about age nine or ten and on, written narrations should become a part of the process.

- Upon finishing a story, a portion of a book, or a reading, simply ask your child to tell you the story. No further prompting is necessary. According to Charlotte Mason, *"A single reading is insisted upon, because children have naturally a great power of attention; but this force is dissipated by the re-reading of passages, and also, by questioning, summarizing, and the like."*

IN OUR HOME...

We have found that narration requires just as much discipline for us as parents as for our children. We are often tempted to "help out" their narration just a little. But it takes parental discipline to stick to the standard of a single reading and no prompting. So, we find that if the parent-reader, before beginning to read, gently reminds the children-listeners in a positive way that they will be asked to narrate, attention is heightened. We don't ask our children to narrate every time we read. Even when we don't, though, they will "narrate" simply talking about a book.

> " *As knowledge is not assimilated until it is reproduced, children should 'tell back' after a single reading or hearing; or should write on some part of what they have read.*
> Charlotte Mason, *A Philosophy of Education*, 1925

> " *Children benefit from working steadily through a well-chosen book. And if they narrate it to you, it will become theirs. But more happens. Because they've tackled a complete book, they become acquainted with its flow and its use of language. They are students of another person—the author.*
> Susan Schaeffer Macaulay, *For the Children's Sake*, Crossway, 1984

> " *Narrating is an art, like poetry-making or painting, because it is there, in every child's mind, waiting to be discovered, and is not the result of any process of disciplinary education. A creative fiat calls it forth...and the child narrates, fluently, copiously, in ordered sequence, with fit and graphic details, with a just choice of words, without verbosity or tautology, as soon as he can speak with ease.*
> Charlotte Mason, *Home Education*, 1935

> " *A single reading is a condition insisted upon because a naturally desultory habit of mind leads us all to put off the effort of attention as long as a second or third chance of coping with our subject is to be hoped for. It is, however, a mistake to speak of the 'effort of attention.' Complete and entire attention is a natural function which requires no effort and causes no fatigue...the concentration at which most teachers aim is an innate provision for education that is not the result of training or effort.*
> Charlotte Mason, *A Philosophy of Education*, 1925

❣ **Narration Requests**—There are numerous ways to ask for a narration. The following are suggestions adapted from an article by Karen Andreola in her quarterly magazine, *The Parents' Review*:

• "Tell me all you know about _____."
• "Explain to me how..."
• "Describe our _____."
• "Describe anything new you learned from this chapter."
• "Tell me five things you learned about _____."
• "Tell me the story back in your own words."
• "Ask six questions about the material in this chapter."
• "What did you learn about _____ in this chapter?"
• "Draw a picture, map or likeness of _____."

• Narration is a creative process, so don't become impatient if your child seems slow. Some children need more time than others to think and to express themselves. Allow your child sufficient time and freedom to narrate as creatively as he desires. At first, your child may have difficulty recalling all the details or getting them in their proper order. The more narration he does, however, the better he will become at attending and retention. If a book has a lot of detail, have your child narrate less material more frequently.

• Some books or readings may include words, names, dates and places that would be difficult to remember when narrating back the reading. This is especially true for younger children. Those pieces of information, though, can be listed on a marker board and noted before the reading. The child is encouraged to refer to the board, if it is needed. Corrections, if necessary, should be offered sparingly, and only *after* the narration. Before discussing corrections, offer some positive affirmations about the narration. Never interrupt a narration, especially if it is to offer a correction.

• Narration is not a strict standard that must be adhered to with legalistic fervor. It is a method and a process. Through it, you are helping your child *learn to learn* from real books. It begins as a formal method, but the more it becomes a natural habit to your child, the more informal it can become.

• Write down your young children's narrations verbatim and collect them in notebooks for each individual child. As writing skills develop, have your children write out their narrations and collect them in a notebook. Use them for reading practice

Narration—A Short Sample
by Sarah Clarkson, age 10
Where the Red Fern Grows, chapter 1

"One day, a man whose name was Billy was walking home from work. It was a beautiful day, and Billy was perfectly happy. As he was nearing his house, he heard the sounds of a dog fight. As he rounded the corner, Billy saw a lot of neighborhood dogs fighting against one old redbone hunting hound. Billy could tell that the dog did not live around there. A hunting hound would have come from the mountains in the country. The hound brought beautiful, sad and happy memories to Billy's heart. He felt sorry for the dog and, taking off his coat, he shooed the other dogs away. He took the dog home with him. As Billy was giving the dog a bath, he found a little tag on which was crudely marked, "Buddy." It was a little boy's handwriting. Buddy must have been sold for much needed money, or maybe he had to be left behind when his family had moved. Whatever it was, Buddy was going home to the master he loved. After the bath, Billy fed Buddy. He ate every last scrap of meat in the house! Billy had to go down to the store to get some more. Later than night, Buddy started out for the rest of his journey. After he had gone, Billy took two beautiful prize cups down from the mantelpiece. One was large and gold, the other was smaller and made of silver. They stirred boyhood memories of two redbone hounds and a red fern."

❏ History

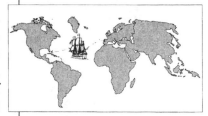

There is only one good reason to study history: *to give your children confidence to follow God (Ps. 78:1-7).* We can prepare our children to be faithful to God by studying the faithfulness of God in the affairs of men and nations. As they come to understand that God has been faithful in the past, they can grow in confidence that God will be faithful in the future. All of history is "His story"—the study of God's providence and sovereignty, and of the obedience and disobedience of men and nations to God's righteous standards. Your teaching goal is not just to impart historical facts, but to help your children see the hand of God in history that brings either blessing or judgment for men (biography) and nations (chronology). The study of history can feed your children's dreams of how God might use them, just as he has used others. History is full of true "heroes" who were used by God who can be examples to your children of godliness, faith, courage, integrity, resourcefulness, sacrifice, perseverance and vision.

How should you begin? With whole and living books. Historical periods are best studied by reading whole books about real people and real events. Biography is the most interesting to a child, especially when told as a story with realistic dialogue and descriptive narrative. Other "living" books can be used to fill in the context with historical color and detail. History textbooks take the life out of history, leaving only bare facts; whole book, literature-based study makes history come alive! The stories of great men and women told well will stir the heart and stimulate the minds of everyone in the family. And you can integrate almost any area of study into your historical reading with context and unit studies—literature, science, fine arts, Bible, character, language arts, social studies and others naturally relate to history with very little effort.

Where should you begin? The Bible is the best place to start a study of history, because Genesis begins at "the beginning" of recorded history. The account of the Fall, the origins of language and governments, the flood, and the birth of Israel, all provide the context for evaluating the rest of world history. Even the seeds of our American and western civilization were planted "in the beginning" in Genesis. For American history, start with Columbus or with the Pilgrims, showing that God used his people in the founding of our country.

IN OUR HOME...

We've joined what appears to be a growing association of home schoolers—families who collect the old Landmark history series that we all grew up with in grade school. We started collecting them relatively recently, but we've run into at least a dozen other families who value them, too, and have many of the 300 books in the series. It's a fun treasure hunt (especially when you can find first edition jacketed copies for $6.00), and they are perfect for historical read aloud or personal reading. The kids are even getting good at spotting Landmark spines at used book sales and stores. They're also fun to trade.

---

66 *There is no history, only biography.*
Ralph Waldo Emerson

66 *Those who do not remember the past are condemned to relive it.*
George Santayana

✎ *Greenleaf Press—* "Twaddle-free history" covering the major periods of biblical and post-biblical world history. GP publishes world history study guides and reprints.

📖 *Landmark History books series—* Highly acclaimed series of elementary historical readers from the 1950's. Most of the 300 or so volumes are now out of print.

📖 *History of the World (Kingfisher)—*One volume encyclopedic history with excellent illustrations and text.

📖 *See Through History series (Penguin)—* Very well done books that illuminate each major period of history with detailed illustrations and overlays.

📖 *Usborne Books—* Usborne publishes dozens of lively books that add historical color and context to the reading of a whole book.

📖 *A Child's History of the World (Hillyer)—*Out of print but worth finding.

♥ **Study Lenses**—You can study history through three different lenses:

- EVENTS (Chronology, or "what happened?") by looking at the context and impact of historical events.
- PEOPLE (Biography, or "who made it happen?") by looking at the lives of famous people through biographies and historical fiction.
- IDEAS (Ideology, or "why did it happen?") by looking at ideas and their movements that have changed and shaped history.

♥ **Time Line**—Post a historical time line on the wall. Use a published one, or make your own using drawings and clip art. The point of it is not for memorizing all the names and dates on it, but to help your child *visualize* where an event being studied fits in history by seeing what comes before and after it, and what else was happening in the world at that time. Fan-folded computer paper works well for a time line. Divide it vertically along the lines of major periods of history (have your children learn the names and order of those periods). You can divide the line by whatever date intervals you want, keeping in mind that shorter intervals will mean a longer time line. You can also create multiple time lines for more detail. You might consider starting out with a time line divided by centuries. You can also divide the paper horizontally into 3-5 areas of influence, such as The Church, The Arts, Ideas, and so on (or use parallel time lines). The center horizontal section or line is the core time line with the events of history written onto it. Whenever you start a new history study, stick a piece of clip art or a symbolic picture on the line to represent what you are studying. Time lines can be folded and stored, too.

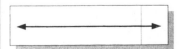

World History

People, events and ideas are the hooks on which your children will hang their growing knowledge of world history. Your teaching goal, through reading whole and living books, is to put as many historical hooks as you can in your children's minds. The more hooks, the easier it will be for them to sort out and make sense of history. In the process, you will be cultivating in their hearts a love and appetite for learning about history through books.

- In the elementary years, focus on your own historical roots. If your ethnic background is not European, you'll also want to study the Orient, Asia, Africa, or South America. Otherwise, follow the streams of history that flow most naturally into your children's lives: the great civilizations of the Old and New Testaments (Egypt, Medo-Persia, Greece, Rome); European history (Middle Ages, Renaissance, Reformation, Enlightenment, Revolution); American history (Colonial, Revolutionary, National, Pioneer, Civil War & Slavery); and others (Vikings, World Exploration & Conquest).

- Children have a natural curiosity to know about the "olden" days of world history, and how people used to live. They want to know what they were like, what they did, and what happened to them. The key to your children's interest in world history, though, is not archeological, but *biographical*—they want to hear about *real people*. They do not have enough experience with events in their own history to understand events in past history, but they can understand people.

- Children also have a natural desire to know who and what came during, before and after. *Chronological* study of world history allows your children to see the steady progress of history across the centuries, instead of just disconnected bits and pieces. Chronology presents world history to children in a logical, understandable sequence.

- Chronological study is preferable, but always remember that it is a servant, not a master. Be flexible; don't become compulsive about chronology. The underlying principle is to study history *sequentially*. In other words, follow the sequence of events in any area of history your study. You will want to break into your chronology of world history throughout the year to teach parts of American, European or church history for holidays, trips or just because your child is interested in something else. When you do, don't be concerned. Your children are learning both globally and linearly in the elementary years. They will put it all together in their own time anyway. So, enjoy your historical side trip and then simply return to the sequence where you left off. A simple time line will help your children orient to the chronological relationship of different historical sequences that you study.

- One of the primary benefits of studying history chronologically is to be able to see the development of ideas. Ideas develop linearly in history. Ideas (whether right or wrong) about origins, science, technology, liberty, the church, or whatever, develop gradually over time. Chronology allows you to study the history, development and impact of ideas on civilization more effectively.

American History

Your children's lives revolve constantly around American history—holidays, traditions, freedoms, language, symbols, museums, geography, pictures, songs, movies, stories, events and more. Even their Christian heritage and history are bound up in American history. They must know world history, of course, but America is the history of which they are a part and in which they must find their own place. It is the most intensely personal realm of history study for your children. You have the privilege of filling in your children's "American identity" with a view of American history that includes God's hand of providence in our past, present and future. That is the America where they must find their place.

- In the elementary years, the theme of study for American history is, predominantly, personal and religious liberty. Your children need to understand the costs, privileges and responsibilities of the freedoms they will enjoy as American citizens, as well as the threats to those freedoms. Study the historical roots of our liberties and the men and women who fought and died for the right to be free. The principles of liberty embodied in our national documents and heritage are solidly rooted in a biblical worldview. Regularly read biographies of great Americans, patriots, leaders and heroes, especially those with a Christian testimony. They are the antidote for the anti-heroes of today's pop culture. They will inspire your children to greatness of character and endeavor.

- Your children's lives constantly revolve around American history (holidays, traditions, language, symbols, museums, songs, stories, movies), so it will be difficult to teach it chronologically. An American history time line is especially helpful to put people and events in time and place whenever American history is being discussed. Cycle American history into your studies regularly, especially biographical studies of Christian colonists and great, patriotic Americans. Teach periods of American history sequentially, but don't worry about the chronology.

- Study state and local history. The best way is to create a unit study for places you visit, or plan to visit. Your library should have plenty of good books and resources to get you started. Call ahead to the historical sites—they often have books no one else carries.

IN OUR HOME...

We turn American holidays into history lessons. On Independence Day, we talk about our freedoms, about the founding fathers and our Christian heritage, about the flag, and other American themes. We read the Declaration of Independence. We might watch a show, such as Johnny Tremain. On Thanksgiving, we tell the story of the Pilgrims and their pursuit of religious freedom. We read from Gov. Bradford's journals, and retell the story of Squanto. And on all these holidays, we see the hand of God's providence in the founding of America.

✎ *Beautiful Feet Books*— Selected living books for literature-based study of primarily American history. BFB publishes useful study guides, time lines, and reprints.

📖 *Mantle Ministries books and tapes*—Excellent source of high quality reprints of out-of-print American history classics and 19th century unburied treasures.

📖 *Childhood of Famous Americans series*— Excellent, easy-to-read historically-based stories.

📖 *Your Story Hour Tapes*— Audio-drama tapes on the lives of great Americans.

📖 *D'Aulaire books*— Award-winning illustrated biographies from American history.

❣ **Dress Rehearsal**—Keep a "role play" locker full of costumes and clothing representing different periods of American history, especially Colonial and Revolutionary. Use them as teaching and learning aids to dramatically "rehearse" key events from American history (especially speeches).

❣ **On Site History**—Make plans to visit nearby historical sites. Coordinate the trip with the reading of a book about the site or event, and a context study. Use the visit as a starting point for broader study and reading about the associated period of American history.

❣ **Historical Holidays**—Use American holidays to teach American history. Use table settings for visual aids, watch a historical video, listen to an audio-drama, sing folk songs from the period. And, of course, read aloud a relevant historical book.

Church History

- In world and American history you are studying about the kingdoms of the world and its people. In church history, you are studying about the Kingdom of God and His people. The church is a spiritual institution that must be studied historically through the eyes of faith.

- For children, the emphasis in church history should not be on chronology (what and when), but on biography (who). Read stories and biographies of great men and women of the faith—ministers, missionaries and martyrs. As in other history studies, locate those you read about both in place (map) and in time (time line).

- Study the events of church history in very broad strokes, emphasizing the early church, the reformation, the church in early America, and the church today. Your goal is not to teach and test the details of church history, but to give your children a sense of continuity with the church through the past two millennia.

Family History

- Family history is all relative. Simply tracing ancestors and descendants, no matter how many names and abstracts you can put on your genealogical record, or how many presidents or princes pop up in your family line, can easily become a meaningless exercise. On the other hand, if it reveals to your children a Christian heritage and legacy that has been passed from one generation to the next, then it has great value (cf. Psalm 78).

- Much more important than facts and data about relatives, though, are their individual stories. Collect interesting stories and insights about your relatives and ancestors—Christian testimony, childhood incidents, history witnessed, impressions about progress and what it was like when they grew up, insights on other relatives now deceased, hopes and dreams. There are commercial products in print and on disk for the computer to help you, or you can just create your own notebook for storing all your genealogical notes.

IN OUR HOME...

Our children are fortunate to have a paternal grandmother (Nana) who is the de facto family historian. She is the curator of a mini-museum of papers, pictures and potpourri that span a century or more. Her hallway walls are literally papered with photographs of familiar and unfamiliar family and relatives. Before their great-grandmother died, the kids' maternal grandmother (Mimi) taped an interview with her mother about her childhood, her memories of being in a wagon train attacked by Indians, and other fascinating insights about her life. It all helps the kids find their place in history.

Sidebar

♥ **God's People**—If you have a historical time line, include a separate line for God's people to place great men and women of faith in historical context.

♥ **Local Church History**—Study the history of your own church. Learn how it started and who its founders were. Trace its theological traditions and distinctives back to their historical roots.

📖 *Trailblazer Books series (Dave/Neta Jackson)*—Historical fiction for children from the lives of great heroes of the faith.

📖 *The Sower Series of Christian biographies*—Good read alouds for Sunday afternoons (not all are well-written).

♥ **Family Tree of Life**—Uncover the Christian heritage and ancestry of your family. Trace the various religious traditions and denominations of your family members over the last one or two centuries. Look especially for Christian testimonies and reports.

♥ **Family History**—Put your ancestors into your history study, especially if you have any "famous" relatives. Bring out photos and stories.

♥ **Family Gallery**—Set aside a wall (hallways work well) for a picture gallery of your extended family. Include a brief biographical or historical note with each one. Try to collect old photos or photographs of portraits of your ancestors.

♥ **Get It On Tape**—Interview older family members who lived through historical periods that your children will study. Have specific questions that will create their life story on an audio-tape.

❏ Geography

Geography is all the rage these days, and our society has decided that the truly educated child can name every country and capital in the world. While there's nothing wrong with such Geo-trivia, it has little to do with true education. Geography is not just land masses and borders, but people and events. The importance of geography is not just in being able to identify a country and its capital, but in knowing its role in history and current events. To say that Vienna is the capital of Austria is a bare fact of little interest. To talk about the classical music associated with Vienna, or its strategic location during wars, or its one-time prominence as the center of an empire makes the geography of Austria worth learning. The study of history provides a natural bridge for the study of geography—they are almost inseparable. When continents, countries, cities, rivers, mountains and such are part of a book or story that you are reading, geography comes alive with meaning. World geography studied for no other reason than to fill in maps, though, quickly becomes tedious and tiresome. But Geography studied in the context of history and current events doesn't even seem like a "geography lesson." It's natural and enjoyable.

- Geography is as much "who" as it is "where." Study the *people* in a geographical area—what are they like, what do they eat, how do they dress, how do they worship, what do they do for work? Study the people living in the various countries where missionaries from your church are ministering.

- Geography should be a part of any context study when you are reading a whole book on history. To see what the geography was like at the time of the story, check the Encyclopedia, a historical Atlas, or a historical reference book on that historical period.

- Whenever you hear of a country mentioned in the news or in other reading, take a minute to find it on the map. Use a reference Atlas to discover more about the people, their customs and culture, the topography of the land (mountains, rivers, deserts, forests, etc.).

- For Bible reading, always keep wall maps or a Bible Atlas close at hand when so you can quickly locate cities, land masses, bodies of water and travel routes. It makes the Bible much more interesting.

> 66 *The teaching of Geography suffers especially from the utilitarian spirit. The whole tendency of modern Geography...is to strip the unfortunate planet which has been assigned to us as our abode and environment of every trace of mystery and beauty. There is no longer anything to admire or to wonder at in this sweet world of ours...[The] questions which Geography has to solve henceforth are confined to how and under what conditions is the earth's surface profitable to man and desirable for his habitation...[But it does not have to be this way.] Perhaps no knowledge is more delightful than such an intimacy with the earth's surface, region by region, as should enable the map of any region to unfold a panorama of delight, disclosing not only mountains, rivers, frontiers, the great features we know as 'Geography,' but associations, occupations, some parts of the past and much of the present, of every part of this beautiful earth.*
>
> Charlotte Mason, *A Philosophy of Education,* 1925

📖 *Children's Atlas of the Bible (Baxter, Greenleaf Press)*—Covers the 11 major periods of Israel's history.

📖 *The Kingfisher Reference Atlas*—Easy to use quick reference for current geography and information.

📖 *The Eyewitness Atlas of the World*—Very visual and informative oversized resource.

IN OUR HOME...

Our geography studies consist mostly of spinning the globe in search of a country, getting more detail in a good children's Atlas, doing some digital drills on the GeoSafari, and playing Where in the Word Is Carmen Sandiego on the computer. You won't hear any modern geography close-ordered drill and review around our house, but you will hear us talking about a country, its people and its resources in the midst of reading a book. We save geography study mostly for times when we are reading history, or when a child expresses a desire or there is a need to know.

📖 *Come Look With Me art book series*—Simple, attractive art books with background and discussion questions about selected artworks in a variety of styles and periods.

📖 *Looking At Pictures*—Child-friendly look at major themes and techniques in art through selected masterpieces.

📖 *Adventures in Art (Cornerstone Curriculum Project)*—Understanding the meaning of art in the flow of history. Selected masterpieces and study guides. Christian perspective.

📖 *Classical Kids audio cassette series*—Audio-drama; historical insights on classical composers with their music woven into a fictional story with young children.

📖 *Masterpiece Collection (Unison)*— Good series of budget classical music cassettes and CDs.

📖 *Music of the Masters (Allegretto)*—Classical music selections with biography and narration.

📖 *A Child's Treasury of Poems (Mark Daniel, Ed.)*—An anthology of children's poetry blended with classic paintings.

❣ **Table Art**—Keep art books out and open on tables (or displayed on a small easel) for easy browsing.

❣ **Gallery de Library**—Your local library probably has a good selection of art books, art posters and music that you can check out. To supplement the art and music, look for corresponding instructional videos there, too.

❑ The Fine Arts: Art, Music and Poetry

The fine arts find their origin in God, the Creator of language, color and music. Fine arts reveals within us an intrinsic need for beauty that is a part of God's image stamped on our being—an attempt to recover a glimmer of what was lost in the fall. God used all the fine arts to express his nature—the beauty of the artists' creations on the tabernacle and temple, the expression of praise through numerous songs, the emotion of poetry in the Psalms. In training your children to appreciate the fine arts, you are tapping into and releasing that part of God's creative nature within them.

In the same way that narration trains your children to hear what an author is saying through a book, you can also train your children to hear what an artist, musician or poet is "saying" through a creative work. In the process, you can train their appetites to hunger after that which is truly "fine" and beautiful, rather than just common or commercial. Fine arts study sharpens the ability to distinguish between mediocrity and a masterpiece.

In studying any of the fine arts, try to provide some personal historical background on the creator of the work—not just raw biographical data, but real stories about the person's life and work, especially as they might relate to the artwork, composition or poem. The more your children see the real person behind the creative work, the more interesting it will be to them. Put the works in historical context, too, using a historical time line. Compare the creator's works with his contemporaries—look at the work of a few other artists, listen to compositions by other musicians, read other poets.

Art

- Your goal in the elementary years is to lead your children into an appreciation and enjoyment of art in all of its varied expressions. Train your children to observe how the artist uses line, form, composition, color, shading, texture and style. Ask what the artist is saying through the artwork—what is his subject—and how the various elements help or hinder his message. Ask your children what they like and don't like about the artwork, and why.

- In order to really get to know an artist and his work, select one artist and study several of his works over a period of several weeks, or even months. Thoroughly examine and discuss one piece of artwork at a time, discovering the "artistic signatures" that characterize the artist's work. If you can study an artist's work chronologically, look for changes or developments in style and subject matter.

- You must set your own standards concerning nudity in studying fine art. Much of it can be avoided in the elementary years, and certainly any base or vulgar use of nudity should be rejected. However, nudity is an almost unavoidable "fact of life" in art, especially if you visit any art museums. Overreacting to nudity can create, rather than prevent, more interest in it. Determine what your threshold of comfort is with artistic nudity and decide ahead of time how to respond when an artist

Music

- As in art, the primary goal of music study is to learn to enjoy music in all of its variety, not just to "study" it academically. Be aware, though, due to so much "background" music in our culture, that your children are already trained to ignore music to some degree. Your first priority, then, is taking time to really *listen* to music—to slow down and to hear the variety of musical nuances that distinguish one piece from another, listening for what the musician was attempting to "say" through music, feeling the emotions expressed in the composition.

- Listen to several compositions by a composer before moving on to another. Try out all kinds of music—symphonic, ensemble, solo instrumental, string quartet, choral, opera, and so on. Baroque and Classical period music are the best place to start for children because the music is more structured and predictable. Read a story of the composer's life to pique your children's interest. Whenever possible, go to classical concerts so they can hear the "real thing" (look for free and inexpensive concerts or recitals in churches and smaller facilities).

Poetry

- Poetry is the most complex form of literary expression, not just for the poet, but also for the reader. The ability to understand the poet's message requires a higher level of concentration, the synthesizing of abstract thoughts and concepts, and the discipline of maintaining both the lyrical meter of the structure and the emotional expressiveness of the content. Good poetry opens the heart to profound thoughts and concepts expressed in new ways. Training your children to appreciate and enjoy the lyrical beauty and emotional power of poetry not only challenges them personally and mentally, but it also prepares them spiritually for reading the primary form and language of worship in the Bible.

- If you give your children an appetite for poetry now, it will stay with them throughout their lives. Start out with simpler verse and work up to longer pieces. Read it aloud expressively and have your children narrate back what they hear and feel. Have them read poems expressively for the rest of family during at tea time or at dinner. Set aside a special time for poetry reading—make it a fun, enjoyable activity.

❦ **Art Smarts**—It is not necessary to be knowledgeable about the fine arts in order to enjoy them with your children. Your attitude will set the pace. If you are interested and excited about the fine arts, your children will be, too.

Comment: The Real Thing
We try hard to give our children appetites for fine art, good music and quality poetry. Our culture tries even harder to give our children appetites for cartoon and pop-culture art, childish and pagan music, and puerile poetry. When they sometimes ask why we don't read a particular book, listen to certain kinds of music, or watch Saturday morning cartoons, we use the illustration below. The subject is the same in each, but which is more interesting? Which is more real? Which tells a story? If we say "No" to some things it is because they are the stick figures. We believe our children's minds are made for better appetites. God doesn't want us only avoiding the ungodly things; he also doesn't want us to let mediocrity crowd out excellence in our minds. He wants us to train our appetites for beauty and excellence.

IN OUR HOME...

Nathan, our youngest, didn't seem very interested in art, until we found him intently studying a Norman Rockwell mural on the family room floor. He had found in the painting's background hidden images of characters from children's literature that we had overlooked. It was a joy to hear him tell about his discovery. In the area of music, there was very little interest in classical music until we played the Classical Kids tapes with dramatized stories about the composer's lives. Once the music became "personal" they wanted to hear more of it.

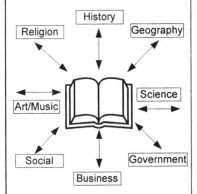

📖 *Usborne Books*—history, geography titles

•

❣ **Life In Context**—You can also use other physical resources to build on a context, such as field trips, museums, historical artifacts, foods, role play, period clothing, musical recordings, poetry readings, and the like.

CONTEXT STUDY

Example
Little House on the Prairie

Geography—map study of 19th century mid-west.
Political—president(s); number of states in the union.
Social—games children played; popular books.
Economics—cost of basic items; personal incomes.
Religion—pioneer churches and Christianity.
Arts&Music—songs of the day; artists and musicians.

❣ **Contextual Books**—Some books are better than others for providing opportunity for interesting context studies, such as biographies and historical literature. The following examples are rich in context:
📖 *The Bronze Bow*
📖 *Adam of the Road*
📖 *A Tale of Two Cities*
📖 *Heidi*
📖 *Caddie Woodlawn*
📖 *The Witch of Blackbird Pond*
📖 *Johnny Tremaine*
📖 *Amos Fortune, Free Man*

One of the many benefits of whole book learning is the very natural way that good books lead into so many areas of study. A good whole book stimulates interest in people, places, ideas and times related to the story it is telling. Context study takes advantage of that natural interest in knowledge to integrate several areas of study and research. A context study is similar to a unit study except that it is tied to a *single whole book* rather than a *single theme*, and it is used only occasionally, rather than as a regular teaching structure. Context study is reading a book for all that it is worth.

- You cannot create a formal context study for every book you read! However, several times a year at your discretion, choose a book that lends itself well to a context study and do it together as a family.

- There are a limitless number of contexts to study: social, political, religious, scientific, geographical, historical, technological, to name just a few. You can take off on just one, some, or a lot of them. *Context studies always return to the original book that is the focus of the study.*

- Context study is a natural way to develop habit patterns that will help later in doing research. Most of the time, context study should be informal, natural and transparent—your children shouldn't even know they are doing it. You simply suggest they find out more about something you are reading and then steer them in the right direction ("Go find out about...", not "Go do a context study on..."). You are helping them to develop a habit pattern of searching out knowledge for greater understanding and insight.

- At your discretion, you can also design a formal context study with a book to read and specific contexts to research. However, your purpose in designing formal context studies for your children is never just to give them "research" assignments. Rather, it is to create a pattern they can follow on their own using the library, the computer, the phone or other research resources you make available. You are helping to build your children's learning confidence and competence. Context studies reinforce the concept that your children can find out what they need to know on their own.

IN OUR HOME...

The hidden message of a context study is that there is always more to learn. When we read a book recently on the life of Eric Liddel, we didn't plan to do a context study. But as we read more, the desire to know more drove us very naturally to the encyclopedia and atlas to find out more about China. Nobody groaned or complained about having to do a research study on China because the desire to know more was already there. There was almost a race to be the one who could report back with something new to illuminate our reading. Our children learned more because they knew there was more to learn.

❑ Unit Study

At the heart of unit study is a very natural learning process. When you really want to know something about a subject, you immerse yourself in it to become knowledgeable. Unit study, which takes that natural drive and creates a systematic approach to education with it, integrates several sources and subjects of learning around a common theme or topic. A unit study on bumble bees, for example, might include: books (reading), coloring (art), observing (science), a poem (writing), listening to "Flight of the Bumble Bee" (music), and so on. Although many use unit study as their primary teaching model, in whole book learning it is best used as a *supplemental teaching method*. When there is a subject of interest to one of your children, or you want to emphasize a certain area of study (history, nature, science, others), you'll find yourself naturally thinking about how to put together a "unit." Children enjoy the variety of learning methods employed in a unit study, and parents appreciate the learning reinforcement resulting from integrated study activities.

- There is a nearly endless supply of units that could be planned, but the ones that will be the most effective are those that take advantage of your children's current interests and desires. Or, if you are planning to study a period of history, plan a "unit" on that time with your children. Units that your children are most interested in can be accomplished in your Discovery Studies and Discretionary Studies. These "Delight Directed Studies," as Gregg Harris calls them, allow your children to study and explore the delights that God has placed in their hearts.

- Unit study is a helpful servant, but can be a demanding master. If your children sense that you are more concerned about the structural details of your unit than you are about the joy of learning, they will not be free to learn. If you are uptight, they will be uptight. Unit study is only one of several methods you will use as a home educator. Flexibility and freedom to change is the key to keeping it effective.

- Many unit studies emphasize "hands-on" and "multi-sensory" activities. However, because they require so much additional planning, effort and time, they can too often take away from time that could be spent reading aloud. And, of more concern, too much emphasis on activity can train your children to *expect* all learning to be "fun," and to become less attentive to reading. If you inadvertently train in an appetite for activity, you might find it difficult to train it out. If you are strong in hands-on activities, you will do them well. If it is not your area of strength, though, don't do them out of false guilt. Your time will be better spent reading a good book with your children and talking about it. Let your Discovery Studies provide the hands-on and multi-sensory activities during informal, more child-directed learning times.

- Every unit needs a "Big Idea" that your studies relate back to. Be careful not to add studies and activities that don't really reinforce the Big Idea of your unit. Example: drinking goat's milk when reading Heidi. Although it may seem a clever thing to do, it has nothing to do with the compelling themes of love and forgiveness in the book.

📖 *How to Create Your Own Unit Study; Unit Study Idea Book (Valerie Bendt, Common Sense Press)*—Good starter manual for unit studies. Emphasizes Charlotte Mason principles and the use of whole books. Contains sample unit studies.

📖 *KONOS curriculum*— A home-schooling standard-bearer for unit studies. Units based on character qualities. Great resource for unit study ideas.

❣ **Unit Study Tools**—Your unit study tool box is overflowing. But when you're building for learning, you use only the tools you need. If a study tool doesn't really fit the unit and it has to be "forced" in, your children will know it and resist that study area.
- Reading books
- Reference resources
- Nature study
- Music
- Art
- Science experiments
- Writing
- Audio/Video tapes
- Bible
- Dictation
- Computer
- Arts & Crafts

UNIT STUDY

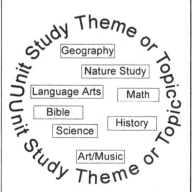

Memorization is a way to fill up the deep reservoirs of your children's hearts and minds with word treasures of beauty, wisdom, inspiration and truth. Recitation is the opening of those reservoirs to let their contents flow out through the expressiveness of speech and emotions. Memorization and recitation not only strengthen your children's mental muscles, but they also shape their hearts by the words that go deep inside and stay there.

- *Memorize for meaning, not just for the sake of memorizing.* Carefully select what you want your children to memorize based on its value for their lives: Scripture, poetry, prose, great words of great men and women, historical writings. Start with short passages and build up to longer ones. Let your children make some selections.

- Memorization should *always* have an audience. Incorporate recitation into your family worship (Scripture), holidays (poems), and history study (speeches and documents). Let your children recite into a tape recorder and send the recording to friends or family. When you have a live audience for your children's recitations, make sure that the audience will be affirming and supportive.

- Avoid memory gimmicks that only add another layer to the memorization process (such as pictures). Children have an almost limitless capacity to memorize in the elementary years. Use key words or hand movements if it is helpful, but keep it simple and uncomplicated.

- If verse references are a roadblock in memory work, remove them. *Verse references are not inspired by God.* It is more important for your children to know the inspired Scriptures and to have the Word in their hearts at this point than it is to get every verse reference right by memory. Try a "graduated learning method." Start out with knowing what book of the Bible the verse is from. Then add chapter references. Then add verse references.

- If ever there were a place to be "twaddle free" it is in memory work. Keep your children's minds free of useless clutter. Don't waste their precious brain cells by using them up with useless words. Make their memory work count! Only have them memorize what they can utilize, or what will edify and strengthen their spirits. Memorization is not for impressing others, but for impressing the memorizer's heart.

- It is good to memorize Scripture verses; but it is great to memorize Scripture passages. God has spoken to us in whole thoughts, which we now find in paragraphs, sections and chapters. Help your children memorize significant, long passages of Scripture. There will never be an easier time in their lives to put large sections of God's Word into their minds and hearts. For individual verses, organize them into meaningful and useful topics (promises, work of Christ, Christian life, speech, etc.). When you memorize a verse, also verbalize about it. Study and talk about the verse so your children will know it as truth, not just a memory verse.

❣ **Commonplace Book**—Students and adults alike used to keep a "Commonplace Book" with quotes, wisdom, and sayings they would read or hear. Have your children keep Commonplace Books and use them for memory work.

❣ **Mental Tapes**—Have your children make and listen to a recording of what they want to memorize. Or, let them listen to a tape with the material they are memorizing recited by a parent or a professional reader.

❣ **A Song to Remember**—Find easy, already published Scripture-only songs, or make up your own tunes for verses. Your children will completely forget they are doing Scripture memory!

❣ **Bible Memory Passages**—
- Matthew 5:3-16 (*The Beatitudes*)
- Matthew 6:5-15 (*The Lord's Prayer*)
- Exodus 20:1-7 (*The Ten Commandments*)
- Ephesians 6:10-20 (*The Christian's Armor*)
- 1 Corinthians 13
- Psalm 1
- Psalm 23
- Psalm 100
Extra Credit:
- Psalm 19
- Psalm 139
- Isaiah 40
- Romans 8:28-39
- Philippians 2:1-18
- 2 Peter 1:3-11

❣ **Good Memory Stuff**—
- Preamble to the Declaration of Independence
- Gettysburg Address
- "If" (Kipling)
- "The Road Less Traveled" (Frost)
- "A Psalm of Life" (Longfellow)
- There Is a Tide ("Julius Caesar," Shakespeare)
- Sonnet CXVI (Shakespeare)
- "The Midnight Ride of Paul Revere" (Longfellow)

❑ Speaking & Presentation

Your children will reach adulthood surrounded by generally literate, but inarticulate peers. In a world of sound-bites and media images, those who are able to present their ideas articulately, succinctly and persuasively will lead; those who cannot will follow. You can give your children an enormous advantage in life simply by developing their speaking and presentation skills. It will put them out in front in every area of their lives—family, ministry, occupation, public service, public speaking, and others. Even more than that, you are preparing them biblically to do what God expects *all* believers to do: proclaim Christ and defend the faith. The very heart of the Christian faith is speaking and presentation.

- Narration is the foundational method for cultivating your children's speaking and presentation skills. Let them know that you expect them to narrate confidently, and with expressiveness. Don't accept a "lazy" narration that is mumbled and disjointed.

- It is important for your children to "be themselves" when they speak or present—to be natural and sincere. However, also teach them that there are four basic elements to an effective presentation, no matter what kind of formal, or informal, speaking situations they might face: 1) eye contact, 2) enthusiasm, 3) clear speech, and 4) relaxed posture. These are easily trained habits of speech, whether for daily discourse or for speaking before an audience.

- The very best early preparation for speaking is to create lots of opportunities to talk at home. Whenever your children have an opportunity to "present" a paper, idea, thought, recitation, song, or whatever, view it as a learning experience and work on their presentation skills. Verbally and publicly affirm your children's speaking abilities. Speaking ability is mostly just the confidence and competence resulting from growing up in a verbal environment. "Skills" just polish the words.

- Drama and music are excellent training grounds for speech and presentation. Find a simple play or musical, and assign parts. Get together with another family or in your support group to put on a dramatic presentation. It's not only educational, it's great family fun!

IN OUR HOME...

Most presentations around our house are of the spontaneous variety. The kids will cook up some kind of play they want to do, or they'll have a nature project they want to show, or an opinion they want to express. We readily affirm these "mini-presentations" knowing that they are the building blocks for more developed and structured presentations. At home-school support group meetings, we often provide time for the children to offer presentations or readings. Or at home-school science fairs, they have an opportunity to present their projects. All these build confidence in speaking and presentation.

---

1 Peter 3:15
But in your hearts set apart Christ as Lord. Always be prepared to give an answer to everyone who asks you to give the reason for the hope that you have. But do this with gentleness and respect...

Colossians 4:6
Let your conversation be always full of grace, seasoned with salt, so that you may know how to answer everyone.

❧ **Play 'n Speak**—On slips of paper, write a variety of speaking situations (interview with the President, commercial for favorite book, Sunday School class, receiving an award, introducing a famous person). Put all in a bowl. Each family member draws one in turn and acts it out.

❧ **Literary Night**—Have several families over for a literary night. Each child prepares a reading, recitation or presentation based on literature. For fun, have them dress to match their presentation.

❧ **Show a Story**—Since they share the same 3-part structure as a speech (introduction, body, and conclusion) have your child write a creative story (real or imagined), and then present it to the family. Older children can choose a topic and write a speech.

❧ **Call to Action**—When your child is ready to write a real "talk," help them write a persuasive speech for a cause of their choice.
- *Attention* First, use an opening that will grab your audience's attention.
- *Interest* Next, give them a reason to be interested in your subject.
- *Desire* Then, show why it is a desirable cause for the audience to adopt.
- *Action* Finally, call the audience to action.

❏ Storytelling

Storytelling is the same as reading aloud, only without a book. You are using your memory and imagination to create a meaningful story with characters, settings and events that are familiar to your children. You children are prepared by God to be your audience, so their attention level is high (narration is not necessary). Like reading aloud, you are demonstrating speaking skills, and you are also modeling creativity, imagination and composition. There is a creative excitement both storyteller and audience experience as they listen to a story unfold that they know is being created right under their ears.

- A story can be short or long, but it should always have a clearly discernible structure: it starts with a *beginning* (introduce characters, set the scene, arouse interest); it builds through a *succession of events* (move the story toward the climax in a smooth flow of action); it reaches a *climax* (the sine qua non and raison d'être of the story, the moral; the meaning); it concludes with an *ending* (resolution, closure, conclusion).

- Use your children's names in imaginative stories. Create a setting with familiar places and activities, or a historical or imaginative setting. Make your child the clear hero of your story.

- Use a book or story you have recently read to your children as the basis for a story. If you're studying history, put them into the historical setting or event and have them interact with great men and women in history. Let them play a part in influencing history in your story.

- Tell real life stories about your own life. Events from your own childhood are especially effective for storytelling and for illustrating a point or illuminating a lesson. Include family stories about parents, siblings, grandparents and other family and friends when they were children.

- At holiday gatherings, tell family stories of faith and of God's faithfulness. Make certain stories a tradition at those holiday events, to be told every year. After a few years, the children can begin telling the stories.

IN OUR HOME...

It was a dark and stormy night. We had just moved to the country. Fears had surfaced. So dad told a story for bedtime. It was a simple little story about a boy called Joel (coincidence?) and his faithful dog Brownie. Joel was hiking the ravine on the property when he slipped down an embankment and sprained his ankle. He was afraid, but he didn't panic. He knew he had to practice self-control. He sent his dog to get help. He had his pocket knife, a walking stick and rocks to protect him. He was a resourceful lad. Soon he was rescued. Joel was recognized in the local paper for his courage and self-control. The end. A simple story (very condensed) that helped Joel over his fears.

❣ **Tape-a-Story**—Get out the tape recorder whenever you're going to tell a story. The kids will love listening to it many times over, especially if they are a part of the story.

❣ **Chain Story**—Get everybody involved in telling a story. Decide together what kind of story it will be (adventure, history, mystery, love, etc.). You can also create a main character, if you choose. Draw numbers, then let the story roll. Each person has a set amount of storytelling time, picking up the story wherever the last person leaves off, and taking it wherever they want it to go. Turn on the tape recorder!

❣ **Sharable Parables**—The parables of Jesus provide a rich source of story outlines. Just substitute the biblical names and places with ones familiar to your children. Afterward, you can read the real parable and watch their lights come on.

❣ **Serial Storytelling**— On the first night, introduce all the characters, create a minor problem/conflict, resolve it, but don't conclude the story. Let them know a series of adventures are to follow. On subsequent nights, continue the story but leave them with an unresolved conflict or situation, to be concluded the next night. Repeat that cycle until you are ready to conclude the stories.

> *Let me tell the stories and I care not who writes the textbooks.*
>
> G. Stanley Hall

EDUCATING THE WHOLEHEARTED CHILD

❏ Asking Questions

There is an art to asking good questions. Whether you are trying to draw out a response, test understanding, or stimulate a good discussion, everything depends on the quality of the question. A well-crafted question will generate stimulating conversation; a poorly thought through question will elicit only awkward silence, uncertain responses, or hopeful "is-that-the-right-answer-daddy" looks.. When interacting with children, a question should be more *invitation* than investigation or interrogation. If invited properly, your children will gladly respond to your question.

- When used with a whole book approach, the purpose of asking questions is to prime and stimulate your children's mental processes. Questions should be used sparingly, and only to assist your children's understanding of a book, not to subvert or circumvent their own thoughts about it. *Always have them do narration before you ask questions.*

- Give your children the opportunity to come up with their own questions about a book or story. It can be a kind of reverse narration that causes them to think about what is important in what they have heard. Be careful not to default into the questioning mode too quickly, though. Give them time to think. And, when you ask a question, give them time to answer. Don't override their thinking process.

- Build on levels of content understanding when using questioning. Start with concrete facts (who, did what, when and where?), move to abstract concepts (why did they do it?), and then to general principles (how should they have done it?). This is a good way to walk your children through a summary of a book (after they have narrated it). They can see how the pieces make up the whole of the book.

- Apart from whole books, challenging or thought-provoking questions can become a way of helping your children learn to think and talk "on their feet." It is a little like narrating in that they are synthesizing and expressing their own thoughts rather than an author's, but the mental processes have to work a little harder since there is no book. Well-crafted questions will challenge them to think well and speak clearly.

IN OUR HOME...

We try to engage our children in "table talk" at dinner time. Sometimes we use discussion-starter type questions, but most of the time good questions simply arise during the process of normal conversation. Whenever the kids tell us about being with other children, we know there will be grist for the question mill! It is easy and natural to pose a hypothetical or similar situation and ask "What would you do?". We also often ask them to evaluate the choices leaders make—such as Joshua with the Gibeonites, or Columbus before Isabella and Ferdinand—to sharpen their ability to discern right from wrong, true from false, and so on. We always expect an answer.

❣ **Good Questions**—Work at asking good questions that are:
- Simple
- Short
- Strategic
- Stimulating

❣ **Questionable Questions**— Avoid the following:
- *Closed-ended questions* that can be answered only with a yes or no, I don't know, or by an either-or response.
- *Loaded questions* that have a hidden agenda, such as to admonish or correct.
- *Rhetorical questions* that raise questions that a child cannot answer.
- *Values Clarification questions* that are morally or ethically vague, or promote moral relativism.

❣ **Answer Angles**—Know what you are asking for:
- Opinion/View
- Feelings/Impressions
- Knowledge/Facts
- Analysis/Interpretation

❣ **Question Box**— Keep a 3x5 file box near the dining table. Keep 3x5 cards with you to write down good questions that come to mind.

❣ **I'm Glad You Asked**— Discussion starters are not that difficult to write. The key is to think like a child and be creative. They can be general questions or tied into a current area of study. A few examples to get you started:
- If you were (name of the family pet) and you could talk, what would you want to say?
- If you were Squanto, how do you think you would feel about the Pilgrims?
- What is the most beautiful thing you have ever seen?
- What person in history would you most like to meet, or be, and why?
- If you could be the child of any person in history, who would you choose and why?

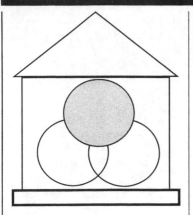

DISCOVERY STUDIES METHODS

❑ The Creative Arts: Music, Art, Drama, Movement

In addition to *studying* and *appreciating* fine art, music and poetry, children should be given the opportunity for *doing* them. In the public schools, "the arts" historically has included music, art, theater and dance. Because of the independent nature of home schooling and the lack of facilities and resources, though, these creative arts are often not emphasized. However, they should be considered a viable part of home education in developing a well-rounded, wholehearted child. The goal is simply exposure and experience, not mastery. If there are budding artists in your family creative troupe, creative arts activities will let their talents come out in the open.

Music

- Singing is the most basic form of making music. Create ample opportunities to try a wide variety of musical styles, rhythms and even harmonies. Sing hymns, praise songs, folk songs or whatever music interests you and your children the most. Form a home school singing group to learn how to sing music from books. Put together a mini-musical or choral presentation.

- Every child enjoys the immediate feedback of a musical instrument, even if it is not always beautiful. For an introduction to musical instruments, try a recorder (end-blown flute), ukulele, 3/4 size guitar, or an autoharp. A piano or keyboard will give them the greatest opportunity for musical exploration. Be sure your child is grounded in basic music theory.

IN OUR HOME...

When we lived in Nashville, the kids had been in Sally's home-school children's choir, and they had even had the opportunity to do professional voice-over work on a musical project Clay was working on. But then we moved to the central Texas countryside and we quickly concluded there would not be too many "real life" performing arts opportunities unless we drove an hour to a major city. When we heard that "The Promise," an outdoor musical production of the life of Christ in our area, was holding auditions, we decided it would be a good experience for our older children (then 7 and 10) at least to audition. We knew they probably would not get the parts, but they really wanted to try. So, we worked with them for several weeks on their audition songs, rehearsed them on their lines from the script, and coached them on expression and projection. They loved the whole process, and what do you know...they actually won the parts! They've played the roles now every weekend during the summer and fall for two years! Mom and dad got in on the act, too. We even all performed the show at the Kremlin Palace Theater in Moscow, Russia.

❧ **Chorale Your Kids**—If your home school support group is large enough, form a children's choir. Teach the kids a selection of songs, or purchase a children's musical, or musical drama, with an instrumental accompaniment track. Perform the music at a nursing home, orphanage, or at church.

❧ **Play It Again, Kids**—Kids love to make music. The more instruments you can have on hand for them to experiment with the more likely it is that music will be a part of their lives. Look for used starter instruments at garage and estate sales, thrift shops and similar sources.
- piano, keyboard
- guitar, ukulele
- recorder
- flute, piccolo
- violin
- trumpet
- clarinet, saxophone
- xylophone, vibes
- autoharp
- drums, bongos
- rhythm instruments

Art

- There is no better way to stimulate artistic expressiveness than with the "canvass" arts. For children, that means lots of opportunities to draw and paint in a variety of media: colored pencils, water colors, charcoal, colored markers, and others. Your goal is not necessarily artistic skill at first, but exposure and experimentation. If artistic skill emerges, then you can consider further art training or lessons.

- Pursue each medium for a long enough period of time to allow your children to become proficient and confident at using it. Give them several different subjects to draw and color so they can experience the range of expressions for each media. With each subject, explore it using a variety of perspective, composition, and lighting. And, of course, display the best works of your budding artists.

Drama

- Drama is an opportunity for your child to learn to express himself verbally and emotionally. Whereas music and art are generally "third person" expressive arts, drama is decidedly "first person." Your *child* is the artistic medium—voice, emotion, attitude, posture.

- Dramatic expression is really an outgrowth of narration and reading. In addition to its mental benefits, narration is also an oral exercise in articulation, and reading aloud is the first step in dramatic expression. If you read aloud dramatically, your children will read aloud dramatically. Start with some books rich in good dialogue—have your children "perform" dramatic readings with the rest of the family playing the part of an audience.

- Start out with improvisation and role play—acting out Bible stories is an easy way to ease into drama, or act out historical scenes and stories. If your children are enjoying dramatic expression and want to go further, try some simple one-act plays written for church, or the narration and dialogue from a church musical, especially ones with humor. Eventually, you might want to stage a small play or musical with some other home-schooling families.

Movement

- God gave us bodies to use for creative expression, too. Traditionally, public schools would teach dance—folk and square dancing—as an area of creative expression. However, that is not practical in a home school setting. You can, though, engage your children in creative expression using movement: reflecting different feelings and attitudes, doing pantomime, interpreting classical music.

- Your goal is to help your children learn that how they use their bodies communicates even more than what they say with their voices. You are training them to use their physical "voice" as expressively as they would use their spoken voice.

A Journey Through Drama (Promise Productions Inc.)— Excellent one-of-a-kind resource for teaching drama to children. Christian product, organized around the fruit of the Spirit. History, helps, activities, and four original, child and family friendly plays.

❏ Drawing and Coloring

In a culture like ours that is increasingly visual and non-verbal, your children will have a distinct advantage if you enable them to acquire the ability to communicate through drawing and color. Unfortunately, most parents, if they think about drawing at all, wrongly equate learning to draw with studying art, so their initial impulse that their children should learn to draw usually results in the purchase of an expensive "art" curriculum. That is like giving your child a dictionary because you want them to learn to read! Despite the claims of many art curricula publishers, most children will not become "artists," so an expensive, comprehensive art curriculum is over-priced overkill. However, *every* child does need to know how to *draw* and how to use *color*. A well-rounded child should be able to express and communicate ideas visually as well as verbally. Your goal is to give your child "visual arts" skills (line, form, perspective, color and so on) in the same way that you are giving them "language arts" skills (alphabet, phonics, writing, and so on). You are teaching them how to *show* as well as *tell*.

- You do not need to prompt your child to draw—it is as natural for a child to draw about his world as it is for him to talk about it. Unfortunately, we try to turn them into artists as they get older, and our desire for them to do it "right" takes away their desire to do it at all. The first rule of teaching drawing is, *let your child draw*. Respond to a drawing, don't try to correct it. Your child is communicating...listen to him.

- At around five or six, introduce your child to an incremental drawing guide that will lead him through the 7-10 basic elements that make up all drawings. At seven or eight, introduce him to color with art quality colored pencils and water color pencils, and a simple book on color. Let your child know that you love to see him draw and thought he would enjoy learning some new ways to express himself. Treat it as an enjoyable Discovery Studies area, not as a Disciplined Study.

- Give your child real-life drawing and coloring opportunities. Have him make his own thank-you notes and greeting cards, letter and color an announcement poster, draw and color a wordless book, make place cards for the dinner table, illustrate and color a letter. Real-life projects reinforce the idea that drawing and coloring is a natural part of communicating.

- Nature is a perfect subject for drawing and coloring. Give your children good sketch books and have them draw and color a variety of plant life, trees and flowers. Some nature coloring books have line art depictions of wildlife to color (animals, birds, butterflies, and so on), with full color examples on the inside covers.

- As they find subjects that they enjoy drawing more than others—cars, rabbits, horses, cartoon people—find a simple step-by-step "I Can Draw" resource that will let them add variety to what they have already learned. Mastering the drawing of one subject with a variety of styles, techniques, details and perspectives will transfer easily to other drawing subjects.

📖 *Mark Kistler's Draw Squad; Mark Kistler's Imagination Station (Fireside)*—Child-friendly approach to drawing that resulted in a PBS series. Makes learning the elements of drawing fun and easy. Self-directed lessons.

📖 *I Draw, I Paint series (Barron's)*—Excellent primers for drawing, colored pencils, water color, markers and more. Includes step-by-step examples.

📖 *I Can Draw series (Simon&Schuster)*—Each title provides step-by-step easy drawings of a single subject (cars, horses, birds, etc.)

📖 *Drawing With Children (Mona Brookes)*—Widely acclaimed book on bringing out the natural drawing skill in all children.

📖 *Dover Coloring Books; Petersen Field Guide Coloring Books*

📖 *How Great Thou Art; Lamb's Book of Art; others (Barry Stebbing)*—Art lessons from a Christian base.

❦ **Drawing Tools**—If you want your children to value drawing and coloring, give them tools that say *you* value drawing and coloring.
- *Pencils*—Any pencil will do at first, but move them into art pencils as they progress.
- *Colored Pencils*—Art quality, wax-based such as Design Spectracolor, or Berol.
- *Water Color Pencils*— Design Water Color Pencils or others.
- *Accessories*—Good art quality erasers, sharpeners, sketch books (Mead Academie) and more.

❑ Creative Play

"When you finish your studies, then you can play." It's an innocent phrase we all use, but it reveals an underlying cultural assumption that *education* and *recreation* are distinctly different activities. We are telling our children in so many words that when they *start* playing they can *stop* learning. And yet, if God designed children to be learning from all of life, then play is an important part of that learning process. In fact, if God has built into children the drive to play, it may be the *best* way for them to learn. With that in mind, then, your goal is to provide creative play opportunities that will be mentally stimulating as well as fun and enjoyable. Loving to learn and loving to play are not mutually exclusive drives in your children—they naturally complement one another and work together.

- Fill your children's play time with "real" things as much as possible, or life-like imitations of real things. Whether they are doing historical dress-up, playing house or store, building a fort in the backyard, or whatever, the more real things they have to play with the more closely their play will resemble real life. If you fill their play time with plastic and toys that have no real life counterpart, their play will tend to become more escapist, and will not reinforce real life for them.

- Provide creative modeling and building materials that let them use their imaginations: wood building blocks, cardboard bricks, Lincoln Logs®, Legos®, wood for carpentry, or similar items. The process of visualizing, designing and building creations is a high-level learning process. Even the couch and chair pillows can become a learning experience in building a pillow tent or maze.

- Give your children access to electronic media: video camera, audio cassette recorder, computer, electronic keyboard, and so on. Let them create movies, recordings, musical productions and whatever else their imaginations will come up with. They can also use other creative play options in their productions, such as historical dress-up.

Comment: Work or Play?

It is interesting that there is no apparent "theology of leisure" or "doctrine of play" in the Bible. The few references to children playing are more often prophetic, with the Millennial Kingdom in view. It seems that the Old Testament feasts are the only God-ordained recreation in Scripture, and their purpose was worship, not just pointless recreation. The "trinitarian" rhythm of life as God intended it would seem to be WORSHIP - WORK - REST. In our modern culture, though, the concept of leisure, or PLAY, has been appended to that balance because of the unprecedented amount of free time we enjoy, but not because of clear biblical teaching. In God's original design, WORSHIP and REST fulfilled the recreational needs of adults. PLAY is attributed naturally only to children in Scripture—children play, adults work. It would seem reasonable to suggest that PLAY as a child becomes WORK as an adult. In other words, child's play is the antecedent to adult work. With that understanding, PLAY is an important developmental time in your child's life. It is, in a way, rehearsal for a life of WORK.

IN OUR HOME...

When we give our children freedom, time and materials for creative play, we're amazed sometimes at the results. Our imaginative middle child Joel loves to fiddle around with the thousands of Legos® we've acquired at garage sales. One afternoon he brought in five Lego® houses he had built representing different historical periods: a pyramid and Sphinx, a Roman villa and bath, a Medieval castle, a contemporary home, and a home of the future. Around the same time, Nathan, our organizationally gifted third child, surprised us one day by showing us the "restaurant" he made on the front porch: tables and chairs, table settings, flowers and decor, a sign, a menu and a waiter outfit. In both cases, the boys had initiated their projects with no prompting from us, but just because it was fun for them. That's how learning should be—as natural as having fun.

❑ Nature Study

Your child is a supernatural naturalist. There is a God-given, built-in curiosity about creation in the heart of your child that naturally wants to observe, ask questions and seek understanding. Your goal in nature study, though, is much more than just to "inform" your children about the details of creation. You greater task is to "form in" them eyes that can see the Creator in his creation (*Rom. 1:20*), an abiding sense of wonder and appreciation of what God has made (*Ps. 8; Ps. 19*), and a passion to care for, subdue and rule over this earth as God's highest expression of created being (*Gen. 1:28*). Nature, or creation, is the most natural realm of science for your children to study because it is an ideal laboratory for studying the things that have been made in their created contexts. God defined the two major areas of nature study for us in Genesis 1:1, "In the beginning, God created the *heavens* and the *earth*." What more could you ask about?

The Heavens (Astronomy, Weather)

- Get in the habit of getting your children to look up at night (especially when you are in the country). The best way is flat on your back, or in tilt-back chairs.Start pointing out constellations, observe the different moon phases, look for the Milky Way, try to spot planets and other heavenly bodies, look for meteors. Any field guide to astronomy will orient you to the night sky.

- Always plan sky watching parties for special events such as the annual Perseid meteor shower, a lunar eclipse, or a conjunction of planets. Plan a unit study on the event in the week before. It will be a really special experience and memory for your children.

- Have your children keep a Night Sky Log to chart the changes during the different seasons of the moon (rise, set, phase), the constellations, and the planets, including unusual phenomena such as halos around the moon. They can also keep a Day Sky Log to chart the changes in weather patterns through the seasons.

IN OUR HOME...

Nature is a natural in our home. We like to take long walks in the country just observing and talking about all that God has made. We recently found a washout that was rich with marine fossils which the kids have enjoyed collecting and classifying, and which also have been the starting point for a number of talks about creation and evolution. All of the kids have contributed to our "nature museum" displays. Our best ones are for butterflies, fossils, and rocks (quartz and agate, to be specific). When the weather is nice, Dad tries to take the kids away for a Saturday morning to browse a local nature center, or to the zoo for a nature walk and picnic. It is a good way to combine learning time, Dad time with the kids, and free time for Mom. And, of course, we never miss a good sunset (Texas has some real blazers).

- If possible, purchase the best telescope you can afford for stargazing. A refractor telescope is usually more powerful but with a narrow field of view. A reflector telescope is usually less powerful but clearer (brings in more light from distant objects) with a much wider field of view. Use an astronomy field guide to check off all the heavenly bodies you are able to locate and view.

The Earth (Plants, Animals, Land, Rocks)

- Take nature walks as a family. Rather than "teaching" about nature, simply talk about things you and your children observe, and stimulate conversation with questions: Have you noticed that some trees lose their leaves and others don't? Why do you suppose God made worms? Why do rabbits have such big ears? Have each child keep a Nature Journal in which they can record their thoughts and impressions, draw sketches of objects found or observed in nature, and consider what they can learn about God from what they see in nature.

- Build up a good nature library: a good assortment of child-friendly field guides (focus first on current interests), quality children's reference books (see column), good literature about nature and animals (ex., books by Ernest Thompson Seton), nature media (software, videos, audiotapes), posters, nature magazines.

- Have your children keep a Seasons Log. Keep it in a nice notebook by a window that allows observation. Identify a selected number of things to observe—temperatures, tree leaves, flowers, garden growth, sunrise/sunset times, location of the sun, stars in the sky. Once a month, on the first day of the month, have them make a record of changes they observe.

- Encourage your children to start simple collections of inanimate objects in nature: leaves, wildflowers, rocks, shells. Use the collections for lessons in observation and classification. Look for Scriptures about the collected objects, as well as about wildlife that is caught or observed. Display the collections at your support group science fair.

- Equip your children with a good set of "tools" for "in the field" nature study: pocket field guides, field binoculars (7x35), compass, magnifying lens, good insect net, walking stick, small pick ax, multi-purpose pocket knife, notebook, collection bag. Supply them with display materials, too: collection boxes and boards, insect pins, killing jar, holding jars, aquarium (for fish) or herpetarium (for reptiles and amphibians), a plant press and notebook.

- Listen for spiritual lessons that God has built into nature. Jesus often illustrated deep spiritual truths from nature. Nature metaphors abound throughout Scripture. That doesn't mean you need to look for a spiritual insight every time you talk about nature! It simply means to be ready to note a spiritual insight when the Spirit gives you one. It might be just what your child needs to understand a biblical principle.

❣ **Nature Library**—Stock up on good field guides and reference resources:
- Audubon Pocket Guides
- Peterson First Guides
- Peterson Field Guide Coloring Books
- Usborne Spotter's Guides
- Eyewitness Books
- Usborne Books
- Golden Press Guides
- Field Guides to Wildlife Habitats
- A Handbook of Nature Study (Anna Comstock, 1991)
- Kingfisher Encyclopedia of Animals
- Reader's Digest Guide to North American Wildlife
- Usborne Illustrated Encyclopedia of the Natural World

📖 *Exploring the Sky by Day; Exploring the Sky by Night*—Introductions to weather and astronomy. Great photographs and graphics.

📖 *First Book of Nature (Usborne)*—Excellent introduction to nature study for early grades. Very visual, short text.

📖 *Kingfisher Visual Factfinder series*—Good introductions to earth, life, space and science.

✎ *The Elijah Co. catalog*—Outstanding science and nature section. Good books and helpful hints and insights.

✎ *Nature Workshop catalog*—Books and products for nature study by the home schooling publishers of *Nature Friend Magazine*.

📖 *It Couldn't Just Happen (Larry Richards)*— Good reasons to believe for young readers. Focus on authority of the Word, and creation.

📖 *Dinosaurs By Design (Gish, Snellenberger)*— Excellent overview of dinosaurs, the flood and creation basics. Award winning illustrations.

📖 *Unlocking the Mysteries of Creation (Petersen)*— Introduction to creation for older children.

📖 *Adam and His Kin (Beechick)*—Novelized history of the early days of man on the earth.

✎ *Creation Ex Nihilo magazine*—Non-technical, short articles on creation evidences; good for all ages; includes a 4-page children's pull-out.

❣ **Creation Mural**—Take seven poster boards and label them Creative Day 1 through Creative Day 7. Write the respective verses from Genesis at the top of each poster. Over a period of weeks, start drawing and cutting out pictures that illustrate elements that God created on each Creation day. When the posters are full, get really creative—find a place to display them!

❏ Creation Science

If nature study helps your children see the pieces of God's creation up close, creation science helps them fit those pieces into the "big picture" within the framework of the book of Genesis—God created the heavens and the earth in six creative days; people are created beings with eternal souls, not just evolved, intelligent animals; the flood of Noah was a world-wide, catastrophic event that reshaped the earth's surface and altered its atmosphere. With the study of creation science, you are providing evidences to your children to show that the biblical account of creation is true and defensible, and that facts do not support evolutionary theories. You are laying the foundations in your children's minds for a biblical worldview of the origins and nature of life, and for our need for a Savior.

• Use the six creative days of Genesis as an outline for science studies: *day 1*, energy (light); *day 2*, atmosphere (pre-flood water canopy); *day 3*, land, seas, vegetation; *day 4*, sun, moon and stars; *day 5*, fish and fowl; *day 6*, land animals, and man. You will reinforce Scripture and show the natural order and progress of God's creative acts.

• Don't be afraid to engage your children in conversations about the bigger issues of biblical creationism vs. secular naturalism: If the universe started with a bang, where did the stuff that exploded come from in the first place (first causes)? If we evolved from monkeys, why aren't there any monkey-men or men-keys running around today (fossil record)? How can there be such obvious design in creation unless there was a Designer (teleology)? Refer them to Romans 1 to show that people who close their eyes to the God of Creation are blinded to the truth. Their refusal to acknowledge God means they must make up truth based only on the teachings of sinful man, such as evolution.

• A study of dinosaurs (always a big hit, especially with boys) from a Christian perspective can lead into a number of creation science study areas. Use some of the excellent illustrated children's books on creation science, especially when considering whether man and dinosaur were created and lived at the same time, contrary to evolution.

• Creation science does not have to be black-and-white dogma for children. They can understand that *ideas* about how creation happened are continually being tested against our understanding of what *Scripture* says and against known *facts*. For instance, although godly, Christian men agree that God created the universe and man, many disagree over whether creation is young (thousands of years) or old (billions of years). Teach your children what you believe, but don't inadvertently label Christians who disagree as false teachers or deceived.

• Train your children to discern truth and error in the matter of evolution. You cannot escape evolutionary references in many of the otherwise very desirable nature and science books, tapes, videos and software. If you refuse to buy such products, you will have a very thin library shelf. Monitor what they are exposed to and avoid obvious evolutionary propaganda, but trust your children.

❑ Hands-On Science

All children enjoy the pop-fizz, whiz-bang, ooh-ahh nature of hands-on science. It's interesting, fun, and captures their attention and curiosity. However, the focus of their attention is nearly always on the secondary *effect*, not on the primary *cause*. Physical science—which deals primarily with the inanimate world, such as chemistry, machines, heat, light, electricity, sound, magnetism—is better studied in later grades when the issue of causes can be better understood. Nonetheless, there is a certain amount of discovery and fascination in experimental science that stimulates in children a curiosity and desire to know. Since it is not generally a required or necessary area of study in the elementary years, though, it is up to you as a home educating parent to determine what role hands-on science will play in your home school. Your children will receive most of what they need if you are laying a solid foundation in nature study and reading.

- When you do hands-on science projects, limit your focus to a single, simple principle, idea or concept that you want to demonstrate. Avoid lots of information, data and details. Let your *children's* hands be on the experiment, not just yours. Encourage them to observe effects, ask questions, and postulate explanations about causes. Know what you want them to learn from the experiment. Review useful vocabulary terms, facts and principles.

- If your children show an interest, pursue science. If they do not, pursue what interests them. If it's not a priority interest to you or them, don't try to make it one. Remember, you're raising a child, not a scientist.

- Increase your audience to make the most of your experiments. Create a monthly study group to which each family brings a hands-on science project to do and observe. You can choose a topic, coordinate the experiments to avoid duplication, and rotate the homes (to share the mess). Also, have your children prepare hands-on science projects of interest to them for your support group science fair.

IN OUR HOME...

Our children were not born into a scientific house-hold. We decided fairly early on, though, that God knew what our children needed most. Ours is a "words and music" family, so whatever our children learn about the physical sciences is primarily from books, media and real life, not from hands-on science experiments. We constantly use real life situations to talk about physical sciences—the nature of water, how a car works, what's in a computer, how gears work, the principle of displacement, how a flashlight works, and so on. These kinds of real life lessons are much more instructional than the entertaining experiments and razzle-dazzle of much of children's hands-on science resources. One of our children may surprise us and someday turn into a scientist, but until then we're focusing on raising wholehearted children.

📖 *Usborne Books*

📖 *The Backyard Scientist*

❝ *(H)omeschoolers usually must live with the traditional style achievement tests and adaptations of them. So it is helpful to know that for elementary grades about half the questions are in the two fields of life sciences and the earth and space sciences. Physical sciences are left largely for the high school years. The other half of the questions include the history, sociology and philosophy of science...as well as elementary questions on physics. To do well on these tests, a student must be able to read and understand in these various fields. And reading space science, for instance, is quite different from reading about plants, mainly because the vocabulary is not the same. Thus your family may want to read and talk and study about a variety of science topics.* **Discussion, especially with adults, is the best known way for children to raise their level of thinking, which raises their test scores.***

Ruth Beechick, *You Can Teach Your Child Successfully*, 1993

Comment: Science Or Not?
First principle of science instruction: you are raising a child, not a scientist. Despite hand-wringing in the public schools over their failure in science, your priority is to focus on training your child to be a confident, self-motivated learner. Once that is in place, learning about science will take care of itself. By around 14 years old (Gr. 8), you should know if your child is inclined toward science or not. If he is, then give him books, tools and resources and point him in the right direction. If he is not, don't try to make him be. Find out what God has put on his heart to do, and point him in that direction.

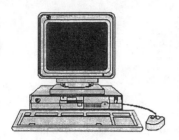

Shareware—Shareware is "try before you buy" software. If you are ordering off the web, most downloads are free. Beware, though—many times the quality is not as high, and you still have to pay for the program if you decide to use it.

♥**Parental Discretion Advised**—The Internet is both a delightful and a dangerous place. It is advisable to use some kind of content filter.
- Software-based—This filter is loaded onto your hard drive and configured by you. It must be updated regularly to be effective. Not as secure as other filters.
- Server-based—This filter is located at your ISP (Internet Service Provider). Unwanted sites never get to your computer. Cost is the same as most ISPs for internet access. Most secure method.
- Web-based—Your search is actively filtered through a another website. Some are free, some charge a fee.
- Portal-based—Some portals offer a "family filter" that can be activated for any searches through their search engine. However, it does not block access by your computer; it only filters that search on their site.

♥**Warning**—All of the main portals (Yahoo!, Excite, AltaVista, Go, Lycos, others) offer "Clubs" and "Photo Albums" on their sites that are easily accessible to anyone, including your children. These sections are often filled with hardcore pornography. Our recommendation: if a portal you use is providing a port for porn, unlink, cast off, and find another harbor.

❑ Computer

It is inevitable that your children will eventually have to tame the silicon beast since they will live as adults in a "digital" world. The earlier they start, the more confident and effective they will be when they enter the adult computing world. After buying books for your library (always the priority), a computer and good software may be the best investments of your educational dollars. However, you need to be clear how a computer will fit into your home education goals. Many parents use a computer only to augment, reinforce, or "computerize" their Disciplined Studies, such as language arts and math. If that is the only reason you want a computer for the children, save your money. The real value of a computer for home education is as a tool for Discovery Studies. A computer is unequaled as an interactive medium for creative expression, mental challenge, and multi-sensory learning, and it is irreplaceable as a tool for exploring the expanding universe of information. As "cyberspace" becomes more accessible, and computers become more of a necessary home utility, computers will play an increasingly important role in your children's lives.

- Good programs (software) are to your computer what good books are to your library. Be as choosy as you would be for any other books or media your children consume. There is just as much disk and digital twaddle as there is paper and ink twaddle. Read reviews carefully and buy only the software that best reflects your educational philosophy and family values. Buy wisely.

- As "curricula" for Discovery Studies, look for programs that allow your child to be creative and expressive in writing and art, or to explore useful information and knowledge stored in words and images (and sound, with multi-media). A good program will provide hours of exploration for your child with minimal parental input.

- The CD-ROM phenomenon created the wonderful world of mutli-media computing and the new generation interactive programs. However, you can pour lots of dollars down the digital drain if you are not careful. Slick packaging can disguise a dull, poorly-designed CD-ROM. Never buy on impulse—you can't tell a disk by its box!

IN OUR HOME...

Each of our children interacts differently with the computer. Sarah became interested at age seven when she used the computer to make materials for a "history club." She is also the best "gamer" in the family, enjoying the competitive component built into many children's programs. Joel is a computer explorer. He is not so much interested as yet in what he can do with a computer, but in what all it will do with him. He tries out everything and thrives on the interactivity. Nathan, on the other hand, though still young, seems to lean toward practical application—signs, cards and the like. Our computer is a different tool for each child, but it fits everyone's hands.

- Make it clear from the start that your family computer is an educational tool for your home school, not just an electronic game box. Many educational and "edutainment" programs have arcade game features your children will enjoy and benefit from, but keep a tight rein on for-entertainment-only games (even ones that come standard in Windows). Good ones can be an enjoyable, even mind-challenging, diversion for your children, but they can also become insidious time thieves. Make game playing time a privilege to be earned.

- Keep in clear view your ultimate goal in providing a computer for your children—to train them to use it as a productivity and communication tool. "Edutainment" and "child friendly" software are appealing, but too much can spoil your children's appetites for *using* the computer when they expect to be entertained by it. Train your children early how to use a *real* word processor, database, desktop publishing program, web page editor, and other tools. Get them keyboarding with a computer typing program, then start them off with some low end or entry level productivity programs or integrated packages. Once they become comfortable with the programs, begin to give them meaningful tasks to accomplish: a family newsletter, posters, a video database, family mailing-list maintenance. They'll be exercising writing, thinking, logic, reading, art and other learning skills, and their confidence will zoom as they successfully use "adult" programs.

- A disturbingly large number of programs for children draw upon occult and demonic figures. It is, of course, a reflection of the growing acceptance and "normalization" of occultism in our culture. Don't buy it! There are many wonderful programs that are occult-free, but you have to do your homework before you do your shopping to keep your computer sanctified and your conscience clean. Read the reviews and visit the websites before you buy.

- A note on interactive story books (children's books that "speak" and interact when you click on certain objects). With only rare exceptions, these products are just digitized twaddle, and do nothing to really improve on the real book. An interactive book can only poorly mimic the role of an interactive parent. *Read books...use computers!*

The Internet and the Web—Going Online

The region of the computer universe sometimes called "cyberspace" is expanding so rapidly that anything said today will be dated by tomorrow. As in any media, there are places to be avoided, and because of that some would say avoid it all. However, there is a rapidly growing Christian and home-school presence on the web, as well as many helpful Christian, research, and educational sites. The web is unlike anything imaginable even just a decade ago, and it will become as common and as integrated into our lives as electricity in just a few years. It is here to stay and your children will want to know how to use it as a source of information and as a medium for communication. Two books that help are *The Homeschool Guide to the Online World* (Dinsmore, Homeschool Press) and *Internet for Christians* (Schultze, Gospel Films). It's a whole new world wide web!

❧**Stay Informed**—Computer magazines will keep you abreast of new software and developments.
- *Practical Homeschooling* (Mary Pride, 800-346-6322, extensive coverage of software, internet and online)
- *Christianity Online* (Christianity Today, Inc., 888-432-5828, now a tie-in to their website www. christianityonline.com)
- *Family PC* (family-friendly and informative for keeping up with trends, and software)

❧**(Home) Educational Software**—Some categories of educational software are better suited to the home than others. Most software you will use falls in one or more of the following categories:
- *Drill*—Test and reinforce math, spelling, etc.
- *Reference*—Encyclopedia, Bible, history, nature, etc.
- *Creativity*—Art, storybooks, music, writing, etc.
- *Discovery*—Interactive with several areas to explore
- *Productivity*—Child versions of real programs
- *Tutorial*—Digital curriculum for specific subjects
- *Edutainment*—Game-based learning of any kind

***Comment: Encyclopedic Wars** Encyclopedias are arguably the premier software product for multimedia family computer users. They are goldmines of interactive learning and information. However, there are also veins of fool's gold in their digital mine shafts, especially concerning the Bible and Christianity. Whichever digital encyclopedia you choose, there will be a trade-off of some kind. Check the reviews in Christian computing magazines before you buy, but more important, check the content when you get it home so no one gets fooled.*

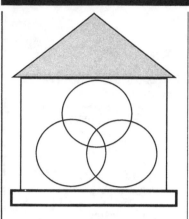

❣ Give A Life—Make practical life skills a regular part of your home schooling. Have your children:
- plan and prepare (or help with) one meal each week, including shopping.
- plant and tend a garden patch and sell the produce.
- help prepare a music and drama presentation to offer to nursing homes.
- plan one hour of childcare activities for a Bible study or support group.
- do their own washing and sorting.
- manage a computer database for VCR tapes.
- keep the tool shed/room neat and organized.

❣ Home Work—If one or both of you have to be away for a day or more without the children, turn over some of your regular responsibilities to them. Examples: plan and prepare dinner; do the daily devotional; read books aloud that you have been working through.

❣ Part-Time Mentors—As your children develop interests and skills, find friends or church members who are knowledgeable in the same areas. See if they would be willing to take a little time to share some of their knowledge with your children as a "mentor." Even if the interest passes, they will benefit from learning from others. You will be training them to seek out expert advice.

DISCRETIONARY AND MISCELLANEOUS STUDIES METHODS

❏ Live and Learn

Everyone learns through life. Real life is immeasurably rich as a source of learning experiences. It is the best "method" you have in your teaching toolbox for developing general living, avocational and even vocational skills in your children. Your home should provide your children an apprenticeship in real living that exposes them to the kinds of experiences and responsibilities they will face as adults. When they graduate from your home school, they should have a clear sense of direction and a confidence that they can handle the basic responsibilities of adulthood. The following are just a few examples of live and learn activities.

- *Business* Start a business for your children that will enable them to learn the basics of manufacture, sales and/or service (use hobbies or existing interests if possible). Examples: make and sell greeting cards, crafts or foods; develop a pet care service; publish a neighborhood newsletter; cut and sell kindling and firewood; grow and sell produce.

- *Ministry* Help your children get involved in a church ministry or community service. Examples: instead of going to Sunday School, let them help you teach a younger grade; take them to help on church work days; visit shut-ins; involve them in whatever ministry you are doing; do "Meals On Wheels;" visit nursing homes and shut-ins.

- *Homemaking* Train your children—both boys and girls—how to take care of a home inside and out. Examples: all areas of housecleaning; laundering and ironing all kinds of clothing; planning, buying for, and preparing nutritious meals; decorations and table settings; babysitting; mowing and trimming the lawn; flower bed and garden care.

- *Finances* Involve your children early on in the family finances. Let them participate in the entire process. Examples: establishing a family budget; evaluating purchases; paying bills; making deposits; reconciling checking accounts; tracking investment values.

IN OUR HOME...

One reason we started a mail order catalog business was to give our children a place to learn some business skills. Sarah began entering invoices and doing database entry when she learned to type at 11 years-old. She also helps with order fulfillment, and with booktable sales at workshops. The boys do a variety of odd jobs: stuffing and sealing newsletter mailings, putting inserts in books, pulling books for orders, putting price tags on books, keeping the inventory in order on the shelves, moving boxes. As the business grows and they grow, they'll take on more challenging tasks. They are apprenticing and they don't even know it!

EDUCATING THE WHOLEHEARTED CHILD

❑ Field Trips

Field trips expose your children to the real world, reinforce current areas of study, and provide opportunities for social interaction with other families and children. However, a field trip can be either a memorable learning experience, or just a fun outing with family or friends, depending on how educational *you* want to make it. The better the planning for a field trip, the greater the return on your investment of time will be.

- Plan to go on *only* those field trips that will be compatible with the age and interests of your children. If you can link a field trip with something you are reading or studying about, all the better.

- Before the field trip, read to your children from some living books that are related to the subject of the field trip. Have them do some research and reading on their own so they will know what they are going to see.

- Encourage your children to plan to ask questions at the field trip, and to go with questions in their minds from their own research. Their questions and the answers they receive can be recorded in a report and saved. Coach younger children with questions they can ask.

- Before leaving for the field trip, review expected behavior at the location, especially if other children will be there. Remind them that the time for play is before and after, but not during, the field trip. Review how they should respond to any leaders of the field trip. Train them to have a good testimony whenever in public.

- After the field trip, have your children write a brief report about what they saw and learned. Keep a notebook of those reports with any pictures taken or materials collected. And have your children write thank-you notes to the field trip leaders and to anyone who helped out at the location. It's a small way to train them in graciousness, and it is a meaningful writing assignment.

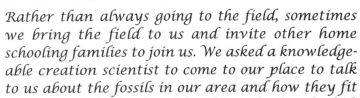

IN OUR HOME...

Rather than always going to the field, sometimes we bring the field to us and invite other home schooling families to join us. We asked a knowledgeable creation scientist to come to our place to talk to us about the fossils in our area and how they fit into a creation model. We had a lot of fossil samples for the kids to examine, and then we took them via tractor and trailer to some washouts where they could go on their own fossil dig. We also want our kids to be exposed to a variety of social settings, so we've had tea parties for the mothers and daughters to provide training in social graces and manners. Everyone dresses up and is on their very best behavior. During political campaigns, we'll have a night when we'll invite local and state candidates to come and speak to us. We'll plan some government and civics learning activities, and maybe even stage a mock election.

❣ **Field Trips To Go**—Here are a just few ideas to get you going:
- Airport
- Auto Garage
- Bakery
- Bank
- Bottling plant
- Central Post Office
- City/County Offices
- Dairy
- Farm or Ranch
- Fire Department
- Homeless center
- Magazine publisher
- Manufacturing plant
- Museums
- Nature Center
- Newspaper
- Nursery
- Parks & Rec. programs
- Police Department
- Print shop
- Radio station
- Recording studio
- Sports stadium
- State Capitol
- Symphony
- Theater
- TV station
- Water Treatment plant

❣ **Field Trip Rules**—
For the children
- Stay with your group, "buddy" or parent at all times.
- Listen quietly when any adult is speaking.
- Touch only what is permitted; ask before you touch.
- Raise your hand to ask a question in a group.
- Look your best and be on your best behavior.

For the adults
- Honor calendar deadlines for keeping FT coordinators informed.
- Arrive 10-15 minutes early.
- Be sure you and your children are clean and dressed appropriately.
- Keep your children with you and under control at all times during a tour.
- Guard your testimony.
- Never use a field trip for "baby-sitting."

📖 *Books Children Love (Elizabeth Wilson)*

📖 *Honey for a Child's Heart (Gladys Hunt)*

📖 *Read for Your Life (Gladys Hunt)*

📖 *A Family Program for Reading Aloud (Slater)*

📖 *Books That Build Character (William Kilpatrick)*

📖 *Great Books of the Christian Tradition (Terry Glaspey)*

✎ *"Whole Book" catalogs—Elijah Co., Greenleaf Press, Lifetime Books & Gifts, others*

Comment: Wrong Way ALA
The American Library Assoc. (ALA) sounds neutral enough, but the 55,000 private member trade association is way out in left field. This notoriously, almost radically, liberal group is securely in control of most libraries through its accreditation of more than two-thirds of full-time librarians. On threat of suspension, members are forced to support and implement the ALA-created "Library Bill of Rights." The LBR is an anti-family statement of library policy that says that any community or parental standards on what a library offers is censorship—pornography, homosexual publications, adult videos, or any other printed matter a child wants to see should be freely available without restrictions on its display and without parental notification. Ask if your library has adopted the LBR and speak out if they have. For more information about ALA and a new alternative accreditation association, Family Friendly Libraries, read the Sept. 18, 1995 issue of Focus on the Family Citizen (Vol. 9 No. 9).

❏ Library

"Going to the library" with your children tells them that you value books and reading. It also instills in them the attitude that the library is an enjoyable, exciting place of learning. While you are building your own home library, it is your best source for new and varied reading materials. Library days should become happily anticipated events as your children's appetites grow for reading whole books.

- Get to know your reference librarian by name. Then get to know your library. Familiarize yourself and your children with the different sections of the library. Each area holds its own treasures to be mined from the shelves, stacks and racks. Create a regular library time when you will go there with your children. Obtain library cards for your children when they can write their name, or when the library allows.

- Learn how to use the library research tools and services: card catalog, Dewey Decimal system, computerized search, printed indexes, periodical guides, inter-library loan service, Books in Print, and so on. Involve your children in the processes so they learn how to use them. Then give them assignments that use the research skills they are learning. Always ask the librarian if you need assistance with anything—they are generally very helpful and knowledgeable.

- Select books that are on Christian and home-school recommended children's reading lists. Award-winning books (usually designated on the cover) can also be good, but always check for objectionable content. Award-winning books are selected for many reasons, most dealing with illustration, literary style, overall excellence and "relevance." However, you will not find many books in the library with awards that recognize traditional, moral or family values. They are there, but they will only rarely be the award-winning titles.

- Select a variety of books on each trip (fiction, history, biography, science, nature, etc.). Give your children guidelines, allow them to choose what they would like to read, but let them know you will make the final decisions. Help them learn how to discern whether or not a book they are looking at is appropriate. Look at the book with them and explain why it does or does not meet your family's standards for reading material. Allow your children to check out as many books as they would like to try to read. In many cases, you (and other home schoolers) will be the only families checking out books, so don't be concerned about checking out the maximum number of books allowable.

- Keep a dedicated basket, bag or box to take to the library for carrying books. When you get home, keep the library books in it, or in a designated special place that is easily accessible for all your children. Keep them there to keep them from getting misplaced before the next trip to the library. Be sure everyone knows how to properly care for the borrowed books. Write the due date and the number of books checked out on your calendar.

❏ Age-Integrated Studies

The instructional methods you choose should allow you to do as much as possible in as little time as possible. That means minimizing as much as possible textbook and workbook based studies, which are inherently more teacher and time intensive in nature, and maximizing whole book centered studies, which naturally integrate all age levels. In a whole book, literature-based approach to home education, all ages can be involved at their own level of ability. It is roughly analogous to the age-integrated one-room schoolhouses of a century ago, except that home and family provide a far better learning environment than a school. When children of varying ages in a family have been trained to listen and learn together, more can be done in less time, leaving more time for other pursuits.

- Age integration can be easily and effectively used for reading aloud of all kinds, history and geography, fine arts, science and nature, and other areas of study. Obviously, it is not as useful for math and language arts studies, which nonetheless can be completed quickly and with a minimum of parental involvement.

- The success of most age-integrated study depends on your providing an age-appropriate way for 4-6 year-olds to participate, especially during a reading time. It might be a specific task to accomplish, or just giving them something that will engage their hands yet leave them free to listen and interact. You also need to develop a tolerance of "the wiggles," especially in little boys. Allow younger children to move around as long as they do not become a distraction, and as long as they are listening to what you are reading or discussing.

- Younger children (under age 6) can be included in narrations if they volunteer their own. Have your children narrate starting with the youngest (of listening age) and progressing up in age. If a younger child wants to narrate like his older siblings but needs help, ask one or two simple questions about the reading to prompt his narration. The older children do not need questions to prompt their narrations.

❣ **Small Suggestions**—Age-integrated study requires both spontaneity and patience on the part of the parent. You need to be prepared to respond spontaneously as the needs arise, but also to be patient with your younger children. The following are some ways to make it work.

- Start reading times with a good illustrated story-book of your younger child's choosing.

- Give younger children something to do while sitting and listening to a reading, such as coloring a relevant picture, or doing a PlayDough® sculpture.

- If older children draw and label a map for a history reading, have the younger ones color a copy of the same map.

- Have your children illustrate on a blackboard or markerboard what you are reading.

- Have an older child read to younger children if you need time to prepare, or to work with a child individually.

- Have a favorite illustrated storybook ready for a child to read in a favorite chair.

- If the younger child becomes tired and distracted during a reading, give him a task to do; don't scold him.

- If you are working through a unit study, always include some picture and story-books that will appeal to your younger children.

IN OUR HOME...

We discovered the power of multiplied siblings with Nathan. Because he is our most active child, we grimmaced somewhat at the prospect of integrating him into our normal reading routines. What we discovered, though, is that even though he needed to move and wiggle much more than Sarah and Joel, he was developing a habit of attention just by being there and listening during reading times. Now, at age 6, Nathan can sit still and listen to a reading for an hour, just like his older brother and sister. He is bearing the fruit of Sally's patient tolerance of his small interruptions, his wiggledy energy, and his budding extraversion. She also trained him early by reading shorter books and story-books to him, and then gradually moving up to chapter books. Patience and progress are the keys with younger children.

❏ Home Workshops

A normal frustration for home-schooling families is how to get Dad involved as a teacher. He is not there during the day when most of the learning and instruction takes place, and it doesn't work to put off some subjects until after dinner just so Dad can be a part. A much more natural way for Dad to get involved is through family workshops. In a workshop, Dad directs a hands-on study of a specific subject or topic that will be of interest to all the family. It's like a family night for learning. It reinforces his role as the head of the home and gives him the opportunity to enjoy the learning process with his children. Mom can lead workshops, too.

- Workshops can be worked into your schedule at random times. However, it is more likely they will get done if you set aside a "workshop night" on a regular basis (usually bi-monthly or monthly) and promote it to your children as a really special time. Plan an early dinner (one the kids will really like) to leave the evening as free as possible.

- Although many workshop subjects can be taught with very little planning, some advanced thought and planning will make the time go much more smoothly. You can lead a series of workshops on a single subject if there is too much to cover in one session, but be sure to plan out the entire series with different emphases and activities for each session. Repetition and too much lecture (a sign of under-planning) will kill a workshop.

- Know what you want your children to learn in the hour or so for each workshop, then create a simple "lesson plan." Find creative visual aids and hands-on projects. Have handouts with learning games. Plan the kinds of questions you can ask. Use a marker board for illustrating. Think ahead about examples and personal illustrations that will clarify areas that might be difficult for children to understand. If you have a friend who is knowledgeable in a particular subject, invite him to be a part of your workshop.

IN OUR HOME...

There is a spontaneous quality to workshops that makes them appealing. It's a little like a mini unit study and lesson combined. The kids were reaching that point with the computer where they could use the jargon of motherboards, hard disk drives, RAM and so on, but they had never actually seen any of these things. So, we had a computer workshop. While Mom was teaching a Bible study, Dad cracked the case on the home computer and gave the kids a circuit-level view of what's inside. We talked about where images on the monitor come from, and how they get there. Then we talked a little bit about the operating system, and how Windows works. Of course, there was a lot of hands-on experimentation. More computer workshops are being planned for the future, but we're off to a good start by demystifying the thing. And the kids love having Dad for some one-on-three time.

❑ Lessons

Lessons outside the home can be a good way to expose your children to a wide variety of new skills and experiences. They also might be just opportunities for interaction with other children. More often than not, they will be disappointing both for your children and for you. If you are truly serious about giving your child lessons for an emerging interest or skill, then private lessons, if affordable, are always to be preferred over group lessons. Individual tutoring is the ideal lesson format for learning. In contrast, the nature of a classroom greatly limits what can be accomplished—too many children for one teacher to give personal attention to them (impersonal), everybody works on the same things (conformity), up front lecture (detached), and a very slow pace of instruction (boring). Once a class gets larger than 3 or 4 children, it begins to become more formal and regimented, and the advantage and benefits of tutoring are lost.

- Lessons work only when four factors are in place: 1) the child is interested in the subject, 2) the teacher is good with children, 3) the teacher knows the subject, and 4) something real is accomplished. Take away any one of those and you raise the risk of a negative experience for your child. There is a slight (though not guaranteed) compensation if a friend is also taking the lessons.

- Limit lessons to one per child at a time. If you try to do more, especially if you have other young children, you will crash your calendar and end up taking time away from your home schooling. Lessons should always be optional and expendable. Home is the priority.

❑ Travel Study

Your car is more than just transportation—it is also a mobile learning environment. Most families spend more time in the car than they care to admit, but it doesn't have to be wasted time.

- Put together a car travel bag of educational and entertaining resources: illustrated story books, drawing materials, challenging puzzle books, favorite magazines, educational activity books, and the like. Leave it in the car or take it with you where you are going. Or assemble a travel bag for each child to use only in the car.

- Always keep a supply of books and stories on tape on hand, especially for trips of 30 minutes or more. Or, keep a book in the car for the passenger parent or the oldest child to read aloud, but only for when you are in the car.

- Make the most of any trip you take as a family, even if it is just for a weekend. Find out in advance about any special history of the city or region, and plan some time for a driving or walking tour. If it is a well-known historical or natural site, plan a unit study or a book and context study. Don't overlook special, out-of-the-way museums, interesting businesses and unusual architecture.

❧ **Lessons to Learn**—If you can come up with a skill that can be taught, there is probably a class somewhere for it. Some of the more common lessons include:

- Art (drawing, painting)
- Music (piano, violin, etc.)
- Sewing (decorative, clothes)
- Horseback riding
- Speech and Drama
- Physical Education
- Sports (team, individual)
- Carpentry
- many more

❧ **Lessons from Life**—Your children can take "lessons" other than in a class. Life offers a wide range of great lessons, especially as your children get a little older.

- Volunteer at a hospital or nursing home to learn about caring for others, medicine, nursing and hospitals.
- To learn about nature and animals, volunteer to help at a nature center, veterinary clinic, or at the zoo.
- If you have a mechanically-minded child, arrange for him to help at a garage.
- Put together a backyard Bible club for neighborhood children. Have your children give their testimonies, or teach a lesson.
- Help with a political campaign or work with your party precinct organization.
- Host an international exchange student in your home.
- Get involved in a moral or social issue as a family. Write letters, hand out materials, help with mailings.

Sensory Teaching Aids

Teaching or study that engages other senses "hooks" what is learned more effectively in a child's long-term memory. For example: looking at pictures of the Swiss Alps (visual aid) and listening to Swiss folk music (auditory aid) when reading Heidi. Some children need sensory reinforcement more than others, but all children benefit from added visual and auditory dimensions, as well as tactile, smell, and taste. Sensory aids include such things as cassette tapes, pictures, chalkboard drawings, manipulatives, foods, maps and globes, items to examine, actions to perform, an animal or insect, or items from nature.

- When using sensory teaching aids, keep them simple and relate them as closely as possible to the topic being studied. Avoid "sensory overload" or creating an increasing appetite for sensory stimulation.

- Whenever possible, use real life for aids rather than imitations and artificial substitutes. Nature abounds with natural aids; the kitchen is full of them. Use your imagination before resorting to "classroom" aids.

- Good sensory aids should do more than just stimulate the senses—they should stimulate learning *through* the senses. In other words, an aid is never an end in itself, but rather a means to an end. It simplified, clarifies or amplifies the book or topic being discussed.

Books on Tape

Listening to books on tape combines the learning value of hearing great literature, with the pure enjoyment and pleasure of listening to a well-told story. Audio books should never be used to replace reading aloud in your home, but listening to a book on tape is a good change of pace from the regular routine, and it is usually, if read by an experienced reader, an excellent example of interpretive and dramatic reading. Although you don't have your children formally narrate what they listen to, you can informally narrate by talking about the book in between chapters and eliciting your children's thoughts and comments about the story.

- It is expensive to build up an audio-tape library, but you will listen to the tapes more than once as younger children come of schooling age, and just for the pleasure of hearing the story again. Some video and book stores rent audio books, as does Blackstone Audio, and you can trade with friends. Unfortunately, there is a dearth of unabridged children's classics and family literature on tape. Numerous abridged versions are available, but they rarely do the real, whole book justice.

- Don't forget the Greatest Book on tape—the Bible. There is a dramatized NIV that is exceptional. Trained actors, sound effects and music add to the readings. Nothing is added to or taken away from the actual Bible text. Other tapes series are no frills readings that tend to be dull and unappealing. Add some drama to your Bible listening.

❣ Book Aid—Books with interesting information and illustrations (such as Kingfisher, Usborne Books or other illustrated fact books) make excellent visual teaching aids. Use them often.

❣ On the Boards—One of your easiest visual aids will be to keep a chalk board and/or a marker board handy (2'x3' or larger) for illustrating, making notes and lists, and such.

❣ Watch Out—Because video is multi-sensory, it is rarely used as a instructional aid in the true sense, but rather as a primary or secondary teaching resource. Use it sparingly.

♥

❣ Tape Drought—There is a paucity of good, unabridged classic children's books or family-friendly literature available on tape. However, you can find them if you look.

✎ *Blackstone Audio (800-729-2665)*—Family business, all unabr'd, excellent children's and classics sections, only evangelical Christian for religion books, many tapes are rentable

✎ *Jabberwocky (800-227-2020)*—All children's and classics, most abr'd for schools

✎ *Listening Library (800-243-4504)*—School oriented, abr'd and unabr'd of popular and classic

✎ *Bookcassette Sales (800-222-3225)*—Some affordable unabr'd classics

❣ Our Favorite Play Alouds—Listening together to a well-told and well-read story is a unifying experience. Our most memorable listens:
- *Where the Red Fern Grows*
- *Great Expectations* (BBC dramatization)
- *Silas Marner*
- *Cheaper by the Dozen*

❑ Scope and Sequence

The concept of scope (topics of study) and sequence (order of study) arose when age-grading became the norm in conventional schools and a system was needed to make sure the teacher "covered" the right material in the right sequence in the right grade level. However, since you do not march lockstep in the age-grade parade, you do not need a scope and sequence. Nonetheless, a scope and sequence can be a handy tool to help you evaluate what your children know and don't know at any given point. It's for the parent's benefit, though, not the child's.

- Trust whole books and home-centered learning to provide all the learning your children will need. Focus your attention on real books and real life, not on a scope and sequence designed for textbooks and classrooms. God designed children to learn in a family and home.

- Use a scope and sequence primarily to evaluate *past* learning, not to plan future learning. Upon reaching an age or grade milestone, check the scope and sequence to see if you've covered most of the material considered necessary up to that point.

- Don't become anxious because of what your child does not yet know. If your child is reading widely, whatever "holes" there may be will be filled in over time. Remember, you are not marching to the beat of the age-grade drum. If you find a topic not yet covered in your reading and other studies, you can simply work it into discussions, nature study, or wherever it most naturally fits, and quickly move on.

❑ Study Groups

A study group is a small group of parents and their children who get together to study a mutually agreed upon subject. Typically, leadership of the study rotates each meeting. The parent leading the group each session plans the lesson, the involvement of other parents, and learning activities for the children. It is, essentially, a group unit study with shared teaching.

- The smaller the group the better. Two to three families is ideal so there is enough, but not too much, time between rotations. Choose families for your study group with the children in mind. If they enjoy their friends, they will enjoy the study group. Also, look for families who share your values to avoid unnecessary conflicts and disagreements.

- Study groups work well for context and unit studies where each child can personally prepare and present a report on some aspect of the study, or contribute in some other way to the learning experience.

- Historical books make good fuel for study co-ops, as do any topics that lend themselves to a unit study. Assign study projects prior to the group. At the co-op, read the chapter aloud, or introduce the subject of the unit, then have the children do their presentations, followed by a learning activity or lesson.

You Can Teach Your Child Successfully (Ruth Beechick)—Insights for teaching grades 4-8 from a veteran teacher and curriculum designer.

How Do You Know They Know What They Know? (Teresa Moon)—A good resource for evaluating your child's progress with other handbook helps for parents.

Teaching Children (Diane Lopez)— A scope and sequence book based on Charlotte Mason's methods. Loaded with details, tips and lists for grades K-6.

♥Group Example—You are leading a study group with two other mothers and their young children. You are studying the Egyptian civilization. You could do any of the following:
- Read aloud *The Egyptian Cinderella*.
- Build a Lego® pyramid with burial chamber and sarcophagus.
- Read aloud and role play parts of the confrontation between Moses and the Pharaoh.
- Make a colored, saltdough map of Egypt.
- Color a line art drawing of King Tut's sarcophagus.
- While reading about Egyptian burial chambers, draw objects described on the chalk or marker board.
- Create hieroglyphic messages that the children must translate.

Before the study group, you could assign responsibilities to the other mothers. Children would either dress up or bring an Egyptian "artifact."

❏ Standardized Tests

❦ **This Is Only a Test**—There are several good standardized achievement tests for grades K-8. Depending upon the requirements of your state, each is an acceptable measurement device. Whichever test you choose or use, it is advisable to stay with the same test from year to year.

- **Iowa Test of Basic Skills (ITBS)**—Testing time in grades 3-8 is 4-5 hours. No listening tests in grades 3-8. Qualified parent may administer.
- **Stanford Achievement Test (SAT)**—Testing time in grades 3-8 is 5-6 hrs. Listening tests and subtests included in all grades. Stricter qualifications for administration.
- **California Achievement Test (CAT)**—Testing time in grades 2-8 is 2-3 hours. No listening tests. No subtests. Reflects more traditional values. Parent may administer.
- **Metropolitan Achievement Test (MAT)**
- **Comprehensive Test of Basic Skills (CTBS)**

✎ *Bob Jones University Press, Testing and Evaluation Service (800) 845-5731—Iowa (ITBS), Stanford (SAT)*

✎ *Christian Liberty Academy Satellite School, Independent Testing Service (312) 259-4444—California (CAT)*

Comment: Standard Brand?
Standardization theoretically levels the playing field so a child taking a "harder" test would score roughly the same as he would on an "easier" test. Tests are standardized based on how the "normed" group (a group representative of the total student population) performs on them. A "harder" test is not a better test.

Standardized achievement tests can be helpful for you, as the parent educator, to evaluate your child's progress. However, it is possible for the results of the tests to wrongly become either a source of over-concern if your child doesn't get above grade level, or of false pride if he's way above grade level. Since the major tests are currently normed against a public-school student population, there is no way to know the actual validity of your children's scores. It is reasonable to assume that most home-schooled students, especially those raised in a verbal and print rich environment, *should* score higher than the public-school-based norm.

- The best use of standardized tests is to help *you* better ascertain where you need to put more emphasis in your teaching. Annual or semi-annual testing gives you a reasonably objective means to measure your child's development. Nonetheless, tests will more than likely only confirm what you already know to be true about your child. In the end, you are the most objective measure of your child's development.

- Many umbrella schools and support groups administer standardized tests for their members. If you have a teaching certificate, or are a graduate of a 4-year degree program, you may be able to administer certain tests for your own children and others. Check with the testing service or with the test publisher.

- A low score does not necessarily mean low comprehension in an area. Take other factors into consideration: Is he a poor test taker? Was he not feeling well, or overly anxious? Had you covered the area in which he scored low? Was there a readiness for the subject (tests do not take into account the concept of learning readiness)? In the end, you are the final judge of your child's comprehension, not an impersonal test.

- Pre-tests are available from testing services and book catalogs to prepare your children for the test. If you don't use written tests in your home school, the pre-test is a good way to familiarize your children with the mechanics of a written test. Buy the test early so you can incorporate the testing methods and concepts in your teaching, but wait until the week before the actual test to give your child the pre-test.

- Coach your child in how to take the test: read directions carefully; look for clue words; answer the questions he knows first; don't spend too long on one item; if there is time, go back and answer unanswered questions (a logical guess is usually better than a blank, but check with the administrator); be sure test item and answer sheet numbers match; mark only one answer per test item; fully erase errors and stray marks.

- Your children will naturally want to know the results of the tests. You should discern whether to give them generalities ("You're doing very well in...We need to work on..."), or specific results in each of the tested areas. Whichever you choose, be especially careful not to compare your children's results ("When Sarah was your age, she scored...", or "Wow, Jack is as smart as Jill in math!").

❑ Tests & Grades

We are so indoctrinated by conventional school methods that the fundamental law of classroom instruction is etched on our minds: "Thou shalt test and grade thy children." Only it is not a fundamental law of home schooling. In fact, it is not a fundamental law of education at all—only of classroom teachers. Testing and grading have gained ascendancy only since the advent of public schooling in the last 150 years or so, and then more as a matter of administrative expediency than instructional necessity. Before that, students were tested orally to determine whether or not they knew a subject—the ability to *discuss a concept* was more important than the ability to *know a fact*. Tests and grades reduce the learning process to one of "getting the right answer." But *your* children can become highly educated and go to most colleges without ever taking a paper test or receiving a grade. The bottomline is, you don't have to test and grade any more than you have to take roll everyday. You're free to do what is best.

- Grades measure both what your children have learned, and what they have *not* yet learned. However, does it make any sense to "grade" your children for what is not yet completely learned or understood? Wouldn't it be just as effective simply to continue teaching until they have learned or acquired the skill?

- If lack of self-discipline is a problem, a poor grade will do nothing to motivate your child to be more diligent. If character is the problem, then your child needs to be properly disciplined and trained, not academically "shamed" by a poor grade.

- Standard grading (A, B, C, D, F) can create a motivation to do better, or to not do badly. But does allowing mediocrity as an acceptable "grade" in your home encourage excellence? Your children's best should be judged by their ability, not by an arbitrary or even a curricular standard. Take away grades and the standard becomes personal excellence in order to please God, parents, and self.

- Testing is just the vehicle for grading. If you ask your child to complete an assignment, does it make it any more effective to call it a "test"? If you want to know what your child has learned, just ask.

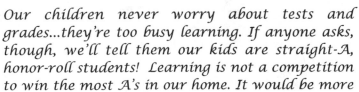

IN OUR HOME...

Our children never worry about tests and grades...they're too busy learning. If anyone asks, though, we'll tell them our kids are straight-A, honor-roll students! Learning is not a competition to win the most A's in our home. It would be more accurate to say it is like any other responsibility we give to our children. One of "Our 24 Family Ways" says, "In our family, we do our work promptly and thoroughly to the very best of our ability." That applies equally to the work of learning. The only "grade" given for work is "well done" when it is correctly completed. We don't allow less than "A" work here.

(cont'd from previous page)

❣ **Testy Terminology**—It is helpful to understand some of the technical terms used on the test report you'll receive.

- *Raw Score*—The number of test items your child answered correctly.

- *Percentile*—Refers to your child's relative ranking to all other tested children; it does not refer to the percentage of correct answers. In a room of 100 children, a 75% percentile ranking means your child did better than 75 other children. Highest is 99 percentile.

- *Grade Level*—Indicates the grade in which your child's score would be average. A 6.4 grade level means sixth grade, fourth month (based on 10 months). It is the score a child at 6.4 grade level would score on the same test. It does *not* mean your child would score average on a sixth grade test.

- *Stanine*—Ranking on a scale of 1-9 based on the percentile groupings. In general, 1-3 is below average achievement, 4-6 is average, and 7-9 is above average. The middle stanine represents about half of the group (based on a bell curve of standard distribution).

❝ ...you can let most children in on test scores and how they are interpreted. This is usually better than being secretive, as though test results are only for parents and teachers. On the profile page of your children's achievement tests they can easily see where their higher and lower scores are, and they can plan with you which scores they should try to raise before the next testing. The scores can be viewed something like golfing or bowling scores, and used for motivation.

Ruth Beechick, *You Can Teach Your Child Success-*

EDUCATING THE WHOLEHEARTED CHILD

CHAPTER SIX

Learning Styles...
Understanding Your Child

Personality and Learning Styles

It doesn't require a college degree to know that children come fully fitted with personality right out of the womb. Time and growth just add new layers of expression to that personality—characteristics that are seminal in the newborn and toddler, become nascent in the pre-schooler, and formative in the young child. A specific personality is there from the start that becomes more refined and defined with age.

The big question, though, is whether or not there are distinct kinds of personalities that can be described and categorized. And then, beyond that, is the question of how personality affects the learning process, and even the teaching process. Those questions have spawned a multitude of opinions, and a multi-faceted educational consulting industry.

One thing is certain—there is no credible theology or doctrine of personality. However, that is not to say that personality is a non- or anti-biblical issue! It is more accurate to say it is simply an extra-biblical subject. Though Scripture nowhere speaks directly to the issue, there are numerous indirect and anecdotal references, such as Jacob and Esau, and Psalm 139, which indicate that one's personality is a part of God's "womb-work." Gifts, too, seem somehow associated with personality. In general, personality seems to be a given in Scripture.

So, in the absence of objective Bible teaching, any attempt to describe and categorize personality based simply on subjective observations of people must be held very loosely. However, as long as a model does not violate Scripture or promote a distorted view of man's nature (sinful and in need of a Savior), it can be assessed and used on its own merits as a helpful tool for better understanding your children and yourself.

For the home educator, personality is a constant factor in learning. It is often referred to as "learning styles." How a child learns, and even how a parent teaches, is all wrapped up with learning modes and personality to some unknown degree. On the following pages, we'll discuss personality and some of the various approaches to learning styles, and then offer our model that integrates learning dynamics and personality.

Psalm 139:13-16
For you created my inmost being; you knit me together in my mother's womb. I praise you because I am fearfully and wonderfully made; your works are wonderful, I know that full well. My frame was not hidden from you when I was made in the secret place. When I was woven together in the depths of the earth, your eyes saw my unformed body. All the days ordained for me were written in your book before one of them came to be.

Genesis 25:27
The boys grew up, and Esau became a skillful hunter, a man of the open country, while Jacob was a quiet man, staying among the tents.

It takes a whole family to raise a whole child.

*T*he Reality of Personality

The study of personality is subjective and observational. There is no reliable way to apply the "scientific method" to "prove" personality. And yet, most people would agree that personality exists, that there are identifiable types of personalities, and even that there may be a certain unknown number of types of personalities.

You are in good Christian company if you accept the reality of personality. Most home schoolers who affirm personality would generally agree 1) that God created what we call personality, and 2) that children's personalities reveal something about how God designed them to learn best. However, though understanding personality is helpful, it should always be a secondary issue in your home education activities. You can study it and use it because it is helpful, and even fun, but it is not necessary for a good education. Whole books and real life will work with any child's personality, whether you know what it is or not.

❑ The Personality Behind the Person

Personality, though difficult to define, is certainly easy to observe—quiet vs. outgoing, visionary vs. details, leader vs. follower, logic vs. personal values, organized vs. non-organized, and so on. However, those kinds of differences comprise only a small part of the intricate creatures called man and woman that God created in his image. We are much more than our *personalities* in God's eyes. We are first and foremost *persons*, eternally stamped with the image and likeness of our Creator. And yet each person created by God is original and unique—a testimony of God's infinite creativity. Each has a distinct personality that sets them apart from every other. In other words, we're all persons with our own personal personalities that, in part, define who we are.

However, studying personality is like studying butterflies. We initially appreciate the natural wonder and beauty of the delicate creatures themselves. Soon, though, we are drawn into separating them into groups according to unifying elements of intricate design and observable behaviors within their diverse numbers. In the same way, we initially see all persons as a unified whole—humanity. But soon, we are drawn into seeing God's personal handiwork in individuals. We begin to observe and soon discover elements of unity within what appears to be at first glance random diversity. We begin seeing patterns of behavior and common traits.

God is a God of order, so it should come as no surprise to see order expressed in his people through common characteristics of personality, just as it is expressed through common physical traits such as eye and hair color, body build, and vocal range. When we talk about personality, we are simply taking part in the great, shared exercise of observing, studying and classifying God's creation. It is a little like nature study—it not only helps us to learn more about ourselves, but to know more about the infinitely creative God who made us (*Romans 1:20; Psalm 19*).

❑ The Person Beyond the Personality

Though we can observe personality and attempt to find patterns, any attempt to define personality is simply a way to *try* to understand our humanity better. Every such attempt, though, is inherently limited in its ability to adequately explain human behavior. There are simply too many other factors and influences that shape our behavior. These variables won't negate or change personality, which is innate and God-given, but they will affect the *expression* of one's personality. It is these kinds of variables that make for a seemingly random diversity among people, even though a theory or model might try to define four, or eight, or however many kinds of temperaments or personalities. Some of the variables include:

- *Character Training* Christian maturity will shape how personality is expressed. A strong aspect of personality might be tempered, or a weak one strengthened.

- *Biblical Values* What a person values shapes behavior that otherwise would be shaped mostly by strength of personality.

- *Weaknesses, Temptation, Sin* Patterns of sinful behavior distort personality. The effects of past sin can also distort personality.

- *Spiritual Gifts* God gives each Christian "spiritual gifts" for ministry in the body. Although gifts may be related to a person's "personality gifts," they are distinct concepts.

- *Life Experiences* Childhood experiences, both positive and negative, can either sharpen or distort personality.

- *Masculine and Feminine Traits* How a person understands and expresses their masculinity and femininity affects their personality.

❑ The Personality of Your Child

You don't need someone to tell you that your children have personalities—it's readily apparent in the way they think, play and relate. One child loves to read and entertain himself quietly; another is always moving and always wants to be with someone. One child excels at routine tasks such as sewing; another dreams up new and interesting projects. One child is very systematic and orderly, but not so relational; another is very relational, but not so organized. One child loves music; another loves sports.

In many ways, children are "pure" personality because they have not yet experienced other shaping influences. That purity, though, disguises the fact that their personalities are still growing and forming. By early adolescence, they will be more comfortable with their personalities; by adulthood, each will have developed a full and mature personality. During childhood, though, they are still learning "to be what they are." Part of your role as a parent is to understand, encourage and direct your children's emerging personality development.

> 66 *Once again, don't label your children. Or if you simply can't resist labeling them, keep an assortment of labels handy...Label your children one way today, another way tomorrow, a third way when appropriate. Use the whole pile of labels to help you understand them and nurture them however they need to be nurtured today, right now. When children are young, only one thing is absolutely certain about them—they are changing and growing. Quicker than we parents can believe.*
>
> LaVonne Neff, *One of a Kind,* Multnomah, 1988

The Reality of Learning Styles

Comment: All for All

Nothing is new under the sun, and no personality theory, regardless how clear or clever or Christian it may appear, is truly original. It is worth noting that nearly every popular approach to personality can be correlated to some degree with the four temperament types originally postulated by Hippocrates (ca. 400 B.C.). The personality model presented in this chapter is no different. It is simply a creative way of understanding personality. There really is no "science" of personality. The striking similarities between the various models serve to reinforce and strengthen the validity of their common elements. It is important to realize, too, that those common elements have generally been defined and described first by observation, rather than by research and testing. The four most common personality descriptions weren't discovered by primary research and statistical analysis—they were simply observed in human behavior, generalized into four categories, and reported.

📖 *Gifts Differing (Isabel Briggs Myers, 1980)*

📖 *Please Understand Me (David Keirsey, Marilyn Bates, 1984)*

📖 *The Way They Learn (Cynthia Tobias, 1994, Christian perspective)*

📖 *One of a Kind (LaVonne Neff, 1988, out-of-print, Christian perspective)*

📖 *God's Gifted People (Gary Harbaugh, 1990, Christian perspective)*

📖 *In Their Own Way (Thomas Armstrong, 1987)*

For all the efforts to define personality, there is no clear consensus on exactly what elements constitute a person's personality. However, there seems to be agreement that a starting point for talking about personality may be the way one thinks—that is, how you gather information, organize it, and make decisions with it. So, while there are certainly other factors that contribute to your personality, your mental processes—the way you think and the mental tasks you prefer to use—could be called the "first cause" of personality.

If how one thinks is somehow intricately bound up with what one is like, then the personality God has given your children will help you understand the way God has designed them to learn. And as a home-schooling parent, you can maximize your teaching efforts by understanding your children's "learning styles." The following is a sampling of some of the more recent and popular personality and learning styles models that have been applied to home education.

❑ Survey of Learning Styles

- **Natural Learning Styles** Widely used traditional approach to learning theory. Children learn by one (or more) natural processes. Most natural models include visual (see it), auditory (hear it), and kinesthetic (do it) learners. Some models also include print (read it), and social (relate it). These styles have also been correlated with other temperament and personality models.

- **Right/Left Brain** This approach is more physiology than it is personality, but it does offer valuable insights on modes of thinking and learning. The brain is divided into two hemispheres, each with its own mode of thinking. You predominantly use either one side or the other. Some children are predominantly "Right-brained" *global* thinkers—they think more intuitively, subjectively, and conceptually. Some children are predominantly "Left-brained" *linear* thinkers—they think more analytically, objectively, and factually.

- **Innate Aptitude (Gardner, Armstrong)** Children are born with one of seven intelligences, or innate aptitudes, that determine what and how they will learn best (musical, artistic, logical-mathematical, linguistic, bodily-kinesthetic, interpersonal, intrapersonal). If given maximum opportunity and cultivation, they will excel naturally in their area of innate aptitude and intelligence.

- **The Gregorc Model (Gregorc)** Children are one of four learning styles based on their Perceptual abilities, or how they prefer to take in information (Concrete or Abstract thinking), and on their Ordering abilities, or how they prefer to use that information (Sequential or Random thinking). Similar to Myers-Briggs. (1982.)

- **Bible Models** Some Christian authors have attempted to create personality models based on various biblical concepts such as spiritual gifts, ways to show love, or Bible characters. These can be useful and helpful, but they tend to read too much into the biblical text. Again, even though personality is a biblical given, there is no definable "theology of personality" in the Bible.

- **Temperaments (LaHaye)** Pastor LaHaye popularized the concept of temperaments, putting them into a Christian framework. He described four temperaments based on categories originally developed by Hippocrates (ca. 400 B.C.)—Sanguine, Choleric, Phlegmatic, Melancholy. He later differentiated each of those even further. Others have followed his lead with differing terminology .

- **Temperament Types (Keirsey & Bates)** Personality and character model based on a variation of Myers-Briggs types. Their book, *Please Understand Me* (1984), is popular in some Christian academic circles. Includes a helpful chapter on temperament in children. Also includes an inventory for determining your type and temperament.

- **Temperaments (Golay)** Dr. Golay developed a model of learning and teaching styles for use in the public schools (1982). Children fall generally into one of four temperaments or learning styles—Actual-Spontaneous, Actual-Routine, Conceptual-Specific, Conceptual-Global. These temperaments are derived from the Myers-Briggs and Kiersey & Bates models of personality type.

- **The 4MAT System (McCarthy)** Children are one of four learning styles (Feeler, Thinker, Sensor, Intuitor). This approach is used extensively in public schools, and in some Christian curricula (Alta Vista). It is based on a synthesis of major personality and learning styles theories and research done in the early 1980's. It is primarily a modification of the Myers-Briggs personality model integrated with Right/Left Brain theory.

- **Personality Type (Myers-Briggs)** Isabel Briggs Myers proposed sixteen personality "types" based on four preferences for thinking and living. The sixteen are often generalized into eight types or, more commonly, four temperaments. Numerous educators and writers, both secular and Christian, have used Myers' type theory as a model for their own learning and personality approaches. The Myers-Briggs Type Indicator (MBTI) is widely used in education. Although some are concerned about the Jungian roots of type theory, the MBTI is non-psychiatric and belief-neutral. It measures only the strength of preference for how one prefers to live, gather information and make decisions. Her book, *Gifts Differing* (1980), summarized a lifetime of work in developing her personality type model and the MBTI. The book contains extensive sections on the applications of type to education and parenting.

❑ Learning Style: Modes of Thinking

Observation, research and common sense indicate that our minds operate in at least two definable modes of thinking. In the *Investigation Mode* of thinking, you are seeking out information in order to gain knowledge. In the *Determination Mode* of thinking, you are sorting out information in order to reach conclusions.

These two modes of thinking can be further broken down by mental tasks—investigating the *facts* or investigating *insights*; and determining by *logic* or determining by *values*. Although you use all four mental tasks, you will prefer and use more skillfully only one of the mental tasks from each mode. "Learning style" is defined by the two mental tasks an adult or child most prefers using. The two tasks in each learning style also provide the defining elements for the four personality profiles provided at the end of this chapter.

Theoretically, the two modes and their four mental tasks would be exercised sequentially under ideal conditions. However, in reality we exercise whichever mental tasks are needed most for a given situation, and in whatever order they are called upon.

The Investigative Mode
(seeking out information to gain knowledge)

- *Task: Investigating FACTS* You seek out information based on your objective five senses. You favor the practical—you look to the proven way. You are comfortable with routine and details. You are a concrete, linear thinker.

- *Task: Investigating INSIGHTS* You seek out information based on a subjective "sixth" sense. You favor the idealistic—you look for a better way. You are comfortable with theories and the "big picture." You are an abstract, global thinker.

The Determination Mode
(sorting out information to reach conclusions)

- *Task: Determining by LOGIC* You sort out information based on impersonal logic. You are systematic, analytical and task-oriented. You strongly value competence and being correct.

- *Task: Determining by VALUES* You sort out information based on personal values. You are relational and people-oriented. You deeply value social skills and harmony in relationships.

❏ Learning Style: Methods of Teaching

Your children need to exercise all four of the mental tasks, not just *their* preferred ones, or the ones *you* prefer. *Your challenge is to use a balance of home-education methods that will exercise all four of the mental tasks, and also to give your children ample opportunities to express their preferred mental tasks.* You want to give them experience in all four areas, but special confidence in the tasks associated with their own learning styles. The key is balanced variety.

In providing a balance of teaching methods that exercise all four mental tasks, don't become formal and rigid. The Home-Centered Learning model, if implemented fully, should exercise all of those tasks naturally. Knowing the four mental tasks, though, will help you provide variety, and avoid inadvertently limiting your methods to those that mostly just reflect your own preferred mental tasks.

The following are just a few suggested methods and learning situations for each of the four mental tasks.

Teaching Methods for the Investigation Mode

- *Methods: Investigating FACTS* Research, context study, hands-on science, planning the logistics for a project, manipulatives, audio-visual aids, using any or all of the five senses.

- *Methods: Investigating INSIGHTS* Reading, role-play, using imagination, considering long-range goals for a project, considering solutions to a problem, brain-storming, independent work.

Teaching Methods for the Determination Mode

- *Methods: Determining by LOGIC* Analyzing, computing, categorizing and classifying, debate and discussion, question and answer sessions, solving problems, thinking skills exercises.

- *Methods: Determining by VALUES* Group discussion and problem solving, relational skills, presentation skills, creative writing, meaningful projects, lecture with personal insights and stories.

❣ **Modes and Methods**—Plan learning activities for study projects that will engage and exercise all four mental tasks. Some examples might be:

Unit Study of Rome
- *Facts:* Read a chapter from a children's reference book on the history of Roman Empire; make a salt-dough map
- *Insights:* Role-play a scene from Shakespeare's Julius Caesar; read aloud a historical novel on Rome
- *Logic:* Evaluate the reasons for the fall of the Roman Empire; write a short report
- *Values:* Discuss "What would I have done as Caesar?"; present a comparison of Rome then and America now

Nature Study of Trees
- *Facts:* Study a field guide to determine types of trees in area
- *Insights:* Determine best way to map the area and record the trees; design mapping material
- *Logic:* Classify and categorize the trees; use leaf samples; evaluate growth patterns
- *Values:* Discuss what new trees should be planted; present reasons why to the group

Study of Vivaldi
- *Facts:* Read aloud a story of Vivaldi's life; listen to the Classical Kids tape; listen to *The Four Seasons*
- *Insights:* Imagine what Vivaldi was picturing in each movement
- *Logic:* Chart and time the movements; note tempo and feel of music
- *Values:* Create dramatic scenes to go with each movement, or select appropriate Bible readings

❑ Learning Style: Mental Focus

It is not unusual to hear someone say about a talkative, gregarious child, "What an extraverted little boy he is." Or, about a quiet, introspective child, "She really is quite introverted, isn't she?" Each is trying to describe a child's "mental focus." However, the psychological terms, though quite useful, can seem somewhat cumbersome. Instead, we would describe the little boy as having an "Active" mental focus, and the little girl as having a "Reflective" one.

- **Active** Active children focus their mental energies and attention on the *external world of people and events*. These children tend to think with their mouths so that whatever is on their minds is on their tongues. Active children are easily distractible, but tend to finish their work quickly in order to move on to something else. They are not as quick to pick up on abstract concepts and ideas, but rather are good with concrete facts.

- **Reflective** Reflective children focus their mental energies and attention on the *internal world of thoughts and ideas*. These children think before they speak, and they tend to be a bit mysterious because so much goes on inside them that they never let out. Reflective children have strong powers of concentration, and are slower to call an effort finished. They more easily pick up on abstract concepts and ideas.

Knowing where your child's mental focus and attention is directed helps you better appraise their learning behaviors, and more easily engage them in learning activities. An active child needs the freedom to "think out loud" without having their thoughts-in-process judged too quickly. A reflective child, on the other hand, needs the freedom to "think it through" before being expected to answer.

IN OUR HOME...

Our family is a real study in personalities. Mom is a Mover and Dad is a Shaper, and we are both Reflectives, so we do a lot of reflecting on ideals together (does it show?). The jury is still out on the kids, but they're beginning to show their personality feathers. Sarah seems to be a Reflective Mover like her Mom. She's an avid reader and loves being a part of important things with friends. Joel is definitely Reflective and Nathan is definitely Active, but beyond that we're still waiting to see what develops. Joel's creativity would indicate a preference for Insights (like Mom and Dad), and Nathan's gift of organization would indicate a preference for Logic (like Dad). Baby Joy is, obviously, a mystery as yet, but she's definitely active for now. Knowing personality preferences has helped us think about how to better love each of our uniquely designed children, how to better motivate them to learn, and how to touch their joys and delights in life. And it's just a lot of fun, too.

❑ Learning Style: Growth and Development

Scripture is clear that, whatever personality is, it is inherent and God-given. However, in the same way that the physical body grows and develops, so do personality and, subsequently, learning styles.

- Children under 13 years old generally have not yet had enough experience with life to know with confidence which mental tasks they prefer and use most skillfully. Around the time of puberty (about seventh grade), however, they begin to differentiate which tasks they most prefer to use. Before that time, since your children are not able to accurately identify their preferences on their own, you can observe them in order to determine patterns of preference that are emerging throughout childhood.

- During the elementary years, your children will routinely use all four mental tasks. They are trying everything on to see what fits best. This is a necessary step in learning development since all four tasks will be used throughout their lives. During this developmental time in their lives, be careful to avoid the temptation to isolate their preferred mental tasks, label them, and then focus your teaching methods exclusively on those emerging preferences. That is not the purpose of knowing your children's learning styles! *Your goal during the elementary years is to plan your methods so as to give your children a balanced experience of all four mental tasks while allowing them to develop confidence and skill in their emerging preferred tasks.*

- As preferred mental tasks emerge, you can begin to use that knowledge to understand your child's learning patterns and frustrations, to increase their motivation for certain subjects, or to make difficult subjects more understandable for them. In Discovery Studies, for instance, you can direct your children to use their own preferred learning styles so they can develop skill and competence in the use of their preferred mental tasks.

- Don't label your children too soon—the label might not fit in another few years! It's fun to talk about personality and learning styles, but keep it general. Let them tell you what *they* think they are. Resist the temptation to evaluate everything they do or say through the grid of their learning style or personality.

- Be especially careful not to show favoritism for certain mental task preferences or personalities. If you are a Mover, you might find it easier to work with a child who is a Mover and inadvertently give that child more affirmation than, say, your Doer child. *It is important for you to learn to value all preferences and personalities equally in your children.*

> 66 *What children need is the conviction that satisfaction can and must be earned. Parents who value this conviction can give it to their children, but the parents must start early and remember both the 'can' and the 'must.'...Both home and school should provide them with the experience of doing particular things well and thereby earning the satisfaction they crave. Because the various types have different gifts and needs, the specific things and satisfactions cannot be the same for all children... [Personality] development is fostered by excellence in almost anything that children can, with effort, do well...The excellence need not be competitive, except as children try to excel their own past performance, and virtue need not be its own reward. The satisfaction earned by the striving can be whatever furnishes the strongest incentive to the child, for example, extra pleasures or possessions for a sensing [facts] child, special freedoms or opportunities for an intuitive [insights] child, new dignity or authority for a thinker [logic], and more praise or companionship for a feeling [values] type.*
>
> Isabel Briggs Myers, *Gifts Differing*, Continuing Psychologists Press, 1980

Learning Style and Personality Type Indicator

An indicator is simply that—a tool to indicate what your child's Learning Style might be. It is based entirely on your own observations, as a parent, of your child's preferences. After all, you are the best and most accurate judge of your child, not a generalized tool. So, use it to help you better understand your child's living and learning preferences, but trust your own instincts concerning your child.

Instructions for Using the Indicator

Evaluate your child's personality using the following scale for all forty characteristics (rate all ten items in each of the four columns). Use the number corresponding to the answer that best describes how consistently your child exhibits each characteristic.

Rating	**Explanation**
1 = Only occasionally	*This doesn't really describe my child.*
2 = Fairly often	*My child does this some of the time.*
3 = Most of the time	*This really describes my child.*

When you have placed a 1, 2 or 3 value in all forty boxes, add the numbers in each column and place the total in the box below it. For each mode, one of the two mental tasks should be stronger. The two *predominant* tasks (one from each mode) indicate your child's personality and learning style might be. For instance, if a child scored 24 for Facts, 14 for Insights, 16 for Logic, and 22 for Values, that child's Learning Style would be "FV" (Facts+Values)—Facts from the Investigation Mode, and Values from the Determination Mode. The child's Personality Profile would be "Helper." Once you have determined your child's indicated Personality Profile, turn to the appropriate page in the section following the Indicator.

Record your child's name, the date of the evaluation, your child's age at that time, his or her Learning Style, and corresponding Personality Type. The Mental Focus is not a scored item. You simply decide which mental focus best describes your child—either Active or Reflective—and record it in the appropriate space.

Values: 1 = Only occasionally   2 = Fairly often   3 = Most of the time

INVESTIGATION MODE
(Seeking out information to gain knowledge)

Investigating FACTS	*Investigating INSIGHTS*
...enjoys familiar activities and regular routine. ☐	...enjoys trying new ways and learning new things. ☐
...wants to know the right way to do things. ☐	...enjoys being different. ☐
...carefully observes, remembers lots of details. ☐	...learns quickly but tends to forget details. ☐
...asks, "Did that really happen?" ☐	...enjoys pretending and making up stories. ☐
...is curious about how things work. ☐	...looks for new ways to do common tasks. ☐
...enjoys books with lots of facts and information. ☐	...enjoys imaginative books and stories. ☐
...cares about clothes and how he or she looks. ☐	...likes to invent and design things. ☐
...is good working with his or her hands. ☐	...is good with words and ideas. ☐
..enjoys puzzles and coloring books. ☐	...uses toys in new and original ways. ☐
...is known to be steady and reliable. ☐	...goes quickly from one new interest to another. ☐

FACTS ☐   **INSIGHTS** ☐

DETERMINATION MODE
(Sorting out information to reach conclusions)

Determining by LOGIC	*Determining by VALUES*
...asks "Why?" a lot. ☐	...likes to talk or read about people. ☐
...insists on logical explanations. ☐	...wants to be praised for caring for others. ☐
...likes to arrange things in orderly patterns. ☐	...shows concern if someone is unhappy. ☐
...shows more interest in ideas than in people. ☐	...tells stories expressively in great detail. ☐
...holds firmly to his or her beliefs. ☐	...tries to be tactful, even if it means avoiding truth. ☐
...not always comfortable with affection. ☐	...shows more interest in people than in ideas. ☐
...wants rules in games established and kept. ☐	...generally agrees with opinions of friends. ☐
...likes praise for doing something competently. ☐	...wants physical and verbal expressions of love. ☐
...can be perfectionistic. ☐	...relates well to other children and adults. ☐
...controls his or her emotions. ☐	...is upset by conflict with family or friends. ☐

LOGIC ☐   **VALUES** ☐

Learning Style (LS), Personality Type (PT) and Mental Focus (MF) Record

Child: _____

Date _____ Age _____ LS _____ PT _____ MF _____
Date _____ Age _____ LS _____ PT _____ MF _____
Date _____ Age _____ LS _____ PT _____ MF _____

Child: _____

Date _____ Age _____ LS _____ PT _____ MF _____
Date _____ Age _____ LS _____ PT _____ MF _____
Date _____ Age _____ LS _____ PT _____ MF _____

Child: _____

Date _____ Age _____ LS _____ PT _____ MF _____
Date _____ Age _____ LS _____ PT _____ MF _____
Date _____ Age _____ LS _____ PT _____ MF _____

Learning Styles:

- **FL:** Facts + Logic
- **FV:** Facts + Values
- **IL:** Insights + Logic
- **IV:** Insights + Values

Personality Types:

- **DOER** (Facts + Logic)
- **HELPER** (Facts + Values)
- **SHAPER** (Insights + Logic)
- **MOVER** (Insights + Values)

Mental Focus:

- **ACTIVE** (Outward on people and activities)
- **REFLECTIVE** (Inward on thoughts and ideas)

Doer

❑ The DOER Child
(Facts + Logic)

- **Mini-Profile** Practical, resourceful. Good at routine physical tasks and details. Does things the proven way. Learns from and relies on experience. Enjoys organizing and making things fit together to work. Consistent and reliable. Uses logic and objective analysis to solve problems. Good with technical tasks. Values fairness (logic) over feelings.

- **Mental Focus** "Active" Doers focus their mental energy on the people and events in their lives. They are usually the children who are the first to get activities organized and directed. "Reflective" Doers focus their mental energy on their thoughts and ideas. These children are very thorough, responsible and precise, and are good at routine work.

- **Learning Style of a Doer** Your Doer child learns best primarily by *investigating facts* and *determining by logic*. This child prefers hands-on subjects and repetitive activity, and does not like subjects that require very much disciplined study.

- **Teaching a Doer** This child is the most hands-on and concrete. Give them something to do or accomplish now. Assign tasks that require practical or repetitive skill, analysis, and organization. Fully explain instructions or directions step-by-step. Your teaching must be factual, organized and orderly to be of use to the Doer. Ask questions that require specific, concrete answers and knowledge. This child likes to accomplish his own work.

- **Reading to a Doer** This child will enjoy action books and dramas based on real events. They are interested in detailed, realistic illustrations.

- **Motivating a Doer** Demonstrate why a task or skill will be useful to this child *right now*; show what function it will play in the child's life. Recognize manual and practical skills. Affirm them for how reliable, resourceful, competent and skilled they are. Rewards must be concrete and immediate to be motivational for this child.

- **Correcting a Doer** Retrace any steps taken in order to find the exact point at which a mistake was made. Start again at that point. Express your confidence in the child to do it correctly the second time. The Doer child often is very active and needs encouragement to develop disciplined study habits.

- **Weaknesses of a Doer** This child can become *impatient* if a lesson takes too long to complete. He or she can also be *inflexible* in how to do a task or lesson.

❑ The HELPER Child
(Facts + Values)

- **Mini-Profile** Practical, resourceful. Good at meeting existing needs that involve people. Does things the proven way. Learns from and relies on experience. Enjoys working with tasks and details to make people fit together more harmoniously. Uses personal intuition to solve problems. Likes to please, avoids conflict, values feelings over logic.

- **Mental Focus** "Active" Helpers focus their mental energy mostly on the people in their lives. These children love either to serve others, or to make sure others are served. "Reflective" Helpers focus their mental energy on their thoughts and ideas. These children thrive working on projects related to the values they hold dear.

- **Learning Style of a Helper** Your Helper child learns best primarily by *investigating facts* and *determining by values*. This child prefers informative subjects such as reading and history, and does not like subjects that require much independent study and imagination.

- **Teaching a Helper** This child is the most willing to serve. Give them something to do or to accomplish that will involve other people. The Helper child is good at practical skills that will benefit others. Create group projects for this child that allow them to offer practical ways to achieve harmony and cooperation. This child wants to be liked and accepted by others.

- **Reading to a Helper** This child will enjoy books and dramas based on real events that involve real people working together harmoniously. They are interested in detailed illustrations of real people.

- **Motivating a Helper** First and foremost, warmly affirm your personal relationship with the Helper child. Put them in group situations that are relationally comfortable and non-threatening. Recognize their ability to get along with others. Affirm their competence and effectiveness in social skills, and their friendliness and caring for others.

- **Correcting a Helper** Express your love and appreciation for the Helper before correcting. Put the subject (especially a difficult one that is resisted) into the context of how much it pleases you to see them learn and grow. The Helper child might need encouragement to become more creative.

- **Weaknesses of a Helper** This child can become *passive* and *resistant to change*. He or she might also resist by *avoiding conflict*.

If God has given you a Helper, he knew you could meet the challenges of educating this servant child. God designed your little boy or girl to help and appreciate others. As a future leader, God will some day use your Helper child to serve others, organize people and, through appreciation and relational skills, help them work together to help others.

If your Helper is a girl, her biblical role model might be Ruth, whose quiet life of service and loyalty to Naomi was rewarded by God. Ruth gave up her life in Moab to follow Naomi and be a daughter to her. Her servant heart and practical skills eventually led her to become the wife of Boaz, and the great-grandmother of David.

If your Helper is a boy, his biblical role model might be Barnabas, who was a behind-the-scenes servant who helped establish the church in Jerusalem and in Asia. He was the "Son of Encouragement" who knew how to work with people and help others become successful. When Paul rejected John Mark, Barnabas took him and turned him into a leader.

Mover

If God has given you a Mover, he knew you could meet the challenges of educating this influential child. God designed your little boy or girl to influence others to do great things. As a future leader, God will some day use your Mover child, through their strong verbal and relational skills, to motivate and move others to join in important ministries and causes.

If your Mover is a girl, her biblical role model might be Deborah, who used her personal influence to lead Israel to victory over the chariots of Sisera. She envisioned what could be done and influenced the people to follow her. She persuaded Barak to take up the battle against 900 chariots. As a result of her vision and plan, Israel routed Sisera.

If your Mover is a boy, his biblical role model might be David, who unified Israel under his leadership. He was a visionary who knew how to move people to action and loyalty through building relationships and connections. Though he had weaknesses, his strength was his close relationship with God, evidenced in the Psalms that still move people today.

❑ The MOVER Child
(Insights + Values)

- *Mini-Profile* Inventive, imaginative. Good at seeing what might be done with, by or for people. Finds new ways to motivate people to aspire to personal ideals. Enjoys promoting worthy causes and persuading others to join in. Uses personal intuition to solve problems. Likes to please, highly idealistic, values feelings over logic.

- *Mental Focus* "Active" Movers focus their mental energy on the people and events in their lives. These children might organize their friends to pursue a cause or make changes. "Reflective" Movers focus their mental energy on their thoughts and ideas. These children tend to try to influence others with their deeply felt ideals.

- *Learning Style* Your Mover child learns best primarily by *investigating insights* and *determining by values.* This child prefers interesting subjects such as reading, writing, and performance arts, and does not like subjects that require routine work such as drill or workbook studies.

- *Teaching a Mover* This child is the most idealistic and possibility oriented. Give them something to believe in, a meaningful reason for learning. Create new, non-routine learning opportunities that enable this child to convince and persuade others to action. Allow them to express their natural leadership abilities. Look for ways to give lessons from an inspirational perspective.

- *Reading to a Mover* This child enjoys imaginative books and drama that are inspiring accounts of people pursuing a cause. They are interested in imaginative and inspiring illustrations

- *Motivating a Mover* Look for the sparks of inspiration and ideals in this child and draw them out. Recognize their verbal and leadership skills. Affirm their insight, enthusiasm and commitment. Affirm your relationship with them and how much you mean to them. This child is motivated by recognition from respected individuals.

- *Correcting a Mover* Engage this child in a *discussion* of incorrect material. Always offer verbal, interpersonal correction, working through the material with them conversationally. The Mover child is very relational and needs to be encouraged to pay attention to nonpersonal details.

- *Weaknesses of a Mover* This child can be *impulsive* and *imprecise* when doing a task or lesson. He or she can also be *overly optimistic* about goals or plans.

❑ The SHAPER Child
(Insights + Logic)

- **Mini-Profile** Inventive, imaginative. Good at any mental task that requires ingenuity. Finds new ways to do things. Looks for new skills to learn. Enjoys thinking about future possibilities and developing strategies to accomplish them. Uses logic and objective analysis to solve problems. Visionary planner. Values fairness (logic) over feelings.

- **Mental Focus** "Active" Shapers focus their mental energy on the people and events in their lives. These children can usually be found engineering new ways to get things done. "Reflective" Shapers focus their mental energy on their thoughts and ideas. These children are the conceivers and architects who design new ways to do things.

- **Learning Style** Your Shaper child learns best primarily by *investigating insights* and *determining by logic*. This child prefers creative and theoretical subjects such as math, science and thinking skills, and does not like subjects that require review, lots of written work or group work.

- **Teaching a Shaper** This child is the most theoretical and abstract, and consequently, also the most independent. Give this imaginative child assignments that allow him to analyze and synthesize a broad range of ideas, concepts and information. Create opportunities that exercise their desire to find new ways to do things. You need to tap into their natural creativity and quest for knowledge.

- **Reading to a Shaper** This child will enjoy fiction and imaginative books and drama that provide new ways to look at the world. They are interested in imaginative, creative illustrations.

- **Motivating a Shaper** Explain how an assignment fits into the "big picture" of learning. Recognize this child's creativity in analyzing and systematizing facts and information. Affirm their competence, intelligence and ingenuity. A challenge met is its own reward for this child, but recognition for competency and innovation also helps.

- **Correcting a Shaper** When possible, direct this child to find and correct his or her own mistakes. Appeal to their sense of competency. Create new assignments or challenges to correct an area of learning. The Shaper child tends to be very individualistic and will need to be encouraged to participate in group activities and work with others.

- **Weaknesses of a Shaper** This child can become *perfectionistic* and negative about the quality of his or her work. He or she can also be *pessimistic*.

If God has given you a Shaper, he knew you could meet the challenges of educating this creative child. God designed your little boy or girl to be the architect of new ideas and concepts, new ways of doing things and unthought of possibilities. As a future leader, God will some day use your Shaper child to envision and plan new and effective ministries for God.

If your Shaper is a boy, his biblical role model might be the Apostle Paul, whom God chose to envision and build his church among the Gentiles. Paul communicated the vision and gave his life to seeing the church grow. He led by the strength, clarity and logic of his ideas and purposes.

If your Shaper is a girl, her biblical role model might be Mary, the mother of Jesus, who saw God's plan for the child in her. In Mary's song, she reveals her grasp of what God was doing in and through her. She committed herself to that plan and to all it entailed. Her obedience would shape eternity.

EDUCATING THE WHOLEHEARTED CHILD

CHAPTER SEVEN

Home Management... Getting It Together

Keeping It All Together...All the Time

Whoever says home schooling is not a full time career obviously has not applied for the job lately. As a home-schooling mom, you are called on to manage your home, teach and train your children, plan for lessons and field trips, shop for and prepare meals, clean and organize your home, do laundry for your entire family, counsel your children, and do planning and record keeping for home education. You may even add a home-based business to the mix in your home. The point is, there is nothing "part time" or easy about the home-schooling lifestyle.

Because your responsibilities are so varied in the home—and so unrelenting—the pressure to get it all together and keep it all together is constant. You feel it all the time. If you ever hope to be both *effective* (doing the right things) and *efficient* (doing things right) in your home-schooling "career," you must get systematic about it—making systems work for you to manage your home and responsibilities.

Personality factors come into play in home management. If you are a *Doer* mom, you probably already have some practical systems in place, but your kids may wonder if they are just pieces in the system. If you are a *Helper* mom, you probably have some systems developed where your children are involved, but the non-personal aspects of your home are in disarray. If you are a *Mover* mom, you're probably so busy influencing your kids that the house and the schedule are in a constant state of flux. If you are a *Shaper* mom, you probably are busier rethinking and redesigning your systems than you are making use of them. The reality is, no personality is the perfect home-schooling mom, so every one has something to learn about home systematics.

This chapter explains "management by the box," a home management approach that will help you move *toward* the ideal of "keeping it all together, all the time." Keep in mind, there is a big difference in *reaching for* the ideal and actually *reaching* it. The approach outlined in this chapter is a doable but imperfect way to reach *for* the ideal. It is purposely uncomplicated, even simplistic. It is easy to understand and implement, but it covers all the major areas of your home management responsibilities. We approach this area with a sense of humor because, let's face it, it's better to laugh at your disorganization than it is to get knots in your stomach because of it. But beyond all that, it will help you get the clutter under control. Whatever your home situation, whatever your personality, whatever your mess—home management by the box can help.

1 Corinthians 14:33
For God is not a God of disorder but of peace.

❝ *To be organized is not synonymous with meticulous. To be organized means you do things for a good reason at the best time and in the easiest way. It doesn't mean that you never get behind, rather that you can stick to it until you have recovered.*

Bonnie McCullough, *Totally Organized*

❣ **Box Mania**—Between 1982 and 1992, the value of one share of Rubbermaid stock rose from $2.41 to $31.00. That is an increase of 1186%! Why did it rise in value so dramatically? The answer in one word—BOXES! Rubbermaid became the leading home storage and container maker in America. "Over-stuffed" American baby-boomer consumers bought them by the case load.

*T*he Science of Home Management

Before explaining the details of home management "by the box," it is worthwhile covering some of the underlying laws and principles that are at work in your home environment.

❏ The Laws of Home Systems Management

Just as there are natural laws that govern the natural universe, so are there home laws that govern the home universe. These laws are a part of the "warp and woof" of your daily life in your home universe—you are either working with them or against them. The astute home manager understands these laws and submits to them. You cannot escape them, but you can learn to use them to your advantage.

Universal Laws of Home Thermodynamics

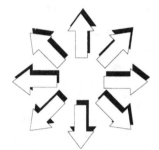

- *First Law:* In home systems, all things tend toward disorder and disarray.

- *Second Law:* In home systems, a finite amount of energy is being dissipated at a constant rate.

Universal Laws of Home Systematics

- *Law:* Systems work.

- *First Corollary:* If you don't work your systems, your systems won't work.

- *Second Corollary:* The more you work your systems, the less you'll work.

Universal Laws of Home Cause and Effect

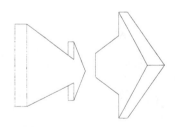

- *Law:* In home systems, every undesirable effect has a cause.

- *First Corollary:* To eliminate an undesirable effect, you must change the cause.

- *Second Corollary:* Causes can be changed only through the application of time and effort.

- *Third Corollary:* Causes are not changed by ignoring, complaining about or rationalizing effects.

❏ The Invisible Energy of Routine

In the same way that there are universal laws that govern your home universe, there are also invisible powers in that universe that hold everything together. In the physical world, subatomic powers keep everything from flying apart (actually, God does, but you get the picture). In the home universe, the invisible power that keeps everything from flying apart is called *routine.*

Routine is simply a habitual pattern of living created by effort applied regularly over time. Once a pattern of living is established in your lifestyle and schedule, it becomes an invisible, self-generating force to hold part of your home universe together. The more you harness the power of routines, the more energy you will generate to apply to other areas of your home. However, if ignored, routine energy rapidly dissipates, and the elements within the home universe begin to disintegrate at rapidly increasing rates of decay. When that happens, even greater amounts of time and effort are needed to regain stability.

The laws of routine are well-established:

- *The Law of Routine* For every action taken to establish routine, there is an equal and similar reaction generating greater amounts of routine energy.

- *The Converse of the Law of Routine* For every action *not* taken to establish routine, there is a corresponding decrease in total home routine energy.

All that to say that it takes a lot less energy to live with established routines than it does to live without them. If your children see you establishing routines in your own life (devotions, exercise, house clean up), they will be more likely to imitate your example in their own. And remember, you are the one who will create the routines for them (Bible reading, home-school assignments, cleaning up room).

IN OUR HOME...

Morning at our house is the most important time for routines. We have observed that if the children get off to a good start with their morning routines—get dressed, make bed, straighten room, read Bible, set breakfast table, clean dishes—then they do better at remembering other routines throughout the day. A good start really sets the pace! Bedtime is another routine time, but somewhat of a wild card time in our day. We're not very consistent on the "time" of the bedtime, so we focus on training in the routine of getting ready for and into bed. If it's early enough, Dad keeps up a reading routine by reading aloud to them. The beauty of routines, theoretically anyway, is that once they become patterns, you won't have to ask (Ha!).

❣ Routinize Your Kids—The goal of routines in your children's lives is to train them to be responsible and to take initiative without being told. In other words, the more routine there is in their lives, the more they should begin to take initiative in other areas, independently and without prompting. Routines also give your children a certain sense of stability and feeling of security that is important in a home-schooling setting.

- Any re-occurring daily event should be cultivated into a daily routine—rise-time, educational activities, mealtimes, bed-times, chores and responsibilities.

- Age-appropriate responsibility for routines (all or part) should be transferred to your children as soon as possible—collecting and putting out the trash, mowing the lawn, vacuuming and mopping and other areas of house cleaning.

- Don't keep or take over an area of responsibility that your child is able to do. Make your children masters of their own routines. While it is not necessary to reward children when routines are maintained, you should be sure there is a "cost" of some kind for broken routines.

- Use routines as "anchors" to stabilize your children's days. The more they know what is expected of them, or what is allowed, at all times of the day the more they will follow the patterns of living you create. Routine becomes automatic so your children are not always looking to you for direction.

- When life throws your routines off temporarily, always get your children back on them as quickly as possible. The longer you delay, the more time and effort that will have to be applied to re-establish them.

*T*he Routine Ups & Downs of Home Life

❏ Home Management Uppers:
    Five Ways to Stay UP on Top of It All

Upper	What	When	Examples
Putting Up	Messes	As You Go	Dishes Arts and Crafts Study materials Projects
Picking Up	Things	Daily	Put away toys Empty dishwasher Pick up rooms Organize kitchen
Cleaning Up	Dirt	Weekly	Vacuum, dust Mop hard floors Wash, iron Change bedding
Keeping Up	Information	Monthly	Bills, finances Clipping, filing Home School papers Correspondence
Catching Up	Organization	As Needed	Library Closets Storage areas Pantry

❏ Home Management Downers:
    Five Ways to Get DOWN from It All

Downer	Why	What to Do	Comment
Lying Down	Laziness	Get going. Get organized.	HS is hard work. There's not much room for taking it easy.
Winding Down	Inactivity	Get healthy. Get fit.	You need a healthy diet and regular exercise to keep going in HS.
Slowing Down	Overcommit-ment	Get free. Get realistic.	An overloaded calendar slows everything down. Put it on a diet.
Falling Down	Weariness	Get rest. Get help.	HS can leave you physically, emotionally and spiritually drained.
Getting Down	Hopelessness	Get counsel. Get support.	Circumstances and Satan can steal your hope. But remember—God is able!

❣ **Child Chores**—Here is a short list of chores that your children can do around the house. For older children, define exactly what you mean by the chore ("The kitchen is clean when..."). For younger children, give them one or two specific tasks at a time ("Organize your toy closet."). Asterisks indicate chores better suited for older children (age 7 and up).

- Make bed
- Clean room
- Set the table
- Do the dishes *
- Clean the kitchen *
- Empty dishwasher
- Fold/distribute laundry
- Change bedding *
- Feed pets *
- Clean sinks/mirrors *
- Scrub toilet *
- Straighten any room
- Vacuum *

❣ **Allowing for Allowances**—Every family has its own philosophy when it comes to money. Here are some of the principles that we use.

- *Allowance* is not tied to chores or responsibilities. It is given just for being part of the family, no strings attached.
- *Chores* are performed without remuneration. They are simply a responsibility attached to being part of the family. Chores are generally defined by daily use—the child helped generate the mess or benefited from it (meals, room, etc.).
- *Extra Help*, on the other hand, is rewarded, usually financially. Extra help is generally defined as work that the child did not generate, or that does not directly benefit the child (yardwork, clean attic). The parent decides when a task should be remunerated. Extra help tasks can also evolve into chores as the children get older.

*T*hree Sources of Stress in Home Management

Even with the perfect management system in place, there is no such thing as a "stress free" home environment, especially for home educators. The "stress free" home is a myth, because the sources that cause what we call stress—that gnawing feeling that you need to keep it all together all the time, but you're not—are constant and unavoidable. However, you can reduce the level of anxiety you feel at home from those stress sources. In other words, you can't control the reality of the stress factors, but you can control your anxiety about them. Essentially, a home management system is a stress reduction system. It enables you to be a better manager of the three primary and constant sources of stress in your home school life: stuff, information, and time.

❏ Stuff management

Stuff is the most easily identified constant in your life because it is so frustratingly visible: clothes, toys, books, games, junk, do-dads, sports gear, kitchen stuff, garden stuff, and so on. Everywhere you look there's a pile of stuff smirking at you, taunting you. And while you're not looking, it has babies! The more it grows, the more burdensome it becomes just having it and having to keep track of it, even if it is never used. It becomes a permanent distraction. And if it isn't controlled, it becomes like a mutating cell that spreads with cancerous oblivion throughout your house. If you don't want your stuff to control you, you need to get your stuff under control!

❏ Information management

Information may be less visible than stuff, but it is even much more pernicious. If your filing system consists mainly of the top of your desk, your dresser drawer, under the bed, somewhere on the bookshelf, or in the "everything" drawer in your kitchen, your information is probably out of control. We are being deluged with papers, forms, records, ads, faxes, magazines, catalogs and more—we are drowning in a sea of information. If you don't channel that flood, you'll be vulnerable to losing information that could have been helpful, or not being able to find information you need because it is buried under the deluge. If you're going to stay above the paper flood, you've got to manage your information flow.

❏ Time Management

Time is the least visible of the three constants, but by far the most demanding and the hardest to manage. You can't put off time until tomorrow, or negotiate with it, or try to hide from it. It demands that you do something about it now...*right* now! In the home-school home, it seems like time is the least available commodity and the most in demand. The time-eating onslaught of scheduled activities, unexpected distractions, unwanted interruptions, and little and big crises provides few breaks from the demands of time. The only way to "make" more time is to use the time you have better. That means time management.

Matthew 6:19-21
Do not store up for yourselves treasures on earth, where moth and rust destroy, and where thieves break in and steal. But store up for yourselves treasures in heaven, where moth and rust do not destroy, and where thieves do not break in and steal. For where your treasure is, there your heart will be also.

Matthew 6:33-34
But seek first his kingdom and his righteousness, and all these things will be given to you as well. Therefore do not worry about tomorrow, for tomorrow will worry about itself. Each day has enough trouble of its own.

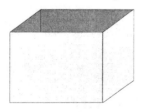

The Box

*H*ome Management "By the Box"

Why the "box"? Simply because it is the most natural way to think about organization. At some point, everything in your life goes into a box, so it seems reasonable to elevate it to an organizational principle. Its beauty and strength are its simplicity. It provides a "minimalist" approach to organizing—no expensive materials to purchase, no fancy hardware to install, no complicated instructions to decipher, no confusing systems to maintain, no thick books to read. It is really just a metaphor that you apply to life. As long as you don't get hung up on the term "box," the principle will serve you very effectively to help you bring your home environment under control and, with systems and routines, keep it in under control.

We have simply applied the organizational principle of the box to the three primary sources of stress in home management—stuff, information and time. For stuff, you will use real boxes; for information, you will use file boxes; for time, you will use time boxes. The suggestions for each of those areas are not comprehensive—they are a few ideas to help get you thinking about how to apply the principle to your own home.

❏ Management by the Box for Stuff

It is imperative to have the right attitude about the much-maligned box before you start using them in your home management. Allow me to sing the praises of boxes for a moment, slightly tongue-in-cheek. *Boxes are good. Boxes are your friends. Boxes will change your life. If you are harboring or holding on to some negative, boxist stereotype, stop! Put a lid on it! Boxes are not confining—that's just boxial prejudice. Boxes are liberating. Applied Boxology will set you free from your bondage to stuff, information and time. Boxlogics is the wave of the future. There's power in the box. Be on the box-cutting edge of home management technology. Get a box!* Having said all that, here are some suggestions for putting boxes to good use in your home management.

IN OUR HOME...

No matter how messy the rest of our learning room is, parents who come by (especially moms) nearly always comment on "the closet." Their object of interest is a converted 8' closet with three deep shelves. In the closet are about 30 small Rubbermaid lidded and labeled boxes filled with the kids' toys, educational stuff, rubber stamp collection, ad infinitum. There are also wing-lidded boxes on the floor full of stuff, and medium and large Rubbermaids full of Legos®. There are banker boxes on the top shelf full of holiday stuff, and boxes with small games on two shelves (big "pre-boxed" games are neatly stacked). There are still messes, but now they are "containable."

- First, become a box-er. Learn to look for boxes and storage containers that you can put to use in your home. If they're in a store, wait until they go on sale and then grab what you need. If they are discards, grab them quickly, before a more dedicated box-er comes along.

- Whenever possible, use a consistent size and type of box for each stuff "piling area" (a piling area is a place in your home where large amounts of stuff accumulate or are stored). Stackable boxes are by far the most space efficient way to box stuff in a closet.

- Keep the contents of boxes generally homogenous (the same kinds of stuff)—crafts, holiday, special papers, little toys, extra home school supplies, and so on. Be sure to label every box with a large removable label that can be read when the boxes are stacked.

- General rule for loose stuff in the house: If it's loose and has friends, box 'em! In other words, as you go around the house, find all the stuff that's loose and make general purpose storage boxes for it if you can.

- Purge your possessions annually. Be merciless. If you haven't used something in a year (or two, or three—whatever you're comfortable with), it's not likely that you're going to use it so why hold on to it. *Always try to make space when you take space.* You cannot displace space infinitely in your home—you've got to make room for more.

The Best Boxes for Home Management

- **Banker Boxes** The most versatile box for larger items, papers and longer term storage. Easy to stack (5-6 high), label and get into. Store in closets, or along walls. Or, get bulk paper (10 reams) boxes from a printer.
- **Rubbermaid Small/Medium Lidded** Good for "little things" that can be collected and grouped. Stackable, so you can store a lot in a small space. Clear plastic lets you see inside, colors let you organize by category.
- **Rubbermaid Large/Shallow** Generally an under-the-bed clothing storage box, but it is perfect if your kids have lots of Legos® (shallow design makes it easier to look for pieces). Good for larger papers, too.
- **Wing-Lid Crates (15 gallon)** The most durable of storage boxes. Good for garage and shed items, but also just right for blocks, Duplos®, marble tracks and other multi-piece building sets. Quick and easy access, stacking.
- **Mini Wing-Lid Crates** Hard to find, but great for kid's rooms for things like the 100's of little cars, ponies, play figures and other "collections," or just for general storage with easy access to small items.
- **Milk Crates** Good for keeping things that you want to move around the house (cleaners, supplies, books, etc.). Sturdy construction with handles makes them easy to carry. They're stackable, too.
- **Mini Milk Crates** Hard to find, but really great for storing cassette tapes and CDs, supplies, letters, and miscellaneous little stuff. Stack nicely for compact storage.
- **"Peach Crates"** If you know a grocer, the wood peach crates are useful for collecting all the children's outdoor stuff in one place.

❦ **Tour du Boxes**—Here is a very brief tour of some of our home box-works.

- 30+ small lidded Rubbermaid boxes with all the kids' little stuff, rubber stamps, supplies, etc.
- uncounted lidded banker boxes for holiday stuff, closet organization, storage, kids' keepsakes, records, and lots of other stuff.
- 10+ mini milk crates for storing CDs, cassettes, office supplies, etc.
- 20+ medium and large lidded Rubbermaid boxes for games, Legos®, crafts, Play-Dough®, blocks, hardware and tools, supplies, etc.
- 6 small milk crate style boxes for loose stuff in the boy's toy closet
- portable hanging file boxes for home-school papers and work, music, records, maps and travel information, manuals, etc.
- 10+ wing lidded storage crates for hardware, garden, bulky toys (and 24 more for books for the catalogue).

Comment: Periodical Control
Periodicals (magazines, newsletters, newspapers) are just paper weeds—they will overtake your home and choke out all signs of new organizational growth if you don't keep them weeded out. Do not save low priority magazines, mail, newspapers, or other paper information, unless you are certain you will recycle it, clip it or file it. If you're not going to, toss it!

❑ Management by the Box for Information

In the past 10-20 years, we have been hit with the initial shock wave of the information explosion. Just consider how much more paper is generated now than a generation ago, in every category—magazines, newspapers, direct-mail advertising, brochures, documents, business letters, church communications, coupons, books, and more. And the main shock wave may still be on the way! However, you can protect yourself with some basic filing systems—information boxes—that will "contain" the blast.

• A filing cabinet is nothing more than a big metal box with moving parts. File folders simply let you subdivide your box for storing information. Create one or as many kinds of files (i.e., file drawers are boxes devoted to a category) as you need to control the information flow—home, home school, action file, business, topical file and such.

• If a filing cabinet does not match or fit into your decor, there are numerous filing options available—portable file boxes, plastic milk crates (with hanging file tracks built in), and one-drawer files (that fit under a table) among others. You might choose different kinds for different tasks—portable for financial, milk crate for home school, and one-drawer for topical research.

• Create a "holding area" where any new information goes until it can be properly boxed (filed). Use whatever you like best—flat files, desktop action files, manila files, just a p.o.b. (plain old box). Look at it as a kind of paper purgatory before it goes either to eternal glory in your filing system, or eternal separation in the wastebasket.

• Use records storage boxes (such as banker boxes) for bulk information, old files, seldom accessed papers, memorabilia, and the like. Label the box clearly with a removable label on the end. Store it out of sight, but where you can get to it if you need it. You can buy banker boxes in five packs that are flat and easy to store.

IN OUR HOME...

We're still trying to tame the paper beast. We have several files that work well, but we still need more. I (Clay) have at least five in my office, plus two vertical files for current projects, and a "paper purgatory" stack of flat files where all the "to be filed" stuff gets stuffed. In no particular order, I manage: an action file (intuitive) for anything current or short term; a family file (intuitive) for financial records and useful information (medical, health, travel, etc.); a future projects file (intuitive) for scraps of ideas and random notes; a topical file (alpha-numeric) for clippings, Bible studies, articles and the like; a business file (intuitive) for Whole Heart Ministries; and a catalog file (alphabetical) for books. Older records are kept in labeled banker boxes. Sally has the home-schooling file and a personal file (both intuitive). You can definitely file it all under "Arrrrgh!"

EDUCATING THE WHOLEHEARTED CHILD

The Best Filing Systems for Home Management

A filing system is, in essence, an extension of your mind. It needs to reflect the way you think about information—how you organize it and keep track of it in your mind. A mismatch will result in misplaced and missing files because your filing system thinks differently than you do. Following are the best.

• Alphabetical File (A/B/C...)

A slightly more organized step up from the Intuitive File system. You need a file folder divider for each letter of the alphabet (or 25, with Mac and XYZ) to separate your file folders. Your divider can be a file, also, for keeping miscellaneous materials that don't need a separate file folder. New material is filed alphabetically behind the file divider corresponding to the first letter of the topic. To prevent the file from looking like it is totally disorganized, file labels should all be placed in one position (usually left or center; or dividers center, and topics left).

• Alpha-Numeric File (1-Reading, 2-Writing, 3-Math...)

Best for large files containing multiple topics, such as a research or topical file. File folders are numbered sequentially starting with "1" and followed by the topic description. Each new topic is entered on the next unused file folder in sequence, typically with five labels across the drawer. Whenever a new topic is assigned to a file number, on an unused ruled 3x5 index card the topic is written in the upper left and the file reference number in the upper right of the card. File cards are then arranged alphabetically in a 3x5 card file box. To find filed material, look under the topic in the card file box to obtain the file number. Cross-referenced files can also be included on the 3x5 card. This method will hold as many files as you have room for.

• Consonant-Vowel File (Aa/Ae/Ai/Ao/Au/Ba/Be/Bi/Bo/Bu...)

A research style file without the need for a 3x5 card file. Use 129 file folders (all must be 1/5 cut). Each set of five is labeled using a letter of the alphabet followed by a vowel (see above for example), for all 26 letters of the alphabet. File material is identified and filed by the first letter and first vowel of its topic (ex.: Family under **Fa**, Children under **Ci**, Internet under **Ie**, and so on). Very quick and easy for filing, but requires being able to recall what topic you would file something under. Cross-reference sheets can be placed in other file folders referring to the file where the information is located.

• Intuitive File (Bills/Correspondence/Pending...)

Everybody's "default" file system. Best for a file with random categories of information that you want to be able to access quickly. The trick with this system is to have enough files, but not so many that you forget what and where they are. Identify the categories of information you need to keep at hand, and then create a file for each one. Arrange the files in whatever order works for you. You can subdivide the file by larger categories using a different color of hanging files for each category. Categories might include Action file (Bills, Current, Pending, ToDo, etc.), Home Schooling, Correspondence, Finances, Consumer Information, Projects, and the like...you decide.

Comment: Hang It All, Get the Best!

Yes, they are more expensive, and yes, they are worth the extra money. Hanging file folders are so much better than those droopy old manila-vanilla file folders that they cannot even be fairly compared (it would be like comparing quill pens and ballpoint pens). Hanging file folders are incredibly versatile since you can move the plastic label holders to any of nine positions. Add color-coding and you can create file systems within file systems. They are also more economical in the long run since you can easily change the paper file labels that slip into the plastic holders. They almost never wear out, and the metal edges make them very easy to handle. They will work with any file system (facing page), and you can even pass them down to your children. They come in standard office-green, or in a variety of different colors. Most file cabinets and portable files are designed now to use them without any modification, or an simple metal frame will fit right in and get you hanging.

❑ Management by the Box for Time

No matter how much you might decry the accelerated pace of life, or how much you try to simplify and de-clutter your calendar, it seems that a planner or organizer has become as necessary as a wristwatch in our time-crunched culture. The calendar becomes even more crowded when you bring the children home to home school! An organizer or planner is simply a useful tool to help you "redeem the time." It allows you to visualize the "time boxes" in your day and week so you can use your time more wisely.

- No matter what kind of calendar, planner or organizer you own, the real test of effectiveness for any of them is: *Will you use it?* A simple weekly planning calendar and an ordinary "to do" list may be all you need to get started in managing time (see Appendix). Or, if you want something more developed, choose a calendar style that provides enough room to break each day into at least three segments (morning, afternoon, evening), such as a two-page-per-week style found in many organizers. You can spend a lot of money on a beautiful organizer, but if it does not "think" the way you do—if it does not fit your own mental patterns—you probably will not use it. Use what you will use.

- Unless you are a veteran organizer user, it is probably best to use a different set of planning sheets for home-schooling lesson plans and records (see samples in Appendix). Use your personal calendar or organizer to map out your week into time boxes, schedule appointments, keep a running ToDo list, and keep other notes and information you need handy (phone directory, grocery list, meeting notes, etc.).

- A calendar or daily planner is just a box for time. To be a good home manager of time, you need to train yourself to think of your week in terms of "time boxes." A time box is a 2-4 hour segment of time that can either be filled with specific tasks, activities or goals, or be left empty. It is a single unit of time, not a series of discreet time segments. For example, Tuesdays from 8:30-12:00 noon is a box for home schooling; 1:00-3:00 is a box for discovery studies; 3:00-6:00 is an unscheduled box; and so on. Each day, because of groups and lessons, will be a little different.

In a sudden flash of reality, Harriett realized that she could save more time if she would just learn to file her papers in the wastebasket.

- Think of meal times and bedtimes as "lids" for your time boxes. Divide each period of time before and after the lids into one or two time boxes (ex., a lunch lid, followed by two two-hour time boxes in the afternoon).

- Group similar events and commitments into each time box whenever possible (ex., errands in a box, home-school time in a box, etc.). Once a time box is closed for that day, don't go back to what you had planned in it until the next day. In other words, don't borrow time from other boxes. If you're behind, it's better to close that box and just wait until the next day to try to catch up.

- Don't try to plan activities by time segments within your time boxes, such as what you will do every 15 or 30 minutes. Rather, plan your general goals for that time box, estimating the time it will take you to complete each goal (so you don't plan 4 hours of goals for a 3 hour time box), and then place them all in that time box without regard to segments of time. Again, see the box as a single unit of time, not as a string of time segments.

- Always leave at least two time boxes empty each week for flexibility and spontaneity. You should always build unscheduled time into your schedule to relax, catch up on missed work, do something new and unplanned, or whatever. The basic principle is: don't overplan. Keep a sheet in your organizer of "things to do to fill an empty time box." You'll be surprised at what you can get done.

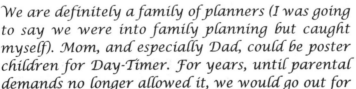

IN OUR HOME...

We are definitely a family of planners (I was going to say we were into family planning but caught myself). Mom, and especially Dad, could be poster children for Day-Timer. For years, until parental demands no longer allowed it, we would go out for breakfast once a week with our Day-Timers in hand just to do planning, even though most of the time we didn't really need to. Now, we really need to do planning, but we have to do it whenever we can—before breakfast, while the kids get ready for bed, in the car, late at night. We do, however, try to set aside a half-day together about once a quarter to do major planning, and to set goals for ourselves and for the children. Sarah is the first child to catch the planning bug. I (Dad) created her very own child-friendly "My Days and Ways" organizer with pages for, among other areas, calendar, planning, financial stewardship, spiritual, and correspondence. I gave her one of my old binders and now she really enjoys piddling in her planner, just like Mom and Dad. My goal now is to create some new pages for defining life goals and plans that she can begin to work on and think through as she approaches her young adult years. Now there are three family members with organizers attached to their fingers. Wonder who's going to be next?

Quick 'n Easy Meals—
Keep a supply of low-prep meals in your arsenal for when you're battling against time or weariness.

- *Snack Dinner* with popcorn, fruit, raw veggies, cheese and crackers, muffins.
- *Toasty Tostados* with chips, refritos, meat, cheese, lettuce.
- *Shepherd's Meal* with soup, wheat bread, cheese, and fruit.
- *Mix 'n Mex* with tortillas, chicken, cheese, refritos and other fixings.
- *Tater Plate* with baked potatoes and green salad with fixings.
- *Breakfast Dinner* with cereal, or eggs and toast.

Cooking to the Max— Depending on your freezer space, use one of the following strategies for making the most of your cooking time.

- *30 Meals Plan* Set aside one day a month to cook and freeze thirty main-course meals for your family. It saves time, energy, clean up, and money. There are several good books available explaining how to do this.
- *Multiple Meals Plan* Whatever you are cooking, always double or triple the batch and freeze the extra in meal-size containers. It's a simple way to cut your cooking and cleaning time by a half or more. Keep a good supply of plastic freezer bags on hand. Always date and label.

The Clean Up Game—
When the house gets out of control, turn the task of cleaning up into a game. Tell the kids you'll set the timer for X minutes. If the house is cleaned up by then, they get a special treat. Use whatever will motivate them the most—cookies, tea party, video.

❏ Moms, You Know Your Home Is Organized When...

Home is your domain, Mom. When it is under control, you are free to fulfill your God-given role to nurture and care for your family. But when it gets out of control, it is a distraction and a constant drain on your spiritual and physical energy. The principles of home management in this chapter can help you get your house under control and keep it that way. If you're distracted, but you're not sure what the problem is, the following list will help you pinpoint where you might need to focus your management efforts. Moms, you know your home is organized when...

❏ ...the clutter is under control, the stuff is subdued, the kids know where things should go.

❏ ...a basic weekly schedule is in place for chores, schoolwork, shopping and other family activities.

❏ ...household routines are predictable so family members know what to expect most of the time.

❏ ...important household and home-school items can be easily located and kept in a dedicated storage area.

❏ ...important information and papers are readily accessible.

❏ ...incoming information is quickly handled with temporary and permanent files.

❏ ...meals are on the table in a timely fashion.

❏ ...children are ready for bed at a reasonable hour.

❏ ...you are in bed at a not-too-unreasonable hour.

❏ ...you have 15-30 minutes for tea in the afternoon. ☺

❑ Dads, You Know Your Wife Is Happy When You...

When it comes to home management, Dad, your God-given role is to insure that your wife is happy and fulfilled in her role as a homemaker and keeper. If you don't fulfill *your* role, nothing will be in control, and your wife will not be happy (and "If Mama ain't happy, ain't nobody happy."). Your role is very simple—it is to be like Jesus to your wife, not looking to be served, but seeking to serve, and to give your life as a sacrifice for her joy (*Eph. 5:22-33*). Dads, you know your wife is happy when you...

❑ ...initiate and lead regular planning times with your wife, without the children (and you plan the baby-sitter!).

❑ ...take the kids regularly for several hours on planned, meaningful outings...i.e., take them *away* (see column). Taking them to McDonald's PlayLand while you have coffee and read the paper does not qualify as an outing. Your wife wants to know that the time will be more than just babysitting.

❑ ...assist with the "Uppers" whenever possible, and be sensitive to the "Downers."

❑ ...defend and protect your wife's time boxes against time consumers (people, distractions, children, calls, etc.).

❑ ...plan in time boxes to be with your children during the day and the week, especially when it gives your wife free time, or when it makes her tasks easier (such as while she is preparing dinner).

❑ ...budget in your heart and mind (and checkbook) for paid household help, if you are able, especially when your children are young. *Any* help goes a long way.

❑ ...prepare an arsenal of ideas that you can do with the children on a moment's notice (see column).

❑ ...are sensitive to the end of the day stress level, planning ahead to take control of the kids at the end of the day even when you are tired.

❣ **Do-Dads**—Activities Dad can do with the kids to give Mom time alone.

Big Times (outings)
- Take them to the park.
- Take them to a nature center.
- Take them to a lake or beach area.
- Take them to a museum.
- Ride bikes in the country with them.
- Take them on a mini field trip.
- Go on a hike with them.
- Go swimming with them.
- Take them to the library reading time.
- Play tennis with them.
- Take them to special events.
- Take them to seasonal festivals.

Little Times (innings)
- Read books to them.
- Play a game with them.
- Throw a ball or shoot baskets with them.
- Take a walk around the block with them.
- Teach them something.
- Clean up the yard together.
- Make a tent with them.
- Build something with them.
- Give them "driving" lessons.
- Play table tennis with them.
- Overhaul bicycles (clean, tighten, etc.) together.

❣ **Dad-dates**—Every child needs individual time with Dad. Plan regular times to take each child on a "date" to be together and talk about life.
- Go out for breakfast, child's choice of restaurant, even if it's the donut shop. Go as early as possible to make it more special.
- Go to a favorite park, playground, or outdoor area. Take a picnic meal or snack. Play and talk.
- With sons, plan an overnight campout. With daughters, plan a dress up night out for dinner.
- Take them for a special shopping trip.

CHAPTER EIGHT

Lifestyle... Making It Work

Mother~The Heartbeat of Your Home!

No one can replace the influence you alone can have on your children! However, your influence won't come from having read all the right books on motherhood, or listened to the latest parenting "experts." It will come because of your *faithfulness*—because you faithfully follow God's design for motherhood. Faithfulness is simply learning to see with God's eyes and seize with God's hands the hundreds of small opportunities you have every day to influence your children—to shape their values and attitudes, build their faith, discipline their disobedience, inspire their genius, nurture their emotions, train their habits, cultivate their character and set their feet on the path of righteousness.

Being that faithful mother, though, is not as idealistic as it sounds—it is, in reality, a daily and hourly challenge. That is why so many mothers confess that the home-schooling lifestyle is so much harder than they had imagined. It is demanding and constant and, with only a few exceptions, there is no time off from the day-to-day responsibility of caring for your children from the time they get up in the morning until the time they go to sleep at night. The reality of home schooling is that God is asking you to become a *servant* to your children, willing to sacrifice your time, body, energy, emotions and expectations for them. That takes more than natural strength—it takes supernatural strength. It takes the kind of faithfulness that comes only from trusting God and depending upon his grace every day. But that's exactly how God wants you to live! He wants to hear you say, every day, *"I can do everything through him who gives me strength."* And as you do you'll find you are becoming a more mature wife—supporting, loving and accepting your husband. You'll find you are becoming a more mature mother—loving and affirming your children, in spite of their immaturity. You'll find you are becoming a more mature woman—weathering with grace the storms of life, and strengthening all within your home domain.

Life will *always* be unpredictable—your schedule *will* fall apart, home schooling *will* occasionally grind to a halt, and the house *will* at times seem like someone detonated a stuff-bomb. Yet if you are trusting in the Lord and depending upon his grace, you can still accomplish your purposes as a mother. If your heart is in conflict with the Lord, no amount of organization, planning or scheduling will make you a more effective mother. If, though, you are nurturing your heart for God, strengthening your faith in him, letting the Spirit control your attitude, and being as faithful as you know how to be, you can be assured you are fulfilling God's purposes for you. Your children will follow your heartbeat.

Proverbs 31:26-31
She speaks with wisdom, and faithful instruction is on her tongue. She watches over the affairs of her household and does not eat the bread of idleness. Her children arise and call her blessed; her husband also, and he praises her: "Many women do noble things, but you surpass them all." Charm is deceptive, and beauty is fleeting; but a woman who fears the LORD is to be praised. Give her the reward she has earned, and let her works bring her praise at the city gate.

66 *There is no nobler career than that of motherhood at its best. There are no possibilities greater, and in no other sphere does failure bring more serious penalties...To attempt this task unprepared and untrained is tragic, and its results affect generations to come. On the other hand there is no higher height to which humanity can attain than that occupied by a converted, heaven-inspired, praying mother.*
Anon, quoted by Elizabeth Elliot, *The Shaping of a Christian Family*, Word, 1992

66 *The mother's heart is the child's schoolroom.*
Henry Ward Beecher

Know Your Purpose

As a Christian home-schooling mother, you need to have a very clear sense of your purpose in life—why you are at home doing what you are doing. Not just to be able to explain or defend your lifestyle, but to be able to better express it in your day-to-day living. *What you believe about God's design for mothers will determine how you live.* Consider the following biblical purposes for mothers as you define God's purpose for your life.

- **To bring order to your home** You have a mandate from God to bring order to your home (to "subdue" it). By God's perfect design, it is your primary domain of influence, and your calling is to bring all aspects of your home life—children, meals, decor, schedule, environment—into subjection to the design for living that God has revealed in his Word. If you want to find fulfillment as a mother, you will find it only in the biblical pattern of motherhood. It's the only way you'll ever feel "at home" as a mother.

- **To nurture your children** Like Eve, the "mother of all the living," you have the God-given ability to impart life to your children. Not only physiological life, but abundant and eternal life. You will place them on the path of life in Christ, and teach them how to walk it in faith. You will gently guide them into a living relationship with Jesus, train them in godly character, and instruct them in biblical truth. What your children become will be in large part because of your nurturing, life-giving influence in their lives. Your children will look to you for sustenance and God has given you the privilege of caring for their needs.

- **To cultivate relationships** God has uniquely equipped women for relationship. Your children will learn much about how to "love God" and, especially, how to "love others" through you. All ministry begins with a commitment to relationship that can be modeled in your home—through opening your home in hospitality, ministering to others in need, or even just through kindness shown in Christ's name.

- **To grow in maturity and obedience** Your example of being "self-controlled and pure" not only creates a pattern for your children to follow, but it also results in a home that is peaceful and Christ-centered. A mother who is growing in maturity and in obedience to God will have a tremendous impact on her children. Your example of virtue will live on in your children, and even your children's children.

- **To respect and help your husband** The Christian life is based on the principle of submission—husbands to God, wives to husbands, children to parents, church members to church leaders, citizens to government, employees to employers. By submitting to your husband, you become a living illustration for your children of what submission looks like. God wants you to love your husband by showing him respect and being his helper. Your attitude toward your husband (and his towards you) will say more to your children than a hundred lessons.

Know Your Priorities

Everyone has priorities. If someone wants to know your priorities, they need only observe how you spend your time. It makes little difference what you *say* your priorities are—it's what you *do* that reveals your true priorities. Of all the opportunities and options before you, your priorities are the ones you *should* and *must* do, so you *do*. The essence of priorities, then, is limitations—you must voluntarily limit other things of less importance in order to accomplish the things that are the most important. Your most pressing limitation is time. You have only one opportunity to "train a child in the way he should go," and once the window of opportunity closes as your child enters young adulthood, *you can never open it again.* However, if you invest yourself in your child's life, shining as much light as you can in the open windows of his heart during childhood, then you can count on God's plan that "when he is old he will not turn from it." It all comes down to priorities, and setting priorities means accepting some limitations.

- **Limit your expectations** There are always other things that you would love to do—working, eating out with friends, a sport or hobby, shopping—things that other mothers with their children in school have time to do. But as a home-schooling mother you have chosen a different set of priorities. Your priorities now revolve around doing everything you can to raise wholehearted Christian children. Your expectations about life must change accordingly.

- **Limit your commitments** Knowing that your priorities are different will limit what you will commit your time and family to doing. Your priorities will lead you to say "yes" to some things and "no" to others, even if the others are attractive, desirable things. You are simply maximizing your efforts and reducing unnecessary commitments in order to do God's will for your life. Whatever you give up will be compensated for by the blessings you gain.

- **Limit your objectives** There will never be enough time to do all that you want to do in your home school, so don't even try to! It will take everything you can muster just to stick to your priorities and still live a balanced Christian life. It takes time—lots of it—to build close, productive relationships with your children. You need time to communicate, build trust, love them; to listen, talk and answer questions; to offer counsel and advice, comfort, encourage. Limiting your objectives allows you more time to do fewer things more effectively.

- **Limit your activities** You need to be at home building an atmosphere that is calm, secure and inviting. That is "priority one" (after your relationship with God, of course). Don't let outside activities rob you of the brief and fleeting time you have to influence your children's minds and hearts. Put personal goals, desires, and activities on hold for a later season of life—this is the time (while they're young) and the place (at home) your children need you most. Limit your activities and spend your time at home.

❝ *God could not be everywhere, and therefore he made mothers.*
Jewish Proverb

Comment: Homeward Bound
New home-schooling moms are often over-concerned about what their kids might be "missing" by being home. This novice home schooler insecurity often leads a mom to overcompensate by getting her children involved in too many replacement activities. The result, of course, is even less time at home and, therefore, even less direct influence on her children—the very reason most begin home schooling in the first place!

❣ Out, Out...—Minimize wasted time in your home by reducing unnecessary distractions—television, telephone, newspaper, magazines, frivolous meetings. You'll be amazed how much time is preserved with just a few controls.

❣ Just Say "I'll Let You Know"—Make it a habit not to commit to anything on the first hearing. Simply say, "Let me ask my spouse." This one little phrase will reap bushels of time by keeping you from making those regretted, hasty commitments that are neither purposeful nor strategic. Learning not to say "Yes" at the first hearing is the first step in becoming proficient in the home-schooling skill of strategic under-commitment.

❣ One Thing?—Try to use the "this one thing I do" principle—one church ministry, one lesson, one sport, one night out, and so on.

Philippians 3:13,14
...But one thing I do: Forgetting what is behind and straining toward what is ahead, I press on toward the goal to win the prize for which God has called me heavenward in Christ Jesus.

♥ Planning Help—The Planning Forms included in the Appendix will help you get a handle on weekly, monthly and quarterly planning. There is also a calendar/planner blank that you can use. The forms will help you get in the habit of planning, and help you establish educational goals and routines.

♥ All In a Year's Work—Flexible year-round schooling allows you to "strike while the iron is hot." During the indoor seasons when the weather prevents going outside as much, focus more on drill and workbook work. During the outdoor seasons, focus more on field trips, nature walks, and outdoor learning experiences. The key is flexibility. Teach several weeks, then take a break when life demands it. Take breaks for holidays, out-of-town company, short trips and catch-up weeks, then return to teaching. Steady progress is the measure of your success—have you accomplished in a year what you planned to finish?

♥ Plan Away—Plan a way to get away to plan. Find a time when you can leave the children with someone and you and your spouse can go for an extended breakfast, evening or overnight to plan for the coming weeks or months. Trade off with another home-school family for overnight childcare. It's good for your family *and* good for your marriage!

Know Your Plans

When you plan your life, it is another way of saying that you are confident and secure enough about your priorities to actually do something about them. By making and following plans, you are making yourself accountable to what God has put on your heart to do. It's axiomatic, but it's as true in home schooling as it is in business management—if you fail to plan, you plan to fail.

❑ Plan your life to accomplish your purposes.

- **Plan and evaluate** In order to be effective in home education, planning is a necessity. That does not mean every 15 minute segment of the day must be scheduled! It simply means that you should know at any time most of what you want to accomplish with your children, and how you're going to do it this week, month, quarter or year. Planning also lets you evaluate what hasn't been accomplished so you can adjust your plans accordingly.

- **Use flexible year-round schooling** Real life is not divided in neat little calendar blocks like in school. Flexible year-round schooling means letting real life set your schedule, rather than trying to fit real life into a rigid schedule of weeks on and off, semesters, quarters or whatever. Home is not school! Real life at home requires flexibility—don't create a rigid schedule that will set you up to fail! Know what you want to accomplish, plan how to do it, then relax, live, learn and enjoy your children. The goal is steady progress.

- **Keep a long-term perspective** Learning is a process, not a procedure. Steady progress, not constant success, is the goal, and that takes time. Progress seems slower when your children are younger, but the reality is that they grow in spurts mentally just as they do physically. Learning to discern their pace and rhythm of learning takes time—time to see what comes easily to your children as well as what is slow to develop, and time to give them individual attention. Perseverance, persistence and patience are the keys to success in home schooling. Keep your eye on the ultimate goal, not on each stride to be run.

Harriett reviews her personal goals for the next quarter. Uh oh, looks like she forgot one!

❏ Plan your home for home schooling.

In order to home school well, your home must be at the center of your life as a mother—the hub of the wheel of life in your family. If you know what you want to accomplish in your children's lives, and you are clear about your priorities, then your home will reflect that. Though it is the center of your life, your home should always be a means to an end, never an end in itself. In other words, it is a tool that you use to build your family. Your home is the primary "domain" that God has given to you to rule over. He wants you to use it skillfully and wisely.

- **Atmosphere** Atmosphere is the attitude of your home. It determines how your children *feel* about being at home—either uptight and anxious in an adult's world, or free and relaxed in a child-friendly world. If you are holding onto "House Beautiful" ideals, they must inevitably give way to "House Useable" realities—the dinner table gives way to a craft, wall space gives way to papers and time lines, floor space gives way to a creative project, shelf space gives way to books and creations. Every room will, in some way, at some time, be affected by the activities related to home education. You cannot avoid it—home schooling is messy because children are messy. If you learn to accept the mess, your children will feel more accepted, too. *Your* attitude will determine the atmosphere.

- **Environment** Environment is the setting of your home. It is whatever is around you that influences you, or your children. Studies show that children grow intellectually in a home environment where they are surrounded by easily accessible books, creative options, music and art. Genius is cultivated in a home environment that encourages a child to read, explore, discover, question, observe and learn. Wherever they turn, your children should run into something that is interesting, challenging or stimulating. But the home environment also needs to be characterized by personal warmth and beauty so your children come to value the special place they'll remember as "home." As with atmosphere, you are the key to creating a unique, personal environment in your home.

> ❝ *I am sure that there is no place in the world where your message would not be enhanced by your making the place (whether tiny or large, a hut or a palace) orderly, artistic and beautiful with some form of creativity, some form of 'art'. It goes without saying, too, that 'The Environment', which is you should be an environment which speaks of the wonder of the Creator who made you.*
>
> Edith Schaeffer, *The Hidden Art of Homemaking*, Tyndale, 1971

❣ **Adapt-a-Home**—If you have a home and don't plan to move, take a fresh look at your floorplan through a home-schooling lens. Ask what you need and then evaluate how your present house can meet those needs. If you decide to remodel, ask what you can do to improve both the atmosphere and the environment of your home for home schooling. If you can't add a room, convert a garage (children are more important than cars!). Keep in mind, remodeling is an investment in your children.

❣ **House Plans**—If you are in the market to build or to buy an existing home, establish some criteria for evaluating the house plans or houses you look at. Decide 1) what features will make the home work *for* you in home schooling, and 2) what features would work *against* you. You'll make trade-offs on the final decision, but you'll move in knowing it is a "home-schooling home."

IN OUR HOME...

When the Lord moved us to family property in the country, he gave us the exciting opportunity to remodel a home to complement our home-centered approach to learning and life. A garage became the "home education room" with floor to ceiling built-in bookshelves and desk units, a deep-shelved closet for games and creative stuff (the "Lego® Lab"), and room for a large reading couch and computer corner. An enclosed porch became a combination breakfast nook and craft center (vinyl floor, of course). We invested, too, in an outdoor playground, especially for our two boys. And, just as important, we carved out a "tea and talk" sitting area in our bedroom. It is such a blessing to be in a home-schooling friendly house.

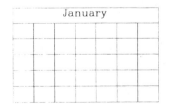
❑ Plan your year around holidays, special days and traditions.

Holidays, special days and traditions should stand out as the bright yellow Hi-Liter marked sections of your life story. They illustrate and accentuate the messages, values and gifts that are unique to your family's Christian heritage. They also emphasize and reinforce the truths and convictions that you want to take root in the hearts of your children, and provide them with rich food for their memories. Everything associated with holidays and traditions—decor, food, child-made crafts, music, readings, sharing, and more—creates an emotional anchor to hold memories deep in your children's hearts for a lifetime. Those anchors also become sources of stability and security for your children as they navigate the sea of life.

- Establish an annual Family Day to remember and celebrate God's faithfulness to your family (see facing page). Make it a special day that your family always looks forward to. Invite other family members or friends to be a part of your day. Show them how to have their own.

- At all holidays and special days, encourage family members to tell stories about their lives, especially the older members of the family who are present. Tell stories of faith that relate to the holiday, or even just add color and warmth to it. Tell stories of history, or just humorous family stories. Encourage the children to share stories and memories, too. Meal time is a convenient time for storytelling. Always turn on a tape recorder when a family "elder" shares a story—you never know if you'll hear it again!

- Select a holiday or special theme for each month. Decorate your dining table accordingly, and plan devotional projects around those days and themes. Use the weeks before certain holidays for an extended study or reading of a longer book. Holidays best suited for extended studies include: Christmas (Advent), Easter, Independence Day, Reformation Day, and Thanksgiving.

- Turn birthdays into family celebrations. Invite families you are close to over for each child's birthday dinner. Have everyone share how they have seen the birthday child grow in maturity during the previous year, new skills and talents they have noticed, and what they especially like about him or her. Then spend some time praying for that child.

- Use holidays and special days to reinforce current study emphases in history, Bible, or other subjects. Save special books and tapes for those times. For example, when studying the Civil War, read a biography about Lincoln for President's Day. Or, when studying Rome, read a historical novel at tea time.

- Create ways for everyone in the family—from the oldest right down to the very youngest—to have a significant role in any holiday celebrations. And always try to give special honor and recognition to the family "elders" (parents and grandparents).

- Make and use centerpieces and decorations that can be used every year. Whatever you purchase or make for a holiday, carefully store it in a clearly labeled box with a lid (such as a banker's box). You'll save yourself the energy of thinking of something all over again the next year! Just pull it out of the box and you're ready for the season.

- Holidays provide a meaningful opportunity for your children to do crafts that everyone will see and admire. Have them make decorations, decorate their rooms, make special place cards for the table, puff-paint tee shirts for everyone, or make special posters. And rather than buying overpriced holiday "greeting cards," have your children make their own cards for birthdays, holidays and such.

- Build on traditions whenever possible by repetition and familiarity. Use the same decorations, play and sing familiar songs, serve the same food, do the same things. Repetition is a fundamental principle of learning for children. Repeated traditions become the moments your children will remember most clearly and vividly, and which will define their memories of childhood and you. Beyond just reinforcing memories, though, the assurance that "we do this every year" also creates a sense of stability and security in a child.

IN OUR HOME...

When our children were still young, we started the tradition of having an annual Family Day. We decided to make ours the Saturday before Labor Day. It was inspired by the account of Joshua's memorial stones which were to remind the children of coming generations of God's power, faithfulness, sovereignty and love (Josh. 4:19-24). We make it a whole day of family togetherness. We start off the day with a special breakfast (Mom's homemade whole-wheat cinnamon rolls). We read some Scriptures on family and take a little time to affirm all the things we like about our family and one another. Then we get out the photo albums from the previous year or two and spend time just remembering the events of our lives. We normally prepare a fun picnic lunch and then go on an outing for the rest of the morning and into the afternoon. Later in the day we might play games or watch a good family movie. Then we have a special dinner to lead into our Family Day "memorial stone" time. First, we read the account of Joshua and the memorial stones to teach the principle of remembering what God has done in our lives. Then we share and discuss all the ways God has been faithful to us that year. Each "memorial stone" of God's faithfulness is written at the top of a piece of paper. Those are parceled out to different family members who then draw a picture to illustrate their memorial. The "memorial stones" are kept in a Family Day notebook and reviewed each year. We also have annual verses selected for each family member. We spend time in prayer, followed by a final fun activity for the kids and a favorite desert.

Holidays are God's idea. He created several for the Jews to celebrate and reinforce the memory of what he had done, and to teach the children. The Jews liked the idea so much, they created more holidays, ones that God had not told them directly to practice. Whatever the reason for the holiday, though, they were always more than just recreational—they were first and foremost educational. In the same way that the Jews followed God's pattern for new holidays, Christianity has developed its own holiday traditions. Holidays such as Christmas and Easter have no biblical mandate, but they are patterned after God's use of holidays as a way to remember and learn about God's actions in history and in our lives. Since the principle of the holiday is trans-cultural and universal, the Christian family can benefit from it as well. For the Christian home-schooling family, holidays can be an effective way of using the God-given seasonal cycles to remember and to learn. God is never opposed to traditions per se—only to empty traditions that serve no purpose for him. When our lives—including our holidays and traditions— reflect his reality, then he is honored. (Rom. 14:5,6a)

❣ **Future Moms & Dads Days**—Use Mothers' and Fathers' Days to talk about the joys of parenting, and to talk to your children about being future parents. On Mother's Day, include your daughters as "future mothers," with both Dad and sons honoring them. On Father's Day, include your sons as "future fathers," with both Mom and daughters honoring them. Recognize your children's future roles as extended family, and as the recipients and guardians of your family's heritage and values. Pray for their future spouses and children, that they would pass on your legacy.

❑ Plan your days around mealtimes.

You have to eat every day, so make that time count. Use those 1,095 opportunities to be together to enhance your home schooling, and to impart your family's values and beliefs. Make meals servants to your goals rather than just "eat and run" breaks. Whether it's cheese and crackers or pot roast and potatoes, each meal can be turned into a strategic session in your home-school schedule—a memory-making hour of discussion, laughter, debate, Bible discovery, narration, book-talk, and life-in-progress wisdom and counsel.

Mealtime Memory Making

Every family's schedule is different, but it is important to sit down together to at least one leisurely meal each day. It's another one of those anchors in your children's lives that they will remember and cherish. When you do eat together, it only takes a little effort to enhance your time together.

- When you eat at the table, whether the meal is casual or formal, show that it is an important occasion by setting a clean, attractive table with a full place setting. Be sure the dining area is clean and neat, too.

- Add personal touches to make every mealtime a special occasion—candlelight in the winter, a variety of background music, place cards with Scriptures or notes, a "You're special today!" red plate, or other memorable touches. Get in the habit of changing your centerpiece periodically to reflect study or holiday themes. Be creative!

- Create special theme nights, with or without advance notice to the rest of the family. Make them different, fun and meaningful—"What I want to be when I grow up" night, "Secret Mission" day, "God's hands in our family" week, and so on. Decorate the table accordingly.

❧ **Center on the Table**—Plan ahead to make meaningful seasonal centerpieces for your table, such as:
- *February/Presidents Day*—Lincoln Log® cabin, picture of President Lincoln, pennies, books on Lincoln. Also for President Washington.
- *July/Independence Day*—Minutemen cut-outs, American flags, Declaration of Independence, books about Revolutionary War.
- *September/Missions Month*—Globe, foreign stamps & coins, foreign artifacts and crafts, pictures and biographies of famous missionaries.

❧ **Set the Theme**—Start making a list of theme ideas that you can use to make meals memorable. Creatively customize the meal and the table to emphasize the theme. A few ideas to get you started:
- *When I grow up I'm going to be a...*—Put a variety of do-dads on the table to represent different professions. Brainstorm occupational names for the meal (ex.: Fireman's Feast, Police Plate, etc.). Each child shares one or more thoughts of what they might want to be. Parents tell how they picture their children.
- *Secret Mission Meal*—Decorate table with a secret agent, spy or detective motif. First night, put everyone's name in one hat and "missions" (clean room, fix a treat, etc.) in another. Each person draws out a name and a secret mission. Each tries to fulfill the mission without being detected. Report on their missions the next night.
- *God's Hands*—Everyone shares how they have seen God's hands at work in their family during a one week period. Decorate with a Bible/prayer theme and motif. Simple meal.

IN OUR HOME...

While living in Europe, our family developed a taste for tea and for tea time! It followed us back to the states, and now Sunday afternoon tea time has become a regular, anticipated, rarely missed fixture in our week. Whether we're just having tea and cinnamon toast, or a full-blown high tea with sandwiches, fruits and a special dessert, we take time to set the table nicely and use our special Austrian tea set (a bit beaten now, but still beloved). We always put on some beautiful or interesting music to provide the proper ambiance. Sometimes, we even practice being "civilized," as though we were taking tea with the Queen and must at least appear that we know how to behave. To make it more enjoyable, we save some special books to be read only during tea time, such as James Herriott's stories or new illustrated story books we have discovered. Everyone in the family looks forward to our Sunday afternoon tea time.

- Keep several books nearby that can be read aloud. You will cover a lot of extra pages of good literature in a year just by getting in the habit of reading a chapter at the table occasionally. Linking good food and good stories is a good way to create a good memory! Have Dad read.

- Regularly prepare special meals that your children will remember as "our family" meals (desserts, too!). Come up with fun, original meals and creative variations to old dishes. It puts the focus on "the meal" and not the food.

Dinner Table Discipleship

Mealtime is a natural time for Dad to lead family devotions, whether they are planned or spontaneous. For a short time, he has a "captive," quiet, relaxed audience. You can help to enhance those times by managing the table environs.

- Keep a Bible, a Bible storybook and child-friendly devotional materials nearby. If it's in sight and in reach, it helps to create both a devotional habit and spontaneity.

- Make a habit of writing down spiritual discussion questions, or Scriptures with discussion questions, on 3x5 index cards. Keep them in a handy file box so you can "put them on the table" with the rest of the meal. Discussion always goes well with dinner.

- Keep a prayer reminder list and/or prayer journal handy to stimulate prayer times. Also keep missionary letters at hand. When you pray for the meal, pray for a missionary or ministry.

Tips for Table Talk

Good conversations don't just happen—they grow in well-cultivated soil. The following tips will create good soil for your table talk.

Manners count. Proper manners show respect for others at the table. Basic civil behavior is a prerequisite for civil, fruitful conversation.

Say it graciously. All conversations should be "with grace." Whatever is said should be said in love. Graciousness edifies.

Seek to build up. The goal of a discussion is never to make points or win arguments—it is to build up and encourage one another.

Avoid negative criticism. A critical attitude can quickly poison a conversation. If it starts, don't let it continue.

Be sensitive. Always consider other people at the table. Be sensitive to what might offend, embarrass or hurt someone else's feelings.

Treat all with respect. Each person at the table is due the same respect. No one's thoughts or opinions are better than another's.

Be inclusive. Everyone at the table should be able to participate in the topic of conversation—young children, elders, visitors.

> *Table talk ought to be such, in every family, as to make the evening hour of mealtime one of the most attractive as well as one of the most beneficial hours of the day to all the children.*
>
> H. Clay Trumbull, *Hints on Child Training*, 1890

Check My Manners— Make and photocopy a list of table manners you want your children to practice. Give them a copy of the list as a reminder. Occasionally, check off the manners on the list that are good, and the ones that need improvement, and give it to them. Each family has its own standards for table manners. Some of them might include:
- Napkin in lap.
- No elbows on the table.
- Sit up straight.
- Use bread or knife to push food, not fingers.
- Clear mouth before speaking.
- Take small bites of food.
- Chew with mouth closed.
- Sip a drink, don't gulp.
- Don't reach, ask.
- Utensils on plate.
- Always ask to be excused.
- Keep free hand in lap, not on the table.
- Always offer the last of something to others first.
- Eat whatever is put in front of you.
- Break your bread before eating it.
- Don't play with food.
- Use a clean utensil, not your own, for serving.
- Wait for the mother to eat before eating.

❏ Plan how to keep adequate records.

Keeping records won't necessarily improve the effectiveness of your teaching, but they will make you more credible to certain education officials. Records are your first line of defense against government intrusion into your home school. In some states records are required of home educators. Nonetheless, keep only as much as what is or may be required by law, unless you have administrative gifts or you actually enjoy keeping records. For non-administrative home educators, though, as long as you are compliant with the law, there is really no compelling need to become compulsive about keeping educational records.

Harriett thought she'd better keep a few extra records this year, just in case someone asked. Now, where did Homer put that dishwasher box?

- **Attendance** An attendance record shows that your child was "in home school" on a given day and that some minimum level of schooling was done. As to the amount of daily hours some states require, count anything that has educational value—actual study time, field trips, cooking, fixing things, computer, piano class and practice, sports, and arts and crafts. If it has a public-school counterpart or equivalent, you can probably count it toward your hours.

- **Curricula and reading** Keep each child's finished workbooks, or a record of their progress and completion. Also, keep a list of books read by each child. In addition to its possible use to defend the credibility of your home school, your children will be greatly encouraged to see how many books they have read, and to see the list growing. An informal record of field trips and "real life" experiences might be useful, too, though not necessary.

- **Health** Keep a minimum record of family health care including vital statistics, shots, and so on. Check with your state as to what is required for your child. If your child has an annual physical, keep a file with those records.

- **Standardized Testing** Keep a file with the results of any standardized tests taken. Unless your state requires annual tests, every two years is sufficient to track your children's development.

IN OUR HOME...

There is, of course, no such thing as a "typical" day in our home, or in any home-schooling home for that matter! Daily routines are routinely subverted by unexpected distractions, teachable moments, lessons from living, and the unrelenting unpredictability of the human child. And yet there is a very definite rhythm that characterizes the home-school lifestyle. It is the rhythm of purpose. It is the rhythm of real life. The schedule on the facing page is really just one of several "typical days" that characterize our home-school lifestyle. It is illustrative, though, of the kind of purpose and rhythm that would characterize other days.

An Untypically "Typical" Day In Our Home

TIME	ACTIVITY
7:30 - 8:00	Get up, make bed, get dressed, read Bible, do morning chores.
8:00 - 8:30	Eat breakfast, family devotions.
8:30 - 9:00	Clean up, make phone calls, children prepare for their day.

9:00 - 12:00
 	
• *Discipleship Studies*
• *Disciplined Studies*
• *Discussion Studies*
	HOME SCHOOLING
	❑ Scripture memory and Bible reading.
	❑ Math, Language Arts.
	❑ Read Aloud and Narration.
	    Mon., Wed. - Literature, History
	    Tue. - Fine Arts (Art, Poetry, Music)
	    Thu. - Science, Nature
	❑ Opt.: Watch an instructional program or video; craft.
	❑ Read to youngest child.

12:00 - 1:30	Prepare and eat lunch, read aloud at table, do chores.
1:30 - 4:00 • *Discovery Studies* • *Discretionary Studies*	Free time for computer, educational or instructional videos, projects, lessons, correspondence, library, drawing, writing. Special projects and assignments.
4:00 - 6:00	Play, dinner preparation.
6:00 - 7:30	Prepare and eat dinner, review, discussion, read aloud. Clean dinner dishes and kitchen, pick up, clean up, tie up loose ends.
7:30 - 8:30	*Winter:* Get ready for bed, read aloud, prayer. *Summer:* Play outside, long walks, yard games/sports.
8:30 - 9:00	*Older children:* Listen to music tapes or read.
9:00 - ???	Parent talk time, relax.

Know Your Principles

❝ *What is a family meant to be? Among other things, I personally have always felt it is meant to be a museum of memories—collections of carefully preserved memories and a realization that day-by-day memories are being chosen for our museum. Someone in the family...needs to be conscious that memories are important, and that time can be made to have double value by recognizing that what is done today will be tomorrow's memory.*

Edith Schaeffer, *What Is A Family?*, Baker, 1975

❝ *I believe it would be much better for everyone if children were given their start in education at home. No one understands a child as well as his mother, and children are so different that they need individual training and study. A teacher with a roomful of pupils cannot do this. At home, too, they are in their mother's care. She can keep them from learning immoral things from other children.*

Laura Ingalls Wilder, *Little House in the Ozarks*

As a home educator, the principles that guide your life will be constantly challenged. The very fact that you home school is viewed as a passive judgment by many of those who don't! The vast majority of parents will choose conventional schooling for their children, and many (Christian and non-Christian alike) will adamantly argue that home schooling is an inadequate, and even unbiblical, educational choice. You will be regularly faced with making decisions about activities, media, playmates and other issues that are in conflict with your principles. You may even be criticized by other home-schooling families. In all these situations and more, you must know your own principles and be ready to defend them when necessary, with confidence and graciousness. You cannot change your lifestyle simply to accommodate those who do not agree with your principles—it will only diminish your choice and deplete your spiritual and emotional energy. Be prepared to stand on principle.

- **About home education** Although many non-home schoolers support home schooling, it is not a neutral issue for many others. Just accept it—you *will be* a "threat" to some people. You may not want to be or feel like one, but you will be. However, when confronted by opposition, you don't have to be falsely humble about your choice. You can confidently testify why home schooling is right for *you*. Be assertive about your choice, not aggressive. Above all, be gracious in your attitude and words.

- **About church activities** Home schooling is a quietly divisive issue in many churches. In a church that is *not supportive* of home schooling, realize that you will be viewed with suspicion, and that you and your family will be under constant scrutiny. Choices you make about your children's activities and companions will cause controversy. If you have the energy to fight for change, do as the Lord leads. However, you and your children, and the church, might be better served by your attending a church with other home-schooling families that is supportive of your choice.

- **About companions** If you have strong principles about the kinds of companions you allow your children to have, it will be a source of conflict. This will be an issue for you whether in your neighborhood, church, or home-school support group. Proceed with caution with new friends for your children until you know the family and their values. You must be prepared to limit your children's relationships if you begin to see negative influences.

- **About media exposure** Prevention is the best means of avoiding a conflict of principle when it comes to media—don't put your children in tempting situations. However, since you don't always know the media standards of other families, train your children to discern when to "just say no thank you" to media your family has decided is unacceptable, wherever it is encountered and whomever is in charge.

*K*now Your Personality

Take it on faith—your personality is suited for home schooling. Your character may need some work, but there is no such thing as a "home-schooling personality" that somehow qualifies some to be better home-schooling mothers than others. There is no "ideal home-school mother" model that you need to become like. It is a phantom. If your husband and children love you, don't worry about what everyone else is supposedly doing. Just be yourself. You will never really relax and enjoy home schooling with your children until you free yourself to be who you are before God, not who you think you should be. Consider the following to give your perspective.

- **Accept yourself** God made you and accepts you unconditionally. And he knew what he was doing when he gave your children to you. Your strengths, skills, knowledge, and abilities are what God knew your children would need—he doesn't mismatch parents and children! Beware of comparing your *weaknesses* with other mothers' *strengths*. Remember that *they* have weaknesses where *you* are strong. Every home-schooling mother has flaws. Whatever you see as your own limitations, God knows them and will work more powerfully in you because of them. God is not limited by your limitations!

- **Be yourself** God gave you your personality for a reason. Because of it, you have a special relationship with your child that is totally distinct from every other mother and child. No one else can nurture your child the same way you can. It is natural and normal, then, that you will home-school differently than other mothers. So, don't compare yourself with other mothers, and don't compare your children with other children! If what you *are* doing is working, don't worry about what others are doing that you are not. Just be yourself and enjoy your children. They will enjoy the relaxed, real you much more.

- **Help yourself** Home schooling is hard. Determine whatever it is you need that will help you persevere in the home-education lifestyle, and then give yourself permission to have it, especially if it provides more rest and energy. You don't have to feel guilty about helping yourself, especially if it makes you more effective as a home-schooling mother. Give yourself the freedom to spend time and money on the things that you need, and that you and your children will enjoy the most—lessons, occasional help with cleaning, an afternoon out, pool passes for the summer, zoo or museum memberships, and so on.

- **Enjoy yourself** If home schooling is God's will for you and your family, then you will have a sense of joy and freedom in it. If, however, home educating your children seems like a joyless burden, then you need to make adjustments. Study what God says in his Word about joy, thankfulness, contentedness, patience and waiting. Do whatever you need to do to cultivate and keep the joy of the Christian life alive in your life. You cannot home school for long without the joy of the Lord. With his joy, though, you can go the whole distance.

> 66 *This above all: to thine own self be true,*
> *And it must follow, as the night the day,*
> *Thou canst not then be false to any man.*
>   William Shakespeare

Philippians 4:11-13
...for I have learned to be content whatever the circumstances. I know what it is to be in need, and I know what it is to have plenty. I have learned the secret of being content in any and every situation, whether well fed or hungry, whether living in plenty or in want. I can do everything through him who gives me strength.

2 Corinthians 12:8-10
Three times I pleaded with the Lord to take it away from me. But he said to me, "My grace is sufficient for you, for my power is made perfect in weakness." Therefore I will boast all the more gladly about my weaknesses, so that Christ's power may rest on me. That is why, for Christ's sake, I delight in weaknesses, in insults, in hardships, in persecutions, in difficulties. For when I am weak, then I am strong.

Psalm 37:3-6
Trust in the LORD and do good; dwell in the land and enjoy safe pasture. Delight yourself in the LORD and he will give you the desires of your heart. Commit your way to the LORD; trust in him and he will do this: He will make your righteousness shine like the dawn, the justice of your cause like the noonday sun.

Know Your Breaking Point

Home schooling is not easy. Though its outward blessings and advantages are evident, they often hide its dark underside—it can be mentally and emotionally demanding, physically exhausting and spiritually frustrating. Most home school mothers at one time or another find themselves struggling with "burn out"—the feeling that says, "I can't do it! It's too much! I quit!" Their flame for home schooling is either flickering, or seems to be extinguished. Whatever the source of those feelings may be—weariness, defeat, immaturity, insecurity—the important thing is what you *do* with the feelings. Here are four ways to prevent your home-school flame from burning out.

- **Lower your expectations** The phantom home-school mom keeps your expectations unrealistically high—orderly home, schedule under control, children who do all their work, lots of field trips, baking bread, keeping a garden, ministry with children, and able to leisurely read all the home-schooling magazines. But she doesn't exist! In reality, all you can do is accept each day from the Lord, live it as wisely as possible, and stay flexible. Learn to expect inconvenient interruptions, incomplete goals, and time-eating bouts of immaturity in your children. Don't expect more of yourself than God does—faithfulness.

- **Accept life's limitations** You'll never accomplish in one lifetime everything you want to do, much less everything you think *others* want you to do. You will always run into limitations—sinful attitudes (yours, your husband's and your children's), insufficient time, inadequate resources, weak skills, poor relationships, ad infinitum. No matter how strong you are in some areas, you will be correspondingly weak in others. Yet God is not limited by your limitations—he will accomplish by his grace all that he intends to accomplish in your life and in the lives of your children, if you trust him. *"With man this is impossible, but not with God; all things are possible with God."*

- **Learn to wait** Time lifts burdens. Whatever is overwhelming you today will probably not seem so burdensome tomorrow, in a week, or in a month. Trusting God is, in essence, *waiting*—patiently depending on him to meet your need. Many times, it is through the waiting that God works in your life to make you stronger. As you grow in faith and perseverance, what once was overwhelming may actually become a normal way of life. Sometimes God changes your circumstances; more often he changes you.

- **Expect adversity** Our generation of "Baby Boomers" was raised to expect prosperity and the good life. And if it didn't provide that, we could simply quit and do something else that would. Scripture, though, reminds us that that never was true. God wants us to experience, prepare for and learn from adversity and difficulty. It is part of his plan for our maturity. If home schooling is God's will for your life, then so is adversity. If you are not surprised by it, then God can use it to strengthen you even more.

Know Your Provider

The better you know your Provider, the easier it will be to trust him to provide for your needs, including the grace and strength to home educate your children. If you really believe that the God of Creation has called you to home school your children, then he will supply your need and sustain your faith. He knows your needs, and he knows your children's needs. However, be aware that God will also use home schooling to bring you to maturity as a parent. In those times when God doesn't answer your prayers as quickly as you'd like, or answer in the way you'd like, he will test how well you know your Provider. In those times, two truths will help you persevere so that you can finish well what he has called you to do.

- **Faithfully trust God**   *"And without faith it is impossible to please God, because anyone who comes to him must believe that he exists..."* *(Heb. 11:6)*. Regardless of the circumstances you face, you have the ability to remain faithful to God. In the end, the measure of your success in home schooling will not be how well your children perform on achievement tests, but how faithful you have been to trust God for his grace and strength in the process of discipling and educating them. Be faithful!

- **Trust God's faithfulness**   *"...and that he rewards those who earnestly seek him." (Heb. 11:6)*. Regardless of the circumstances you face, you can trust God because he is faithful. Do a Bible study on God's faithfulness to his people. Then, take some time to take inventory of all the ways he has shown his faithfulness *to you* in the past. He has been faithful to his people in every generation. He is looking for faith in ours, and he will bless it when he finds it. Trust God!

IN OUR HOME...

As the home-school mother of the house, I have found that a few simple "little" things can keep me going (especially if I need to keep going for another 15 years!). Adequate rest is a key priority, because there is never a time to "catch up" on lost sleep. An important time of my day is my mid-afternoon, private, "do not disturb!", take the phone off the hook, one woman "tea time." It is during the kids' rest-or-read hour, so I give myself however many minutes of time alone every afternoon that God will allow me to have (usually 15-30 minutes). If I get exhausted from sick children (like triple chicken pox), I just plan to get less done. Or, if my desk disappears under a pile of papers and stuff, I give myself time off to get it under control. I live for Clay's weekend outings with the kids so I can have the house all to myself! And, of course, I am active in a support group where both the kids and I can regularly enjoy good fellowship. These "little" things may not seem like much, but they add up to a weary sigh when they're missing, and a big sigh of relief when they're there.

Hebrews 10:35-39
So do not throw away your confidence; it will be richly rewarded. You need to persevere so that when you have done the will of God, you will receive what he has promised. For in just a very little while, "He who is coming will come and will not delay. But my righteous one will live by faith. And if he shrinks back, I will not be pleased with him." But we are not of those who shrink back and are destroyed, but of those who believe and are saved.

Hebrews 12:1-3
Therefore, since we are surrounded by such a great cloud of witnesses, let us throw off everything that hinders and the sin that so easily entangles, and let us run with perseverance the race marked out for us. Let us fix our eyes on Jesus, the author and perfecter of our faith, who for the joy set before him endured the cross, scorning its shame, and sat down at the right hand of the throne of God. Consider him who endured such opposition from sinful men, so that you will not grow weary and lose heart.

66   *If I am willing to be still in my Master's hand, can I not then be still in everything? He's got the whole world in His Hands! Never mind whether things come from God Himself or from people— everything comes by His ordination and/or permission. If I mean to be obedient and submissive to the Lord because He is my Lord, I must not forget that whatever He allows to happen becomes, for me, His will at that moment.*

Elizabeth Elliot, *The Elizabeth Elliot Newsletter*, July/August 1994

Psalm 46:10
Be still, and know that I am God; I will be exalted among the nations, I will be exalted in the earth.

Page 185

CHAPTER EIGHT—LIFESTYLE

CHAPTER NINE

Support...
Keeping It Going

What You See Is What You'll Get

There is a final critical element in home education. It is the shaping force behind everything in this book. Its presence, or absence, will shape everything you do in home education. Without it, you will likely grow weary and give up after a year or two. With it, though, you will be more likely to endure, persevere and overcome, keeping going even beyond the scope of this book until you usher your home-school graduates into adulthood. The critical element is vision. *Your* vision.

Vision is how you think about your *whole life*, not just about today or tomorrow. It is what you see with the eyes of your spirit when you look ahead to the end of your life and then look back to the present from that perspective. Vision is your *raison d'être*, your reason for being. Unfortunately, you cannot learn from a book how to have vision for Christian home education. Vision is the by-product of your own walk with God. The closer your walk with the Lord, the clearer your vision will be for your family's life. This book is an incomplete attempt to communicate our own family's vision for home education. Obviously, it is written to influence your vision for the education of your children, but ultimately that vision must come from God working in your own heart and mind. You must find your own vision for your life as a family.

If your vision—the "what you see"—is clear, then you will begin to make the kinds of decisions that will cultivate and strengthen that vision—the "what you'll get." In other words, if your vision is clear, then you're going to be sure to "get" whatever you need to carry out your vision. This final chapter discusses what you should be sure to "get" to keep moving ahead in your decision to home educate. The more you "get" to keep your vision for home schooling sharp and clear, the more you'll "see."

If you are a brand new home-schooling parent, we want you to know that you have made the right choice for your family. God will reward your step of faith many times over. May he richly bless your first years of living and learning in his will in your home. If you are a veteran home-schooling family and you have been in the grip of curriculum, we encourage you to take a step of faith and give real books and real life a try. You may just find the freedom and joy of home schooling that your heart knows God wants you to experience. If you're already a home-centered whole-booker, just keep the faith. You are giving your children a gift of inestimable value—your home. Whatever your situation, may God grant you the joy of seeing your vision for home schooling fulfilled as you bring up whole-hearted children for his glory.

Philippians 1:9-11
And this is my prayer: that your love may abound more and more in knowledge and depth of insight, so that you may be able to discern what is best and may be pure and blameless until the day of Christ, filled with the fruit of righteousness that comes through Jesus Christ -- to the glory and praise of God.

66 *Husbands and wives need a common vision of the purpose and priority of the family. They need help in understanding and performing their God-given tasks in nurturing their children... There is a desperate need to think Biblically, creatively, and drastically about our homes; they are quickly being relegated to bit parts in the twentieth-century drama.*

Bernie A. Schock, Ed.D, *Remodeling the Family*, Wolgemuth&Hyatt, 1989

Get With the Program, Dad!

It's no secret in the home schooling community—moms are the engines of industry when it comes to the education of their children. The burden of home schooling falls mostly on the backs of moms who are already burdened with managing, nearly single-handedly, a room and board facility with round-the-clock daycare. Since most of it happens during the day while dads are at work, the role of fathers in the home schooling "program" has stayed relatively (conveniently, sometimes) undefined. What dads have been lacking, though, is what every manager knows to provide for co-workers—a job description! So, dads, here is a condensed job description to help you get with the program in your own home school. There is no salary and no time off, but the fringe benefits are eternally rewarding.

❑ Home School Principal

As the principal of your home school, you represent and oversee the whole program. You make sure your "teaching staff" has all she needs to do her job, and you love and discipline your students. As the God-appointed head of your home, you take personal responsibility for the effectiveness of your home school. Your teacher and students are looking up to you for leadership. You must take the initiative to be involved in planning and evaluating your home school, fixing problems, and offering input on fine tuning it. You do not need to micromanage your home school—your wife is a capable manager of the day-to-day responsibilities. Just be available and be involved. Also, as the head of your family, you represent your home school. You are its spokesman in the community, at church and, if ever called upon, before government officials. The buck stops with you.

❑ Adjunct Instructor

As an adjunct instructor, you are available to step in as needed to teach areas of special interest and knowledge. You can plan special workshops for your children in the evenings on areas that you, personally, are interested in (ex., computers), or for which you have special insight or ability (ex., math or science). Or, you can plan a short nature outing to observe wildlife, stars, or whatever. Best of all, you can read books aloud at meals and bedtimes. However it is possible, you help carry some of the teaching load with your wife, not just for your wife's sake, but for your children's sake as well. They need your fatherly involvement, instruction and perspective as much as your wife needs your help.

❑ Daily Reviewer

Your job as daily reviewer is to listen to your children tell what they have learned that day. By proudly and patiently hearing their presentations and reports, encouraging them in their new skills, and affirming their academic and other work, you can give them a sense of worth they can get only from you, their dad. They are looking and listening for your approval.

❑ Teacher's Helper

Even the best teachers need helpers. You can be there for your home-schooling wife to offer real, practical help when it is really needed. It may require sacrificing some of your own desires or plans, but you are called to be your helper's helper. Whether it is with academics (reading, writing, math, science), logistics (taking some children so she can work with others; driving children to an activity), projects (working on art or science fair projects with children; directing an outdoor project; guiding a child through a computer project), or some other area (organizing the learning room; systematizing the library), you can actively look for ways to help.

❑ Recreational Director

You can't lose with this job. Just have fun with your children. Teach them sports, play outside with them, take a walk, play a board game, go on an extended outing. Plan regular times throughout the week to be actively involved with your children, especially when they are young, whether they are planned times or just doing whatever the children want to do. Just before dinner is a good time for dads to take over for awhile.

❑ Guidance Counselor

Your children want to spend time with you alone. There is guidance and counsel they need to hear that God has designed you alone to give to them, especially from the ages of about seven years old and up. Their development as healthy young men and women is largely dependent upon your involvement in their lives during the formative years before adolescence. Set aside special times with each of your children to talk. Think ahead about some areas of interest and concern that you can probe in their lives. Offer personal affirmation and encouragement for ways they are growing up and maturing. Share your vision for their lives as your children.

IN OUR HOME...

There is a nearly universal experience shared by home-schooling dads. I call it the "so many hours, so little time" syndrome. What I find happening in my own life is an acceleration of projects that need to be done yesterday or sooner, and steadily expanding needs for me to be involved in the lives of my children. It seems there are always too many hours of things to do, and too little time to do them. The only solution I have found is a business management approach. If I don't actually schedule activities, I end up getting involved in whatever is most urgent or visible. So, I put my kids on the calendar, and show them when and what I'll be doing with them. Then I am almost certain to do it because I have made a specific commitment. Some dads are more hang loose than that, I realize, but if you find you are more involved in projects than with your children, try the calendar. It can help!

Comment: Dadmonitions

God has spoken succinctly to dads in Scripture. It's certainly not because fathering was low on God's priorities—after all, he is God the Father! Perhaps it was because he knew dads would choke on "101 Ways to Be a Better Dad." So, God put only a few choice admonitions directed specifically to fathers in his Word. But they are enough. Taken together, they can be expressed in six simple admonitions to dads. Call them "dadmonitions." They are all a dad needs to know for becoming the godly father God the Father wants him to be.

1. Be a dad who consistently models godliness for his children. *(Deut. 6:4-9; Prov. 14:26, 17:6)*

2. Be a dad who faithfully trains and instructs his children. *(Eph. 6:4; Prov. 22:6)*

3. Be a dad who lovingly disciplines his children. *(Prov. 13:24; Heb. 12:7-13)*

4. Be a dad who tenderly sympathizes with his children. *(Ps. 103:13; 1Thes. 2:10-12; Col. 3:21)*

5. Be a dad who confidently leads his children. *(1Tim. 3:4, 5:8; Tit. 1:6; Gen. 18:19)*

6. Be a dad who loyally pursues his children. *(Mal. 4:5-6; Lk. 1:17; Prov. 17:6; Ps. 78:1-7)*

Get In the Home School Network

Comment: Support Group Unity

In a typical small, informal home school support group, there will often be a wide range of church and cultural backgrounds. Even though the real source of unity is Jesus Christ and a common commitment to home schooling, the diversity can foster interpersonal conflicts. To guard against conflict, following are some suggested "rules" for small support groups:

- *Group goals should be determined and evaluated each year at a meeting of the group members, not by one person. A group leader can be recognized then.*
- *All planning and general communication should go through the group leader. That person oversees the group calendar and coordinates with other members in charge of events or field trips.*
- *All involvement should be voluntary. If there are no volunteers for an event, then there is not sufficient interest in it. Mandatory attendance and assigned responsibilities don't work. Legalism will kill a small group.*
- *Group activities should never be used as "childcare" opportunities at which children are dropped off.*
- *Group members should agree together not to gossip among themselves about each other.*

❑ Support Groups

A home schooling parent without a support group can become isolated and vulnerable. A support group provides the encouragement and social contact that most home-schooling mothers need to keep going. And it provides an important source of group identity, friends and activities for your children. Don't stay home without one!

- Wherever two or more Christian home schoolers are living in an area, there is usually a support group. Some support groups are organized around a common home-education approach or curriculum (such as Whole Books, or Konos), others around fellowship and field trips.

- A small, informal support group (10 families or less) is easy to establish. Invite several home-schooling families to meet together. Find out what the common needs and desires are—fellowship, field trips, activities, cooperative learning? Decide together on the scope of the group, and any requirements for participation in the group. Make a calendar, ask for volunteers, and get started. Leadership usually flows to the one most willing to create a calendar and/or newsletter for the group.

- An alternative small support group is a "Whole Book" or similar fellowship that meets regularly to review and discuss books, materials and resources. In addition, the children can do readings, recitations and presentations. It is informal and infrequent (monthly).

- A large support group can often offer more special events, speakers, special classes for the children, and other services, but these benefits typically require a financial commitment. There are usually smaller sub-groups within the large one with which to get involved.

❑ Conferences and Fairs

Conferences and Curriculum Fairs are a highlight of the year for most home schoolers. It is where you see hundreds and sometimes thousands of home schoolers like yourself in one place. You can be inspired and challenged by state and national home-school speakers and leaders. Publishers and suppliers offer workshops addressing practical issues of home schooling. But best of all, vendors by the score display their products and promote their services. It is your opportunity to review material you might be considering, and to see new products and services entering the market.

❑ Organizations

- Home School Legal Defense Assoc. (HSLDA)
- State and Local home-schooling associations
- Umbrella schools (where applicable)
- National Challenged Home Schoolers Assoc. Network (NATHHAN)

Starting a Larger Support Group

Starting or leading a small, informal support group is relatively easy and painless. However, a larger, more formal support group can provide much more. If you desire the advantages of a larger group, and you live in an area with a substantial number of home-schooling families, you can create your own group. We started a weekly support group in Nashville that offered two classes for each of three age groups, childcare (nursery and preschool), field trips and activities, and a mothers' Bible study. We charged a monthly fee, hired skilled teachers (art, music, gymnastics, science, and others), and required mothers to participate as helpers. We had 40 families and 120+ children the first year, and limited the enrollment to 25 families the next. It was a lot of work and time, but it was worth it. The following are some general suggestions, based on our experiences, for starting a similar group.

- Wait until you have home schooled full time for two or three years before attempting to start a group. Leadership will be very demanding.

- Plan six months to a year in advance. The most important task in the beginning is to find others willing to be a part of your leadership team who will share the responsibilities. You should not try to start a larger group without a committed, reliable leadership team.

- If you plan to offer classes, you will need a facility. Find a church open to home schooling that has adequate rooms and a meeting area. Don't overlook nursery and rooms for the women's Bible study, if needed.

- If you plan to be a Christian home-schooling group, create a very simple statement of faith to insure agreement on areas of essential doctrine (deity of Christ, authority of Scripture, the trinity, salvation by grace, and others). If using a church facility, review your statement with the church leadership.

- Create a support group policies statement that all participants in the group must agree to and sign. Clearly explain the responsibilities and expectations for every member mother, and the expected behavior of the children. Also, create job descriptions for each of your leadership team positions—Treasurer, Field Trips Coordinator, Facility Coordinator, Nursery Coordinator, and so on.

- Promote the group during the summer for the following school year. Set a maximum enrollment based on facility capacity and leadership depth. Create a waiting list if necessary.

- Set a tuition price that gives you sufficient income to make the program worth the price. Pay well for good teachers! If there are quality classes for the children, families will be willing to pay for them. Give your leadership team members reduced or free tuition.

- If you are a program of your church, your finances will be handled by the church. This added accountability can be to your advantage, but it can also become an undue constraint if the church leadership is not entirely pro-home schooling. You need a key contact and supporter in church leadership.

- If you are an independent group, you will need a bank account. Consult a lawyer and accountant about incorporation as a non-profit organization, or running it as a sole proprietorship. Be sure you ask about and understand all of the liability, tax and payroll issues.

Comment: Preparing for Bookfairing

If you live in or near a large metropolitan area, there is very likely a large, annual home-schooling conference and bookfair that is held near you. They often have over 100 vendors and are very crowded. Here are a few suggestions for going to a large (or small) bookfair to get the very most out of your day.

- *If at all possible, make arrangements for your children. You'll be much freer to make decisions and to enjoy the bookfair if it's just you. Some large fairs do not allow strollers, or children under a certain age.*

- *For two or three day book fairs, Saturdays tend to be a little slower, and less crowded. However, used book booths will be well picked over by the second day. Whole book vendors might have some holes in their inventory by then, too.*

- *Plan ahead. Make a list of specific materials, or kinds of materials, that you need or want. If you're on a budget, take cash and spend only as much as you have.*

- *Arrive early. Take some time to study the bookfair map. If you know some items you definitely want, go to those booths first, since vendors do run out of some materials.*

- *Take a small notebook and pen to record prices at different booths, and a calculator. Be sure to take your checkbook since some vendors will not accept bankcards.*

- *Wear comfortable clothing and tennis shoes. Take something to carry your purchases (large fabric bag, backpack, or shoulder bag).*

- *Pack some snacks and a small water bottle. If the fair is at a convention center, pack a lunch to eat outside unless you are willing to pay their prices.*

*G*et On the Right Mailing Lists

❏ Publications

- ✍ Practical Homeschooling
- ✍ Homeschooling Today
- ✍ The Teaching Home

❏ Catalogs and Suppliers (Whole Book)

- ✍ Whole Heart Catalogue
- ✍ Lifetime Books and Gifts
- ✍ God's World Books
- ✍ The Elijah Company
- ✍ Greenleaf Press
- ✍ Beautiful Feet Books

❏ Businesses and Ministries

- ✍ Home School Legal Defense Assoc. (HSLDA)
- ✍ National Center for Home Education (NCHE)

❏ Activities Calendars

- ✍ Chambers of Commerce
- ✍ Local newsletters, newspapers
- ✍ Library
- ✍ Museums, Zoo, Nature Center
- ✍ Symphony, Theater
- ✍ Churches, Ministries
- ✍ Colleges, Seminaries
- ✍ Recreational facilities
- ✍ Tourist areas or attractions
- ✍ Local professional associations

❏ State/Regional Newsletters

- ✍ Support group(s)
- ✍ State/regional organization
- ✍ Political action organizations
- ✍ Informational organizations

Sidebar (left column)

- ✎ Whole Heart Ministries
  Whole Heart Catalogue
  P.O. Box 67
  Walnut Springs, TX
  76690

- ✎ Homeschooling Today
  P.O. Box 1425
  Melrose, FL 32666

- ✎ Practical Homeschooling
  P.O. Box 1250
  Fenton, MO 63026

- ✎ The Teaching Home
  P.O. Box 20219
  Portland, OR 97220

- ✎ Elijah Company
  Rt. 2, Box 100-B
  Crossville, TN 38555

- ✎ Greenleaf Press
  1570 Old LaGuardo Rd.
  Lebanon, TN 37087

- ✎ Lifetime Books & Gifts
  3900 Chalet Suzanne Dr.
  Lake Wales, FL 33853

- ✎ Beautiful Feet Books
  139 Main St.
  Sandwich, MA 02563

- ✎ God's World Books
  P.O. Box 2330
  Asheville, NC 28802

IN OUR HOME...

Our family has been in nearly every conceivable kind of home-school support group: an umbrella school and support group, a small "whole-book" group, a church-based cooperative school and support group (one we started and one we didn't), a big-city "multi-functional" support group, and a small-town "fellowship and field trips" support group. Though very different, each has provided the support, fellowship and help we needed. From these groups, we have made lifetime friends we keep up with, and whose children our children write to and visit when possible. We're less mobile now that we've settled into the country, so our support groups (we're in two right now) have become even more important to us. We'll never outgrow the need for support.

Get Out the Books

The home-school lifestyle, by its nature, will limit your contact with the community in which you live. You will be less involved socially not only because of time constraints, but also because of differing goals for your children. A certain degree of isolation is the price you will pay for the choice to give your children the opportunity to learn at home. You will need regular encouragement to strengthen your convictions and to keep going as a home educator, so do what you tell your children to do—look to your books. Start building a library section of books on home schooling. Even though they're just paper and ink, they'll become some of your best friends the longer you home school.

❏ Family and Parenting

There are only a few family and parenting books around that reflect or affirm the values of a home educating family. When you find one, it is a rare jewel—you'll find yourself going back often for more encouragement and insight. *Hints On Child Training* is a must read from 1890.

❏ Home-Schooling Introductions

These are the home-schooling "primers" that give you the "why to" from a variety of perspectives. They reinforce and sharpen your convictions, and remind you why you are home schooling. *For the Children's Sake* is an excellent whole book primer.

❏ Home-Schooling Methods

Read books that reinforce your own methods. If you adopt a Home-Centered Learning approach, look for books that promote a "whole book" or literature-based method, and that emphasize learning through real life experiences. *A Family Program for Reading Aloud* is filled with practical, natural insights.

❏ Home Schooling Testimonies

Reading "real life" war stories from the home-schooling "home front lines" can be a shot in the arm. The methods may vary, even the spiritual values, but the commitment is the same. It helps to hear what others have gone through.

❏ Home-Schooling Resources

Even if you don't need any new resources, reading about all the resources available is a learning experience all in itself. Major on books with good reading lists, and "full service" catalogs and "magalogs" that specialize in whole books. Mary Pride's *Practical Homeschooling* magazine specializes in resources.

Family

- 📖 *Hints on Child Training (H.C. Trumbull)*
- 📖 *What Is a Family? (Edith Schaeffer)*
- 📖 *Shaping of a Christian Family (Elizabeth Eliott)*
- 📖 *The Child Influencers (Dan Adams)*

Introductions

- 📖 *Educating the WholeHearted Child (Clarkson)*
- 📖 *A Charlotte Mason Companion (Karen Andreola)*
- 📖 *For the Children's Sake (Susan Schaeffer Macaulay)*
- 📖 *All the Way Home (Mary Pride)*
- 📖 *Home Grown Kids (Dr. Raymond Moore)*

Methods

- 📖 *You Can Teach Your Child Successfully (Ruth Beechick)*
- 📖 *Charlotte Mason Study Guide (Penny Gardner)*

Resources

- 📖 *How to Grow a Young Reader (Lindskoog, Hunsicker)*
- 📖 *Books Children Love (Elizabeth Wilson)*
- 📖 *Books That Build Character (Kilpatrick, Wolfe)*
- ✎ *The WholeHearted Child*
- ✎ *The Elijah Company*
- ✎ *Greenleaf Press*
- ✎ *Lifetime Books & Gifts*
- ✎ *Beautiful Feet Books*

Get Off to a Good Start!

It is not necessary to approach home schooling as though you are reading off the pre-flight check-list for a Boeing 757 about to take off—books, check!...materials, check!...blackboard, check! You don't need to create more pressure for yourself with an elaborate checklist! All you really need to do is get oriented and headed in the right direction. If you get started in the right direction, momentum will keep you going from there. The following will help you get off to a good start. The rest is up to you.

❏ Agree and pray with your spouse.

Christian home education is a ministry to your children. You and your spouse must be of one heart and mind that it is God's will for your family. If you are divided, it is not God's timing. Set aside a day to get away together alone to talk and pray about your family.

❏ Set goals and make plans.

Determine some general goals for your children: academic, spiritual, social, physical. Then write out a general plan for reaching those goals. Don't be overly detailed—just create a broad overview that you can use to keep you on track.

❏ First, work on devotion and discipline.

Discipleship is the foundation of education. Your first priority of home education is to establish patterns of family devotion, Bible study and Bible reading. You must also determine together your approach to discipline and training, and then be consistent and supportive of one another.

❏ Next, begin reading to your children every day.

Reading is the lifeblood of Home-Centered Education. Make it a daily priority to read aloud and to have your children read alone. Add read aloud at meal times or bed times. Even if the rest of your day falls apart, always try to spend some time with your children reading aloud and narrating.

❏ Then, establish routines for living and learning.

Determine what your days will be like organized around the focused study areas of the Home-Centered Learning model. Establish a daily routine so your children know what you expect of them throughout the day and week.

❏ Set up your learning room and discovery corners.

Your learning room and discovery corners are like an educational garden for your children. Wherever they plant themselves, they will grow a little more inside by drawing from that soil. Create a learning environment.

❑ Build a quality home library.

Your library will become the heart and soul of your home school. Start filling it up with whole and living books, and child-friendly reference books. The more you have in your library, the more your children will have to draw upon. In all things moderation...except books!

❑ Choose your instructional materials carefully.

Some learning—like language arts and math—just takes more diligence and discipline than others. However, be careful that your learning materials do not create additional, unnecessary work. Curricula for the basics may take work, but they should not be drudgery.

❑ Enjoy life with your children.

Above all, relax. Take time to just enjoy your children and get to know them. Begin to enjoy family the way God always intended it to be. You were designed to be living, learning, loving and growing together at home. Home schooling is the natural extension of the family that simply brings back into the home what never should have been given away. If you and your children are feeling tense, stressed and burdened by home schooling, then you probably are trying to do too much, or you are trying to use burdensome textbooks and workbooks. Home schooling does not have to be complicated or overwhelming. The Home-Centered Learning model will liberate learning in your home.

❑ Care for yourself and your children.

Take care of your kids. Make sure they get plenty of exercise and fresh air. Give them a healthy, balanced diet with plenty of water. Be sure they get sufficient sleep. Healthy children will be happier children, and happy children make much better students. And take care of yourself in the same way—you'll need all the energy you can muster to keep going.

IN OUR HOME...

We home school year-round, but September always starts a new "school year" for us. One of the things our children noticed early-on is that their schooled friends always got a bunch of new stuff when they started school. Now, we're not ones to "imitate the world," but we both had fond memories of those early school days of shopping for new notebooks, paper, stuff to fill up the plastic pencil pouch, a lunchbox and new school clothes. We decided it was a worthwhile investment in home-school motivation, so every year we go shopping for the new school year. We give them a list of the things they can buy and head for Target or WalMart. Then we let them pick out a new outfit and maybe a new pair of sneakers. It's a fun way for them to start the school year, and gives them the same fond memories we remember.

❣ **Annual Tune-Up**— Summer is a good time for a 365-day tune-up of your home schooling home. Set aside a week and get everybody involved. Here are a few suggestions for tuning up the home front for a new year of home schooling.

- **Purge** Get rid of all the books, papers, used workbooks, unused workbooks, broken pencils, and useless stuff that is just taking up space in your learning room.
- **Organize** Systematize (again!) your storage so there is a place for everything (at least for a while). Bring in whatever organizers and boxes will help.
- **Arrange** Put the library back together with an accessible arrangement. Arrange desktops for maximum efficiency and minimum clutter potential. Give each child a study area all his own.
- **Plan** Determine your first quarter goals for each child, write them out and post them. Plan for any new materials you need to acquire.
- **Schedule** Fill in monthly calendar blanks with all known event and commitment dates. Post the calendar where all can see it and add to it as necessary.
- **Shop** Set aside a day to shop for school supplies and clothes. Stock up on often used items and materials. Go to the Teacher Supply store or a warehouse store to get supplemental workbooks and coloring books.
- **Simplify** Take stock of your commitments and determine which ones can be dropped. Consider simpler ways of doing things at home—meals, clean up, chores, etc..
- **Relax** Don't be so hard on yourself. Keep the long range goals in mind, not just the short range plans. Resolve to find some time each day to relax.

Get Your Heart Right Before God

We began this book by challenging your convictions about home education. We went on to discuss the relationship of discipleship and education, our "Home-Centered Learning" model and methods of home education, and the practical issues of personality, planning and organization, and lifestyle. Now, as we reach the end, we come full circle back to you, the home-educating parent.

When all the philosophy, methods and materials are stripped away, it is clear that Christian home education is an issue of the heart...*your* heart. If you really believe home schooling is a matter of obedience to God's will in your life, then you should do it with your whole heart—driven by the conviction it is right, doing it in the power of the Holy Spirit, with confidence that the full authority of God and his Word is behind you.

If you are to keep your heart right before God for the godly task of home educating your children, you will need a daily supply of his grace. Different church traditions have promoted a variety of "means" for obtaining God's grace, but the Bible is clear about three:

❑ God's Word

God speaks to you through his Word, the Bible. This is the first and most abundant source of his grace. You go to it to find God, to seek wisdom, to know his promises, and to follow his ways. All that you need to know for life and godliness, God has revealed in his Word. It is not just a reference manual, though, it is God's *living* Word. You receive grace when the Word is alive in your heart through the Spirit. Make it your priority to spend time in God's Word daily.

❑ Prayer

You speak to God through prayer. Grace for daily living comes through an ongoing, personal conversation with God. You express praise and thanksgiving, confess sins, and seek his help and power. God is not a prayer machine or a detached sovereign, but a *person.* He longs to share his grace with you through a personal relationship with him. Prayer is a channel for that grace. When you pray, you become a part of the spiritual drama of his grace and providence working through you and your children. Make it a habit to pray often during the day.

❑ Fellowship

God ministers to you and through you through fellowship. He is present in his people, the body of Christ. Believers who are receiving God's grace through the Word and prayer become channels of that grace to you and others. You receive grace from God through the encouragement, biblical counsel and prayers of other believers. Make time regularly for meaningful fellowship with other like-minded believers.

For this reason I kneel before the Father, from whom his whole family in heaven and on earth derives its name. I pray that out of his glorious riches he may strengthen you with power through his Spirit in your inner being, so that Christ may dwell in your hearts through faith. And I pray that you, being rooted and established in love, may have power, together with all the saints, to grasp how wide and long and high and deep is the love of Christ, and to know this love that surpasses knowledge—that you may be filled to the measure of all the fullness of God.

APPENDIX

Home Schooling Directory

Publications

These publications generally support a Home Centered Learning approach to home schooling. There are certainly others that could be included, and new ones seem to come out every month. These provide a good starting point, though. If you run across others you like, let us know about them. Listed alphabetically.

Magazines

- *Homeschooling Today*
  P.O. Box 436, Barker, TX 77413
  (281) 492-6050 / (866) 804-4HST
  www.homeschooltoday.com
  service@homeschooltoday.com
  Bi-monthly magazine for home schoolers with articles on a variety of approaches, including classical, unit studies and whole books. Practical helps for home schooling. Reformed theology.

- *Practical Homeschooling*
  Home Life, P.O. Box 1250, Fenton, MO 63026
  (800) 346-6322
  www.home-school.com
  svc@home-school.com
  Mary Pride's quarterly magazine. Regular columnists for a variety of educational areas. Excellent and very helpful reviews of dozens of home schooling products and resources. Clay and Sally were regular columnists for several years.

- *The Teaching Home*
  P.O. Box 20219, Portland, OR 97220
  (503) 253-9633
  www.teachinghome.com
  tth@teachinghome.com
  The original Christian home schooling magazine. Good source of information about speakers, issues, and ideas. Each issue includes a special section on a featured topic.

- *The Old Schoolhouse Magazine*
  P.O. Box 185, Cool, CA 95614
  (530) 823-0447
  www.theoldhomeschoolhouse.com
  info@tosmag.com
  Quarterly magazine filled to overflowing with a wide variety of articles, columns, reviews, and more. Very eclectic in approach, with something for everyone. High quality and a treasure trove for lovers of ads, too. Paul and Gena Suarez.

Websites and E-Letters

- *Charlotte Mason Research & Supply*
  www.charlottemason.com

- *Christian Homeschool Fellowship*
  www.chfweb.com

- *Crosswalk Homeschool*
  www.crosswalk.com

- *Eclectic Homeschool Online*
  www.eho.org

- *Heart of Wisdom*
  www.heartofwisdom.com

- *Homeschool World*
  www.home-school.com

- *Whole Heart Online*
  www.wholeheart.org

Your Personal Favorites

-
-
-
-
-
-
-
-

Catalogs & Publishers

The catalogs and publishers in this list are "whole book" oriented in approach, or provide supplementary material for Home Centered Learning. Textbook publishers and catalogs that rely primarily on a curricular or textbook approach are not listed. Listed alphabetically.

- *Whole Heart Ministries*
  P.O. Box 3445, Monument, CO 80132
  Phone: (800) 311-2146
  Fax: (866) 311-2146
  www.wholeheart.org
  Email: whm@wholeheart.org
  Whole Heart Ministries no longer publishes the Whole Heart Catalogue. However, you can purchase any of the products we write and publish on our ministry website. As we are able, we will offer more books there to help in all areas of your Christian parenting. You can also sign up there for our ministry e-mail letter, and for Sally's personal e-mail letter, and add your name to our print mailing list to receive our bi-annual (spring and fall) ministry letter in the mail (Whole Heart Letter). You can also learn about and register for any of our seminars, conferences, and speaking engagements online.

"Whole Book" Catalogs

- *Beautiful Feet Books*
  139 Main Street, Sandwich, MA 02563
  (800) 889-1978, (508) 833-8626
  www.bfbooks.com
  Small whole book catalog emphasizing quality books on American and European history. Great study guides for history and geography, and reprints of classic juvenile history books. Rus & Rea Berg.

- *The Elijah Company*
  1053 Eldridge Loop, Crossville, TN 38571
  (888) 235-4524
  www.elijahco.com
  "Full service" catalog from home school and catalog veterans Chris and Ellyn Davis. Good selection of children's literature and nature resources.

- *Greenleaf Press*
  3761 Highway 109N, Unit D, Lebanon, TN 37087
  (615) 449-1617
  www.greenleafpress.com
  Whole books and "twaddle free" history from Rob and Cyndy Shearer. Best source for history books from every period of history. Great history study guides. Full color catalog.

- *Lifetime Books and Gifts*
  3900 Chalet Suzanne Dr., Lake Wales, FL 33853
  (800) 377-0390
  www.lifetimebooksandgifts.com
  The Always Incomplete Catalog, Bob and Tina Farewell's wonderfully diverse collection of whole books and everything else. Text only, but full descriptions of books.

General Catalogs

- *Bethlehem Books*
  10194 Garfield St. S, Bathgate, SD 58216
  (800) 757-6831
  www.bethlehembooks.com
  Selection of hard-to-find children's books, including regular reprints. Catholic in orientation.

- *Bluestocking Press*
  P.O. Box 2030, Shingle Springs, CA 95682
  (800) 959-8586, (916) 621-1123
  www.bluestockingpress.com
  Interesting selection of whole books. Emphasis on history and the foundations of our liberty. Text only.

- *Charlotte Mason Research & Supply Co.*
  P.O. Box 758, Union, ME 04862
  www.charlottemason.com
  Karen Andreola is the original Charlotte Mason lady in the homeschool movement. Her website tells about her books and articles.

- *Cornerstone Curriculum Project*
  2006 Flat Creek Pl., Richardson, TX 75080
  (214) 235-5149
  www.cornerstonecurriculum.com
  Unique selection of products for math, music, art, language arts and others created by David and Shirley Quine. Excellent Worldview curriculum.

- *Farm Country General Store*
  412 North Fork Rd., Metamora, IL 61548
  (800) 551-3276 (FARM)
  www.homeschoolfcgs.com
  A real "general store" of home schooling books and resources. Larry Schertz.

- *Lamplighter Publishing*
  P.O. Box 777, Waverly, PA 18471
  (888) 246-7735
  www.lamplighterpublishing.com
  Mark Hamby's catalog of outstanding reprints of Victorian Christian moral stories, and many other family-friendly books and resources.

- *Mantle Ministries*
  140 Grand Oak Dr., San Antonio, TX 78232
  (210) 490-2327
  www.mantleministries.com
  Richard "Little Bear" Wheeler's catalog of reprinted, hard-to-find classics of history and literature. Text only.

- *Rushton Family Ministries*
  1225 Christy Lane, Tuscumbia, AL 35674
  (888) 472-6657 (HSBOOKS)
  www.cindyrushton.com
  Rich source of Charlotte Mason inspired books and articles by Cindy, and many other resources.

- *The Book Peddler*
  P.O. Box 1960, Elyria, OH 44036
  (800) 928-1760
  www.bookpeddler.us
  Full range of products with good literature. Text only on newsprint.

- *Timberdoodle Company*
  1510 E. Spencer Lake Road, Shelton, WA 98584
  (360) 426-0672
  http://www.timberdoodle.com
  Good discovery studies resources. Published by home schooling family for over ten years.

- *Veritas Press*
  1250 Belle Meade Drive, Lancaster, PA 17601
  (800) 922-5082
  Beautiful color catalog. Resources geared to "Classical" education method. Heavy on Reformed.

- *Vision Forum*
  32335 U.S. Hwy. 281 N., Bulverde, TX 78163
  (800) 440-0022
  Hard to find books and reprints for families. Color catalog. Very heavy on Reformed.

  Your Personal Favorites

-

-

-

Organizations & Individuals

These are just a few of the organizations you should know about as a home schooling family.

- *Whole Heart Ministries*
  Clay and Sally Clarkson
  P.O. Box 3445, Monument, CO 80132
  Phone: (800) 311-2146
  Fax: (866) 311-2146
  www.wholeheart.org
  Email: whm@wholeheart.org
  Whole Heart Ministries is a 501(c)(3) non-profit Christian ministry dedicated to "encouraging and equipping Christian parents to build a biblical home and a godly heritage by nurturing, discipling and educating their children at home." WHM serves Christian parents and their children worldwide through ministries of speaking, teaching, training, writing and publishing that focus on the biblical and practical aspects of building a Christian home. Our ultimate objective is to come alongside Christian parents to help them prepare their children to become Christian leaders in the next generation. For more information about our ministry, or to make a donation, visit our ministry website, Whole Heart Online.

♥ ♥ ♥

- *Bob Jones University Press, Testing and Evaluation Service*
  Greenville, SC 29614-0062
  (800) 845-5731
  Standardized testing for all grades.

- *Christian Liberty Academy Satellite School, Independent Testing Service*
  502 W. Euclid Ave., Arlington Heights., VA 60004
  (847) 259-4444
  Standardized testing for all grades.

- *Home School Foundation*
  P.O. Box 1152, Purcellville, VA 20134
  (540) 338-8899
  www.homeschoolfoundation.org
  Home School Foundation is sponsored by HSLDA. Its mission is "to preserve parental freedoms, promote home schooling, provide assistance to needy home schooling families, and support like-minded organizations." It manages several specific funds for widows, families in need, projects, and more.

- *Home School Legal Defense Association (HSLDA)*

    Michael Smith
    P.O. Box 3000, Purcellville, VA 20134
    (540) 338-5600
    www.hslda.org
    HSLDA fights the legal battles for home schooling member families in every state. Don't stay home without this team of home school legal eagles on your side! Fees are very reasonable, and discounted through approved state organizations, support groups and umbrella schools. It is a small price to pay for your freedom to home school.

- *National Challenged Home Schoolers Associated Network (NATHHAN)*

    P.O. Box 39, Porthill, ID 83853
    (208) 267-6246
    www.nathhan.com
    NATHAN offers support and encouragement for home schooling parents with special needs and learning challenged children. Membership includes a magazine, access to lending library, and a member family directory. Christian, non-profit.

- *National Center for Home Education (NCHE)*

    One Patrick Henry Circle, Purcellville, VA 20132
    (703) 338-7600
    NCHE is a non-profit organization of HSLDA that lobbies congress and monitors legislation. It operates the Congressional Action Program (CAP) and coordinates a national phone and fax alert network.

- *National Home Education Research Institute (NHERI)*

    Dr. Brian Ray
    P.O. Box 13939, Salem, OR 97309
    (503) 364-1490
    www.nheri.org
    A research and education organization. Publishes a research journal, as well as reports on primary and secondary (anecdotal) research concerning the home schooling movement.

Add Your Own

-
-
-
-
-
-
-
-
-
-

These are the resources that we have found most helpful in our own home schooling experience. This list represents, of course, only a very few of the many excellent resources available. Those that we regularly use and most often recommend are marked with a ✔ (you can find many of the checked titles in the Whole Heart Catalogue). Titles are listed alphabetically.

Home Schooling Books and Resources

✔ *Educating the WholeHearted Child (Clay and Sally Clarkson, 1994, 1996)*

Introductions

✔ *A Charlotte Mason Companion (Karen Andreola, CMR&S Co., 1998)*
> Karen's insights into the Charlotte Mason Method based on her research and articles from The Parent's Review. Excellent introduction to the method.

• *All the Way Home (Mary Pride, Crossway, 1989)*
> How to make family the center of your life. Home schooling is an important part of restoring the family to God's design.

✔ *Charlotte Mason Study Guide (Penny Gardner, 1998)*
> Excellent summary of the content found in the 5-volume Mason series. Good primer.

✔ *For the Children's Sake (Susan Schaeffer Macaulay, 1984)*
> An explanation of Charlotte Mason's living books and real life approach to education. The book that started the whole book movement.

• *Home Grown Kids (Raymond/Dorothy Moore, Word, 1981)*
> An overview of home-centered teaching and learning theory for newborns through nine year-olds. A pivotal book that helped fuel the Christian home schooling movement in the early 1980s.

• *The Original Home Schooling Series, 6 volumes (Charlotte Mason, ca. 1900)*
> These turn of the century books are a treasury of wisdom and educational insight.

Reading Lists

✔ *Books Children Love (Elizabeth Wilson, Crossway, 1987)*
> A comprehensive listing of the best books for children. Based on Charlotte Mason's concepts.

✔ *Books That Build Character (Kilpatrick, Simon & Schuster, 1994)*
> Recommended books that emphasis or illustrate character development. Over 300 titles.

• *A Family Program for Reading Aloud (Rosalie J. Slater, F.A.C.E., 1991)*
> Read aloud program for the Principle Approach. Includes reading lists.

• *Great Books of the Christian Tradition (Glaspey, Harvest House, 1996)*
> Over 500 books that have shaped our faith and our world. Includes good list of children's books.

• *Honey for a Child's Heart (Gladys Hunt)*
> "The imaginative use of books in family life." Ideas for family reading aloud with recommended books list.

✔ *How to Grow a Young Reader (Lindskoog, Hunsicker, Harold Shaw, 1999)*
> Excellent reading list book from a distinctively Christian perspective.

Teaching Methods & Helps

✔ *Design-A-Study Guides (Kathryn Stout)*
> Series of resource books that allow you to create your own curriculum and studies. Almost like an encyclopedia of ideas. Flexible and helpful.

✔ *Five-in-a-Row Guides (Jane Lambert)*
> Series of study guides each built around five pieces of children's literature. Various levels and themes of study, including character.

• *How to Create Your Own Unit Study; The Unit Study Idea Book (Valerie Bendt)*
> Practical suggestions for unit studies with a strong emphasis on using whole books.

- *Teaching Children (Diane Lopez, Crossway, 1988)*

  Practical insights on Charlotte Mason teaching methods and a grade-by-grade scope-and-sequence covering all subjects.

- *The Three R's (Ruth Beechick)*

  Three books—Reading, Language, Arithmetic—for grades K-3. Presents an easy, non-curricular way to start your children learning.

- ✔ *You Can Teach Your Child Successfully (Ruth Beechick)*

  A 400-page resource for teaching and learning theory for grades 4-8. Covers all subject areas with a whole book, natural, non-curricular approach.

Christian Home Books and Resources

- ✔ *Beautiful Girlhood (M. Hale, revised by Karen Andreola, 1994)*

  A unique reprint especially for girls who are about to become young ladies. Excellent resource for reading with your pre-adolescent daughter on the qualities of being "lady like."

- *The Child Influencers (Dan Adams, Home Team Press, 1990)*

  Looks at the shift in primary influences upon children from family, books and home learning, to peers, TV, and public schooling. Great for dads.

- *Children of a Greater God (Terry Glaspey, Harvest House, 1995, out of print)*

  An easy-to-read and to-do exploration of how to develop your children's "moral imagination."

- *The Duties of Parents (J.C. Ryle, 1888)*

  A surprisingly insightful little booklet (excerpted from *The Upper Room*, by Ryle) about the role and responsibilities of Christian parents.

- ✔ *Family Celebrations at Christmas; Family Celebrations at Easter; Family Celebrations at Thanksgiving (Ann Hibbard, Baker)*

  Covers every major holiday with suggestions for how to make each one meaningful and inspirational. Provides background on each holiday with lots of ideas for Bible readings, activities, arts and crafts. (WHC)

- *Family Devotions for the Advent Season; Preparing for Easter (James Evans, Tyndale)*

  Easy-to-use guides for Advent and Lent. Includes Scripture, suggested discussion with object lesson, prayer and application assignment.

- ✔ *The Hidden Art of Homemaking (Edith Schaeffer, Tyndale, 1971)*

  A classic on expressing your creativity through the "hidden art" within your home.

- ✔ *Hints On Child Training (Henry Clay Trumbull, 1890)*

  Trumbull was a leader in the Sunday School movement in the late 1800's. This book is full of pure, simple, biblical wisdom for training your child. A must read for dads.

- *If Teacups Could Talk (Emilie Barnes, Harvest House, 1994)*

  A beautiful book full of lovely ideas for reviving the art of teatime in your home, and lovely pictures and artwork that will revive your spirit.

- *Remodeling the Family (Bernie Schock, Ed.D., 1989, out of print)*

  "A radical plan for restoring the home" that advocates home-centered living and learning.

- *The Shaping of a Christian Family (Elizabeth Elliot, Word)*

  Elizabeth Elliot looks back at her own family experience to suggest the characteristics of a strong Christian family. (H.C. Trumbull, above, was her grandfather).

- ✔ *Seasons of a Mother's Heart (Sally Clarkson, WHM, 1998)*

  Sally's personal and inspirational insights and reflections on being a home schooling mother. Includes a full Bible study after each of the 12 chapters. Good for personal reading or group discussion.

- ✔ *What Is a Family? (Edith Schaeffer, Baker, 1975)*

  A classic on the family by the wife of the late Dr. Francis Schaeffer. She paints illustrative word pictures of what the Christian family should be. Lots of wisdom and anecdotes from their life at L'Abri.

Discipleship Studies

Bible Reading

✔ *The Bible (NIV, NKJV, NASB)*
    The New International Version is the easiest to understand and often preferred by families for reading. The New American Standard Bible (update) is the most accurate translation and is preferred by many for Bible study. The New King James Version is often preferred for memory work.

✔ *The Child's Story Bible (Catherine Vos, Eerdmans)*
    A time-tested Bible story book first published in 1935 that is faithful to the biblical texts. This is not your typical "childish" beginner Bible story book. Vos' well-written text reads like a whole book and covers all major Bible content. Excellent for read-aloud. Recently re-published. (WHC)

• *The Narrated Bible (Harvest House)*
    The NIV Bible harmonized and arranged in actual chronological, historical order with narrative comments throughout. Good for reading aloud through the entire Bible. Includes a daily reading guide.

Bible Study

• *Bible Reader's Companion (Richards, Scripture Press)*
    Quick reference resource for insight on every chapter of the Bible. Includes chapter summary, commentary on key verses, outlines, cross references, definitions, contextual insights, and illustrations.

• *The Children's Illustrated Bible (Dorling Kindersley)*
    Beautifully illustrated Bible story book with hundreds of detailed illustrations, photos and information.

• *The International Children's Bible Dictionary (Lynn Waller, Word)*
    Over 1000 simple definitions of Bible words, phrases and events. Nicely illustrated with drawings and photographs. A good first reference work for Bible study.

✔ *The International Children's Bible Handbook (Larry Richards, Word)*
    Answers to many of the questions children ask about the Bible. Covers all Bible books, Genesis to Revelation. Apologetics primer.

✔ *What the Bible Is All About for Young Explorers (Scripture Press)*
    Handbook of the Bible for older children. Excellent content and helpful line-art illustrations.

Devotions

✔ *Children's Bible Basics series (Carolyn Nystrom, Moody)*
    Brightly illustrated storybook on various Bible doctrines for younger children. Referenced Scriptures can be used with any age.

✔ *Hero Tales (3 volumes, Jackson, Bethany House)*
    Profiles of 45 Christian heroes with a biographical sketch and three vignettes that illustrate character qualities. Short chapters with devotional helps.

✔ *Leading Little Ones to God (Marian Schoolland, Eerdmans)*
    Series of readings for younger children on Bible doctrines. A child-friendly systematic theology without theological language. Good for read aloud and family devotions.

✔ *Stories to Share—A Family Treasury of Faith (Patricia St. John)*
    Collection of devotional stories with Scripture readings for all children (and adults!) from the beloved author of Christian fiction for children. Every story is captivating and well-written.

• *Stepping Stones to Bigger Faith for Little People (Joyce Herzog, Greenleaf Press)*
    Devotional for children. Full-page illustration with each short devotional. Mature concepts and Bible truths presented simply in child-friendly language.

Training

✔ *A Child's Book of Character Building (2 volumes, Coriel, Baker)*
    Each character quality is illustrated for the child by one-page stories with drawings showing how it is lived out in the Bible, at home, at school and at play, with character "challenges" for application.

✔ *Developing Godly Character in Children (Hands to Help)*
    Handbook and resource guide for teaching and training your children in biblical character.

✔ *For Instruction in Righteousness (Pam Forster, Doorposts)*
> Unrivaled biblical reference resource for discipline and training. Bible instruction for 50 different sins in seven categories.

• *How to Have Kids With Character (Nadine Brown, Tyndale, out of print)*
> Easy to use parental primer for character development. Twelve character qualities, training for 2-7 and 8-12.

✔ *Our 24 Family Ways (Clarkson, Whole Heart)*
> A discipleship tool for training in Christian character. Includes four rules ("ways") for each of six areas—authority, relationships, possessions, work, attitudes, choices—with six Scriptures for each rule, 240 fully-scripted devotions.

✔ *Pearables series*
> Original and reprinted character and moral stories to use in Christian training..

Disciplined Studies

Beginning Reading

• *Alpha-Phonics (Samuel Blumenfeld)*
> A word-family phonics approach using extensive word lists and practice sentences. Short lessons (128), teacher's guide in back.

✔ *Christian Eclectic Readers (McGuffey, Eerdmans)*
> The venerable McGuffey Readers updated by veteran home schoolers Charles and Betty Burger with added Christian content. Good follow-up to *Teach Your Child to Read in 100 Easy Lessons*.

✔ *Noah Webster's Reading Handbook (Christian Liberty Press)*
> Phonics primer for beginning reading skills. Revised and updated version of Noah Webster's handbook. Excellent supplemental text for review of phonics fundamentals.

✔ *Teach Your Child to Read In 100 Easy Lessons (Simon & Schuster)*
> Just what the title says—no preparation, completely scripted, 20-minute lessons. A nationally recognized, phonics-based approach to beginning reading skills. Highly recommended.

Handwriting

• *The Italic Handwriting series (Getty/Dubay, Continuing Education Press)*
> Excellent K-6 handwriting curriculum. Based on learning classic italic manuscript and then adding joins to make cursive (no new letters to learn for cursive). Consumable workbooks.

• *A Reason for Writing series (Concerned Communications)*
> A K-6 handwriting curriculum using Scripture and traditional manuscript and cursive approach. Consumable workbooks with Scripture poster practice sheets.

Language Arts

• *Learning Language Arts Through Literature (Common Sense Press)*
> Comprehensive, literature-based language arts curriculum. Integrates all areas of language arts studies in single daily lessons: phonics, grammar, writing mechanics, spelling, vocabulary, creative writing.

✔ *English from the Roots Up (Joegil Lundquist, Literacy Unlimited)*
> Good supplement to language arts. Shows the Latin and Greek etymological roots of common English words. It's fun, too, for the children to see how words develop.

✔ *How to Teach Any Child to Spell; Tricks of the Trade (Gayle Graham, Common Sense Press)*
> A unique approach to spelling that builds lists based on child's own writing. This is a sensible, no-groaner way to build better spelling skills.

✔ *Simply Grammar~An Illustrated Primer (Karen Andreola, CMR&SCo)*
> An updated and revised version of the oral grammar used in Charlotte Mason's schools. Fifty wonderful 19th century lithographs illustrate the lessons.

Writing & Composition

✔ *Wordsmith series (Common Sense Press)*
> Self-directed creative writing and composition workbooks for elementary (*Wordsmith Apprentice*), junior high (*Wordsmith*) and high school (*Wordsmith Craftsman*). Good balance between instruction in writing skills and techniques, and application to real writing. Also, a *Wordsmith Teachers Guide*.

- *Right Words~The Grace of Writing; Guidelines for Teaching Right Words~A Relational Approach to Writing (Adams/Stein, Truth Forum)*

  Excellent creative writing curriculum. Whole family participates in workshop approach. Focus on releasing your children's writing "voice." Writer's revision handbook also available.

- *Homestead Children: A Sampler of Children's Writings (Truth Forum)*

  Nearly 200 writing samples from children of all ages, personalized with over 200 photographs. Interesting, inspiring writings about real life close to family and the land. Accompanies *Right Words* series.

Math

- *CalcuLadder (The Providence Project)*

  Simple, pencil and paper math tool for timed drills to develop and test math competencies.

- *Making Math Meaningful (David Quine, Cornerstone Curriculum Project)*

  Excellent math program, Elementary through High School emphasizing understanding concepts and manipulatives.

- *Math-U-See*

  Popular math program employing instructive videos, manipulatives and workbooks.

- *Miquon Math*

  Good beginning math in a consumable workbook format. Takes your child up to 4th grade level math.

- *Saxon Math*

  Excellent K-12 textbook and workbook math program. Uses an effective incremental learning model.

Thinking Skills

- *Building Thinking Skills (Critical Thinking Press)*

  Series of graded manuals with thinking skills problems. Good mental exercisers. Short lessons, no preparation required, teacher's manuals available.

- *Connections: Working With Analogies (The Continental Press)*

  Series of consumable workbooks at different age/ grade levels to develop thinking skill.

- *Developing the Early Learner, Vols. 1-4 (Simon Bibeau)*

  Consumable workbooks that exercise several areas of your children's thinking skills.

- *Gifted and Talented series*

  Conumable workbooks with exercises for range of skills and learning, including thinking skills.

Discussion Studies

Literature

See "Our Family's Favorite Books" for list of recommended whole books for reading and reading aloud, and for poetry.

History

- *Eyewitness Books series (Dorling Kindersley)*

  Popular series known for its use of vivid photographs and concise text.

- *The Kingfisher Book of the Ancient World (Kingfisher)*

  World history up to the fall of Rome. Detailed, colorful illustrations, photographs. Insightful text.

- *The Kingfisher Encyclopedia of World History (Kingfisher)*

  Outstanding, encyclopedic history resource. Detailed, colorful illustrations, photographs. Insightful text.

- *See Through History series (Viking)*

  Excellent resources for unit studies. Informative text and excellent illustrations bring time period alive covering all major periods of history and many more selected historical topics. Each book includes four transparent overlay pages.

- *The 100 Most Important Events in Church History (Revell)*

  Just what the title says. Historical profiles in short chapters make excellent home study resource.

- *Usborne Books (EDC)*

  Popular publisher known for the use of bright, colorful hand-drawn illustrations and short, easy-to-read text.

Art

✔ *Come Look With Me art book series: Enjoying Art With Children; Exploring Landscape With Children; Worlds of Play; Animals In Art (Gladys Blizzard)*
Simple, attractive art books with background and discussion questions about the selected art works in a variety of styles from masters to moderns.

✔ *Famous Artists series (Barrons)*
Very visual and text-full studies of the life and works of a variety of artists.

✔ *Looking At Pictures (Abrams)*
Child-friendly book on art that explores understanding the themes and techniques used by the great artists by examining twelve recognized masterpieces.

✔ *Adventures in Art (David Quine, Cornerstone Curriculum Project)*
A biblically-based look at selected masterpieces to discover the role of art in the flow of history.

Music

✔ *Classical Kids cassette series: Mr. Bach Comes to Call; Vivaldi's Ring of Mystery; Mozart's Magic Fantasy; Beethoven Lives Upstairs; Tchaikovsky Discovers America; Hallelujah Handel! (Susan Hammond)*
Dramatized stories with classical music by the composers skillfully interwoven throughout. Kids love these imaginative and engaging tapes. Highly recommended!

✔ *Famous Children series of books (Rachlin/Hellard, Alladin)*
Humorous stories from the childhood of several famous composers. Lively illustrations.

✔ *Getting to Know the World's Greatest Composers series (Children's Press)*
Good introductions to the best composers for younger children combining text, art and photgraphs.

✔ *The Spiritual Lives of the Great Composers (Kavanaugh, Zondervan)*
Twenty profiles on the world's greatest composers with insights into their spiritual beliefs.

✔ *Music and Moments with the Masters (David Quine, Cornerstone Curriculum Project)*
Outstanding 5-year introduction to the classical composers and their music.

● *Masterpiece Collection (Unison Music)*
Numerous collections on CD/Cassette by composer, style and period. Budget priced but high quality.

● *Music Masters (Allegretto)*
A set of 18 cassette tapes, each containing portions of musical selections with narration about the composer.

Discovery Studies

Audio Tapes

✔ *Family Radio Theater series (Focus on the Family, Tyndale)*
Audio drama at its finest. Historical events and great literature dramatized with state-of-the-art sound effects and music..

● *The NIV Dramatized Bible*
Dramatized reading of the entire NIV text using ten actors with background music and sound effects.

● *The World's Greatest Stories from the World's Greatest Book (4 tapes, George W. Sarris)*
One-man dramatization of a variety of Bible stories in either NIV or KJV. Unusually vivid style with music and sound effects.

✔ *Your Story Hour Tapes*
Numerous albums of audio drama cassette tapes from the syndicated radio program. Dramatized Bible stories, history and biography, and character/morality stories.

Science and Nature

● *Audubon Pocket Field Guides (Audubon Society)*
Small format (6"x9", approximately 200 pages), easy-to-carry field guides with full page photographs for easy identification, and enjoyable browsing.

● *Bible Animals (Tyndale)*
A journey into nature study through the animals of the Bible. Beautifully illustrated.

● *Creation Ex Nihilo Magazine*
Creation Science Ministries, P.O. Box 6330, Florence, KY 41022; (800) 350-3232
A colorful, fascinating Creation Science magazine for the whole family. Filled with bite-sized news, articles, and evidences of creation. No paid advertising. Full color. $22.00/year (4 issues).

- *Dinosaurs By Design (Gish/Snellenberger)*
  Great illustrations of all major dinosaurs with text. Answers many common questions about creation science.

- *A Handbook of Nature Study (Anna Comstock)*
  Originally published in 1911, nearly 900 pages of lesson plans and information for all areas of nature study.

- *First Book of Nature (Usborne Books)*
  Excellent beginning nature study books. Bright, vivid illustrations and readable text.

- ✔ *It Couldn't Just Happen (Larry Richards, Word)*
  Apologetics for young minds. Clear answers to hard questions for children on creation, science and the authority of Scripture. Colorful layout, readable text.

- *Kingfisher Encyclopedia of Animals (Kingfisher)*
  A paper zoo of over 2000 animals with over 1000 illustrated with color photographs or drawings.

- *Kingfisher Visual Factfinder series: Planet Earth; The Living World; Stars and Planets; Science and Technology (Kingfisher)*
  Overviews of major areas of science and nature with informative text and attractive, modern graphics and illustrations. Great for browsing and unit study.

- *Nature Friend Magazine*
  P.O. Box 73, Goshen, IN 46527-0073
  A small monthly magazine for children 5-12 about nature with a Creationist perspective. Stories, nature articles, letters, activities. Spot color. $22.00/year (12 issues).

- *Peterson Field Guide Coloring Books (Houghton Mifflin)*
  Full color pictures on inside covers. Line art colorable drawings throughout with descriptive text.

- *Unlocking the Mysteries of Creation (Peterson, Master Books)*
  Shows why evolution fails to explain the fossil, archaeological and geological data.

Drawing and Coloring

- *Berol Prismacolor Colored Pencils*
  Art quality colored pencils with wax-based pigments. Brilliant color, expressive, blendable.

- ✔ *Dover Coloring Book series (Dover)*
  Dozens of historical, literary and thematic coloring books with excellent line art drawings and instructive text. Great for study supplements.

- ✔ *How Great Thou Art (Barry Stebbing)*
  Christian-based drawing and art workbooks for all ages. Covers all aspects of drawing and color.

- *I Draw, I Paint series (Barron's)*
  Excellent starter books for drawing, colored pencils, watercolors, and markers. Good introductions to materials, basics, and color.

- *Keepsake Bible Story Coloring Book (Emilie Barnes, Harvest House)*
  Bible stories accompanied by full-page line art illustration of the story. Hardbound. Color and keep.

- *Mark Kistler's Draw Squad; Mark Kistler's Imagination Station (Fireside)*
  High energy "how to draw" books for kids using an incremental, cartoon-style approach. Lots of fun.

Creative Play

- *Aristoplay Games*
  Aristoplay; 800/634-7738
  Creative, educational games. Well done, but a bit pricey. *Made for Trade* (Colonial America); *Knights and Castles* (Medieval Europe); *By Jove* (Greek mythology); *Alpha Animals* (naming and categorizing animals); others

- *Crafts for Kids: A Month by Month Idea Book (Dondiego/Cawley, Tab Books)*
  Seasonal arts and crafts projects for elementary children.

- *Kids Create! (Laurie Carlson, Williamson)*
  Arts and crafts projects for younger children.

- *Klutz Books products*
  Lots of fun, interesting and instructive books of skills, hobbies, crafts, and games. *Boondoggle*; *Cat's Cradle*; *String Games from Around the World*; *Book of Knots*; *TableTop Football*; *The Foxtail Book*; *Classic Board Games*; numerous others.

Learning Tools

- *GeoSafari*
  Educational Insights; 800-955-4436
  Popular drill-and-review alternative for kids. Great for geography, but also for nature, science, history, and reading. Or, make your own cards.

- *Understanding Machines I&II*
  Innovative Education; 817-259-3311
  Step-by-step learning guides that illustrate basic principles of machines using Lego Dacta Technic I (Simple Machines) and Techic II (Motorized Machines) sets. Very well done by Richard Meyers, a high school math teacher.

- *Journey Through Drama*
  Promise Productions, Inc.; 800-687-2661
  An interactive theater-drama activity book for grades 4-6 that incorporates the fruits of the spirit, as well as other areas of elementary study. Drama skills, reproducible activity pages, history of theater, four original plays. No other product like it. Good for a support group or multiple family project.

- *Learning Seeds Activity Cards*
  Home Team Press; 216-928-8083
  A 4x6 index card collection of do-it-now ideas for family learning. Numerous subject areas, 300 cards.

- *Lego® Technic and Dacta Kits*
  For creating real models with moving parts. Cards in Activity Centers show how.

Reference Books

- *American Heritage Student Thesaurus (Houghton Mifflin)*
  High quality thesaurus for middle-school years. Good tool for the budding writer. They also make a Children's Thesaurus.

- *The Kingfisher Illustrated Children's Dictionary (Kingfisher)*
  The colorful, detailed illustrations and encyclopedia style articles set this dictionary apart from all the others on the shelf. Extremely child friendly and appealing.

- *The Kingfisher Illustrated Thesaurus (Kingfisher)*
  Recently updated and revised to make it even easier to use. This is a child-friendly thesaurus that will put words into your children's mouths (and minds).

- *Kids Discover Magazine*
  Full-color 20-age magazine for children. Each of the monthly issues covers a different topic from Science, Nature or History with fascinating facts and visually-appealing illustrations and photographs. 12 issues, $22.00.

- *Websters American Family Dictionary (Random House)*
  Newly created dictionary designed to reflect the language and cultural values of mainstream American families. No offensive language, 116,000 entries.

Our Family's Favorite Books

These are just a few of our favorite books, a very abbreviated sampler. They are some of the best of the whole and living books that are enriching our family. Books that are family-affirming, or are morally or spiritually inspiring are marked with a ♥. Titles are listed alphabetically by the title or by the author's last name.

Classic Literature for Children

♥ *Louisa May Alcott books*
    Little Women, Little Men; others

♥ *Anne of Green Gables; Anne of Avonlea* (Lucy Maud Montgomery)

• *At the Back of the North Wind* (George MacDonald)

• *Black Beauty* (Anna Sewell)

• Frances Hodgson Burnett books
    A Little Princess; The Secret Garden; Little Lord Fauntleroy; others

• *The Call of the Wild* (Jack London)

• Charles Dickens novels
    Great Expectations; A Tale of Two Cities; Oliver Twist; David Copperfield; The Curiosity Shop; others

♥ *Hans Brinker, or the Silver Skates* (Mary Mapes Dodge)

♥ *Heidi* (Johanna Spyri)

• *Ivanhoe* (Scott)

• *Jane Eyre* (Charlotte Bronte)

• *Jungle Book* (Rudyard Kipling)

• *Just So Stories* (Rudyard Kipling)

• *Johnny Tremain* (Esther Forbes)

• *Kidnapped* (Robert Louis Stevenson)

• *Peter Pan* (James Barrie)

♥ *Pilgrim's Progress* (John Bunyan)

• *Pinnochio* (Collodi)

♥ Eleanor H. Porter books
    Pollyanna; Just David, others

♥ Gene Stratton Porter books
    Freckles; A Girl of the Limberlost; others
    (W□C)

♥ *Rebecca of Sunnybrook Farm* (Kate Wiggin)

♥ *Robinson Crusoe* (Daniel Defoe)

♥ *The Swiss Family Robinson* (Johann Wyss)

• *Tales from Shakespeare* (Charles and Mary Lamb)

• *Treasure Island* (Robert Louis Stevenson)

• Mark Twain books
    The Prince and the Pauper; A Connecticut Yankee In King Arthur's Court; others

• *The Wind in the Willows* (Kenneth Graham)

Contemporary Children's Fiction

♥ *All of a Kind Family* books (Sydney Taylor)

♥ *Chronicles of Narnia* (C. S. Lewis)

♥ *Elsie Dinsmore* books (Martha Finley)

♥ *Five Little Peppers* books (Margaret Sidney)

• *Great Dog Stories* (Albert P. Terhune)

• Marguerite Henry horse books
    Misty of Chincoteague; Stormy-Misty's Foal; Sea Star-Orphan of Chicoteague; Black Gold; King of the Wind; Justin Morgan Had a Horse; others

• Holling C. Holling nature books
    Minn of the Mississippi; Sea Bird; Paddle to the Sea; Pagoo; Tree in the Trail

- ♥ *Little House* books (Laura Engels Wilder)
- A.A. Milne books
  Winnie the Pooh; House at Pooh Corner; Now We Are Six; When We Were Very Young
- ♥ *The Little Lame Prince* (Dinah Maria Mulcock)
- ♥ Ralph Moody novels
  Little Britches; Father and I Were Ranchers; Man of the Family; others
- Walt Morey Adventure books
  Gentle Ben; Home Is the North; Scrub Dog of Alaska; Year of the Black Pony; Runaway Stallion; Run Far Run Fast; Angry Waters; Deep Trouble; Gloomy Gus
- *The Railway Children* (E. Nesbit)
- ♥ Patricia St. John books
  Treasures of the Snow; The Tanglewoods Secret; Rainbow Garden; The Secret of the Fourth Candle; The Secret at Pheasant Cottage; Star of Light; Three Go Searching; others
- ♥ Wilson Rawls books
  Where the Red Fern Grows; Summer of the Monkeys
- ♥ *Uncle Arthur's Children's Stories* (Arthur Maxwell)
- E.B. White books
  Charlotte's Web; Trumpet of the Swan; Stuart Little
- *A Wrinkle In Time* (Madeleine L'Engle)

Picture Books and Illustrated Story Books

- ♥ *All the Places to Love* (Patricia MacLachlan)
- ♥ *The Bear That Heard Crying*
- *Billy and Blaze* series (C.W. Anderson)
- ♥ *The Blue Hill Meadows* (Cynthia Rylant)

- *The Boy Who Held Back the Sea* (Locker)
- ♥ *Brother Francis and the Friendly Beasts* (Margaret Hodges)
- ♥ *Dangerous Journey* (John Bunyan, condensed Pilgrim's Progress)
- *Don Quixote and Sancho Panza* (Margaret Hodges, condensed Don Quixote)
- *Five O'Clock Charlie* (Marguerite Henry)
- *Follow the Drinking Gourd* (Jeannette Winter)
- ♥ *Island Boy* (Barbara Cooney)
- *James Herriot's Treasury for Children* (James Herriot)
- ♥ *Least of All* (Carol Purdy)
- ♥ *Love You Forever* (Robert Munsch)
- ♥ *Lucy's Summer* (Donald Hall)
- Robert McCloskey books
  Make Way for Ducklings; Time of Wonder; One Morning In Maine
- ♥ *Miss Rumphius* (Barbara Cooney)
- ♥ *My Great Aunt Arizona* (Gloria Houston)
- ♥ *Only Opal* (Barbara Cooney)
- *Oxcart Man* (Donald Hall)
- ♥ *The Relatives Came* (Cynthia Rylant)
- ♥ *Robin Hood* (Margaret Early, Abrams)
- *Roxaboxen* (Alice McLerran)
- ♥ *Song and Dance Man* (Karen Ackerman)
- ♥ *St. George and the Dragon* (Margaret Hodges)
- ♥ *The Velveteen Rabbit* (Rose Reed)
- *When I Was Young and In the Mountains* (Cynthia Rylant)

- ♥ *Wilford Gordon McDonald Partridge* (Mem Fox)
- ♥ *William Tell* (Margaret Early, Abrams)
- • *Yonder* (Johnston/Bloom)
- ♥ *The Young Artist* (Locker)

History and Biography

Ancient World

- • *The Bronze Bow* (Elizabeth Speare)
- • *The Children's Homer* (Padric Colum)
- • *The Golden Fleece* (Padric Colum)
- • *Cleopatra* (Stanley/Vennema)
- • *The Golden Goblet* (Eloise Jarvis McGraw)
- ♥ *Joel, A Boy of Galilee* (Johnston)
- • *The Children's Homer* (Padraic Colum)

Middle Ages

- • *Adam of the Road* (Elizabeth Gray)
- • *The Door in the Wall* (Marguerite de Angeli)
- • Howard Pyle books
  Otto of the Silver Hand; King Arthur and His Knights; Champions of the Round Table; Sir Lancelot and His Champions; The Grail and the Passing of Arthur; The Merry Adventures of Robin Hood
- • *Ivanhoe* (Sir Walter Scott)
- ♥ *Joan of Arc* (Lucy Foster Madison)
- ♥ *Saint Valentine* (Robert Sabuda)
- • *Sir Gawain and the Green Knight* (J.R.R. Tolkein)
- • *The Trumpeter of Krakow* (Eric P. Kelly)

Renaissance

- • *Good Queen Bess: The Story of Elizabeth of England* (D. Stanley, P. Vennema)
- • *William Shakespeare: Bard of Avon* (D. Stanley, P. Vennema)
- • *Peter the Great* (D. Stanley)

Reformation

- ♥ *The Hawk That Dare Not Hunt By Day* (Scott O'Dell)
- ♥ *Morning Star of the Reformation* (Andy Thompson)
- ♥ Louise Vernon books (Greenleaf Press)
  Ink on His Fingers; Thunderstorm in Church; The Bible Smuggler; Night Preacher; The Secret Church; A Heart Strangely Warmed; The Man Who Laid the Egg

Colonial America

- • Aliki books
  The Story of William Penn; The Many Lives of Benjamin Franklin; others
- • *Benjamin West and His Cat Grimalkin* (Marguerite Henry) (WᴏC)
- • Clyde Bulla historical fiction
  A Lion to Guard Us; Pocahontas and the Strangers; Squanto, Friend of the Pilgrims
- ♥ Alice Dalgliesh historical fiction
  The Courage of Sarah Noble; The First Thanksgiving; Homes In the Wilderness
- • *Justin Morgan Had a Horse* (Marguerite Henry)
- ♥ *Little Maid of New England* (Alice Turner Curtis)
- • *The Matchlock Gun* (Edmonds)
- • *The Pilgrims of Plimoth* (Maria Sewall)

- Robert Lawson whimsical historical fiction
  I Discover Columbus; Ben and Me; Mr. Revere and I

- Elizabeth Speare historical fiction
  The Witch of Blackbird Pond; Calico Captive; The Sign of the Beaver

- *Stranded At Plimouth Plantation 1626* (Gary Bowen)

- *Squanto* (Fennie Ziner)

- ♥ *Three Young Pilgrims* (Cheryl Harness) (WᴑC)

- *Obadiah* books (Brinton Turkle)
  Thy Friend, Obadiah; Obadiah the Bold; Rachel and Obadiah; Adventures of Obadiah

- *Traitor: The Case of Benedict Arnold* (Jean Fritz)

Revolutionary America

- *America's Paul Revere* (Esther Forbes)

- ♥ *Amos Fortune, Free Man* (Elizabeth Yates)

- *By the Dawn's Early Light~The Story of the Star Spangled Banner* (Kroll/Andreasen)

- ♥ *Carry On, Mr. Bowditch* (Jean Lee Latham)

- *Early Thunder* (Jean Fritz)

- *Guns for General Washington* (Seymour Reit)

- *Johnny Tremain* (Esther Forbes)

- *Paul Revere's Ride* (Longfellow, Ted Rand)

- *Sarah Bishop* (Scott O'Dell)

- *Toliver's Secret* (Esther Wood Brady)

- *Yankee Doodle Boy* (Jospeh Martin)

- ♥ *Young John Quincy* (Cheryl Harness)

Pioneer America

- *A Gathering of Days* (Joan Blos)

- *Abe Linclon Grows Up* (Carl Sandburg)

- *The Cabin Faced West* (Jean Fritz)

- ♥ *Caddie Woodlawn* (Carol Ryris Brink)

- *Diary of an Early American Boy* (Eric Sloan)

- ♥ *Johnny Appleseed* (Steven Kellogg)

- *Magical Melons* (Carol Ryris Brink)

- *On to Oregon* (Morrow)

- *Sarah, Plain and Tall* (Patricia MacLachian)

- *Thee, Hannah* (Marguerite de Angeli)

History Sets, Series, Specials

- *American Girls* historical fiction series (Pleasant Company, numerous titles)

- *Childhood of Famous Americans* biography series (Alladin, numerous titles/authors)

- *I Can Read* series
  Sam the Minuteman; George the Drummer Boy; The Boston Coffee Party; The Long Way Westward; numerous others

- *Ingri and Edgar Parin D'Aulaire* books
  Abraham Lincoln; Benjamin Franklin; Christopher Columbus; George Washington; Leif Erikson; Pocahontas

- *Jean Fritz history readers (Putnam)*
  And Then What Happened, Paul Revere; Can't You Make Them Behave, King George?; What's the Big Idea, Ben Franklin?; numerous others

- *Landmark Books* (200+ history titles)

- ♥ Mantle Ministries reprints
  Gaining Favor With God and Man (Thayer, 1893); Great Americans and Their Noble Deeds (Hadley); The Price of Liberty (Whipple, 1910); One Nation Under God; Foxe's Book of Martyrs

- ♥ *Men and Women of Faith* Christian biography series (Bethany House, numerous titles and authors)

- ♥ Peter Marshall books (Baker)
  The Light and the Glory for Children; From Sea to Shining Sea for Children

- ♥ *The Sower Series* biography books (Mott Media, numerous titles/authors)

- • *Step Up* biographies ("Meet" books)
  Meet Christopher Columbus; Meet Thomas Jefferson; Meet George Washington; Meet Benjamin Franklin; Meet Abraham Lincoln; numerous others

- ♥ *Trailblazer Books* Christian historical fiction series (Bethany House, numerous titles by Neta and Dave Jackson)

- • *Troll Easy Biography* series (Troll, numerous titles/authors)

Poetry, Prose, Art

- • *Aesop's Fables* (various versions)

- • *Best Loved Poems of the American People*

- ♥ *The Book of Virtues* (William Bennett)

- ♥ *A Children's Book of Virtues* (William Bennett)

- • *A Child's Garden of Verses* (Robert Louis Stevenson) (W▫C)

- • *A Child's Treasury of Animal Verse* (Mark Daniel, Ed.)

- ♥ *A Child's Treasury of Poems* (Mark Daniel, Ed.)

- • *A Child's Treasury of Seaside Verse* (Mark Daniel, Ed.)

- ♥ *A Christian Treasury* (Crossway Books) (W▫C)

- • *Imaginary Gardens: American Poetry and Art for Young People* (Abrams)

- • *Favorite Poems Old and New* (Doubleday)

- ♥ *The Moral Compass* (William Bennett)

- • *Who Has Seen the Wind? An Illustrated Collection of Poetry for Young People* (Rizzoli, out of print)

Early Readers, Fairy Tales, and Everything Else

- • *AlphaBears; Numbears* (Kathleen Hague)

- ♥ *Andersen's Fairy Tales* (Children's Classics, collection of Hans Christian Andersen)
  The Little Match Girl; The Mermaid; The Ugly Duckling; The Steadfast Tin Soldier; The Emperor's New Clothes; Thumbelina; others

- • *Each Peach Pear Plum* (Ahlberg)

- • *Friends* (Helme Heine)

- • *Fritz and the Beautiful Horses* (Jan Brett)

- • *Galimoto* (Karen Lynn Williams)

- • *Illuminations* (Jonathan Hunt)

- • Leo Leoni books
  Alexander and the Windup Mouse, Swimmy, Frederick

- • *The Light Princess* (George MacDonald)

- • *The Lost Princess* (George MacDonald)

- • *Petunia Beware (Roger Davidson)*

- • *Quick As a Cricket* (Audrey Wood)

- • *Rainbow Crow* (Nancy Van Laan)

- • *Usborne ABC Book*

Home Education Planning Forms

The forms on the pages that follow are simply tools to help you clarify your goals, stay organized and cultivate productive routines in your home school. However, they are not necessary—you can effectively home educate your children and never use these or any other forms. If you need them, they can help. If you don't need them, they won't make you a better home educator. The last thing we want to do is add yet one more layer of "one more thing I have to do" to your home schooling responsibilities. You may reproduce any of the forms for your personal use at home. Please do not reproduce any of them for distribution to other individuals or groups without calling first for permission. The following are brief explanations about each form, and ideas on how to use them.

- **One Month Calendar and Planner**

  This is a universal calendar blank that you can put in a notebook, on the refrigerator or on the bulletin board. It shows you your month in a single glance. Simply fill in the "Month" and "Year" boxes, and write in the appropriate dates for each day of the month. Use the memo boxes at the bottom of the page to notate dates and descriptions of important "Events and Activities" and "People and Projects." Then, use a number or symbol of your choice to reference it on the calendar.

- **One Week Calendar and Planner (1 page)**

  This is a universal calendar blank that is best used in a notebook, but can also be posted in a convenient location. First, fill in the "Month," "Week," and "Year" boxes. Then enter commitments, appointments and time blocks (using a vertical arrow to indicate an entire block) in the spaces provided. Use the memo box at the bottom of the page for special notes or reminders.

- **Home Education Goals (2 pages)**

  This form is based on the Home Centered Learning model. It is designed to give you an quick and easy form for planning quarterly educational goals for each child, and for determining what resources you will need. Fill in the "Child," "Quarter," and "Year" boxes, one form for each child. Referring to chapter four, determine your educational goals for each child in each of the focused studies areas. Then note what resources or materials you will need, indicating if they are on hand or if you will need to obtain them.

- **Home Education Studies Planner (2 pages)**

  This form is based on the Home Centered Learning model. It is designed to give you a quick and easy form for planning monthly home education studies for each child. Fill in the "Child," "Month," and "Year" boxes, one form for each child. Referring to chapter four, determine the kinds of educational studies for each child in each of the focused studies areas. Use horizontal arrows to indicate continuation over a period of weeks. Blank "Subject" boxes are provided if you want to add your own areas of study.

- **Home School Weekly Planner (1 page)**

  This comprehensive form is designed to be used by your child during the week to self-regulate his or her learning and study assignments. Before the start of the week, fill in any relevant assignments at the top of the chart. Include number of pages to read on Reading List section. At the bottom, indicate the study material and which pages/lessons should be completed on which days for any relevant subjects. Allow your child to work ahead.

- **Universal Home Education Planner (2 forms)**

  This is a universal planning blank that allows you to look at the overall picture of your home education activities in a single glance. It can be used for a quarter ("Qtr"), month ("Mo") or week ("Wk"). Simply fill in the appropriate box for time range, the name of each child in a "Child" box. Subjects can be listed in the left hand column, and assignments in the other columns.

- **LifeGIFTS Planner (1 page)**

  Use this form to plan your home discipleship strategies for each child. In the "Training" column beneath each of the GIFTS, describe specific training you can do to help your child grow. In the "Instruction" column, plan a Bible study, Scripture memory, or other ways to instruct your child in Bible knowledge.

- **"Fish & Bread" Character and Values Planner (1 page)**
  Use this form to plan character and values training, and to identify areas of weak character and values in which your child needs to grow or be strengthened. Describe the character or value in the center column; reference relevant Bible passages in the "Scripture" column.

- **My Assigned Reading List (1 page)**
  When you assign reading for a child, use this form to record the list of books. Have your child write his or her name in the box, the title and author of each book, and the date the book was assigned. Whenever a book is completed, you child will simply place a check in the check box.

- **Books I Have Read (1 page)**
  Use this form to keep a running record of the books your child reads. Have your child write his or her name in the box, the title and author of each book, the number of pages, and the date the book was completed.

- **My Home-School Work for This Week (1 page)**
  Have your child write his or her name in the box, a description of the assignments or studies that need to be accomplished that week, and the date they are due. When an assignment is completed, you child will simply place a check in the check box.

- **My "Check Me Out" List (1 page)**
  This form is designed to help your children develop personal habits of responsibility and self-discipline. The form is a *self-evaluation* tool for your *child* to use, not for you to keep for your child. A check mark is just a way for your child to say "I did it!"—it is not for reward or punishment. The check marks will help your children see patterns of behavior in their lives. Mom or Dad should always, before bedtime, review each child's "check me out" list for the day, offer words of encouragement, and pray about areas needing work. Use the space following each line to highlight a specific behavioral goal or concern. For example, after "Read my Bible and pray?" you might want to add "for 10 minutes before breakfast." Or, after "Get along well with others?" you might want to add "did not argue with my brother." Additional spaces are provided to write in other "check points" for your own family situation. *This form is not meant to be used permanently.* It is a temporary training tool. The most effective way to use this form is as a one-month training project. Do it religiously, every day, for four weeks in a row, then take a break from it. After a month or two, do the four week emphasis again. Use this process to help your children see the patterns of behavior in their lives. Determine a reward that the family will enjoy together at the end of four weeks *if* everyone completes the list *every day*. Remind them that the reward is not based on the number of "checks," but on being consistent to fill out their "checklist" every day.

- **Bible Reading and Devotional Journal (1 page)**
  This form is designed to help your child engage their heart and mind in their devotional reading. Ask them to read one paragraph each day. First, they will summarize (written narration) what they have read. Then have them note one verse or passage that caught their attention and have them answer the "know, be, do" question in a short journal-style entry. Finally, have them write down several words or thoughts suggested by the passage as prayer reminders.

- **Bible Study Notes: TOPIC Study (1 page)**
  This form is designed to help you or your child do a simple topical study in the Bible.

- **Bible Study Notes: BOOK Study (1 page)**
  This form is designed to help you or your child do a simple study of a book of the Bible.

One Month Calendar and Planner

Month: | **Year:**

Sun	Mon	Tue	Wed	Thu	Fri	Sat

Events and Activities Dates	**People and Projects Dates**

One Week Calendar and Planner

Month:	Week:	Year:

	Morning	Afternoon	vening
SUNDAY			
MONDAY			
TUESDAY			
WEDNESDAY			
THURSDAY			
FRIDAY			
SATURDAY			

To Be Done

Home Education Goals

Child: **Quarter:**   **Year:**

	Learning Goals	Resources Needed
DISCIPLESHIP STUDIES		
DISCIPLINED STUDIES		

Subject	Week 1		Week 2		Week 3		Week 4		Week 5
DISCUSSION STUDIES									
Read Aloud Literature									
History & Geography									
Art, Music & Poetry									
Science and Nature									
DISCOVERY STUDIES									
Nature Study									
Computer									
DISCRETIONARY STUDIES									

Home School Weekly Studies Planner

Name:

Month: Week:

Subject	Monday	Tuesday	Wednesday	Thursday	Friday
Discipleship Studies					
Bible Reading					
Bible Study					
Disciplined Studies					
Reading					
Creative Writing & Composition					
Language Arts					
Math					
Thinking Skills					

Subject	Monday	Tuesday	Wednesday	Thursday	Friday
			Discussion Studies		
Read Aloud					
History & Geography					
Fine Arts, Music & Poetry					
Science and Nature					
			Discovery Studies		
Nature Study					
Computer					
			Discretionary Studies		

Home School Weekly Studies Planner

Name:

Month:

Week:

Subject	Monday	Tuesday	Wednesday	Thursday	Friday
Discipleship Studies					
Bible Reading					
Bible Study					
Disciplined Studies					
Reading					
Creative Writing & Composition					
Language Arts					
Math					
Thinking Skills					

Subject	Monday	Tuesday	Wednesday	Thursday	Friday
Discussion Studies					
Read Aloud					
History & Geography					
Fine Arts, Music & Poetry					
Science and Nature					
Discovery Studies					
Nature Study					
Computer					
Discretionary Studies					

Home School Weekly Planner

Name		Week	

Bible Study & Research Topics	Family & Special Responsibilities
Bible Reading:	Meal Time:
Bible Topic:	Afternoon:
Bible Book:	Check Daily:
History Research:	As Needed:
Science Research:	Cleaning:

Reading List	Special Instructions & Calendar
History:	Morning:
Biography:	
Church History:	Afternoon:
Literature/Fiction:	
Science/Nature:	Evening:
Christian:	Weekend:

Subject	Book, Resource, Curriculum	✔	MON	✔	TUE	✔	WED	✔	THU	✔	FRI
Bible											
Language Arts											
Handwriting											
Writing & Composition											
Math											
History											
Geography											
Science & Nature											
Art, Music & Poetry											
Computer & Keyboard											
Government & Civics											
Worldview & Apologetics											

Universal Home Education Planner

QTR MO	Child	Child	Child
QTR MO	Child	Child	Child

LifeGIFTS Discipleship Planner

Child		Date	
Training		**Instruction**	
GRACE			
INSPIRATION			
FAITH			
TRAINING			
SERVICE			

"Fish & Bread" Character and Values Planner

Child

Date

"FISH"	CHRISTIAN CHARACTER	SCRIPTURE
Faithfulness		
Integrity		
Self-Discipline		
Humility		

"BREAD"	CHRISTIAN VALUES	SCRIPTURE
Bible		
Relationships		
Eternal Perspective		
Authority		
Disciplines		

My Assigned Reading List

✔	Book & Author	Date Entered

Books I Have Read

#	Title & Author	Pages	Date
1			
2			
3			
4			
5			
6			
7			
8			
9			
10			
11			
12			
13			
14			
15			
16			
17			
18			
19			
20			

My Home-School Work for This Week

✔	Assignment, Project, Practice	Due Date

My "Check Me Out" List

SOW YOUR SEED IN THE MORNING...

DID I...	MON	TUE	WED	THU	FRI	SAT
Make my bed neatly?						
Dress my self nicely?						
Groom my self well?						
Read my Bible and pray?						
Do my morning chores?						

AND AT EVENING LET NOT YOUR HANDS BE IDLE...

DID I...	MON	TUE	WED	THU	FRI	SAT
Pick up all my clothes and things?						
Put up all my home school work?						
Clean up all my messes?						
Straighten my room and bath?						
Get my self ready for bed quickly?						

WHATEVER YOU DO, DO IT ALL FOR THE GLORY OF GOD...

DID I...	MON	TUE	WED	THU	FRI	SAT
Honor and obey my parents?						
Get along well with others?						
Use my time wisely?						
Guard my tongue (words)?						
Guard my heart (attitudes)?						

Comments:

Bible Reading & Devotional Journal

Name		Page	

Today's Passage: **Day:**

Write a one sentence summary of this section: **Date:**

Today's Verse: ___ **Meditated?**

What does God say that I need to KNOW, BE or DO?   ___ **Memorized?**

Prayer Words:

Today's Passage: **Day:**

Write a one sentence summary of this section: **Date:**

Today's Verse: ___ **Meditated?**

What does God say that I need to KNOW, BE or DO?   ___ **Memorized?**

Prayer Words:

Today's Passage: **Day:**

Write a one sentence summary of this section: **Date:**

Today's Verse: ___ **Meditated?**

What does God say that I need to KNOW, BE or DO?   ___ **Memorized?**

Prayer Words:

Today's Passage: **Day:**

Write a one sentence summary of this section: **Date:**

Today's Verse: ___ **Meditated?**

What does God say that I need to KNOW, BE or DO?   ___ **Memorized?**

Prayer Words:

Today's Passage: **Day:**

Write a one sentence summary of this section: **Date:**

Today's Verse: ___ **Meditated?**

What does God say that I need to KNOW, BE or DO?   ___ **Memorized?**

Prayer Words:

Today's Passage: **Day:**

Write a one sentence summary of this section: **Date:**

Today's Verse: ___ **Meditated?**

What does God say that I need to KNOW, BE or DO?   ___ **Memorized?**

Prayer Words:

Bible Study Notes: TOPIC Study

Name	Date	Page

Bible Topic	
Related Topics	

Key Words	
Cross Refs	

Define Topic	

Key Passages	Summary

Notes

Bible Study Notes: BOOK Study

Name		Date		Page	

Bible Book	
Passage	

Key Verse(s)	
Key Word(s)	

Cross Refs	

Passage Theme	

Outline Refs	Outline Content

Notes

Thank You!

We appreciate your purchase of *Educating the WholeHearted Child*. We'd like to hear what you think after you've had a chance to read it. You can write to us at the address below.

Whole Heart Ministries is a non-profit Christian parenting ministry dedicated to encouraging and equipping Christian parents to build a biblical home and a godly heritage by nurturing, discipling and educating their children at home. Whole Heart Ministries is located in Monument, Colorado.

If you enjoyed this book, you will also enjoy other Whole Heart Ministries Press published products:

- **Seasons of a Mother's Heart:** This personal book by Sally is being read and used for Bible study and discussion by home school mothers groups around the country and the world. It is a collection of 12 inspiring essays from Sally's experience as a home schooling mother that get to the heart of motherhood.

- **Our 24 Family Ways Family Devotional Guide:** A easy-to-use devotional and discipleship resource for families that teaches 24 family values. This resource provides 120 scripted devotionals that can be done with no advance preparation. There is also a companion **Kids Color-In Book** for young way-makers.

- **Journeys of Faithfulness:** Our daughter Sarah wrote this book at 17. It is a fictionalized retelling of the stories of four young women in Scripture (Esther, Ruth, Mary of Bethany, and Mary), with personal insights and journal pages. It is a great book for mothers and daughters, for teen girls of all ages.

- **Whole Heart Classics:** These reprints of classic Christian works of fiction, devotion and instruction for families were published in the 19th and early 20th centuries. These are rediscovered treasures for a new generation of families in a quality hardcover series for the family legacy library.

- **Whole Heart Audio:** Listen to Sally's messages to mothers recorded at her WholeHearted Mother Conferences 1998-2005, and her WholeHearted Child Workshop 1997. All of our audio is available in CD and Cassette in any combination from **www.Best-Christian-Conferences.com**.

- **The WholeHeart Letter:** Sent as we are able to keep you up-to-date on the ministry of WHM, let you know about new books and resources, and inform you when Sally will be speaking in your area.

To add your name to our mailing list, or to order any of the WHPress products above, contact us at:

Whole Heart Ministries
P.O. Box 3445
Monument, CO 80132

Phone: 719-488-4466
Fax: 866-311-2146
Orders: 800-311-2146

Send an e-mail: whm@wholeheart.org
Visit our website: http://www.wholeheart.org